SAMS Teach Yourself

Microsoft® Office Word 2003

in 24 Hours

Heidi Steele

SAMS   800 East 96th Street, Indianapolis, IN 46240

Sams Teach Yourself Microsoft® Office Word 2003 in 24 Hours

Copyright ©2004 by Sams Publishing

International Standard Book Number: 0-672-32556-X

Library of Congress Catalog Card Number: 2003103644

Printed in the United States of America

First Printing: September 2003

06   05   04   03   4   3   2   1

Trademarks

Warning and Disclaimer

Bulk Sales

Sams Publishing offers excellent discounts on this book when ordered in quan-tity for bulk purchases or special sales. For more information, please contact

U.S. Corporate and Government Sales
1-800-382-3419
corpsales@pearsontechgroup.com

For sales outside of the U.S., please contact

International Sales
1-317-428-3341
international@pearsontechgroup.com

ASSOCIATE PUBLISHER
Greg Wiegand

ACQUISITIONS EDITOR
Michelle Newcomb

DEVELOPMENT EDITOR
Laura Norman

MANAGING EDITOR
Charlotte Clapp

COPY EDITOR
Margaret Berson

TECHNICAL EDITOR
Helen Bradley

TEAM COORDINATOR
Sharry Lee Gregory

INTERIOR DESIGNER
Gary Adair

COVER DESIGNER
Gary Adair

PAGE LAYOUT
Plan-it Publishing

GRAPHICS
Tammy Graham

Contents at a Glance

Contents

About the Author

Heidi Steele is a freelance writer and software trainer. She specializes in demystifying computer concepts and making programs such as Microsoft Word accessible to home users and professionals alike. Heidi Steele is the author of numerous other computer books, including *How to Use the Internet*, *Easy Word 2003*, and *Sams Teach Yourself Word 2000 in 24 Hours*. She lives in Port Orchard, Washington.

Dedication

*This book is dedicated to my partner Doug, whose kind and generous nature
is a continued source of inspiration.*

Acknowledgments

Once again, I truly enjoyed working with my acquisitions editor Michelle Newcomb. She makes her job look effortless, although I am sure it is not. Thanks also to my development editor Laura Norman, who was available with answers to my questions almost before I asked them. I'd also like to thank my technical editor Helen Bradley and copy editor Margaret Berson for their many excellent suggestions. On the home front, Doug put on his software engineer hat to write the chapter on XML, as well as contributing his own photographs and documents for use in the examples. My friend Chris Smith graciously allowed me to use his gardening articles as examples in this book, and Deborah Craig once again permitted me to use her paper on Imogen Cunningham. Finally, I'd like to thank my son Gaelan and my stepchildren Isaac and Rachel for the joy and warmth they bring to our family.

We Want to Hear from You!

As the reader of this book, *you* are our most important critic and commentator. We value your opinion and want to know what we're doing right, what we could do better, what areas you'd like to see us publish in, and any other words of wisdom you're willing to pass our way.

As an associate publisher for Sams Publishing, I welcome your comments. You can email or write me directly to let me know what you did or didn't like about this book—as well as what we can do to make our books better.

Please note that I cannot help you with technical problems related to the topic of this book. We do have a User Services group, however, where I will forward specific technical questions related to the book.

When you write, please be sure to include this book's title and author as well as your name, email address, and phone number. I will carefully review your comments and share them with the author and editors who worked on the book.

E-mail: feedback@samspublishing.com
Mail: Greg Wiegand
         Associate Publisher
         Sams Publishing
         800 East 96th Street
         Indianapolis, IN 46240 USA

For more information about this book or another Sams Publishing title, visit our Web site at www.samspublishing.com. Type the ISBN (excluding hyphens) or the title of a book in the Search field to find the page you're looking for.

Introduction

Word is the most popular word processing program available. Its primary mission is to help you type and format text documents, but it also offers a host of other powerful features that let you create tables, work with graphics, create mass mailings, design Web pages, and more. This book teaches you to use the most recent incarnation of the program, Word 2003.

What This Book Will Do for You

If you rank learning new software right up there with trips to the dentist, you're not alone. Many people feel less than enthusiastic about exploring new programs because the "how-to" books they use are unclear or intimidating. This book aims to give you a much more positive learning experience. In it, you learn a good portion of the Word program—enough to create just about any type of document you need—in a thorough and systematic way.

Sams Teach Yourself Microsoft Word 2003 in 24 Hours is organized in 24 sessions that should take approximately one hour each to complete. Depending on your previous experience with Word and your areas of interest, some sessions may take less than an hour and others may take more. The exact amount of time is not important. After you've practiced and absorbed all the information in a session that is relevant to your work, you're ready to move on.

What Is Word Designed to Do?

Word's fundamental mission is simple: to help you type, revise, and format text. To this end, it offers a complete set of tools that enable you to create just about any type of document imaginable. You can produce anything from basic letters and memos to complex documents such as reports, papers, newsletters, brochures, résumés, mass mailings, envelopes, and mailing labels. You can even compose e-mail messages and design Web pages in Word.

Each person who uses Word needs a slightly different combination of features. If you're an administrative assistant, you may need to use Word's mail merge feature to generate mass mailings. If you're a student, you'll want to learn about footnotes and endnotes for your term papers. If you're a marketing executive, you may want to use the table feature to present information in charts. Depending on the documents you create, you'll use some parts of Word constantly, and others you will never venture into. This is to be expected. Learn the areas of Word that you need, and don't feel compelled to explore every nook and cranny.

Word is part of Microsoft Office, a suite of business applications. The other key players in Office are Excel, a spreadsheet program, and PowerPoint, a presentation program. Depending on the edition of Office you have, you may also have a database program called Access, a personal information manager (PIM) and e-mail application called Outlook, and possibly a few others. All the Office applications have a similar look, and they are tightly integrated to let you use them in combination with one another (see Hour 20, "Integrating with Other Office Products").

What Came Before Word 2003?

Microsoft has been producing Word for years, so several versions of the program are floating around. To make things more confusing, there is more than one way to refer to some versions. Table 1.1 lists the most recent versions of Word to help you understand where Word 2003 fits in. You can run all these versions on Windows 98, Windows ME, Windows 2000, and Windows XP. In contrast, Word 2003 only runs on Windows XP and Windows 2000.

TABLE 1.1   The Recent Incarnations of Microsoft Word

Name	Version	Description
Word 97	Word 8.0	Word 97 was sold separately and as part of Office 97.
Word 2000	Word 9.0	Word 2000 was sold separately and as part of Office 2000.
Word 2002 or Word XP	Word 10	Word 2002 is sold separately and as part of Office XP.

You may work with people who haven't yet upgraded to Word 2003. If you do, you probably will have to open documents created in earlier versions of Word and save documents in a format that older versions of Word will be able to read. In Hour 18, "Collaborating on Documents," you learn how to cope with these situations.

Conventions Used in This Book

Sams Teach Yourself Microsoft Word 2003 in 24 Hours uses a few conventions to present concepts and skills clearly:

- Menu commands are separated by commas. For example, if you need to click the Save command in the File menu, you will see instructions to choose File, Save.

- Keyboard shortcuts that require you to hold down the first key or keys and then press a letter key are shown combined with a + sign, like this: Ctrl+B. (It doesn't matter whether Caps Lock is turned on when you type the *b*, but you should not use the Shift key to make the letter uppercase.)

- In numbered steps, commands or options that you need to click or select are shown in **boldface**.

- For simplicity's sake, procedures that involve the operating system describe the steps that are required in Windows XP. If you are using Windows 2000 (or have turned on the Classic Start menu in Windows XP), your operating-system–related procedures will differ to some degree. Furthermore, this book assumes that you are using Microsoft Office 2003 and not a standalone version of Word 2003. If you are using a standalone version of Word, you may see some minor differences between the procedures described in this book and the ones you need to follow.

Each hour ends with common questions and answers. In addition to the explanatory text and the question-and-answer section, each hour also includes four elements:

Notes provide additional information related to the topic of discussion.

Tips offer alternative or time-saving ways to do things.

Cautions warn you about potential pitfalls and tell you how to avoid them.

PART I

Getting Started

Hour

HOUR 1

Getting Acquainted with Word

Whether you use a computer at home or at the office, if you work with text documents of any sort, you will probably come to view Word as your "home base" on the computer. Word gives you quick access to the commonly used commands, while also providing a host of more advanced features that enable you to create a variety of specialized documents. You can "talk" to Word in a variety of ways—with menus, toolbars, and keyboard shortcuts. The exact methods that you use are a matter of personal preference. Experiment with all of the methods described here and see which ones you like best.

Highlights of this hour include

- Pointers on installing Word
- Starting Word
- Elements of the Word window
- Getting around in Word
- Working with task panes
- Moving and resizing the Word window
- Getting help
- Closing documents and exiting Word

Installing Word

If you are installing any edition of Office, Word is included in the installation. To start the setup process, insert the Office CD in your CD-ROM drive. The setup dialog box appears automatically. When prompted, enter your product key and user information, accept the license agreement, and then choose the desired installation option (descriptions of each option are provided onscreen). Click the Install button to continue with the installation, and then click Finish when the installation is complete. (For a detailed discussion of modifying or repairing your Word installation, refer to Appendix A on the book's Web site.)

> If the setup dialog box doesn't appear automatically, you can start the installation process by displaying the contents of the Office CD in a My Computer window or the Windows Explorer and double-clicking the file Setup.exe (if your computer is set up to hide file extensions, your file will appear as Setup).

By default, the Office installation procedure does not install all features to your hard disk. Rather, it installs some features that aren't used as frequently on a "first use" basis. For example, the help files for WordPerfect users, page border art, and some templates and wizards are installed on first use. The first time you issue a command in an Office application that requires one of these features, the application displays a message box stating that the feature is not currently installed and asks whether you would like to install it now. If this happens when you're using Word, insert the Office CD and click the Yes button. Word will then copy the files that it needs for the feature from the CD.

> Depending on how your CD-ROM drive is configured, it may automatically display the opening screen for the Office installation process. You can close this screen because you don't need to see it when Word is copying files to install a new feature. To prevent this screen from displaying, press the Shift key for a few seconds while the CD is loading.

Depending on your installation of Office, other features may be set to run from the Office CD or, if you work on a network, from a location on your network. If you issue a command that requires one of these features, you may receive a prompt to insert your Office CD or connect to the network location that contains the Office setup files.

Starting Word

When you want to start a new Word document or continue working on an existing document, you need to open a Word window. As with just about anything Microsoft, you can do this in more than one way. Experiment to see which method you like the best.

The most basic way to start any Windows application, including Word, is from the Start menu:

1.   Click the **Start** button at the left end of the taskbar to display the Start menu.

2. See if Microsoft Word appears in the main Start menu. If it does, click it to start the program (see Figure 1.1).

FIGURE 1.1

Starting Word from the main Start menu.

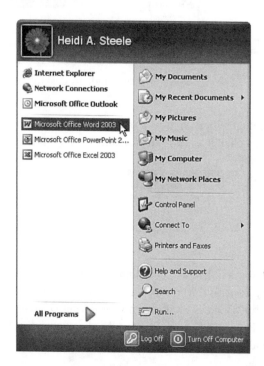

3. If it doesn't, point to All Programs in the Start menu, point to Microsoft Office, and then click **Microsoft Office Word 2003** (see Figure 1.2).

FIGURE **1.2**
Starting Word from the
Start, All Programs
menu.

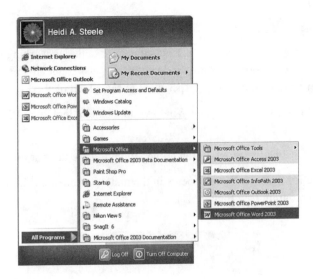

If you have a shortcut icon for Word on your Windows desktop, double-click it to start Word.

If your system is set up with a Word icon in the Quick Launch toolbar to the right of the Start button, you can click it to start the program (see Figure 1.3).

FIGURE **1.3**
You can start Word by
clicking its icon in the
Quick Launch toolbar.

You can also click (or double-click, depending on the way you've configured your Windows operating system) a Word document icon anywhere you see it—on your Windows desktop, in Windows Explorer, in your Recent Documents submenu, in a My Computer folder window, and so on—to start Word and open the document. Figure 1.4 shows a folder window that contains several Word document icons.

Elements of the Word Window

Learning the names of the elements of the Word window may not be the most stimulating part of learning the program, but it's essential for understanding the instructions throughout the rest of this book, and in Word's help system. Figure 1.5 labels the most important parts of the Word window.

FIGURE **1.4**

You can click any Word document icon to start Word and open the document.

Word document icons

FIGURE **1.5**

It's a good idea to learn the names of the different parts of the Word window.

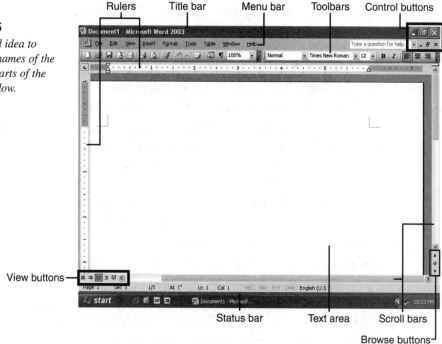

Rulers   Title bar   Menu bar   Toolbars   Control buttons

View buttons

Status bar   Text area   Scroll bars

Browse buttons

Here is a description of these elements:

- *Title bar.* The title bar of any Windows application lists the name of the application—in this case, Microsoft Word 2003. Word's title bar also contains the name of
  the open document. As you'll see in the section "Controlling the Position and Size
  of the Word Window" later in this hour, you can use the title bar to move the Word
  window around the desktop, or to minimize or maximize the window. When the
  Word window is active, the title bar is colored. When another area of your screen is
  active, the title bar is dimmed.

- *Menu bar.* The menu bar contains a set of pull-down menus that you use to issue
  commands.

- *Toolbars.* The toolbars contain buttons that you can click to issue commands.

- *Rulers.* The vertical and horizontal rulers show you where your text is on the page.
  The shaded sections at the ends of the rulers indicate the margin areas. You can use
  the rulers to change some formatting, including tabs, indents, and margins (see
  Hour 7, "Formatting Paragraphs," and Hour 8, "Formatting Pages"). Depending on
  which *view* you're using, you may see only a horizontal ruler. (You'll learn about
  views in Hour 4, "Viewing and Printing Your Documents.") To hide the rulers,
  choose View, Ruler. To display them, choose View, Ruler again.

- *Text area.* This is the area in which you can type text.

- *View buttons.* You can use these buttons to switch views (see Hour 4).

- *Status bar.* The status bar tells you about the current status of your document. The
  left section tells you the current page number and the total number of pages. The
  middle section tells you the location of the insertion point (the cursor), and the
  right section tells you whether some special features are turned on.

- *Scrollbars.* The horizontal and vertical scrollbars let you bring different parts of a
  document into view. You'll learn how to use them in the next hour.

- *Control buttons.* These buttons let you control the Word window.

- *Browse buttons.* You can use these buttons to navigate sequentially through your
  document in various ways (see the next hour).

In addition to these basic elements of the Word window, you may also see the *Getting
Started task pane* when you first start Word (see Figure 1.6). This and other task panes
are discussed in "Working with Task Panes" later in this hour.

Getting Started task pane

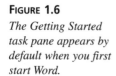

FIGURE 1.6
The Getting Started task pane appears by default when you first start Word.

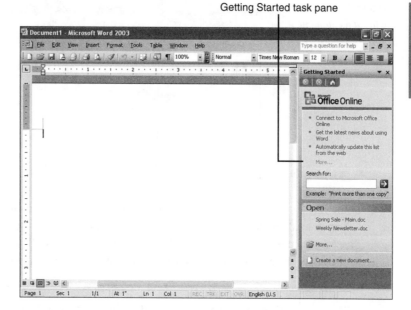

Working with Menus

The menu bar at the top of the Word window contains nine pull-down menus—File, Edit, View, and so on. You can issue all of the commands in Word via these menus. Chances are that you'll use toolbar buttons or keyboard shortcuts for many commands, but you can always fall back on the menus if you forget the alternate methods.

Menu Basics

To display a menu, click its name in the menu bar. For example, to display the Format menu, click Format in the menu bar, as shown in Figure 1.7. Then click a command in the menu to instruct Word to carry it out. If you want to close a menu without issuing a command, click anywhere outside the menu in the text area. (If your Format menu looks different from what you see in Figure 1.7, you may be using *full menus*, not *personalized menus*. See "Using Personalized Menus" later in this hour for more information.)

FIGURE **1.7**

Click a menu name to display the menu.

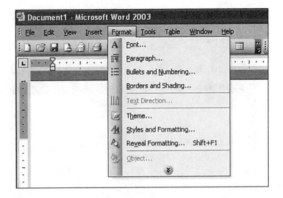

Some menu commands, such as the ones shown in the Format menu in Figure 1.7, are followed by three dots (…). These commands lead to dialog boxes, which you use to give Word more information before it carries out a command. If a menu command is not followed by three dots, Word performs the command as soon as you click it.

Commands that are followed by three dots are safe to click when you're exploring Word on your own, because you can always back out of the resulting dialog box by clicking the Cancel button. And just looking over the options in a dialog box can give you a sense of what the command does. If you have an important document onscreen, it's a good idea to refrain from clicking a command that is not followed by three dots, unless you know what it does. (You can undo many actions, as you'll learn in Hour 2, "Entering Text and Moving Around," but a few actions cannot be undone.)

If a menu command has a small triangle at its right, it leads to a submenu. To display the submenu, just point to the command. In Figure 1.8, the Insert, Picture submenu is displayed.

FIGURE **1.8**

Menu commands with triangles lead to sub-menus.

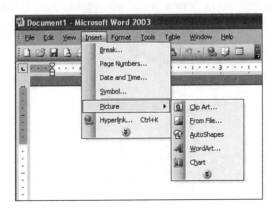

When a menu command is light gray, it is not currently available. In Figure 1.9, the first three commands in the Edit menu are grayed out.

FIGURE 1.9
Light gray commands are not currently available.

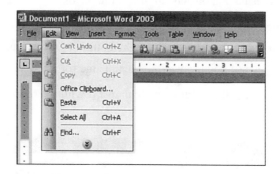

Many menu commands list keyboard shortcuts to their right. For example, in Figure 1.9, the keyboard shortcut Ctrl+A is listed to the right of the Select All command. You can use these keyboard shortcuts as an alternative to clicking the commands in the menus. See "Using Keyboard Shortcuts" later in this hour for more information. Furthermore, menu commands that have equivalent toolbar buttons show the toolbar buttons to the left of the command in the menu. In Figure 1.9, all of the commands but Select All have toolbar equivalents.

Using the Keyboard to Issue Menu Commands

You can use the keyboard instead of the mouse to display menus and issue commands in them. To display a menu, press the Alt key, and then press the underlined letter in the menu name. For example, to display the Format menu, you press Alt+O. After the menu is displayed, press the underlined letter in the command that you want to issue. For example, to issue the Paragraph command in the Format menu, press P. When a menu is displayed, you can press the right or left arrow keys to display the other menus in the menu bar. To close a menu without issuing any command, press the Alt key again.

 You can also use the keyboard to interact with dialog boxes. See "Working with Dialog Boxes" later in this hour for more information.

Using Personalized Menus

Word offers two choices for controlling how your menus behave: *personalized menus* and *full menus*. When the personalized menu feature is enabled, clicking a menu name displays a *short menu* that contains only the commands you use frequently. This reduces

clutter in your menus and makes it easier to find the commands you use all the time. If
you want to use a command that is not visible in the short menu, use one of these methods to expand the menu and display all of its commands:

- Double-click the menu name.
- Point to (or click) the down arrow at the bottom of the menu.
- Hover your mouse pointer over the menu name for a few seconds.

Figure 1.10 shows the full Format menu (contrast it with the short menu shown previously in Figure 1.9).

FIGURE 1.10

*When personalized
menus are turned on,
you can still display
the full menus.*

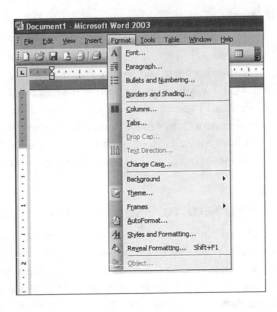

If you display the full menu and click one of the commands that was hidden in the short
menu, Word adds it to the short menu. By the same token, if you don't use a command in
the short menu for a period of time, Word may remove it from the short menu.

If you want to restore the default set of commands in your short menus, follow these
steps:

1. Choose **Tools, Customize**.
2. Click the **Options** tab.
3. Click the **Reset Menu and Toolbar Usage Data** button.
4. Click **Yes** in the message box that appears, and click **Close**.

Turning Off Personalized Menus

For some of you, personalized menus may be the best thing since sliced bread. For others, they may be an irksome distraction.

If you want to turn off personalized menus and always see the full menus instead, follow these steps:

1. Choose **Tools, Customize** to display the Customize dialog box.
2. Click the **Options** tab.
3. Mark the **Always Show Full Menus** check box.
4. Click the **Close** button.

Now you will see the full menus all of the time. (If you need any help with these steps, see "Working with Dialog Boxes" later in this hour.) If you want to turn personalized menus back on at some point, follow these same steps, but clear the check box in step 3 instead of marking it.

> To keep things simple, the remainder of this book assumes that personalized menus are turned off. If you prefer to keep this feature turned on, remember that some of the commands referred to in this book may not be included in your short menus; you might have to display the full menus to see them.

Displaying Context Menus

In addition to using the pull-down menus at the top of the Word window, you can also use *context menus* (sometimes called *shortcut menus*). These are menus that you display by clicking the right mouse button. The commands in a context menu vary depending on where you right-click. For example, if you right-click text, you get commands for editing and formatting text (see Figure 1.11), and if you right-click a toolbar, you get a list of available toolbars (see Figure 1.12).

To choose a command in a context menu, use a left-click. To close a context menu without choosing a command, click anywhere outside it (or press the Esc key).

FIGURE 1.11

Right-clicking text displays a context menu with commands for working with text.

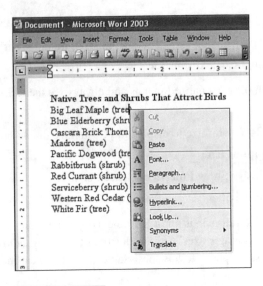

FIGURE 1.12

Right-clicking a toolbar displays a context menu that lists available toolbars.

Working with Toolbars

For many people, the fastest way to issue commands in Word is by using the toolbars. Word comes with a large set of toolbars. By default, it displays two of them—the Standard and Formatting toolbars, as shown in Figure 1.13. The Standard toolbar contains buttons for performing file-management tasks, such as starting, saving, opening, and printing documents. The Formatting toolbar contains buttons for common formatting tasks, including changing the font and font size, and adding boldface, italic, or underline to your text.

Standard toolbar   Formatting toolbar

FIGURE 1.13

The Standard and Formatting toolbars are displayed by default.

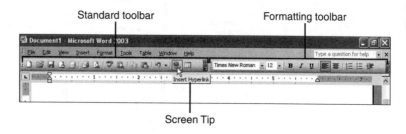

Screen Tip

To see what a toolbar button does, rest your mouse pointer on it for a moment. A ScreenTip appears with the button's name, as shown in Figure 1.13.

Displaying and Hiding Toolbars

The toolbars that aren't displayed by default can help you with all kinds of tasks. For example, the Tables and Borders toolbar has buttons for creating and formatting tables, and the Reviewing toolbar contains buttons that are useful if you're editing someone else's document. Some of these toolbars appear automatically when needed, but you can also display any of them "manually" whenever you like. You may also want to hide toolbars that you never use, to create more space in the Word window.

To display or hide a toolbar, choose View, Toolbars (see Figure 1.14). The toolbars that are currently displayed have check marks next to them. The ones that are currently hidden do not. Click the toolbar that you want to display or hide. (Depending on your Word installation, your available toolbars may not exactly match the ones shown in Figure 1.14.)

You can also display or hide a toolbar by right-clicking any toolbar that's currently displayed, and then clicking the desired toolbar in the context menu that appears (refer to Figure 1.12).

Accessing Hidden Toolbar Buttons

Depending on the size of your Word window, the number of toolbars that are sharing the same row, and so on, Word may not have room to display all of a toolbar's buttons. If you want to use a toolbar button that's currently hidden from view, click the Toolbar Options arrow at the right end of the toolbar (or at the bottom of the toolbar if you've docked it on one of the sides of your Word window). Word displays a list of all the hidden buttons (see Figure 1.15).

FIGURE 1.14

Use the Toolbars sub-menu to display or hide toolbars.

FIGURE 1.15

Word puts any toolbar buttons that are currently hidden in the Toolbar Options list.

Toolbar Options button

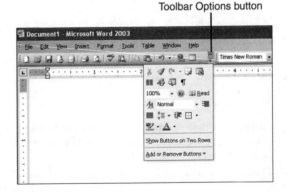

Click the button that you want to use. As soon as you click it, Word removes it from the Toolbar Options list and places it in a visible spot on the toolbar. (See "Moving Buttons Around a Toolbar" later in this hour if you want to adjust the button's position in the toolbar.)

If you want to restore the default set of visible buttons in your toolbars, follow these steps:

1. Choose **Tools, Customize**.
2. Click the **Options** tab.
3. Click the **Reset Menu and Toolbar Usage Data** button.
4. Click **Yes** in the message box that appears, and click **Close**.

Adding and Removing Toolbar Buttons

In addition to accessing hidden toolbar buttons, you can also use the Toolbar Options list to add new buttons to a toolbar, or to remove buttons that you never use. Click the Toolbar Options arrow at the right (or bottom) end of the toolbar, click Add or Remove Buttons, and then click the name of the toolbar whose buttons you want to add or remove (see Figure 1.16). Buttons that don't have check marks are not currently included in the toolbar; those that do have check marks are included. Click the button that you want to add or remove.

FIGURE 1.16

Click a button in the Add or Remove Buttons list that you want to add to or remove from the toolbar.

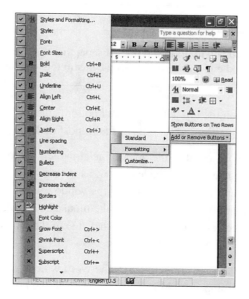

If you've made a mess of a toolbar, you can reset it to the state it was in when you installed Word. Click the Toolbar Options arrow, and then click Add or Remove Buttons. Click the name of the toolbar whose state you want to reset, and then click Reset Toolbar at the end of the Add or Remove Buttons list. (You may have to point to the down arrow at the bottom of the list to scroll to the end of the list.)

Moving Toolbars Around the Word Window

You can position your toolbars anywhere you like in the Word window. One reason to move a toolbar is to make it easier to see. If you have several toolbars displayed at the top of the Word window, they may seem to merge into one jumbled clump of buttons. You can visually separate the toolbars by spreading them out in different parts of the Word window.

Another reason to move a toolbar is to bring all of its buttons into view. If a toolbar is sharing a row with other toolbars, some of its buttons are probably hidden. If you want to access all the buttons without using the Toolbar Options list (see "Accessing Hidden Toolbar Buttons" earlier in this hour), you can move the toolbar onto its own row.

A quick way to put the Standard and Formatting toolbars on separate rows is to choose Tools, Customize, and then click the Options tab. Click to mark the Show Standard and Formatting Toolbars on Two Rows check box. Click the Close button when finished.

The remaining hours in this book assume that the Formatting toolbar is positioned on its own row, directly beneath the Standard toolbar.

You can *dock* toolbars on the top, left, right, and bottom edges of the window, or *float* them over the screen (see Figure 1.17). By default, most toolbars in Word are docked.

To move a docked toolbar, point to the dotted line at the left (or top) end of the toolbar. The mouse pointer becomes a four-headed arrow, as shown in Figure 1.18. If you want the toolbar to float, drag it into the text area of the window, and release the mouse button. To move the toolbar after you've released the mouse button, drag its title bar. If a toolbar is floating, you can quickly dock it on the edge of the window where it was most recently docked by double-clicking its title bar.

Another way to dock a toolbar on the edge of the Word window is to drag it toward that edge until its title bar disappears and it "flattens out," and then release the mouse button.

You can change the size of a floating toolbar by dragging one of its outside borders. Point to the outside edge of the floating toolbar and when the cursor changes to a double-headed arrow, drag the edge in or out.

FIGURE 1.17

You can dock toolbars or let them float.

Floating toolbar

Docked toolbars

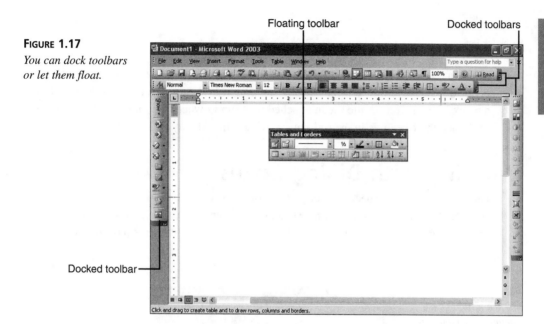

Docked toolbar

FIGURE 1.18

Drag the dotted line at the top (or left) end of a docked toolbar to move it.

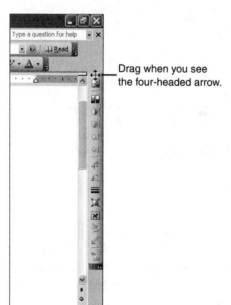

Drag when you see the four-headed arrow.

Moving Buttons Around a Toolbar

You can rearrange the order of the buttons on a toolbar if you like. To move a button, point to it and hold down the Alt key as you drag it to the desired position. As you drag, a black I-beam with a button icon attached to it shows where the toolbar button will end up. When the I-beam is in the right place, release the Alt key and your mouse button.

Working with Dialog Boxes

Dialog boxes let you specify exactly what you want Word to do before it carries out your command. Dialog boxes have some standard elements that you use to set options. The Print dialog box (choose File, Print), shown in Figure 1.19, contains most of these.

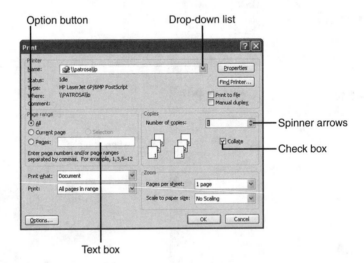

FIGURE 1.19

The Print dialog box contains common dialog box elements.

Here is a description of these elements:

- *Drop-down list.* Click the down arrow at the right end of a drop-down list to display a set of choices, and then click an item in the list. As soon as you click an item, the list closes. If you display a drop-down list and then decide not to change its current setting, click the down arrow again to close the list (or click anywhere else in the dialog box).

- *Option button.* To mark an option button, click it. A black dot appears in its center. To clear an option button, you have to click another option button in the same group. Only one option button in a group can be marked. (Option buttons are sometimes called *radio buttons*.)

- *Check box.* To mark a check box, click it. A check mark appears in the box. To clear the check mark, click the check box again. If you see a group of check boxes, you can mark as many of them as you like.

- *Text box.* A text box is a box in which you can type text. Click in a text box to place the insertion point in it, and then start typing. If there is already text in the box, you can replace it by dragging over it with the mouse to select it before you start typing.

- *Spinner arrows.* Some text boxes have spinner arrows. You can click the up and down arrows to increment the number in the text box up or down. Alternatively, you can just type the number in the box.

Some dialog boxes also contain *tabs* across the top of the dialog box. Each tab contains a separate set of options. Figure 1.20 shows the Options dialog box (Tools, Options), which contains 11 tabs. To bring a tab to the front, just click it.

FIGURE 1.20

In many dialog boxes, related sets of options are organized in tabs.

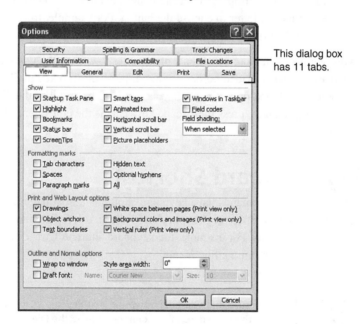

This dialog box has 11 tabs.

After you've made your selections in a dialog box, click the OK button to tell Word to carry out the command. (If a dialog box doesn't have an OK button, look for another likely candidate, such as a button labeled Close or Insert.) If you decide not to go ahead with a command, you can back out of the dialog box by clicking the Cancel button. Clicking the Close button (the X) in the upper-right corner of a dialog box is the same as clicking the Cancel button.

You can also use the keyboard to make selections in a dialog box. To do so, first press the Tab key to move to the option that you want to change. (To move in the reverse direction, press Shift+Tab.) When the option is selected, it will be highlighted or have a dotted box around it. Then make your choice by using one of these methods:

- To choose an item in a drop-down list, press the down-arrow key to display the list, use the up- and down-arrow keys to select the desired item, and then press Enter.
- To mark an option button, use the up- and down-arrow keys to mark the button.
- To mark or clear a check box, press the Spacebar.
- To type in a text box, move to it using the Tab key (if the text box is currently empty, an insertion point appears in the box; if it contains text, the text will be selected), and then type your text.
- To choose a button in a dialog box, move to it using the Tab key and then press Enter. If the button name has an underlined letter (or *hot key*), you can press the Alt key plus that letter to choose the button. For example, to choose the Properties button in the Print dialog box (refer to Figure 1.19), you can press Alt+P.

After you've made your selections, press Enter to choose the OK button. (If the OK button doesn't have a shaded border around it, press the Tab key until the button gains a dotted border, and then press Enter.) If you decide to back out of the dialog box without making any changes, press the Escape key. This is the equivalent of clicking the Cancel button.

Using Keyboard Shortcuts

Many common commands have keyboard shortcuts that you can use instead of the menus or toolbars. Some of these keyboard shortcuts are listed to the right of the commands in the menus. For example, the keyboard shortcut Ctrl+O appears to the right of the Open command in the File menu.

Make sure that you hold down the first key in a keyboard shortcut as you press the second key. For example, to issue the File, Open command with the keyboard, you press and hold down the Ctrl key as you press the letter O. If there are three keys in a keyboard shortcut, such as Shift+Ctrl+End, keep the first two held down as you press the third.

For a complete listing of keyboard shortcuts in Word's help system, search the help system for *keyboard shortcuts*, and then click the *Keyboard Shortcuts* topic in the results list. If you like, you can print the shortcuts and keep the list next to your computer for reference. (See "Getting Help" later in this hour.)

Working with Task Panes

By default, when you start Word the Getting Started task pane appears at the right edge of your Word window to give you a quick way to open a document, start a new document, or ask for help (refer back to Figure 1.6). This task pane is one of many that appear automatically when you perform certain actions, such as starting Word, inserting clip art in your document, or beginning a mail merge. Task panes typically contain information and options that are relevant to what you are doing. They give you a handy way of accomplishing tasks without leaving your document.

If you'd rather not see the Getting Started task pane on startup, choose Tools, Options to display the Options dialog box. Click the View tab, clear the Startup Task Pane check box, and click OK.

You can also deliberately display any of the task panes whenever you'd like. To do so, choose View, Task Pane (or press Ctrl+F1). The task pane that was most recently displayed will appear again. (Figure 1.21 shows the New Document task pane.) To switch to a different task pane, click the Other Task Panes button to display a list of the other task panes, and click the one you'd like to use. If you'd like to scroll through the various task panes that have been displayed so far in the current Word session, click the Back and Forward buttons. To quickly display the Getting Started task pane, click the Home button. When you want to close a task pane, click its Close button or press Ctrl+F1 again.

You can display some task panes by clicking toolbar buttons. For example, the Research button on the Standard toolbar (the ninth button from the left) displays the Research task pane, and the Styles and Formatting button on the Formatting toolbar (the button on the far left) displays the Styles and Formatting task pane.

FIGURE 1.21

Task panes give you a convenient way of performing tasks without leaving your document.

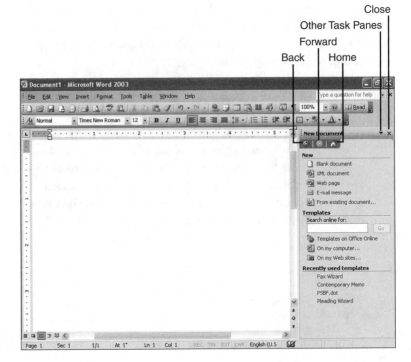

Controlling the Position and Size of the Word Window

You can change the appearance of the Word window in a variety of ways. You can make it disappear temporarily so that you can see what's behind it on the Windows desktop, or make it fill up the screen to give you more room to work. You can also move the Word window around on your desktop, or adjust its size.

Using the Control Buttons

The Control buttons appear in the upper-right corner of the Word window. The function of these buttons is the same for all Windows applications.

Click the Minimize button to temporarily hide the Word window, leaving only its taskbar button. To redisplay the Word window, click its taskbar button. If you want to make the Word window cover the entire desktop, click the Maximize button (see Figure 1.22).

FIGURE 1.22

The Minimize button shrinks the Word window to a taskbar button; the Maximize button enlarges it to cover the desktop.

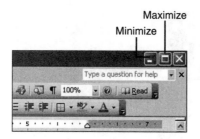

As soon as the Word window is maximized, the Maximize button becomes a Restore button (see Figure 1.23). Click the Restore button to return (restore) the window to the size it was before you maximized it.

FIGURE 1.23

Click the Restore button to return the window to the size it was before it was maximized.

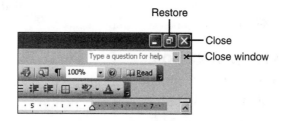

For information about using the Close button (the red X) and the Close Window button (the smaller, black X underneath the Close button), see "Closing Documents and Exiting Word" later in this hour.

Moving and Resizing the Word Window

If the Word window isn't maximized, you can move it around the Windows desktop or change its size.

To move the Word window, point to its title bar, drag the window to a different location, and release the mouse button.

To resize the Word window, point to the lower-right corner of the window. The mouse pointer becomes a diagonal black arrow, as shown in Figure 1.24. Drag in the desired direction to enlarge or shrink the window. (You can actually drag any edge or corner of the Word window to resize the window—the lower-right corner is just the most convenient spot.)

FIGURE 1.24

Drag a border or corner of the Word window to resize the window.

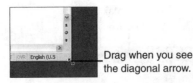

Drag when you see
the diagonal arrow.

Getting Help

If you putter around in Word trying to figure things out on your own (which you are strongly encouraged to do!), you are bound to have some questions once in a while. Maybe a feature isn't working as you think it should, or you know that a particular task must be possible, but you don't know how to approach it. This book will cover the most common issues you will run into; however, there may be a time where you are trying to tackle a more advanced topic and need further assistance. At these times, familiarity with Word's help system might be of some assistance. You can often find the information you need without pestering your coworkers or family members.

Using the Help Text Box

The simplest way to ask for help is to use the Help text box in the upper-right corner of the Word window (see Figure 1.25).

Help text box

FIGURE 1.25

Use the Help text box to tell Word what information you are looking for.

Click in the Help text box, type a keyword or two to describe your question, and press Enter (see Figure 1.26).

FIGURE 1.26

Type your question in the Help text box and press Enter.

Word searches its help system for information related to your question, and then displays links to the topics it finds in the Search Results task pane (see Figure 1.27).

FIGURE 1.27

Word displays links to relevant help topics in the Search Results task pane.

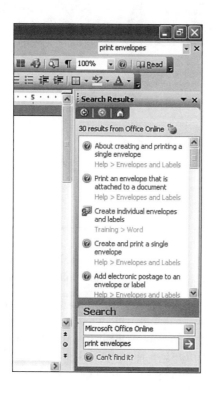

 If your computer is connected to the Internet, Word accesses its help information at the Microsoft Web site. However, you can still get help when your computer is not connected to the Internet—Word just accesses help information stored on your own computer instead. If you don't want Word to search help content on the Microsoft Web site, click the Online Content Settings link at the bottom of the Word Help task pane (see the next section). In the Service Options dialog box that appears, clear the Show Content and Links from Microsoft Office Online check box, and click OK.

Click the topic you are interested in to display it in a Microsoft Office Word Help window (see Figure 1.28).

To print a help topic, click the Print button at the top of the Microsoft Office Word Help window. In the Print dialog box that appears, click the Print button.

FIGURE **1.28**

Word displays help topics in the Microsoft Office Word Help window.

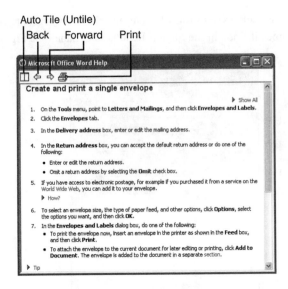

If you want to browse through other help topics that you've accessed during your current trip into the help system, use the Back and Forward buttons to bring them into view.

The Auto Tile button rearranges the size and position of the Microsoft Office Word Help window and the Word window so that the help window appears along the left side of the Word window. This enables you to refer to the help topic as you work in your document. When the Microsoft Office Word Help window is tiled, its Auto Tile button becomes an Untile button, which you can use to once again let the window sit "on top" of the Word window.

Using the Word Help Task Pane

If you like, you can also enter the help system by choosing Help, Microsoft Office Word Help (or clicking the Microsoft Office Word Help toolbar button toward the right end of the Standard toolbar). This command opens the Word Help task pane shown in Figure 1.29.

From here, you can use the Search text box to ferret out the information you need, or click the Table of Contents link to download the table of contents for the help system from Microsoft's Web site (see Figure 1.30). The table of contents organizes help topics into "books." Click a book to display the topics, and possibly other books that it contains. (The topics have question mark icons.) Click a book again when you want to hide its contents. When you find a topic that you want to read, click it to display its contents in the Microsoft Office Word Help window, described in the previous section.

FIGURE 1.29
The Word Help task pane provides another entry way into the help system.

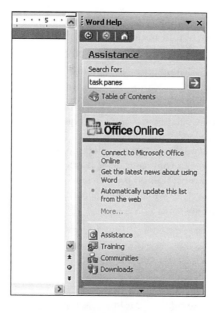

FIGURE 1.30
The table of contents organizes topics into "books" that you can expand and collapse.

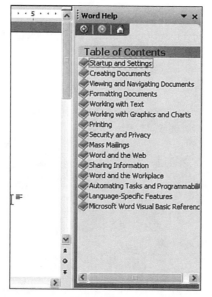

Closing Documents and Exiting Word

If you want to close all the Word documents you have open and exit Word, choose File, Exit. As Word is closing documents, it will stop to prompt you to save any that have unsaved changes.

If you want to close just the document that you're working on, but leave other Word documents open, click the Close button in the upper-right corner of the window (the red X). If your document contains any unsaved changes, you will be prompted to save it (you'll learn about saving in Hour 3, "Managing Documents").

> If your Word installation has been configured to display all open documents in one Word window (by choosing Tools, Options, clicking the View tab, and clearing the Windows in Taskbar check box), the Close button will behave just as the File, Exit command does; it will close all open documents and exit Word. If Word is configured this way and you want to close the current document but leave the remaining documents open, use one of the two methods described next.

Here are two other ways to close the current document but leave Word open:

- Choose **File**, **Close**.
- Click the **Close Window** button (the black X under the Close button in the upper-right corner of the Word window).

If you only have one Word document open, either of these methods closes the document but leaves the Word window open (see Figure 1.31).

No document is currently open.

FIGURE 1.31

Choose File, Close or click the Close Window button if you only have one Word window open and you want to close the document but leave Word open.

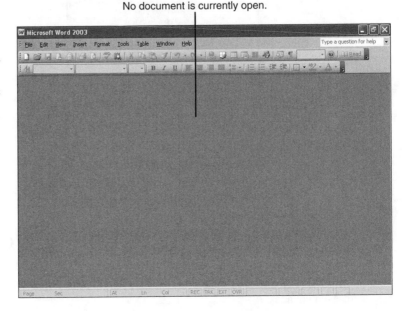

Summary

Word's mission is to help you create documents. Word is rich enough in features to let you produce all manner of specialized documents, yet simple enough that you can type a basic letter or memo without having to remember an esoteric sequence of commands. The Word window is quite customizable. If you like an uncluttered work environment, you can pare its contents down to the bare minimum. If, on the other hand, you feel most comfortable working with all kinds of tools close at hand, you can create an environment suitable for yourself as well. In the next hour, you will master a set of skills related to typing and editing text, including cutting and pasting, undoing mistakes, getting a word count, and more.

Q&A

Q **If I already have Office XP, can I install Office 2003 without uninstalling Office XP?**

A Yes. If you install Office 2003 on top of Office XP, Office will retain your customized settings in Office XP so that you don't have to redo them in Office 2003. Refer to Appendix A for more information.

Q **I'd like to single-click my Word shortcut icon instead of double-clicking it to start the program. How do I do that?**

A Click the Start button, and click My Computer. Choose Tools, Folder Options in the My Computer window. In the General tab, mark the Single-click to Open an Item (Point to Select) option button, and click OK.

Q **Should I close Word before I shut down Windows?**

A In general, it's a good idea to save and close your Word documents and exit Word before shutting down Windows. However, if you do issue the command to shut down when you have open Word documents that have unsaved changes, Word will prompt you to save the documents before the computer shuts down.

HOUR 2

Entering Text and Moving Around

For all the bells and whistles that come with a word processing program, you spend the bulk of your time with a much more mundane activity: typing and editing your text. In this hour, you first learn the basic principles of typing in Word. After you know how to get text onto the page, you then practice moving around the document. Finally, you learn all of the skills required to polish your text, including inserting new text, deleting text, and moving or copying text from one spot to another.

The highlights of this hour include

- Starting new paragraphs and creating blank lines
- Starting a new page
- Moving the insertion point in a document
- Jumping to a particular page
- Inserting new text into existing text
- Selecting text in preparation for doing something to it
- Deleting text
- Undoing mistakes, including restoring deleted text
- Moving and copying text

Typing Text

When you start Word, it gives you a blank document to let you start typing right away. Word makes some assumptions about how the document will look, so you don't need to worry about formatting at all unless you want to change the default settings. Here are the most important ones:

- 8 1/2- by 11-inch paper
- 1-inch margins on the top and bottom of the page, and 1 1/4-inch margins on the left and right sides of the page
- Single spacing
- Times New Roman, 12-point font

Later in this book, you learn how to change all of these formatting options. For now, you can just focus on typing.

Typing Paragraphs and Creating Blank Lines

The key to having a happy typing experience is knowing when to press Enter. Follow these two rules for typing paragraphs of text:

- When your text reaches the right margin, just continue typing. When Word can't fit any more text on the line, it automatically wraps the text to the next line for you. You should not press Enter at the ends of the lines within a paragraph.
- When you reach the end of the paragraph, you do need to press Enter. This brings the insertion point (the cursor) down to the next line.

Figure 2.1 illustrates these two rules.

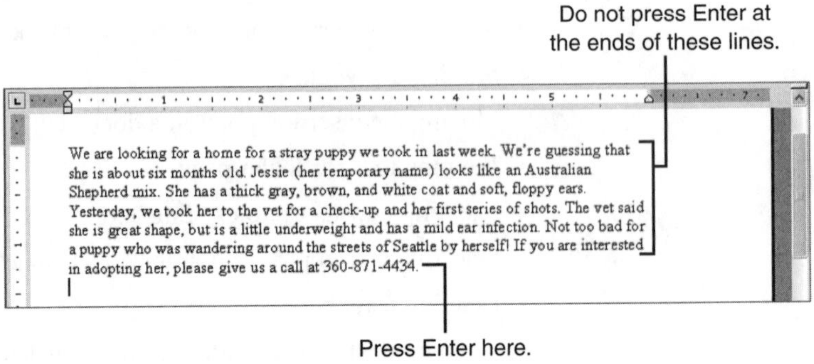

Do not press Enter at the ends of these lines.

FIGURE 2.1

Do not press Enter within a paragraph. Do press Enter at the end of the paragraph.

We are looking for a home for a stray puppy we took in last week. We're guessing that she is about six months old. Jessie (her temporary name) looks like an Australian Shepherd mix. She has a thick gray, brown, and white coat and soft, floppy ears. Yesterday, we took her to the vet for a check-up and her first series of shots. The vet said she is great shape, but is a little underweight and has a mild ear infection. Not too bad for a puppy who was wandering around the streets of Seattle by herself! If you are interested in adopting her, please give us a call at 360-871-4434.

Press Enter here.

> If you do accidentally press Enter at the end of lines within a paragraph, your line breaks go haywire as soon as you add or delete any text. If your paragraph has some lines that are much shorter than they should be (a telltale sign that you pressed Enter within the paragraph), follow the instructions in "Viewing Paragraph, Tab, and Space Marks" later in this hour to hunt down the offending paragraph marks and delete them.

2

When you press Enter, you actually insert a hidden character called a *paragraph mark*, which tells Word to end the paragraph. Word's definition of a paragraph may be a little broader than yours. It considers a paragraph to be any amount of text that ends with a paragraph mark. So as far as Word is concerned, blank lines and short lines of text—such as headings or the lines in an address block—are separate paragraphs.

To create lines between your paragraphs, press Enter twice at the end of the paragraph: once to end the paragraph you just typed and once to create the blank line. If you need several blank lines, just continue pressing Enter. If you press Enter too many times and need to delete a blank line, press the Backspace key. You'll learn much more about deleting paragraph marks later in this hour.

Figure 2.2 illustrates when to press Enter to create short lines of text and blank lines.

Press Enter to end these short lines.

FIGURE 2.2
Press Enter to end short lines of text and create blank lines.

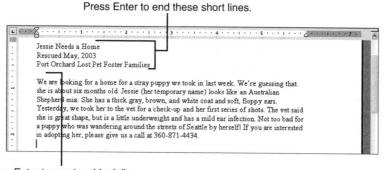

Press Enter to create a blank line.

> In "Adding Paragraph Spacing" in Hour 7, you'll learn how to automatically add a blank line after each paragraph without pressing Enter a second time.

As you type, you may see a variety of nonprinting underlines and buttons popping up automatically in your text. Here is a list of what they are and where you'll learn about them:

- Red or green wavy lines. These lines indicate possible spelling or grammatical errors. They are discussed in Hour 11, "Checking Your Spelling and Grammar and Using the Thesaurus."
- Purple dotted lines, often accompanied by small "i" icons, called Smart Tag Action buttons. These represent *smart tags*, and they are discussed in the "Working with Smart Tags" section at the end of this hour.
- Clipboard icons. These are Paste Options buttons, and you will learn about them in the "Cutting, Copying, and Pasting Text" section later in this hour.
- Lighting bolt icons (which first appear as a small blue bars). These are AutoCorrect Options buttons, and they are discussed in Hour 12, "Handy Editing Techniques."
- Purple wavy lines. These are XML schema violation markers, and they only appear in XML documents. They are discussed in Hour 24, "Smart Documents and XML."

Inserting Tabs

Word gives you default tab stops every one-half inch across the horizontal ruler. (If you don't see your rulers, choose View, Ruler.) Each time you press the Tab key, the insertion point jumps out to the next tab stop. Any text to the right of the insertion point moves along with it. Figure 2.3 shows the beginning of a memo in which the Tab key was pressed after the labels To:, From:, Date:, and Re: to line up the text at the half-inch mark on the horizontal ruler. When you use tabs, you can align your text far more precisely than you can by pressing the Spacebar multiple times.

Default tab stops (every half inch)

FIGURE 2.3

Press the Tab key to push text out to the next tab stop.

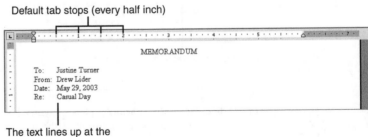

The text lines up at the half-inch mark on the ruler.

You can also press the Tab key at the beginning of a paragraph to indent the first line by one-half inch. Figure 2.4 shows a document whose paragraphs are indented in this way.

FIGURE 2.4

Press the Tab key at the beginning of each paragraph to indent the first line.

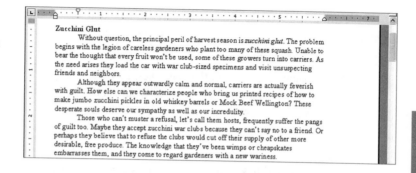

2

If you need to line up your text at precise locations along the horizontal ruler, you may want to replace the default tab stops with *custom tab stops.* You'll learn how to do this in Hour 7, "Formatting Paragraphs."

Viewing Paragraph, Tab, and Space Marks

As you're typing your document, you may occasionally want to check to see whether you accidentally pressed Enter at the end of a line within a paragraph, or pressed Enter too many times between paragraphs. Or, maybe you think you might have pressed the Tab key one time too many, or typed an extra space between two words. You can use Word's Show/Hide ¶ feature to solve these mysteries. To turn it on, click the Show/Hide ¶ button on the Formatting toolbar (or press Ctrl+Shift+*). This is a *toggle* button, meaning that you click it once to turn it on, and again when you want to turn it off (see Figure 2.5).

FIGURE 2.5

The Show/Hide ¶ feature lets you see your paragraph, tab, and space marks.

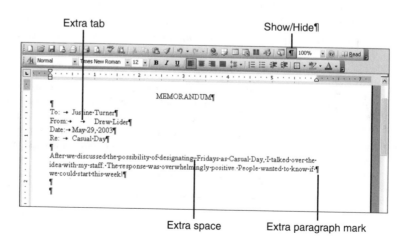

The Show/Hide feature uses the paragraph mark symbol to indicate where you pressed Enter, a right arrow to show where you pressed the Tab key, and a dot to mark where you pressed the Spacebar.

Figure 2.5 shows a document that has an errant paragraph, tab, and space mark. The user accidentally pressed the Tab key a second time on the From: line, typed an extra space between the words *designating* and *Fridays*, and pressed Enter at the end of a line within a paragraph.

To delete any of these characters, click immediately to the left of the character and press the Delete key (or click immediately to the right of the character and press the Backspace key). Figure 2.6 shows the same document after these three problems were fixed.

FIGURE 2.6

The extra paragraph, tab, and space marks have been deleted.

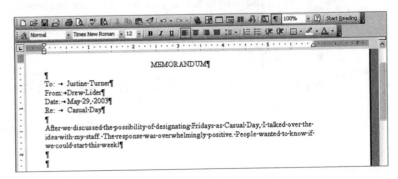

Typing onto the Next Page

As you're typing, Word calculates how many lines fit on a page. When the page you're on is full, Word automatically inserts a page break and starts another page. Figure 2.7 shows the break between two pages of text, as it appears in Print Layout view. (If your page breaks look different than what you see in Figure 2.7, choose View, Print Layout.)

As you add or delete text, Word adjusts the page break so that it is always in the right place. This type of "adjustable" page break is called a *soft page break* (or *automatic page break*). Sometimes you may need to break a page even though it is not yet full. For example, you might want to start the next section of a report on a new page, or create a title page. To do this, you have to insert a *hard page break* (or *manual page break*). You'll learn more about page breaks in Hour 8, "Formatting Pages."

FIGURE 2.7

Word breaks pages for you.

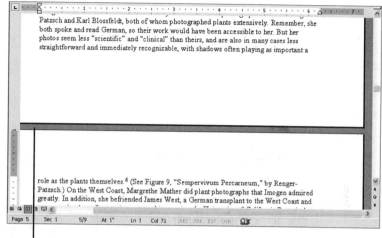

Patzsch and Karl Blossfeldt, both of whom photographed plants extensively. Remember, she both spoke and read German, so their work would have been accessible to her. But her photos seem less "scientific" and "clinical" than theirs, and are also in many cases less straightforward and immediately recognizable, with shadows often playing as important a

role as the plants themselves.[6] (See Figure 9, "Sempervivum Percarneum," by Renger-Patzsch.) On the West Coast, Margrethe Mather did plant photographs that Imogen admired greatly. In addition, she befriended James West, a German transplant to the West Coast and

Page break

Navigating Through Text

As you're typing a document, you will surely want to revise what you've written. Maybe you want to add a paragraph earlier in the document, change some wording, or delete a sentence or two. Before you can edit your text, however, you have to move the insertion point (*navigate*) to the location where you want to make the change. Word enables you to navigate with both the keyboard and the mouse. In the remainder of this hour, you will practice both types of navigation techniques.

It's important to differentiate between the *insertion point* and the *I-beam* (see Figure 2.8). The insertion point is the flashing vertical bar that shows where text will be inserted or deleted. When you navigate with the keyboard, the insertion point moves as you press the navigation keys. The I-beam is the mouse pointer that appears when you move the mouse over text. It does not show you where text will be inserted or deleted. In fact, its sole mission in life is to move the insertion point when you click. (If you're using the click-and-type feature, you need to double-click. This is discussed in "Inserting New Text into Existing Text" later in this hour.)

I-beam

FIGURE 2.8

The insertion point shows you where text will be inserted or deleted; the I-beam lets you move the insertion point.

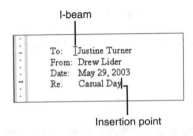

To: Justine Turner
From: Drew Lider
Date: May 29, 2003
Re: Casual Day

Insertion point

Navigating with the Mouse

To navigate with the mouse, simply point to the location where you want to place the insertion point and click. If the location is currently offscreen, you need to scroll the location into view by dragging the scroll box or clicking the up/down arrows in the scrollbars, or by using the Browse buttons. These techniques are described in the next two sections.

> If your mouse has a wheel between the buttons, you can roll the wheel to scroll up and down. (It doesn't matter where the mouse pointer is in the Word window when you do this.) If you click the wheel instead, the mouse pointer changes to two black arrows with a dot in between. You can then scroll by simply moving the mouse without rolling the wheel. To get out of this mode, click the wheel again. (You will probably find it easier on the eyes to scroll by rolling the wheel.)

Using the Scrollbars

Word provides a vertical scrollbar on the right side of the Word window and a horizontal scrollbar across the bottom of the window. You will frequently use the vertical scrollbar to scroll up and down through your document. By default, the entire width of your document is visible in the Word window, so you rarely need to use the horizontal scrollbar.

> When you use the scrollbar to scroll a document, the insertion point doesn't move to the portion of the document that you've scrolled onscreen until you click there.

You can click the up and down arrows at either end of the vertical scrollbar to scroll approximately one line at a time. To scroll more quickly, point to the up or down arrow and hold down the mouse button. To move longer distances, it's faster to drag the scroll box along the scrollbar. As you drag, a ScreenTip tells you what page you are on. If your document has headings, the ScreenTip also shows what section of the document you're in (see Figure 2.9).

Figure 2.9

Page 8 of this nine-page document is scrolled into view.

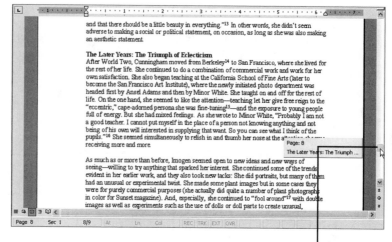

Drag the scroll box to travel longer distances.

To scroll up one screen at a time, click directly on the scrollbar above the scroll box; to scroll down one screen at a time, click the scrollbar below the scroll box.

Using the Browse Buttons

Browsing is a fast way to move sequentially through your document. You can use several types of objects as the focus point for browsing—including pages, headings, graphics, and footnotes—and you can change the browse object at any time. To browse, you use the three Browse buttons in the lower-right corner of the Word window (see Figure 2.10).

Figure 2.10

The Browse buttons let you move sequentially through your document.

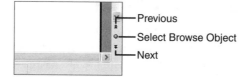

Previous
Select Browse Object
Next

The default option is to browse by page, so the ScreenTips for the Next and Previous buttons are Next Page and Previous Page. Click the Next Page button to travel directly to the top of the next page; click the Previous Page button to go to the top of the previous page.

If you want to browse by a different type of object, click the Select Browse Object button. Word displays a grid containing various browse objects (see Figure 2.11). Point to each square to see its description in the gray area at the bottom of the grid. Some objects, such as Field and Comment, are useful only if you have used certain features in your document. The two squares on the left end of the lower row, Go To and Find, display the Find and Replace dialog box.

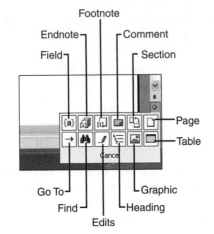

FIGURE 2.11
Click the Select Browse Object button and choose an object to browse by in the grid.

Select the browse object that you want to use. As soon as you choose an object other than Page, the Next and Previous buttons turn blue, and their ScreenTips change to reflect the currently selected object (Next Heading and Previous Heading, for example). Clicking these buttons now takes you to the next or previous instance of the browse object you selected.

Navigating with the Keyboard

If you prefer not to have to take your hands off the keyboard, you can move the insertion point through an entire document by using only the four arrow keys (see the first four items in Table 2.1), but you won't get anywhere fast. To navigate more efficiently, use the keyboard shortcuts listed in Table 2.1. Learning these shortcuts will save you huge amounts of time later on as you're editing documents.

TABLE 2.1   Keyboard Techniques for Moving the Insertion Point

Keyboard Technique	Moves the Insertion Point
↓	Down one line
↑	Up one line
→	One character to the right
←	One character to the left
Ctrl+→	One word to the right
Ctrl+←	One word to the left
Ctrl+↓	Down one paragraph
Ctrl+↑	Up one paragraph
End	To the end of the line
Home	To the beginning of the line
Page Down	Down one screen
Page Up	Up one screen
Ctrl+Page Down	To the top of the next page (or to the next browse object if the current browse object is something other than Page)
Ctrl+Page Up	To the top of the previous page (or to the previous browse object if the current browse object is something other than Page)
Ctrl+End	End of document
Ctrl+Home	Beginning of document

> With the keyboard techniques that involve pressing two keys, you can continue to travel in the same direction by holding down the first key as you press the second key repeatedly. For example, to move the insertion point word by word to the right, hold down the Ctrl key as you press the right-arrow key repeatedly.

Take a moment to practice the keyboard techniques now. You might want to jot them on a Post-it and stick the "cheat sheet" on your monitor. That way, you can refer to the shortcuts easily until you have them memorized.

Jumping to a Specific Page Using the Go To Command

When you're typing a long document, you often need to get to a particular page to make a change. You can, of course, navigate to that page by using the standard mouse and keyboard techniques described in this hour. However, it's often faster to use Word's Go To feature, which enables you to jump directly to any page in your document.

To use the Go To command to jump to a specific page, follow these steps:

1. Choose **Edit, Go To** to display the Go To tab of the Find and Replace dialog box.

2. If Page is not currently selected in the **Go to What** list, click it now, and then type the number of the page in the **Enter Page Number** text box (see Figure 2.12).

FIGURE 2.12

Type the desired page number in the Enter Page Number text box and press Enter.

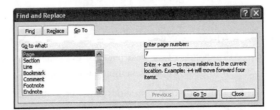

3. Click the **Go To** button (or press Enter). Word jumps to the page you specified. (You can check the page number in the status bar to confirm this.)

4. Repeat steps 2 and 3 if you want to go to other pages. Otherwise, click the **Close** button.

One unusual aspect of the Find and Replace dialog box (and a few other dialog boxes as well) is that you can click outside of the dialog box and edit your text while the dialog box is open. Most dialog boxes close as soon as you click the OK button, and you can't edit your document while the dialog box is displayed.

Word leaves the Find and Replace dialog box open after you click the Go To button so that you can continue using the dialog box to jump to other pages in the document. If you need to edit text on the current page, click outside of the dialog box to deactivate it and activate the document. The dialog box's title bar turns a lighter color to let you know that it no longer has the focus. Revise your text, and then click the title bar of the dialog box to activate it again. You can then use the Go To command to travel to another page. When you're finished using Go To, click the Close button in the dialog box.

As you can see in Figure 2.12, the Go to What list in the Go To tab of the Find and Replace dialog box lets you go to other items besides pages. When you click a different item in this list—Line or Footnote, for example—the options on the right side of the dialog box change to enable you to tell Word which specific instance of the item you want to go to.

Inserting New Text into Existing Text

2

When you want to insert text in the middle of a sentence or paragraph that you've already typed, Word assumes that you want the existing text to move out of the way to make room for the new text. Word calls this default behavior *insert mode*. To insert text, you simply move the insertion point to the place where you want the text to go and start typing. Any text to the right of the insertion point shifts over as you type. Note that when you insert text, you usually need to add a space either at the beginning or the end of the insertion.

If you are revising text throughout your document and want to return to the previous editing location, press Shift+F5.

Typing over Existing Text

Once in a while, you might want the text that you insert to replace existing text. To do this, press the Insert key on the keyboard to switch to *Overtype mode*. When you're using Overtype mode, every character you type replaces the character immediately to the right of the insertion point. The Insert key is a toggle, so you press it again when you want to return to Insert mode.

Watch your screen carefully when you're using Overtype mode. If you forget that you're in Overtype mode and merrily type away, you'll probably replace not only the text you wanted to delete but a sizable chunk of text that you wanted to keep as well.

The Insert key is right next to the Home, Delete, and End keys on the keyboard, so it's easy to press it accidentally when you mean to press another key. If you notice that your existing text is getting "gobbled up" as you type, it's a sure sign that you inadvertently switched to Overtype mode. Press the Insert key again to switch out of it, and then click the Undo button in the Standard toolbar one or more times to restore the deleted text.

You can also switch to Overtype mode by double-clicking the letters OVR in the right half of the status bar. The letters turn dark to indicate that you're in Overtype mode (see Figure 2.13). To return to Insert mode, double-click OVR again.

FIGURE 2.13

When you're in Overtype mode, the letters OVR in the status bar are dark.

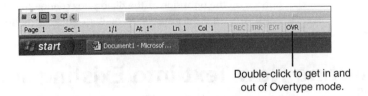

Double-click to get in and out of Overtype mode.

Double-Clicking to Move the Insertion Point Anywhere on the Page

Word's *click-and-type* features enable you to start typing in a blank area of your document by simply double-clicking at the desired location. For example, you can double-click in the middle of the page to center your text, double-click on the right margin to make the text flush right, or double-click several lines below your last line of text to create a large block of white space above the text. You don't have to first change your alignment, insert custom tabs, or press Enter repeatedly to create white space at the end of the document. (You will learn about alignment and custom tabs in Hour 7, "Formatting Paragraphs.") Word makes these changes for you when you double-click.

Click-and-type works only in Print Layout view and Web Layout view. To make sure you're using Print Layout view, choose View, Print Layout (Web Layout view is useful only if you're using Word to design Web pages).

To practice using click-and-type, start a new document, and move your I-beam to the right margin of the page. After a moment, an icon appears next to the I-beam indicating that your text is right-aligned (see Figure 2.14). Double-click to move the insertion point to this spot. If you start typing, your text is flush against the right margin.

If double-clicking doesn't move the insertion point, make sure you are in Print Layout view (choose View, Print Layout) and then choose Tools, Options, click the Edit tab, make sure the Enable Click and Type check box is marked, and click OK.

FIGURE 2.14

This click-and-type I-beam indicates right alignment.

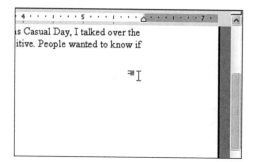

Now position the I-beam about halfway across the page. The I-beam icon changes to indicate center alignment. Double-click to move the insertion point. Any text you type now is centered horizontally on the page.

Next, point to a location anywhere on the page but about one-half inch from the left margin, on the right margin, or in the center. (Pointing to one of these locations would display an I-beam icon that indicates, respectively, left alignment with the first line indented, right alignment, or center alignment.) The I-beam icon indicates left alignment. Double-click to move the insertion point. If you start typing now, your text is left-aligned at the location you double-clicked.

Now position your I-beam about one-half inch in from the left margin. The I-beam icon changes slightly to indicate that it will create a *first-line indent* for you when you double-click (see Figure 2.15). If you do this, the first line of your paragraph will be indented one-half inch.

FIGURE 2.15

This click-and-type I-beam indicates a first-line indent.

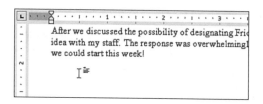

Finally, move the I-beam several inches down from the top margin of the page, and double-click. Word moves the insertion point down to the line you double-clicked on. If you start typing now, you have several blank lines above your text.

You don't have to use click-and-type if you don't want to. You can still move the insertion point into blank areas of the page by using the traditional formatting methods, which you'll learn about in Hour 7. If you'd like to disable click-and-type because the changing I-beam is distracting, choose Tools, Options, click the Edit tab, clear the Enable Click and Type check box, and click OK.

Combining and Splitting Paragraphs

As you're typing, you may at times want to combine two paragraphs into one, or split a longer paragraph into two or more shorter ones. Although there is nothing mysterious about doing this, it can be a little puzzling to beginners.

To join two paragraphs, click at the very end of the first paragraph, just past the period, and press the Delete key one or more times until the second paragraph moves up to join the first. (Alternatively, you can click at the very beginning of the second paragraph and press the Backspace key one or more times.) You may need to add a space where the two paragraphs come together.

 When you press the Delete or Backspace key to join paragraphs, you're actually removing the hidden paragraph marks separating the paragraphs. (See "Deleting Text" later in this hour for more about deleting hidden characters.) Remember that you can click the Show/Hide ¶ button in the Standard toolbar to make paragraph marks and other hidden characters visible.

To split a paragraph into two separate ones, click just before the first letter of the sentence that should begin the second paragraph, and press Enter. If you want blank lines between the two paragraphs, press Enter again for each blank line you need.

Selecting Text

Selecting (highlighting) text is an essential word processing skill. In many situations, you have to select text before issuing a command so that Word knows what text you want the command to affect. For example, you have to select text before cutting and pasting it or applying many kinds of formatting.

Using the Mouse

The most basic way of selecting text is to drag across it with the mouse. To do this, you position the I-beam at the beginning of the text you want to select, press and hold down the mouse button, drag across the text, and then release the mouse button. When text is selected, it becomes white against a black background, as shown in Figure 2.16. If you want to deselect text (remove the highlighting) without doing anything to it, click anywhere in the text area of the Word window, or press a navigation key such as one of the arrow keys, Home, or End.

FIGURE 2.16

Selected text is white against a black background.

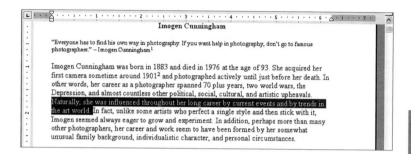

If you accidentally drag over too much text, you can remove the extra text from the selection by keeping the mouse button held down as you drag back up and/or to the left.

If you select some text, release the mouse button, and then realize that you selected too much or too little, you can't point to the end of the selection and start dragging to extend or shorten it. If you do this, you end up *moving* the selected text. (Dragging selected text performs a type of cutting and pasting called *drag-and-drop*.) Instead, you need to either click elsewhere to deselect the text and then start the highlighting process again, or press the Shift key and then click with the mouse to extend or shrink the selection.

Word assumes that when you're dragging with the mouse, you want to select entire words at a time. This can make it difficult to be precise about what you're selecting. If you find this behavior vexing, follow these steps to turn it off:

1. Choose **Tools**, **Options**.
2. Click the **Edit** tab.
3. Clear the **When Selecting**, **Automatically Select Entire Word** check box.
4. Click **OK**.

Using the Keyboard

Although dragging always works to select text, it is often not the most efficient method. Table 2.2 lists some shortcuts for selecting different amounts of text.

TABLE 2.2 Selection Shortcuts

Amount of Text to Select	Shortcut
One word	Double-click the word.
One sentence	Ctrl+click the sentence. (This only works if nothing else is currently selected.)
One line	Click in the selection bar to the left of the line.
One paragraph	Double-click in the selection bar to the left of the paragraph. (You can also triple-click directly on the paragraph.)
Entire document	Triple-click or Ctrl+click anywhere in the selection bar. (Ctrl+click only works if nothing else is currently selected.)
Any amount of text	Click at the beginning of the text you want to select, and then Shift+click at the end of the text.

Three of the shortcuts involve clicking in the *selection bar*, the white area in the left margin of the page (see Figure 2.17). When the mouse pointer is in this area, it becomes a white arrow angled toward your text.

FIGURE 2.17
The selection bar is the white area to the left of your text.

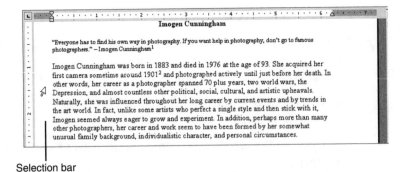

Selection bar

Selecting Multiple Blocks of Text

You can select more than one nonadjacent block of text at the same time. You might do this if you want to apply the same formatting to several words in a paragraph, or cut and paste several sentences from one location to another. To select multiple blocks of text, select the first block using whatever method you like, and then hold down the Ctrl key as you drag over the second block. If you want to add more blocks of text to the selection, just Ctrl+drag over them as well (see Figure 2.18).

FIGURE 2.18

*Ctrl+drag to select
multiple blocks of text.*

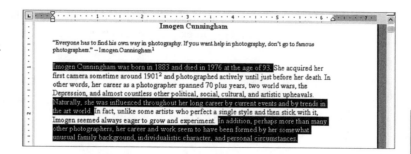

If you like using the keyboard, you may prefer to select text by using only the keyboard. All of the keyboard selection techniques involve adding the Shift key to a navigation keyboard shortcut (whichever one travels the distance that you want to select). Table 2.3 lists some of the most common keyboard selection techniques.

TABLE 2.3   Keyboard Selection Techniques

Keyboard Technique	Amount Selected
Shift+→	One character to the right
Shift+←	One character to the left
Shift+↓	One line down
Shift+↑	One line up
Shift+Ctrl+→	One word to the right
Shift+Ctrl+←	One word to the left
Shift+Ctrl+↓	One paragraph down
Shift+Ctrl+↑	One paragraph up
Shift+End	From the insertion point to the end of the line
Shift+Home	From the insertion point to the beginning of the line
Shift+Ctrl+End	From the insertion point to the end of the document
Shift+Ctrl+Home	From the insertion point to the beginning of the document
Ctrl+A	The entire document (same as choosing Edit, Select All)

When using the keyboard techniques that involve pressing an arrow key, you can quickly add to the current selection by keeping the other keys in the combination held down as you repeatedly press the arrow key. For example, to select six words to the right, you would hold down the Shift and Ctrl keys as you pressed the right-arrow key six times.

One of the handiest uses of keyboard selection techniques is to adjust the size of a selection after you've already released the mouse button. For example, if you dragged over a couple of sentences, but accidentally didn't include the period at the end of the last sentence, you can press Shift+→ to extend the selection one character to the right to include the period.

> You can also press the Shift key and then click with the mouse to extend or shrink the selection.

Deleting Text

Knowing how to delete text is almost as important as knowing how to type it in the first place. Although you can delete any amount of text if you bang on the Delete or Backspace key enough times, it's much more efficient to use other methods when you want to select more than a few characters. Table 2.4 lists techniques for deleting different amounts of text.

TABLE 2.4   Techniques for Deleting Text

Technique	Result
Delete key	Deletes character to the right of the insertion point
Backspace key	Deletes character to the left of the insertion point
Ctrl+Delete	Deletes word to the right of the insertion point
Ctrl+Backspace	Deletes word to the left of the insertion point
Select text and press the Delete key	Deletes selected text (can be any amount)
Select text and start typing	Deletes selected text (can be any amount) and replaces it with the text you type

To delete several words, hold down the Ctrl key as you press Delete or Backspace several times. If you want to delete only the end of a word—for example, you want to change the word functionality to *function*—click in front of the part you want to delete (before the letter *a* in this example) and press Ctrl+Delete. If you want to delete the beginning of a word—to change the word *ultraconservative* to *conservative*, for instance—click just after the part you want to delete (just past the letter *a* in this example) and press Ctrl+Backspace.

Word treats paragraph marks, tabs, and spaces just like other characters, so you can delete them with the Delete and Backspace keys, just as you delete other characters. In most cases, it's obvious where they are even though they are hidden. At times, however, you may find it helpful to display these hidden characters onscreen so that you can see exactly where they are. To do this, click the Show/Hide ¶ button in the Standard toolbar. (You learned about the Show/Hide feature in the section "Viewing Paragraph, Tab, and Space Marks" earlier in this hour.)

Undoing Mistakes

If you know how to delete text, you surely want to know how to restore it when you delete it accidentally. Word's Undo feature enables you to bring back deleted text as well as undoing many other actions. You are not limited to undoing the most recent action you performed; Undo enables you to undo multiple actions. For example, if you delete a paragraph by mistake and then go on to issue a few more commands before realizing that the paragraph was gone, you can undo all of your actions back to, and including, restoring the deleted text.

> Word can undo most actions related to editing and formatting your document. Two actions that Word can't undo are saving and printing.

To undo the most recent action, click the Undo button on the Standard toolbar (see Figure 2.19) or press Ctrl+Z. To continue undoing previous actions one by one, keep clicking the Undo button or pressing Ctrl+Z.

Click to display a list of actions you can undo.

Undo ─┐   ┌─ Redo

FIGURE 2.19
Click the Undo toolbar button to undo your most recent action.

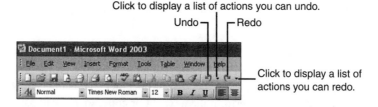

Click to display a list of actions you can redo.

If you know that you want to undo something you did a few minutes ago and don't want to click the Undo button several times, click the down arrow to the right of the Undo button (refer to Figure 2.19). This displays a list of all of your actions, with the most recent action at the top (see Figure 2.20). Scroll down the list and click the action that you want to undo. Word reverses all of your actions back to and including the one you click in the undo list.

FIGURE 2.20

Click an action in the Undo drop-down list to undo everything back to that point.

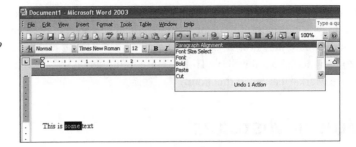

If you undo an action and then decide that you want to perform it after all, click the Redo button on the Standard toolbar (refer to Figure 2.20) or press Ctrl+Y or F4. As with Undo, you can redo multiple actions by clicking the button repeatedly, or by choosing an action in the Redo drop-down list.

Cutting, Copying, and Pasting Text

The capability to move and copy text from one place to another is one of the most appreciated features of word processing programs. The term *cutting and pasting* actually refers to both moving and copying text. When you *move* text, you remove (*cut*) it from one location in your document and paste it in another. When you *copy* text, you leave the text in its original location and paste a duplicate of it somewhere else.

The location that contains the text you want to move or copy is called the *source*, and the place you want to paste it is called the *destination*. The destination can be in the same document, another Word document, another Office document (such as an Excel spreadsheet or a PowerPoint presentation), or a document created in another Windows application.

When you cut or copy text, it is placed on the Windows Clipboard, a temporary storage area available to all Windows applications. Issuing the Paste command copies the text from the Windows Clipboard into your document. (It actually stays on the Windows Clipboard until you perform the next cut or copy, so you can paste the same text multiple times if you like.)

A major limitation of the Windows Clipboard is that it can hold only one selection at a time. Each time you cut or copy another block of text, it replaces the text that was previously on the Windows Clipboard. As you'll see in "Moving and Copying Multiple Items" later in this hour, Office offers a way around this restriction with the Office Clipboard.

Moving Text

When working with documents, you often need to restructure the text. Rather than delete text and retype it, you can move a word or phrase within a sentence, reorganize the flow of sentences within a paragraph, or change the order of some paragraphs.

Follow these steps to move text:

1. Select the text that you want to move. (Use any method described in "Selecting Text" earlier in this hour.)
2. Click the **Cut** button on the Standard toolbar (see Figure 2.21) or press **Ctrl+X**. The text disappears from its current location.

2

FIGURE 2.21

Click the Cut button to remove the selected text from its current location.

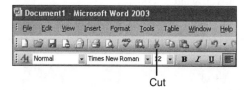

Cut

3. Navigate to the destination, and place the insertion point exactly where you want the text to appear.

If the destination is in a different document that is currently open, click the document's taskbar button to switch to it, and then navigate to the place where you want to insert the text. If the destination document isn't open, open it now (see "Opening Documents" in Hour 3).

4. Click the **Paste** button in the Standard toolbar (see Figure 2.22) or press **Ctrl+V**. The text is pasted into the destination, and existing text to the right of the insertion point moves over to make room for the inserted text.

FIGURE 2.22

Click the Paste toolbar button to paste the text into the destination.

Paste

If you're trying to move text and the Cut toolbar button is dim, you forgot to select the text you want to move. The Cut and Copy toolbar buttons become active only when you have text selected.

Copying Text

If you want to insert a block of text that you've already typed somewhere else, it's much faster to copy it than to type it from scratch.

Follow these steps to copy text:

1. Select the text that you want to copy.
2. Click the **Copy** button on the Standard toolbar (see Figure 2.23) or press **Ctrl+C**. The original text remains in its current location.

FIGURE 2.23

Click the Copy button
to make a copy of the
selected text.

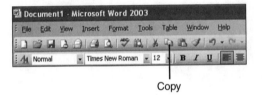

Copy

3. Navigate to the destination, and make sure that the insertion point is exactly where you want the text to appear.
4. Click the **Paste** button in the Standard toolbar or press **Ctrl+V**. The text is pasted into the destination, and existing text to the right of the insertion point moves over to make room for the inserted text.

If you want to copy an entire file into the current document, click at the location where you want to insert the file, choose Insert, File, select the file in the Insert File dialog box, and click the Insert button.

Moving and Copying with Drag-and-Drop

If you are handy with the mouse, you may find it easiest to move and copy text with *drag-and-drop*. This feature enables you to select text and then drag it to its destination. Drag-and-drop is best suited for moving or copying small amounts of text a short distance.

To move text with drag-and-drop, follow these steps:

1. Select the text that you want to move or copy and release the mouse button.

2. Point to the selected text. The mouse pointer becomes a white arrow.

3. To move the text, drag it to the destination. As you drag, the mouse pointer changes to indicate that you're performing a drag-and-drop (see Figure 2.24). Drag until the dashed insertion point attached to the mouse pointer is in the right place, and then release the mouse button.

FIGURE 2.24
A special drag-and-drop mouse pointer shows where the text will be inserted.

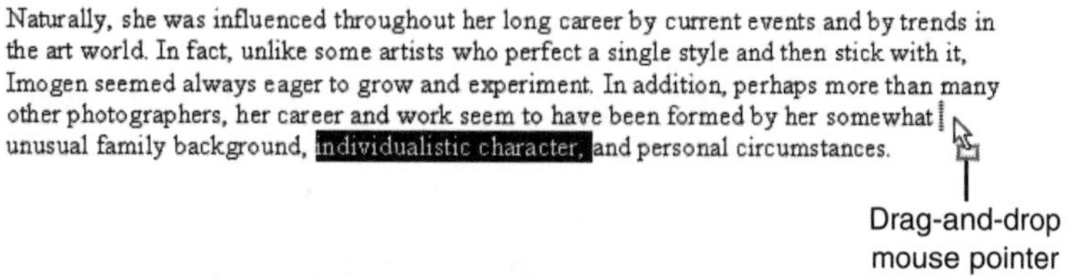

Naturally, she was influenced throughout her long career by current events and by trends in the art world. In fact, unlike some artists who perfect a single style and then stick with it, Imogen seemed always eager to grow and experiment. In addition, perhaps more than many other photographers, her career and work seem to have been formed by her somewhat unusual family background, individualistic character, and personal circumstances.

Drag-and-drop mouse pointer

4. To copy the text, **Ctrl+drag** it to the destination (hold down the Ctrl key as you drag). The drag-and-drop mouse pointer gains a plus sign to indicate that you're performing a copy, not a move (see Figure 2.25). When the dashed insertion point is in the right place, release the mouse button and then the Ctrl key. (If you release the Ctrl key before the mouse button, Word performs a cut instead of a copy.)

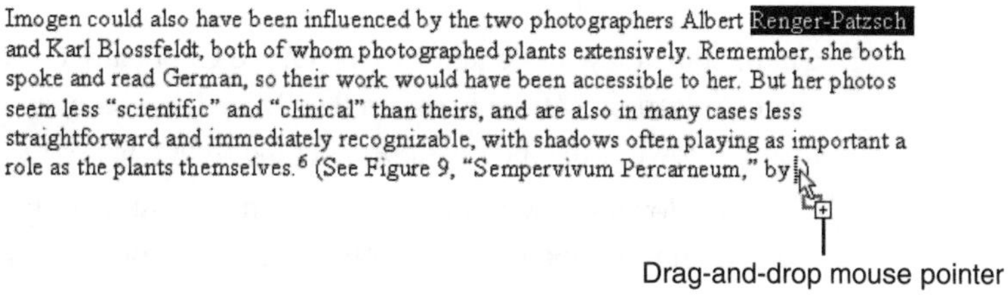

FIGURE 2.25
The drag-and-drop mouse pointer includes a plus sign when you're copying text.

Imogen could also have been influenced by the two photographers Albert Renger-Patzsch and Karl Blossfeldt, both of whom photographed plants extensively. Remember, she both spoke and read German, so their work would have been accessible to her. But her photos seem less "scientific" and "clinical" than theirs, and are also in many cases less straightforward and immediately recognizable, with shadows often playing as important a role as the plants themselves.[6] (See Figure 9, "Sempervivum Percarneum," by

Drag-and-drop mouse pointer

5. Click anywhere to deselect the text.

If you accidentally drop the selected text in the wrong place, click the Undo button on the Standard toolbar.

Moving and Copying Multiple Items

With the traditional cut-and-paste procedure, you can cut or copy only one selection at a time. The Office Clipboard enables you to "collect" up to 24 selections of cut or copied data from any application and then paste them in any order into any Office document. The Office Clipboard can handle all of the standard data types, including text, numbers, graphic images, and so on.

To practice using the Office Clipboard, follow these steps:

1. Select a block of text in a Word document, and click the **Cut** or **Copy** button on the Standard toolbar. Repeat this action by cutting or copying another block of text in the document. The Clipboard task pane automatically appears with two Word icons to represent the two items that you've cut or copied (see Figure 2.26). In addition, the Clipboard icon appears at the right end of the Windows taskbar.

FIGURE 2.26

Each item you cut or copy appears as an icon in the Clipboard task pane.

The Office Clipboard contains two items.

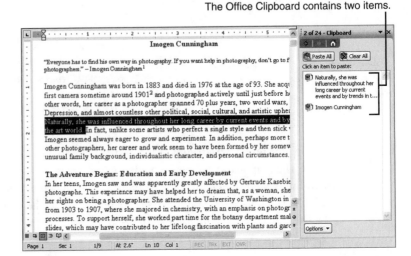

2. Cut or copy a few more items to the Office Clipboard, click in a location where you want to insert one of the items on the Office Clipboard, and then point to one of them. A down-arrow button appears at the right edge of the item (see Figure 2.27).

3. Click the down arrow to display a drop-down list, and then click **Paste** to insert the item in your document (see Figure 2.28). (You can also just click the item to insert it.)

4. Paste some of the other items in the Clipboard task pane if you like, and then click the **Close** button in the upper-right corner of the task pane.

If you want to paste all of the items in the Clipboard task pane at once, click the Paste All button at the top of the task pane. To remove all of the items from the Clipboard task pane, click the Clear All button. (To remove an individual item from the task pane, click its down arrow and choose Delete.)

FIGURE 2.27

Point to an item to display its down arrow.

The down arrow appears when you point to an item.

FIGURE 2.28

Choose Paste to paste the item into your document at the location of the insertion point.

You can bring up the Clipboard task pane at any time by choosing Edit, Office Clipboard. If you don't want the Clipboard task pane to appear automatically, click the Options button at the bottom of the task pane and clear the check marks next to Show Office Clipboard Automatically and Show Office Clipboard When Ctrl+C Pressed Twice.

When the Clipboard task pane is visible, you can cut or copy items from any Windows application to the Office Clipboard. Items that you've cut or copied from applications other than Word have different icons. In Figure 2.29, the Office Clipboard holds five items: one from Paint Shop Pro (a graphics program), one from a PowerPoint presentation, one from an Excel spreadsheet, one from a Web page, and one from a Word document.

FIGURE 2.29

You can cut or copy items from any Windows application.

Options for Formatting Pasted Text

When you paste text, a Paste Options button appears next to the pasted text as soon as you issue the Paste command (see Figure 2.30).

FIGURE 2.30

The Paste Options button shows up as soon as you issue the Paste command.

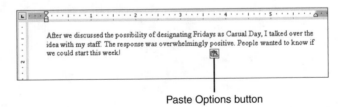

Paste Options button

To display various paste options, click the down arrow that appears to the right of the bottom when you point to it. The commands in this list will vary depending on the program you are pasting from, the formatting of the text surrounding the pasted text, and the type of content you're pasting. The list shown in Figure 2.31 appears when you're pasting text into a paragraph. As soon as you choose a command from the list, the button disappears.

FIGURE 2.31

The items in the Paste Options list vary depending on what you are doing.

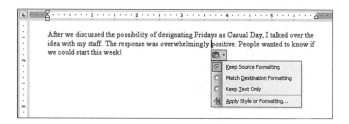

If you don't use the Paste Options button when it appears, it disappears automatically when you take the next action (such as typing, selecting, or deleting text). If you want to "manually" hide the Paste Options button, press the Escape key. To turn off this feature entirely, follow these steps:

1. Choose **Tools**, **Options** to display the Options dialog box.
2. Click the **Edit** tab.
3. Clear the **Show Paste Options Buttons** check box.
4. Click **OK**.

Getting a Word Count

Whether you've been asked to submit a biography of 100 words or fewer, or to write a paper no longer than 4000 words, you will appreciate Word's ability to serve up these statistics with a click of the mouse. To check the number of words in your document, choose Tools, Word Count. The Word Count dialog box, shown in Figure 2.32, appears with a word count, as well as a count of pages, characters, paragraphs and lines.

FIGURE 2.32

The Word Count dialog box reports the number of words in the text you've selected.

If your document contains footnotes or endnotes, you can mark the Include Footnotes and Endnotes check box to include that text in your word count. If you need to check your word count frequently, click the Show Toolbar button, and then click Cancel.

The Word Count toolbar appears on top of your document (see Figure 2.33). Display the drop-down list to see the same statistics that are presented in the Word Count dialog box, and click the Recount button whenever you need to update the numbers.

FIGURE 2.33
The Word Count tool-bar gives you quick access to your word count statistics.

Working with Smart Tags

Word has a penchant for "decorating" your text with various gizmos that give you access to tools it thinks you might find handy. The purple dotted underlines and little "i" icons represent *smart tags* (see Figure 2.34). Word marks certain pieces of text it recognizes—such as names, addresses, financial symbols, and so on—with smart tags to indicate that you can perform actions on them.

FIGURE 2.34
Smart tags are indi-cated with a purple dotted underline and a Smart Tags Action button.

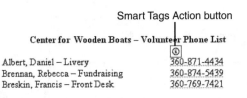

Smart Tags Action button

To use a smart tag, move your mouse pointer over purple underlined text such as a phone number as seen in Figure 2.34, to display the Smart Tag Actions button. Point to the button and click the down arrow that appears to its right to display a list of possible actions, and then click the action you want to perform. In Figure 2.35, choosing Add to Contacts will display Outlook's Contact dialog box to enable you to add the phone number to your Outlook contact information without leaving Word.

Other companies have also designed smart tags that you can download from the Web. To see what's available, choose Tools, AutoCorrect Options, click the Smart Tags tab, and click the More Smart Tags button.

To remove an individual smart tag from a piece of text, click the Smart Tag Actions button and choose Remove This Smart Tag.

If you want to control which types of text get marked with smart tags, choose Tools, AutoCorrect Options, and click the Smart Tags tab (see Figure 2.36). Mark or clear the appropriate check boxes, and click OK.

FIGURE 2.35

Choose the action you want to perform in the Smart Tag Actions drop-down list.

Center for Wooden Boats – Volunteer Phone List

Albert, Daniel – Livery
Brennan, Rebecca – Fundraising
Breskin, Francis – Front Desk
Mangahas, Gabrielle – Shop
Olsen, Christina – Front Desk
Peterson, Jacob – Shop
Ramsey, Menghua – Livery
Rutherford, Janice – Shop
Sullivan, Kai – Fundraising

Telephone Number: 360-871-4434
Add to Contacts
Remove this Smart Tag
Stop recognizing "360-871-4434" ▶
Smart Tag Options...

206-821-3315
360-871-5337

FIGURE 2.36

You can specify what types of text get marked with smart tags.

If you want to use the smart tags feature, but you don't want to see the purple dotted underlines, you can choose Tools, Options, click the View tab, and clear the Smart Tags check box. If you do this, the Smart Tag Actions button will still appear over text that the smart tags feature has recognized, but you will no longer see purple underlines.

To remove all smart tags from the current document, choose Tools, AutoCorrect Options, click the Smart Tags tab, click the Remove Smart Tags button, and click OK. (If you later want to see them again, you can click the Recheck Document button.) To turn off the smart tags feature entirely, clear the Label Text with Smart Tags check box, and click OK.

Summary

Revising text is at the heart of word processing. When the techniques explained in this hour become second nature, you'll be able to place your attention squarely on the content of your document, where it belongs, rather than the commands required to edit text. Don't worry too much about formatting your text yet. You will learn many ways to format in Part 2 of this book. The most pressing task at the moment is learning how to save your documents so that you can come back to them later. You'll learn this and other document-management techniques in the next hour.

Q&A

Q How much of the page can I see onscreen?

A Assuming that you're using Word's default settings, you can probably see about one third of a page onscreen at a time.

Q How can I tell how many pages long my document is?

A The left third of the status bar shows you the current page and the total number of pages, separated by a slash. If you see 5/14, for example, you are currently on page 5 out of 14 pages.

Q When I tried to move text with drag-and-drop, it didn't work. What is wrong?

A Some people disable drag-and-drop if they find that they are moving text accidentally. If someone turned this feature off on your computer, you can turn it back on by choosing Tools, Options, clicking the Edit tab, marking the Drag-and-Drop Text Editing check box, and clicking OK.

Q If I use the Office Clipboard in a Word document and then close Word, does the Office Clipboard remain available?

A The Office Clipboard is available as long as you have at least one Office application open. If you want to use the Office Clipboard to cut or copy data in a non-Office application, display the Clipboard task pane first, and then switch to the application in which you want to cut or copy data. Select the item that you want to cut or copy and issue the Cut or Copy command. When you switch back to the Office application, you will see an icon for the item you just cut or copied on the Office Clipboard. When you close all Office applications, the Office Clipboard is cleared.

Q How exactly does the Office Clipboard relate to the Windows Clipboard?

A The Office Clipboard and Windows Clipboard are separate, but their functions overlap. When you cut or copy items to the Office Clipboard, the last item is placed on the Windows Clipboard. When you click the Paste button in the Standard toolbar (or choose Edit, Paste or press Ctrl+V), the item in the Windows Clipboard (the last item in the Office Clipboard) is pasted into your document. If you keep issuing the Paste command, this same item is pasted each time, until you cut or copy another item. Clicking the Clear Clipboard button in the Clipboard toolbar also clears the Windows Clipboard.

2

HOUR **3**

Managing Documents

In this hour, you learn how to manage your Word documents. The topics in this hour read like a file clerk's job description: You learn how to store (save) files for later use, open existing files so that you can revise them, quickly access your favorite folders and files, and so on. You may already know how to use Windows Explorer or My Computer to create new folders and rename, delete, move, and copy files. Here you learn how to perform these same tasks in Word so that you can handle them without leaving the Word window.

The highlights of this hour include

- Saving and opening files
- Accessing favorite folders and files
- Creating folders
- Changing your default documents folder
- Switching among open documents
- Starting new documents
- Renaming and deleting files
- Moving and copying files

Saving Documents

When you are typing a new document, it exists only in your computer's memory. Memory (or RAM) is a temporary storage area. In other words, it is dependent on electricity. As soon as you turn off your computer, memory is wiped clean and everything in it is lost. For this reason, you need to save your documents to a permanent storage medium, such as your hard disk, a removable disk such as a floppy disk, Zip disk, CD-R/CD-RW (a writeable CD-ROM), or a network drive (if you're on a network). These storage devices are not dependent on electricity, so the files stored on them remain there whether your computer is turned on or off.

You can think of your disk drives as filing cabinets. Just as a physical filing cabinet holds hanging folders that can contain other folders or files, so can your permanent storage devices contain folders, which can in turn contain other folders or files.

A *disk drive* is basically a disk player. It's the device that plays the disk, just as a tape player plays a cassette tape. Because you can't remove a hard disk from the drive, the terms *hard disk* and *hard drive* are often used interchangeably. (In contrast, you can remove a floppy disk, Zip disk, or CD-R/CD-RW from its disk drive.) If your computer is on a network, your own hard drive is often called your *local drive* to distinguish it from *network drives*, which are storage locations on other computers on the network.

Saving a Document for the First Time

Before you save a document for the first time, it has a temporary name such as Document1, Document2, or Document3. When you save the file, you replace this name with one of your choosing. Here are the rules for filenames:

- They can contain up to 256 characters.
- They can include spaces.
- They cannot include these characters: / \ > < * . ? " | : ;
- They are not case sensitive; as far as your computer is concerned, the filenames *Letter to mom* and *letter to Mom* are the same.
- You can have only one file of any given name in a folder.

The number following *Document* in the temporary filename doesn't mean that you have that number of documents open. For example, if your document is named *Document8*, it doesn't mean that you have eight documents open. It means only that you've started eight documents in this session of using Word. (You may have closed some of them.) When you close all of your Word windows and start Word again, the temporary filenames start over at *Document1*.

As soon as you decide that the document you're typing is worth saving, follow these steps:

1. Click the **Save** button on the Standard toolbar (or choose **File, Save**). Because this is the first time you are saving the document, Word displays the Save As dialog box to ask what you want to name the file and where you want to store it (see Figure 3.1).

FIGURE 3.1

Use the Save As dialog box to choose a name and location for your file.

Places list   Save In box   Up One Level

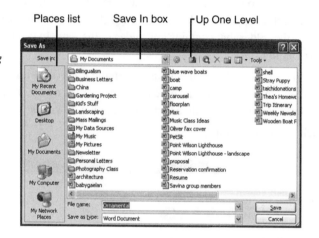

2. Look at the location in the Save In box. If you want to save the file in this location or in a subfolder it contains (the subfolders appear as folder icons in the main area of the dialog box), skip to step 4. Otherwise, continue with the next step.

3. Click the down arrow to the right of the Save In box, and click the location in which you want to save the file (see Figure 3.2). For example, click the drive letter for your CD-R (or CD-RW) drive to save your file to your writeable CD. If you want to save the file in a location on your network, choose **My Network Places**. The main area of the dialog box then lists the drives and folders to which you have access on your network.

FIGURE 3.2

Choose a location in the Save In list.

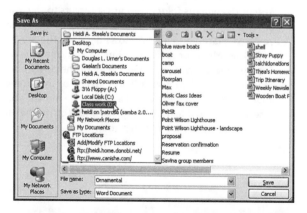

If there are multiple users on your machine, your personal My Documents folder will be listed in the Save In drop-down list both as My Documents and as *User Name's* Documents, for example, *Heidi A. Steele's Documents.*

4. If necessary, double-click folders in the main area of the dialog box until the desired folder appears in the Save In box. If you want to move back to a parent folder (the folder that contains the folder in the Save In box), click the **Up One Level** button.

5. Type the filename that you want to use in the File Name text box (see Figure 3.3). Word automatically adds the extension .doc to the name. (Depending on your Windows settings, your file extensions may not be visible.)

6. Click the **Save** button.

FIGURE 3.3

Type the name for your file in the File Name text box.

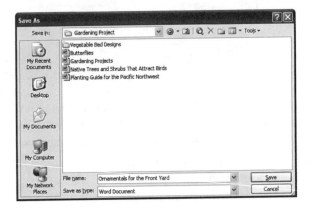

The Places list on the left side of the Save As dialog box contains buttons for some locations in which you are likely to want to save your files. The My Recent Documents folder contains shortcuts to the last couple of dozen documents you have worked on. The Desktop folder contains the documents you have placed on your Windows desktop. The My Documents folder is the default location for saving documents you create in Word. The My Computer icon gives you access to all of the drives and folders on your own computer, and My Network Places lists all of the locations you can access on your network. (My Network Places will be empty if your computer is not on a network.) You'll learn how to add shortcuts to the Places list for locations you frequently use later in this hour.

Word saves your document. If it finds an existing document in the same folder with the same name, it displays the message box shown in Figure 3.4.

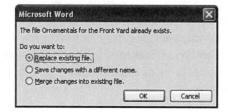

If you keep the Replace Existing File option button marked and click OK, Word replaces the existing file with the one you're saving. (After you replace the existing file, you can't get it back.) If you mark the Save Changes with a Different Name option button, Word redisplays the Save As dialog box to let you choose a different name and/or location for the file so that it won't overwrite the existing file. Finally, if you mark the Merge Changes into Existing File button, Word compares the document you're saving against the one with the existing file of the same name, and marks up the existing file to show you all of the differences between the two files. You'll learn about this *track changes* feature in detail in Hour 18, "Collaborating on Documents." You will most often choose one of the first two options. If you aren't sure, choose the second option so that you retain both the existing file and the one you're saving.

Saving As You Work

After you've saved your document for the first time, you need to continue to save it every few minutes as you work on it. Each time you save, Word updates the copy of the file on your hard disk with the copy on your screen (in memory). If you save religiously, then in the event of a crash or power outage, you lose, at most, a few minutes' worth of work.

To save your document periodically, choose File, Save (Ctrl+S). It looks as if nothing is happening when you issue the Save command because Word assumes that you want to keep the same filename and location, so it automatically overwrites the original file on disk without asking you any questions.

If you live in an area with frequent power outages, consider buying an uninterruptible power supply (UPS). This gizmo sits between your computer and the wall socket, and kicks in when there is an outage, at which time it powers your computer by battery for approximately 10 to 20 minutes—enough time to save and close your documents and shut down Windows. Some UPS devices also come with software that saves and closes your documents and shuts down for you if an outage occurs when you aren't at home.

Saving a Document with a New Name or Location

If you want to create a document that is very similar to one you have already saved, you don't need to type the new document from scratch. Rather, you can open the first document, make changes to it, and then save the new document under a different name. Because you're giving the document a new name, it won't overwrite the original file. For example, you can create monthly invoices for a particular company by opening the previous month's invoice, changing the invoice number and other details, and then saving the revised invoice under a new name.

> If you frequently use one document as the "jump-off point" for creating others, consider creating a template for this type of document, as described in Hour 10, "Working with Templates."

A variation of this idea is to open a document and then save it with the same name but in a different location. This is one way to copy a file from one place to another. For example, if you have a document on your hard drive that you want to put on a floppy disk, you can open the document from your hard drive, and then save it to your floppy drive.

To save a file with a different name and/or location, follow these steps:

1. Open the file (see "Opening Documents" later in this hour).
2. Choose **File, Save As** to display the Save As dialog box.
3. If you want to save the new file to a different location, navigate to it so that it appears in the Save In box. If you're keeping the same location as the original file, type a different name for the new document in the File Name text box so that you do not overwrite the original file.

> See the steps in "Saving a Document for the First Time" earlier in this hour if you need help figuring out how to locate a drive or folder in the Save In box.

4. Click the **Save** button.

Recovering Documents After Crashes or Power Outages

When you're typing a document, you might notice that at periodic intervals, the Save icon (the icon that appears on the Save toolbar button) flashes briefly at the right end of the status bar. When this happens, Word's AutoRecover feature is taking a "snapshot" of your document (saving a copy of the file in its current state). By default, the AutoRecover feature updates this snapshot every ten minutes when the document is open. If you close the document normally, it deletes the AutoRecover information.

However, if a computer crash or power outage prevents you from saving your document before Word closes, Word keeps the most recent snapshot for you. If you did not save for a long period of time before the crash or outage, the snapshot can contain a much more current version of your document than the one you most recently saved.

When Word crashes, it displays an error message such as the one shown in Figure 3.5. By default, Word will restart and try to recover your documents. If you see a check box offering to restart and recover your documents automatically, you have the option to clear it and not have Word restart and attempt to recover your work. However, unless you are sure that there were no unsaved changes in any Word documents that were open at the time of the crash, it's best to allow Word to attempt to recover your files.

FIGURE 3.5

Word politely informs you that you will lose all unsaved work—a compelling reason to save frequently.

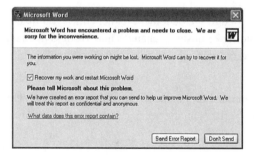

If you want your computer to send Microsoft a report about the crash, click the Send Error Report button. Otherwise, click the Don't Send button.

Microsoft analyzes the error reports it receives from crashes and may occasionally send you information about how to prevent the crashes you are experiencing. For example, if you are running another program that conflicts with Word, you may receive a message from Microsoft that contains a link to an article at Microsoft's Web site describing the problem and suggesting a fix.

When Word restarts, it displays the Document Recovery task pane, which lists all of the documents that were open at the time of the crash, as well as different versions of the same document, where applicable (see Figure 3.6).

FIGURE 3.6

The Document Recovery task pane appears automatically the first time you start Word after a crash.

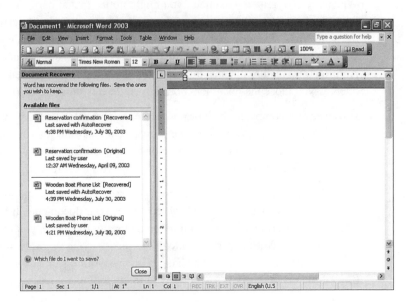

If [Original] is appended to the document name, either you made no changes since you last saved, or you did make unsaved changes and Word is displaying the original version to contrast with the recovered version (this is the case with both documents shown in Figure 3.6).

If [Recovered] is appended to the document name, you made changes since you last saved, and Word is offering you the version it saved with its AutoRecover feature.

Follow these steps to save as much of your work as possible:

1. Click each file listed in the Document Recovery task pane to open it on the right side of the Word window. The name of the open file in the Document Recovery task pane appears in bold to indicate that it's the one you're currently viewing.

2. View each file to see which one contains your changes.

3. When you find a file you want to save, choose **File, Save As**. Keep the same name and location if you want to overwrite the original file. Otherwise, save the file with a different name and/or location.

4. If you want to close a document, open it on the right side of the Word window, and choose **File, Close**.

5. When you are done, click the **Close** button in the lower-right corner of the Document Recovery task pane.

> If you want AutoRecover to take a snapshot of your document more frequently (perhaps you're working on a critical document during a storm, you don't have a UPS, and you're less than diligent about saving), choose Tools, Options to display the Options dialog box. Then click the Save tab, make sure the Save AutoRecover Info Every X Minutes check box is marked, change the number of minutes to a shorter time frame, and click OK.

Opening Documents

When you want to work on a file that has previously been saved to disk, you have to tell Word to open it.

Follow these steps to open a document:

1. Click the **Open** button on the Standard toolbar (or choose **File, Open**) to display the Open dialog box (see Figure 3.7).

2. Check the location in the Look In box. If the file you want to open is in this location or in one of the subfolders it contains, skip to step 4. Otherwise, continue with the next step.

3. Click the down arrow to the right of the Look In box, and click the drive that contains the file (see Figure 3.8). For example, click 3 1/2 Floppy (A:) if the file is on your floppy disk. (If you want to open a file from a location on your network, choose **My Network Places**. The main area of the dialog box will then list the drives and folders to which you have access on your network.)

FIGURE 3.7

Use the Open dialog box to open a file that you want to revise.

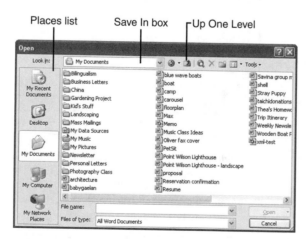

FIGURE **3.8**

Choose a location in the Look In list.

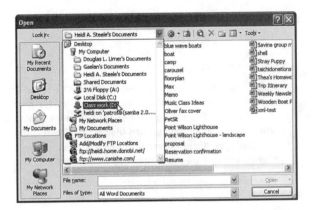

The Open dialog box has a Places list just like the one in the Save As dialog box. If the file that you want to open is in one of the folders in the Places list, click the folder icon in the Places list to have it appear immediately in the Look In box.

4. If necessary, double-click folders until the desired folder appears in the Look In box. If you want to move back to a parent folder, click the **Up One Level** button.

5. Double-click the filename, or click it and then click the **Open** button (see Figure 3.9).

FIGURE **3.9**

Double-click the file that you want to open.

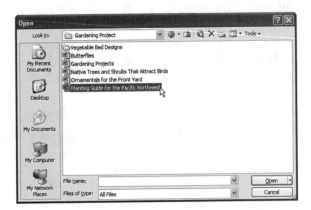

If you accidentally click twice instead of double-clicking the file in step 5, Word thinks you're trying to rename the file. (See "Renaming Documents and Folders" later in this hour.) If a thin box appears around the filename, indicating that you're in rename mode, press the Esc key or click on a blank area in the dialog box, and then double-click the file.

> When you open a file, a copy of the file is placed in your computer's memory. The original file is still on disk. If you close the file without making any changes, you don't need to save because the onscreen copy is no different from the one on disk. You need to save only if you revise the file.

Opening Multiple Documents at Once

If you want to open several files in the same folder at once, you can select all of them in the Open dialog box before clicking the Open button. To select several files, use these techniques:

- If the files are adjacent to one another, click the first file, and then Shift+click (hold down your Shift key as you click) the last file.

- If the files are not adjacent, click the first file, and then Ctrl+click (hold down the Ctrl key as you click) the additional files.

You can also delete, move, or copy multiple files by selecting them as described here before issuing the appropriate command. See the sections "Deleting Documents" and "Moving and Copying Documents" later in this hour.

> The four documents that you most recently opened are listed at the bottom of the File menu. If you want to open one of these files, you can dispense with the Open dialog box altogether. Just display the File menu and click the document that you want to open.

Viewing Files in the Save As and Open Dialog Boxes

Word enables you to choose among eight views to use when displaying folders and files in the Save As and Open dialog box. To change views, click the down arrow to the right of the Views button (see Figure 3.10), and then click the desired view in the list that appears. (Alternatively, you can click the View button itself one or more times to switch among all of the views.)

The various views are described here in the order in which they appear in the list:

- Thumbnails view displays thumbnails of image files. It is not particularly useful for Word documents.

3

- Tiles view displays a large icon for each file, accompanied by the filename, the file type, and the file size.
- Icons view displays medium-sized icons for each file, along with the filenames.
- List view (the default option) lists the names of the folders and files.
- Details view displays the size, type, and date modified for each file or folder, in addition to its name.
- Properties view displays the information from the Properties dialog box (File, Properties) in a pane on the right side of the dialog box.
- Preview view shows a preview of the selected document in a pane on the right side of the dialog box (see Figure 3.10); in this view, you can take a peek at the contents of your file without actually opening it. (Some types of files don't have a preview available. If this is the case, the message "Preview not available" appears in the Preview pane.)
- WebView enables users to navigate through a Document Library on a SharePoint site. It is dimmed out except when the current folder is a Document Library. (This feature will not apply to you unless your company has a SharePoint site.)

FIGURE 3.10

Use the Preview view to see what's in a file before opening it.

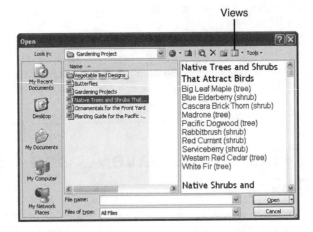

By default, files and folders in the Save As and Open dialog boxes are ordered by name. To sort them by type, size, or date instead, right-click on a blank part of the dialog box, point to Arrange Icons By in the context menu, and choose the desired option in the submenu.

Getting to Your Favorite Folders

If a folder that you use frequently is buried deep in the structure on your hard disk or is on another network computer, it can be time-consuming to navigate to it in the Open and Save As dialog boxes. Fortunately, you can avoid this hassle by creating a shortcut to the folder in your Places list. The shortcut simply points to the folder; clicking it opens the folder just as if you clicked the item itself.

Follow these steps to create a shortcut to a folder in your Places list:

1. Display the Open or Save As dialog box. Using the Look In or Save In box if necessary, navigate until the folder that you want to create a shortcut for appears in the main area of the dialog box, and then select it.

2. At the top of the dialog box choose **Tools, Add to "My Places"**. The shortcut is added to the bottom of the Places list. (You may need to click the down arrow at the bottom of the Places list to scroll it into view.)

3. Click your shortcut in the Places list. The contents of the folder appear in the dialog box (see Figure 3.11).

4. If you don't want to have to scroll your Places list, right-click any of the shortcuts in the list and choose **Small Icons** in the context menu.

5. To rearrange the shortcuts in the list, right-click the one you want to move and choose **Move Up** or **Move Down** in the context menu.

6. To rename a shortcut, right-click it and choose **Rename** in the context menu. In the Rename Place dialog box that appears, type the new name and click **OK**. (You can't rename the default shortcuts in the Places list.)

7. To delete a shortcut, right-click it and choose **Remove**. Deleting a shortcut does not remove the file or folder to which the shortcut pointed. (You can't delete the default shortcuts in the Places list.)

FIGURE 3.11

Click your shortcuts in the Places list to access your favorite folders.

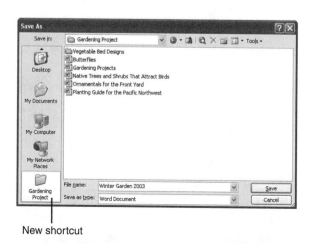

New shortcut

Creating Folders

Just as you might add a new hanging folder to a physical filing cabinet to hold a new group of related files, so you can create new folders on your hard drive (or a network drive) to store groups of related Word documents. For example, you might want to create a folder for your personal correspondence, or one for your child's homework assignments. You can create folders in either the Save As or the Open dialog box, although you're most likely to create them in the Save As dialog box when you're in the midst of saving a file.

Microsoft Office automatically creates the My Documents folder on your hard drive as a convenient place for you to store data files including Word documents, Excel spreadsheets, PowerPoint presentations, and so on. You can create a set of subfolders within My Documents for the various types of documents you create. You aren't required to use the My Documents folder, but it's a good idea to designate one folder for your data—whether it be the My Documents folder or different one—and then store all of your files in subfolders of that folder. (If you want to use a different folder to store all of your data files, see the next section.) If you are on a network, ask your network administrator where you should save your Word documents.

To create a folder, follow these steps:

1. In either the Save As or the Open dialog box, navigate to the folder that you want to be the parent of the new folder so that it appears in the Save In or Look In box.

2. Click the **Create New Folder** button.

3. The New Folder dialog box appears (see Figure 3.12). Type the name you want to use, and click **OK**. (The rules for naming folders are the same as for naming files—see "Saving a Document for the First Time" earlier in this hour.)

Create New Folder

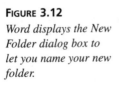

FIGURE 3.12

Word displays the New Folder dialog box to let you name your new folder.

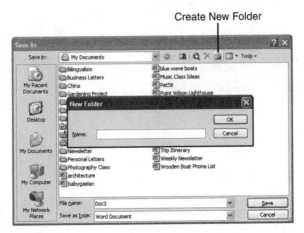

If you are in the middle of saving a file when you create your new folder, it will become the location in the Save In box, so you can simply continue the save process. If you created the new folder in the Open dialog box, click the Cancel button to close it.

Changing Your Default Documents Folder

By default, Word assumes that you want to store documents in the My Documents folder or one of its subfolders, so it automatically displays the contents of the My Documents folder when you first display the Open or Save As dialog box. If you use a different folder for your data files, you will probably want Word to automatically display its contents in the Open and Save As dialog boxes instead.

To change your default documents folder, follow these steps:

1. Choose **Tools**, **Options**.
2. In the Options dialog box, click the **File Locations** tab.
3. Select **Documents** under File Types, and then click the **Modify** button.
4. In the Modify Location dialog box that appears, navigate to and select the folder that you want to be the default documents folder. When its name appears in the Look In text box, click **OK**.
5. Click the **Close** button in the Options dialog box.

Now when you display the Open dialog box, the folder you designated appears by default in the Look In box. By the same token, when you display the Save As dialog box, this folder appears in the Save In box.

Switching Between Open Documents

You can open as many Word documents at a time as you like. (Issue the File, Open command or click the Open toolbar button in any Word window to open additional documents.) In general, however, it's best to use a little restraint. The more documents you have open, the more slowly your computer runs. When you have more than one Word document open, you can switch among them by using the techniques described in the next three sections.

Taskbar Buttons

By default, each document that you open appears in its own Word window, with its own button on the taskbar at the bottom of your screen. The simplest way to switch from one to another is to click their taskbar buttons. In Figure 3.13, three Word windows are open. The active Word window is maximized, so the other Word windows are hidden behind it.

FIGURE 3.13

Click the taskbar button of an open document to switch to it.

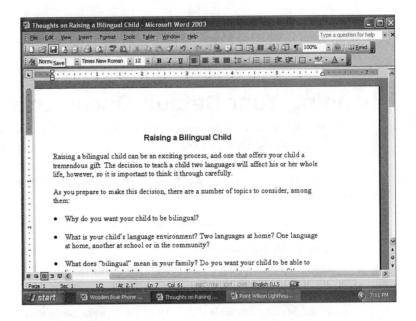

The keyboard shortcut for switching among open Word documents is Ctrl+F6. Each time you press Ctrl+F6, Word brings another open document to the top.

Depending on your display settings and the number of Word documents you have open, Windows may decide that you don't have enough room to display a separate taskbar button for each document. When this happens, it displays only one Word taskbar button that contains a number indicating the number of open documents. When you click the button, a list of all of the open documents pops up. To switch to one of the documents, simply click it in the list.

If you have several Word documents open at once, you may have difficulty telling which document is which because the taskbar buttons are so small that the document names have to be truncated. You can always point to a button to display the entire filename in a ScreenTip. If you prefer, you can also display all of your open documents in one Word window, which means you will see only one Word taskbar button that lists the name of the currently active document. To do this, follow these steps:

1. Choose **Tools, Options**.
2. In the Options dialog box, click the **View** tab.
3. Clear the **Windows in Taskbar** check box, and click **OK**.

If you take these steps and are now displaying all of your documents in one Word window, you need to use the Window menu method described in the next section to switch among them.

> If you don't see your taskbar, either someone dragged it out of view, or it has been set to hide when a window is active. To bring it into view, rest your mouse pointer on the edge of the desktop where it normally appears. If it was set to hide automatically, it will pop up right away. If it doesn't, drag toward the middle of your screen when you see a double-headed black arrow. If your taskbar was set to auto hide and you want it to be visible all of the time, right-click the Start button and choose Properties. In the Taskbar and Start Menu Properties dialog box, click the Taskbar tab, clear the Auto-hide the Taskbar check box, and click OK.

Window Menu

You can also switch among open documents by using the Window menu in any Word window. All of your open documents are listed at the bottom of the Window menu (see Figure 3.14), and a check mark appears next to the one that's currently active. Click the desired document to switch to it.

FIGURE 3.14

Click the document that you want to switch to at the bottom of the Window menu.

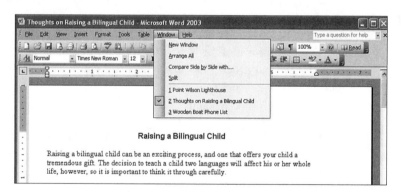

Keyboard Shortcut

When you have more than one window open, you can switch among all of your windows, including the Word windows, by using the Alt+Tab keyboard combination. Press and hold down the Alt key as you press the Tab key to display a small window containing icons for each open window. An outline appears around the icon for the active window (see Figure 3.15). Keeping the Alt key held down, continue to press Tab until the icon for the document that you want to switch to is outlined, and then release the Alt key. (If you are displaying all of your documents in one Word window, as described in the previous section, you will only see one icon for your Word window in the Alt+Tab list.)

FIGURE 3.15

*Release the Alt key
when the desired docu-
ment icon is outlined.*

Point Wilson Lighthouse - Microsoft Word 2003

Starting New Documents

Word presents a new blank document when you start the program. If, after you've started typing in this document, you decide to begin another new document, click the New Blank Document button at the far-left end of the Standard toolbar (or press Ctrl+N). A second Word window opens with a new blank document.

When you use the New Blank Document toolbar button to start a document, Word assumes that you want to base the document on the *Normal template*. All Word documents are based on a template, which is like a blueprint for a document that includes formatting and possibly text. The Normal template produces a plain-vanilla blank document with all of Word's default formatting. Unless you specify otherwise, Word also uses the Normal template to store items you create such as AutoText entries, styles, and macros so that they will be available in all documents based on the Normal template. (You'll learn to create these items in later hours in this book.) Word also comes with many other templates (including special templates called *wizards*) that can help you create a wide variety of documents, including letters, memos, fax cover sheets, reports, and so on. If you want to base your new document on one of these templates, you have to use the File, New command instead of the New Blank Document toolbar button. You learn how to use other templates in the next hour, and in Hour 10 you'll learn how to create your own templates.

Renaming Documents and Folders

You can rename your files in the Save As or Open dialog box. Make sure that the file you want to rename is not open. Then display either of these dialog boxes, and use one of these methods to switch to rename mode:

- Right-click the file and click Rename in the context menu.
- Select the file and then click it again.
- Select the file and press F2.
- Select the file, click the Tools button at the top of the dialog box, and choose Rename.

A thin box appears around the filename to inform you that you're in rename mode, and the current name is highlighted so that you can easily replace it (see Figure 3.16). Type the new name and press Enter. You can't rename a file while it's open, or rename a folder while a file contained in the folder is open.

FIGURE 3.16

The Music Class Ideas file is ready to be renamed.

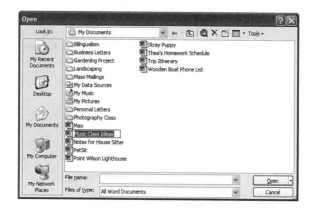

 You can rename folders in the exact same way that you rename files.

Deleting Documents

You can delete files in either the Save As or Open dialog box. Make sure that the file you want to delete is not open. Display either dialog box, and delete the file by using one of these methods:

- Right-click the file and click Delete in the context menu.
- Select the file and click the Delete toolbar button at the top of the dialog box (the black X).
- Select the file and press the Delete key.
- Select the file, click the Tools button at the top of the dialog box, and choose Delete.

The Confirm File Delete message box appears to ask whether you want to send the document to the Recycle Bin. Click the Yes button. If you later want to get the document back, you can double-click the Recycle Bin icon on your Windows desktop, right-click the file, and choose Restore in the context menu. The file reappears in the folder in which it was originally stored.

If you want to delete more than one document, select them all before issuing the Delete command. (To select adjacent documents, click the first one and Shift+click the last one. To select nonadjacent documents, select the first one and then Ctrl+click the remaining ones.)

> If you delete a file from a network drive or a removable drive (a floppy or Zip drive, for example), it does not go to the Recycle Bin—once it's gone, it's gone.

Moving and Copying Documents

As with creating folders, renaming files, and deleting files, you can move or copy files in either the Save As or Open dialog box. When you move a file, you remove it from its current location and place it in a new location. When you copy a file, you leave it in its current location and place a duplicate copy in the new location.

To move or copy a document, follow these steps:

1. Make sure that the file you want to move or copy is not open, and then display either the Save As or the Open dialog box.
2. Navigate to the folder containing the file you want to move or copy so that the folder appears in the Save In or Look In box.
3. Right-click the file and choose **Cut** or **Copy** in the context menu. (You can also press Ctrl+X to cut or Ctrl+C to copy.)
4. Navigate to the folder in which you want to paste the file so that the folder appears in the Save In or Look In box.
5. Right-click a blank part of the main area in the dialog box and choose **Paste** in the context menu (or press Ctrl+V).

If you want to move or copy more than one document, select them all after step 2. Then right-click any of the files, and continue with step 3.

Summary

In this hour, you learned everything that you need to know to manage your Word documents. You can save them to disk, open them when you want to revise or print them, and perform other standard file-management tasks. In the next hour, you learn a wide variety of techniques for viewing and printing your documents.

Q&A

Q **I have Excel spreadsheets and Word documents in my My Documents folder. Why do I see the Word documents in the Open dialog box only when the My Documents folder is in the Look In box?**

A By default, Word displays Word documents (files with an extension of .doc) only in the Open dialog box. If you want to see all of the files in a folder, including non-Word documents, choose All Files in the Files of Type drop-down list at the bottom of the dialog box.

Q **How can I record tracking information about my documents when I save them?**

A Choose File, Properties, enter information about the document (its title, subject, and so on) in the Summary tab of the Properties dialog box, and click OK. If you want Word to prompt you to fill in this information each time you save, choose Tools, Options, click the Save tab, mark the Prompt for Document Properties check box, and click OK. You can display (but not edit) the properties of any document from the Open and Save As dialog boxes. Simply select the document in the dialog box, click the Tools button at the top of the dialog box, and click Properties.

3

HOUR 4

Viewing and Printing Your Documents

Word offers a wide assortment of options for changing the appearance of your document onscreen. If you type only simple letters and memos, you may never need to change these settings. However, if you create documents with sophisticated formatting, have trouble reading small print, or want to view different parts of a document or more than one document at the same time, you can tailor the view options to suit your preferences. And when you've finished typing your documents and like their appearance onscreen, you'll probably want to print them out. In this hour, you explore a whole host of viewing and printing options.

The highlights of this hour include

- Switching views
- Magnifying your document
- Viewing separate parts of your document at the same time
- Arranging multiple Word documents on the desktop
- Previewing your document before you print
- Printing your document
- Printing envelopes and labels

Selecting a View of Your Document

Word's view options are so plentiful that you can surely find one or two that work well for you. You can use any of these seven views to work with your documents:

- Print Layout (View menu)
- Normal (View menu)
- Reading Layout (View menu)
- Full Screen (View menu)
- Print Preview (File menu)
- Web Layout (View menu)
- Outline (View menu)

You'll learn about Print Layout, Normal, Reading Layout, and Full Screen view in the next four sections. Print Preview is discussed in "Previewing a Document Before Printing" later in this hour. Web Layout view is covered in Hour 23, "Word and the Web," and Outline view is explained in Hour 13, "Working with Long Documents."

You can switch among Normal, Web Layout, Print Layout, Outline, and Reading Layout views by using the five View buttons in the lower-left corner of the Word window (see Figure 4.1).

FIGURE 4.1
Using the View buttons to switch among five of the views.

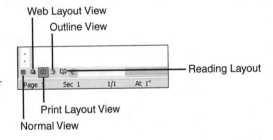

Web Layout View
Outline View
Reading Layout
Print Layout View
Normal View

 Word remembers the view you choose for a document and uses it the next time you open the document.

Using Print Layout View

Print Layout view is the default view option. If you aren't sure whether you're using it, choose View, Print Layout or click the Print Layout View button in the lower-left corner of the Word window.

Print Layout view gives you the sense that you're typing directly onto a piece of paper (see Figure 4.2). It includes horizontal and vertical rulers so that you always know where your text appears on the page, and it shows you the top, bottom, left, and right margin areas. If you have typed text in the headers and footers (you learn how to do this in Hour 10, "Working With Templates"), it will be visible in the top and bottom margins. All page breaks (regardless of type) appear as a gap between the bottom edge of one page and the top edge of the next.

FIGURE 4.2

Print Layout view enables you to see the margin areas of your document.

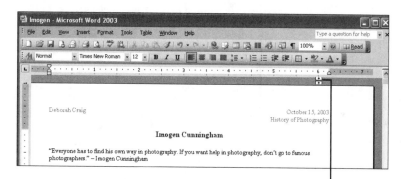

Click at the top of the page to hide white space

When you are using Print Layout view, you can hide the white space at the top and bottom of each page. Point to the lower edge of the horizontal ruler, and click when the mouse pointer changes shape to become double arrows facing inward (refer to Figure 4.2). To bring the white space back into view, point to the same place and click when the mouse pointer changes shape to become double arrows facing outward.

You don't have to use Print Layout view if you're typing documents with simple formatting. However, you do need to use it if you're working with more complex formatting such as columns, tables, and graphics. (These features do not display correctly in Normal view.)

Using Normal View

Normal view is useful for documents in which you just want to type and format text. The simple, uncluttered layout makes it easy to quickly scroll through the document and edit your text. To switch to Normal view, choose View, Normal or click the Normal View button in the lower-left corner of the Word window.

Normal view displays only the horizontal ruler, not the vertical ruler. And it doesn't display the margin areas of the page, so you can't see headers and footers (see Figure 4.3).

FIGURE 4.3

Normal view doesn't display the margin areas of your document.

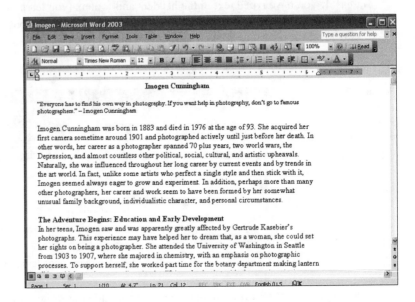

One advantage of Normal view is that unlike Print Layout view, it shows you what type of page breaks are in your document. A soft page break appears as a dotted horizontal line running across the page. A hard page break appears as a dotted horizontal line with the words *Page Break* on it. Figure 4.4 shows a soft and a hard page break in Normal view.

Normal view also displays *section breaks*, which you have to use to apply certain kinds of formatting to only a portion of your document. You learn more about page and section breaks in Hour 8, "Formatting Pages."

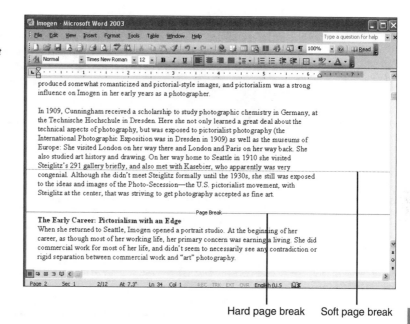

FIGURE 4.4

Switch to Normal view if you need to see what kind of page breaks are in your document.

Hard page break   Soft page break

Using Reading Layout View

In Reading Layout view, text is enlarged and displayed in "screens" rather than actual pages to make it easy to read (see Figure 4.5). This view is well suited for long documents, especially ones that people have collaborated on using the Track Changes feature. This feature enables you to see who made what changes in a document. You'll learn about it in Hour 18, "Collaborating on Documents." To switch to Reading Layout view, choose View, Reading Layout, click the Reading Layout button in the lower-left corner of the Word window, or click the Read button at the right end of the Standard toolbar.

In Reading Layout view, the Reading Layout and Reviewing toolbars appear in place of the Standard and Formatting toolbars at the top of the Word window, and Word displays one or two screens of your document text.

If you want to view only one screen at a time, click the Allow Multiple Pages button to turn it off (see Figure 4.6). To switch back to viewing two screens at once, click the Allow Multiple Pages button again to turn it back on.

To view the next screen press the Page Down key. Page Up brings you to the previous screen. Use any of the arrow keys or the arrows at the top and bottom of the vertical scroll bar to move one screen at a time through your document (you will only scroll one screen at a time even if Allow Multiple Pages is turned on).

FIGURE 4.5

Reading Layout view is designed for reading long documents.

Reading Layout toolbar   Reviewing toolbar

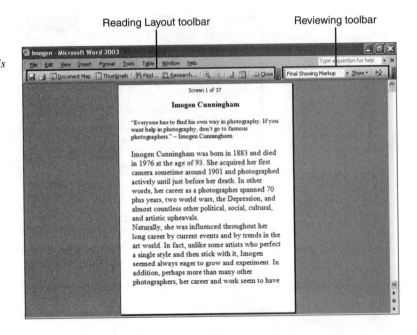

Decrease Text Size ⌐ Actual Page

Increase Text Size ⌐ ⌐ Allow Multiple Pages

FIGURE 4.6

You can view two screens at once, and adjust the text size.

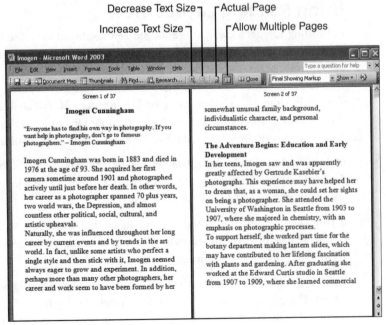

To adjust the size of the text as it's displayed on screen (this doesn't change how it prints), click the Increase Text Size and Decrease Text Size buttons.

If you want to view the document in actual pages as they would print instead of in screens, click the Actual Page button. (Click it again to turn it off.)

When you are finished, click the Close toolbar button to switch back to the previous view.

The remaining features of Reading Layout view are all explained in other parts of this book:

- Document Map toolbar button (Hour 13, "Working with Long Documents")
- Thumbnails toolbar button ("Viewing Thumbnails" later in this hour)
- Find toolbar button (Hour 12, "Handy Editing Techniques")
- Research toolbar button (Hour 11, "Checking Your Spelling and Grammar and Using the Thesaurus")
- Reviewing toolbar (Hour 18, "Collaborating on Documents")

Using Full Screen View

If you like working in a completely uncluttered environment, you'll appreciate Full Screen view. To switch to this view, choose View, Full Screen. (You can't switch to Full Screen view from Reading Layout view.) Your document window enlarges to cover the entire desktop (see Figure 4.7). The title bar, menu bar, and toolbars in the Word window are temporarily hidden to give you as much room as possible to see your text, and a little Full Screen toolbar appears to let you easily switch out of Full Screen view.

If you want to issue a menu command, point to the thin gray line running across the top of your screen to slide the menu bar into view.

Full Screen view works in conjunction with whatever other view you are using, not in place of it. In Figure 4.7, the document is in Print Layout and Full Screen view. While you are in Full Screen view, you can switch among the other views as you like. When you are finished using Full Screen view, click the Close Full Screen button on the Full Screen toolbar (or bring the menu bar into view and choose View, Full Screen again).

Viewing Thumbnails

Regardless of what view you are using, you can choose View, Thumbnails to display a vertical pane along the left side of the Word window that contains thumbnails of each page (or screen in the case of Reading Layout view) in the current document (see Figure 4.8).

Point to the thin gray line to
bring the menu bar into view.

FIGURE 4.7
*Full Screen view gives
you an uncluttered
view of your document.*

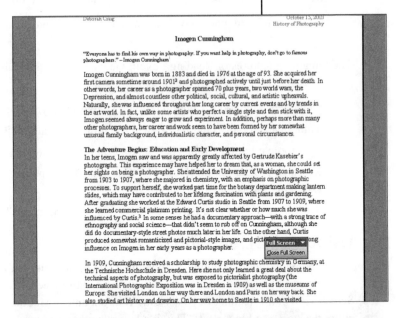

FIGURE 4.8
*Thumbnails enable you
to quickly jump from
one spot to another in
your document.*

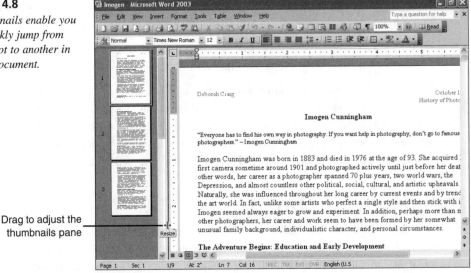

Drag to adjust the
thumbnails pane

If you want to enlarge the Thumbnails pane to see more thumbnails at one time, drag the
right border of the pane to the right. When you want to hide the thumbnails, drag the
border all the way to the left edge of the Word window. You can also choose View,
Thumbnails again to hide the Thumbnails pane.

Magnifying Your Document

Word normally displays text at approximately the size it is when printed. In some situations, you might want to enlarge or shrink the text onscreen to make it easier to read, edit, and format. You change your document's magnification by adjusting the Zoom setting.

You might want to change your Zoom setting if your document has especially large or small fonts, if you're printing on a paper size other than 8 1/2 by 11, or if your eyesight isn't what it used to be. When you shrink the magnification to anything less than 100 percent, the text appears smaller and you can see more of your document at once. When you enlarge the magnification to anything over 100 percent, the text appears bigger and you can see less of your document in the window. Changing the magnification of your document onscreen does not affect the way it prints; it only affects the way you view the document on your monitor.

To change the Zoom setting, click the down arrow in the Zoom box at the right end of the Standard toolbar to display the Zoom list (see Figure 4.9), and then click the desired setting.

FIGURE 4.9

Choose the desired magnification setting in the Zoom list.

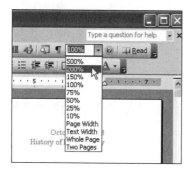

In Figure 4.10, the document has been zoomed to 200 percent. Word remembers the setting and uses it the next time you open the document.

If you enlarge the magnification of your document, as shown in Figure 4.10, you may need to use the horizontal scrollbar at the bottom of the Word window to bring the right side of the document into view.

The four options at the bottom of the Zoom list also come in handy. They automatically adjust your document's magnification just the right amount to display the full width of the page (Page Width), the width of the text only (Text Width), the entire page (Whole Page), and two entire pages (Two Pages). In Normal view, the Text Width, Whole Page, and Two Pages options are not available.

FIGURE **4.10**

The Zoom setting was changed to 200 percent.

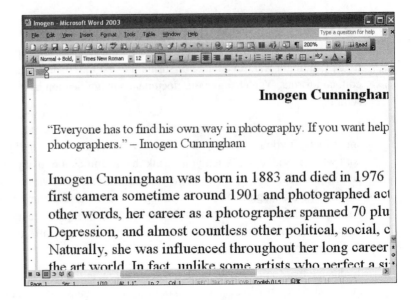

You aren't limited to the magnification percentages shown in the Zoom list. If you want to magnify your document at a setting not in the list, 85 percent, for example, click in the Zoom box and type over the current setting with the percentage you'd like, and press Enter.

Viewing Separate Parts of Your Document at the Same Time

With a longer document, you may find it convenient to view separate parts of it at the same time. For example, if you're typing a report that begins with a table of contents, you may want to keep it in view as you're typing later portions of the report to make sure that you're sticking to your outline. (This feature does not work when you're viewing thumbnails, or from Reading Layout view.)

To practice using this feature, open any document that is too long to fit onscreen. Then point to the *split bar*, the short horizontal bar directly above the up arrow at the top of the vertical scrollbar (see Figure 4.11).

Split bar ┐

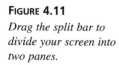

FIGURE 4.11

Drag the split bar to divide your screen into two panes.

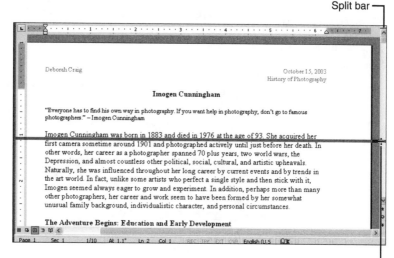

Drag to create the split ┘

When you point to the split bar, your mouse pointer changes to two horizontal lines with a vertical double arrow. Drag about halfway down the Word window. As you drag, a gray horizontal line shows where the window will be split (see Figure 4.11). When the line is in the right place, release the mouse button.

Word divides the window into two panes. Each pane has its own rulers and scrollbars. Click in the lower pane to activate it, and then use its vertical scrollbar to scroll down in the document. As you scroll, the portion of the document displayed in the upper pane doesn't change. If you want to scroll the upper pane, click in it and then use its vertical scrollbar. The status bar at the bottom of the Word window shows you the page number of the active pane (the pane containing the insertion point). In Figure 4.12, the first page of a 9-page document is displayed in the upper pane, and the last page is displayed in the lower pane. The lower pane is active, so the status bar lists the last page of the document.

When the Word window is split, you can use the Go To feature in the active pane to scroll only that pane to the page you specify. (See the section "Jumping to a Specific Page" in Hour 2, "Entering Text and Moving Around.")

Also, you can drag and drop text from one pane into the other. This makes it easy to use drag-and-drop to move or copy text in a multiple-page document.

If you want to adjust the relative size of the two panes, point to the gray dividing line and drag it up or down. To remove the split, double-click the gray line or drag it all the way up to the top of the Word window.

4

FIGURE 4.12

The first and last pages of a nine-page document are visible at the same time.

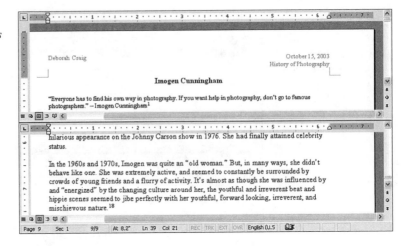

Another way to create a split is to choose Window, Split. Word displays a gray horizontal line and moves the mouse pointer over it. Move the mouse to get the line in the right spot, and then click to create the split. When you want to remove the split, choose Window, Remove Split.

Arranging Word Documents on Your Screen

If you have more than one Word document open, you may want to display the two documents next to one another to compare their content, or to drag and drop text between them.

Displaying All Open Documents on Your Desktop

To arrange your open Word documents so that all of them are visible, choose Window, Arrange All. Word tiles the documents so that they cover your entire desktop (see Figure 4.13). If you want to create more room to see your text in tiled Word windows, you can hide the rulers and place the Standard and Formatting toolbars on one row, as shown in Figure 4.13.

To hide the rulers and combine toolbars, follow these steps.

1. To hide the rulers, choose **View**, **Ruler**.

2. To put the Standard and Formatting toolbars on the same row, choose **Tools**, **Customize**, click the **Options** tab, and clear the **Show Standard and Formatting Toolbars on Two Rows** check box.

3. Click the **Close** button.

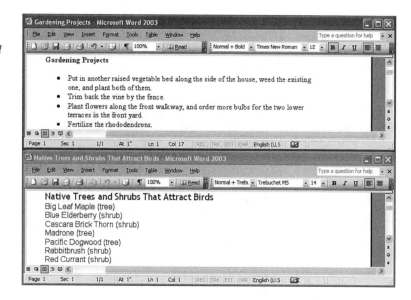

FIGURE 4.13

The two open Word windows are arranged vertically on your desktop.

To return to viewing only one Word window, click the Maximize button in the upper-right corner of the window that you want to use.

Comparing Two Documents Side By Side

When you have two versions of a document and want to compare them side by side, you can easily do so with a click of the mouse. When the two documents are aligned side by side, scrolling or zooming one of them scrolls or zooms them both, so you can scan both documents at the same time.

To compare two documents side by side, follow these steps:

1. Open the two documents that you want to display side by side. For now, open only these two documents.

2. Choose **Window**, **Compare Side by Side with *document name***. Word knows which document you want to compare with because it's the only other open document (see Figure 4.14).

FIGURE 4.14

When you only have two documents open, Word knows which one you want to display.

3. The documents are now arranged side by side and the title bar of the active document is dark (see Figure 4.15). To activate the other document, click anywhere in its window.

Synchronous Scrolling

FIGURE 4.15

*The two open Word
windows are arranged
side by side.*

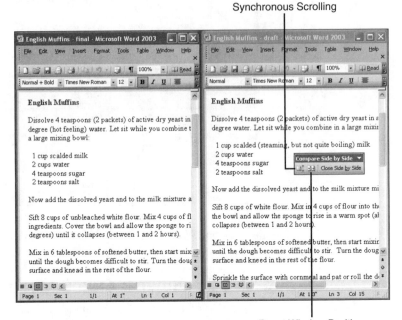

Reset Window Position

4. Use the scroll bars and change the zoom setting on one document to control both documents at the same time. (If you want to disable this behavior, click the **Synchronous Scrolling** button in the Compare Side by Side toolbar.)

5. To break the side-by-side arrangement, click the **Close Side by Side** button on the Compare Side by Side toolbar.

When only two documents are open, Word assumes that you want to compare one with the other. When more than two are open, you will tell Word which one you want to compare. To see how this works, open a third document and click on one of the documents that you want to compare. Then open the Window menu. This time, no document name is included in the Compare Side by Side With command. When you click the Compare Side by Side With command, the Compare Side by Side dialog box appears (see Figure 4.16). Select the document you want to compare with the current one, and click OK.

FIGURE 4.16

Select the document that you want to compare.

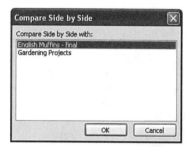

If you adjust the size and position of the windows after you've arranged them side by side, Word remembers the new arrangement the next time you issue the Compare Side by Side command. To reset the windows to their default side-by-side positions, click the Reset Window Position toolbar button in the Compare Side by Side toolbar (shown in Figure 4.15).

Previewing a Document Before Printing

Word's Print Preview feature enables you to see what a document looks like before you send it to the printer. Using Print Preview is a great way of saving paper because you can catch things that you'd like to change before you print. To use Print Preview, click the Print Preview button on the Standard toolbar (see Figure 4.17) or choose File, Print Preview.

FIGURE 4.17

Click the Print Preview button in the Standard toolbar to switch to Print Preview.

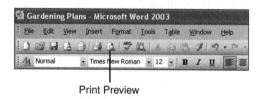

Print Preview

Word switches to Print Preview. When you're using this view, the title bar contains the word *[Preview]*, and a Print Preview toolbar appears (see Figure 4.18).

To scroll through the document page by page, press the Page Down and Page Up keys. If you want to view several pages at once, click the Multiple Pages toolbar button and drag through the desired number of squares in the grid that drops down (each square represents a page). To go back to viewing one page, click the One Page toolbar button. If you want to print your document directly from Print Preview, click the Print toolbar button.

FIGURE 4.18
Print Preview gives you a good idea of what your document will look like after it's printed.

Magnifier
Multiple Pages
Full Screen

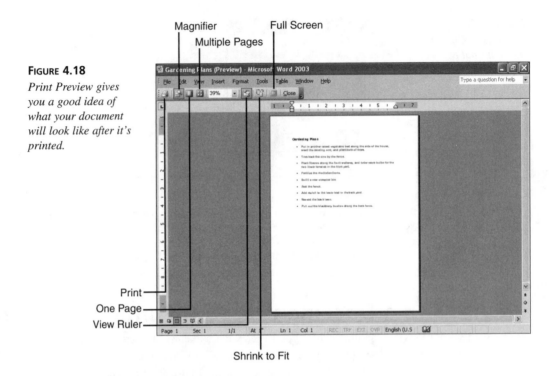

Print
One Page
View Ruler

Shrink to Fit

Another handy feature in Print Preview is Shrink to Fit. To make your document fit on one page (or you if want it to fit onto two pages and it's spilling onto three, and so on), click the Shrink to Fit toolbar button to make it fit on one less page than it currently does. Word accomplishes this by making small adjustments to your document's formatting (reducing the font size, decreasing the amount of white space, and so on).

> You can edit your document while you're viewing it in Print Preview. Click the Magnifier toolbar button to turn it off. An insertion point appears in the document. You can now type and revise your text as usual. You may want to use the Zoom box in the Print Preview toolbar to increase the magnification so that you can see your text more clearly. You can also click the Full Screen toolbar button to switch to Full Screen view. Click the Magnifier button again when you are finished.

When you're finished using Print Preview, click the Close button at the right end of the Print Preview toolbar to return to the view you were using previously.

Printing Your Document

Word assumes that you frequently want to print a complete copy of your document, so it provides the Print button on the Standard toolbar enabling you to do just that (see Figure 4.19). Clicking this button sends your document to the default printer immediately using the printer's default settings for print quality, color, and so on.

FIGURE 4.19

Click the Print button on the Standard toolbar to print one copy of the entire document.

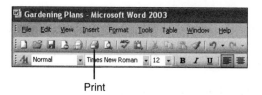

Print

If you want to customize your printing at all—by printing only certain pages or printing more than one copy, for example—you need to use the Print dialog box.

Follow these steps to print from the Print dialog box:

1. Choose **File**, **Print** or press **Ctrl+P** to display the Print dialog box (see Figure 4.20).

4

FIGURE 4.20

Use the Print dialog box to customize your printing.

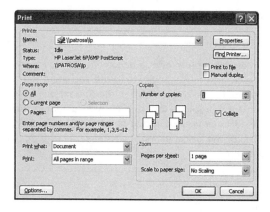

2. Check the printer listed in the **Name** drop-down list. If you have only one printer, you won't need to change this setting. If your computer is hooked up to multiple printers, you can select a different printer in this list.

3. Under Page Range, the All option button is marked by default. This option prints your entire document. You can select other options to tell Word which pages to print, for example

- To print only the page containing the insertion point, mark the **Current Page** option button.
- To print more than one page but not the entire document, type the page numbers you want to print in the **Pages** text box.
- Use commas to separate nonsequential pages and dashes to indicate a range of pages. For example, you would type *1,3-6,8* to print pages 1, 3, 4, 5, 6, and 8.
- If you want to print only one block of text in your document, select the text before displaying the Print dialog box, and then mark the **Selection** option button.

4. If you want to print more than one copy of your document, enter the number in the Number of Copies text box by typing it or clicking the spinner arrows.

5. Under Zoom, click the desired number of pages in the **Pages per Sheet** drop-down list if you want to print more than one document page on a sheet of paper. (You might do this to conserve paper.) Select a paper size in the **Scale to Paper Size** drop-down list to print on a different paper size than the one that's set for the document. (You learn how to set a document's paper size in Hour 8.)

6. Click the **OK** button to send the document to the printer. (If you decide not to print, click the **Cancel** button.)

Word enables you to print a document without opening it. To do so, display the Open dialog box, navigate to the document that you want to print, right-click it, and choose Print in the context menu. To print more than one document in a folder, Ctrl+click each document in the Open dialog box (or, if the documents are adjacent to one another, click the first document and Shift+click the last one). Right-click any one of the selected documents and choose Print.

Printing Envelopes

Printing envelopes in Word is simple. You check the recipient's address and the return address, load your envelope in the printer, and issue the command to print. Word assumes that you want to print on a standard business-size envelope, but you can choose a different envelope size if necessary.

Instead of printing one envelope or label at a time, you can also print a bunch of them at once as part of a mass mailing. You learn how to do this in Hour 14, "Generating a Mail Merge."

Follow these steps to print an envelope:

1. If you used Word to type the letter addressed to the recipient, open the letter now.
2. Choose **Tools**, **Letters and Mailings**, **Envelopes and Labels**.
3. Click the **Envelopes** tab in the Envelopes and Labels dialog box (see Figure 4.21).

FIGURE 4.21

Use the Envelopes tab of the Envelopes and Labels dialog box to specify the addresses to print on your envelope.

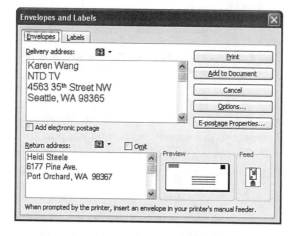

4

4. Word finds the address in the document you have open onscreen. Edit it in the **Delivery Address** box if needed.
5. Word automatically includes your return address on the envelope. If you have envelopes with a preprinted return address, mark the **Omit** check box.
6. If you want to print a return address, check the address in the **Return Address** box, and edit it if necessary.
7. If your envelope is not the standard business size, or if you want to change the font or position of the addresses, click the **Options** button to display the Envelope Options dialog box (see Figure 4.22). Use the **Envelope Size** list to choose a different envelope size. To change fonts, click the **Font** button under Delivery Address or Return Address. To adjust the position of the return or recipient address, click the spinner arrows to the right of the appropriate **From Left** and **From Top** text boxes. When you're finished, click **OK** to return to the Envelopes and Labels dialog box.

FIGURE **4.22**

The Envelope Options dialog box enables you to customize your envelope.

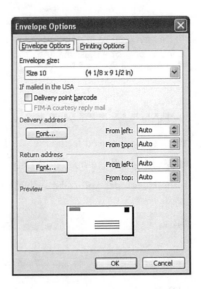

8. Put the envelope in your printer and click the **Print** button to print it. Alternatively, you can click the **Add to Document** button to add the envelope to the top of the current document so that it prints every time you print the document. (If you do this, remember to always have an envelope loaded when you print the document because it prints as the first page.)

If you aren't sure how to feed your envelope into the printer, check the Feed Method area in the Printing Options tab of the Envelope Options dialog box. The diagram is usually correct. If it's not, check your printer's documentation for the right way to load the envelope.

9. If you changed your return address in step 6, Word asks whether you want to save the new address as the default return address. Click the **Yes** button if you want to use this return address in the future, or click **No** to use it just this once.

Word finds your return address in the User Information tab of the Options dialog box. If you change it while printing an envelope, Word updates your address here. You can edit your return address and other user information at any time. To do so, choose Tools, Options. Then click the User Information tab, revise the information, and click OK.

Printing Labels

The steps for printing labels are very similar to those for printing envelopes. The one difference is that you'll probably need to choose another label type because labels come in such a wide variety of sizes.

Follow these steps to print a label:

1. With a document open, choose **Tools**, **Letters and Mailings**, **Envelopes and Labels**.
2. Click the **Labels** tab in the Envelopes and Labels dialog box (see Figure 4.23).

FIGURE 4.23

Use the Labels tab of the Envelopes and Labels dialog box to specify the address to print on your label.

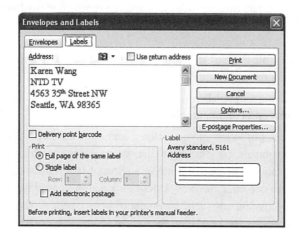

3. Type or edit the address in the **Address** box. If you want to print your return address instead, mark the **Use Return Address** check box.
4. Click the **Options** button to display the **Label Options** dialog box (see Figure 4.24).

FIGURE 4.24

The Label Options dialog box enables you to specify the type of labels you're using.

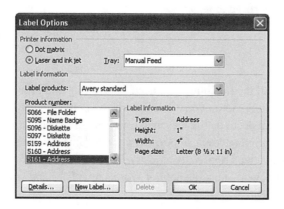

5. Select the product number for your labels in the **Product Number** list, and click **OK**. (If you don't have standard Avery labels, choose a different label from the **Label Products** drop-down list.)

> The product number for most labels is printed on the packaging. If you can't find your labels' product number or it isn't in the Product Number list, click the New Label button in the Label Options dialog box. In the New Custom Laser dialog box (or New Custom Dot Matrix if you marked the Dot Matrix option button in the Label Options dialog box), type a name for your labels, enter their dimensions, and click OK. Your new label type is added to the Product Number list so that you can choose it in the future.

6. Mark the **Full Page of the Same Label** check box if you want a whole page of labels with the same address on each one.

7. If you want a single label, mark the **Single Label** option button, and then enter the label's row and column number.

8. Put the sheet of labels in your printer, and click the **Print** button to print the label or sheet of labels. (If you aren't sure which paper tray to use, check your printer's documentation.) If you are printing a sheet of labels and want to print them in the future, you can click the **New Document** button instead of the Print button. Word creates a separate one-page document of your labels. Save this document, print as many copies as you need, and then close it. You can open this document at any time in the future to print more of these labels.

> Even though Word enables you to print a single label at a time, it is not a good idea to run a sheet of labels through a laser printer more than once. Doing so can cause labels to come off inside the printer, something that is not cheap to repair.

Summary

Word gives you all the flexibility you need for viewing and printing your documents. In addition to switching views, you can adjust the magnification of your documents, display different parts of a document at the same time, and tile open Word documents on the desktop. Before printing, you can preview your document to make sure it looks the way you want it to, and then optionally adjust your print job in a variety of ways. In the next hour, you learn how to enlist the help of Word's templates and wizards to produce nicely formatted documents.

Q&A

Q In Print Layout view, header and footer text appears dim. Will it print that way?

A No. Header and footer text appears dim because the header and footer areas are not active in Print Layout view by default. If you want to edit your header or footer, double-click it to activate it. The text turns dark. When you are finished, double-click the document text to reactivate it. You'll learn more about headers and footers in Hour 8.

Q I use a high-resolution setting on my monitor, and the text in Word documents is too small to read easily. Will the Zoom feature help in this situation?

A Yes. A small high-resolution monitor may make the text too small if you use one of the higher resolution settings. You can compensate for this by increasing the Zoom setting, although you will lose the benefit of seeing more text on the screen.

Q Can I print Word documents without opening Word?

A Yes. If you have a shortcut to your printer on your desktop, you can drag the document icon from Windows Explorer or My Computer and drop it onto the printer shortcut. If you don't have a printer shortcut on your desktop, open your Printers and Faxes folder (located in your main Start menu), right-drag the icon for your printer onto the desktop, release the mouse button, and choose Create shortcuts here.

4

HOUR 5

Creating Documents from Existing Documents, Templates, and Wizards

You can type and format all of your documents from scratch, but you don't have to. If you have an existing document that resembles the document you want to create, you can simply base your new document on the existing one and then revise the new document as needed. If you don't have an appropriate document on hand, Word's templates can help you out. A *template* is a rough blueprint for a document that includes some combination of text and formatting. The default template, Normal, produces a blank document with "plain-vanilla" formatting. But Microsoft provides literally hundreds of other templates, for creating everything from memos, letters, and fax cover sheets to résumés, reports, and more. In this hour, you learn to use two of these other templates, and you also try out a couple of wizards. A *wizard* is a special kind of template that asks you a series of questions, and then creates a "made-to-order" document based on your answers.

The highlights of this hour include

- Creating a new document based on an existing document
- Finding out how templates and wizards can help you
- Selecting a template or wizard for a new document
- Creating a document with a template
- Creating a document with a wizard

Basing a New Document on an Existing One

The most obvious advantage of using an existing document as the basis for a new one is that you don't have to retype the text that will stay the same or apply the same formatting over again. When you use the steps outlined here to create a new document based on an existing one, the new document has a temporary name of *Document1, Document2,* and so on, just as if you created a new blank document. Therefore, when you are ready to save, you can use the Save command without risking overwriting the original document.

In Hour 3, you learned that when you click the New Blank Document button in the Standard toolbar to start a new document, Word assumes that you want to base the document on the Normal template. If you want to use an existing document (or a different template or wizard), you have to use the File, New command.

To create a new document based on an existing one, follow these steps:

1. Choose **File**, **New** to display the New Document task pane (see Figure 5.1).

FIGURE 5.1

The New Document task pane appears when you choose File, New.

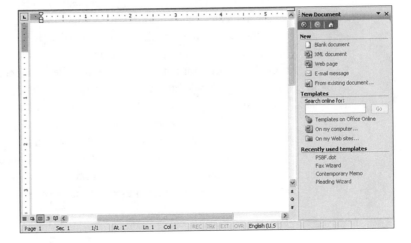

2. Click **From Existing Document** in the New Document task pane.

3. In the New from Existing Document dialog box, shown in Figure 5.2, navigate to and select the file on which you want to base your new document, and click the **Create New** button.

FIGURE 5.2

Select the existing document you want to use in the New from Existing Document dialog box.

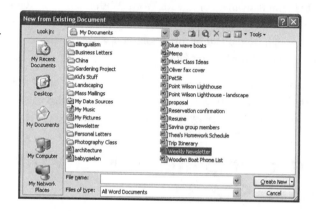

4. A new document with a temporary name such as *Document1* or *Document2* appears with all of the text and formatting from the document you selected in the previous step. Revise it as you like, and then choose **File**, **Save** or **File**, **Save As**.

5. In the Save As dialog box, choose a location and name for your file, and click **Save**.

As an alternative to the preceding steps, you may be inclined to open an existing document that you want to use as "boilerplate text" with the File, Open command, revise it, and then use the Save As command to save the file under a new name. By using Save As, you don't overwrite your boilerplate file with the new one. The problem with this technique is that sooner or later you will probably have a brain lapse and use the Save command instead of Save As. When you do, the existing document will get replaced with the revised version, and you will have to re-create your boilerplate file. You can avoid this potential problem by using the steps described here instead, or by using a template or wizard.

5

The Advantages of Using a Template or Wizard

As with basing a new document on an existing one, a major benefit of using a template (or wizard) is that it's fast. If you use a template that includes the standard text that doesn't change from one document to the next, you can avoid the tedium of typing this text yourself.

Another benefit of using templates is that the formatting is handled for you. Professionals who know how to use Word's formatting features to their best advantage designed the templates that come with Word. With the help of templates, you can produce documents with sophisticated formatting that you haven't yet learned how to apply yourself (although by the end of this book, you will know how to apply most of the formatting included in Word's templates).

Templates also enable you to create a consistent look for all of your documents. This is especially helpful in an office, where you can use templates to standardize the letters, memos, reports, and so on that you and your coworkers generate.

Selecting a Template on Microsoft's Office Online Web Site

Microsoft offers a large number of templates on its Office Online Web site. The quickest way to locate one you want to use is to search for it by keyword, as described in these steps:

1. Choose **File**, **New** to display the New Document task pane.
2. In the **Search Online For** text box, enter the type of template you are looking for and click the **Go** button (see Figure 5.3).

FIGURE 5.3

Type a keyword or two describing the type of template you're looking for.

3. A list of likely matches appears in the Search Results task pane (see Figure 5.4). Click one that interests you to preview it in the Template Preview dialog box (see Figure 5.5).

FIGURE 5.4

The Search Results task pane lists the templates on Office Online that most closely match your search criteria.

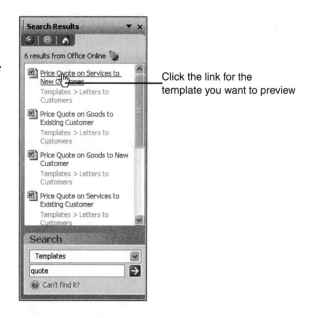

Click the link for the template you want to preview

FIGURE 5.5

You can browse the results of the Office Online search in the Template Preview dialog box.

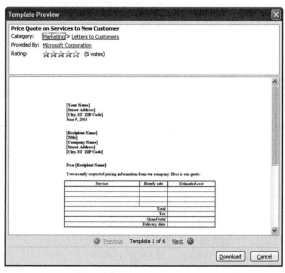

5

4. Use the Previous and Next links at the bottom of the Template Preview dialog box to continue browsing the search results. When you find a template you'd like to use, click the Download button in the lower-right corner of the dialog box.

As the template is downloading, you may see a message from Microsoft Office Online asking whether you want to see links to additional assistance and information about the template. If you click Yes, these links (if any are available), will be displayed in the Template Help task pane, which appears automatically when you use a template from Office Online.

A document based on the downloaded template opens in Word (see Figure 5.6). Revise it as desired, and then save it as you would any other document. (You'll learn more about filling in templates and wizards later in this hour.)

FIGURE 5.6

A document based on the downloaded template appears in your Word window.

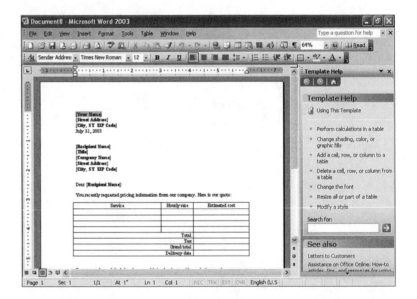

Selecting a Template on Your Own Computer

If you already have a template you want to use on your own computer, follow these steps to select it:

1. Choose **File**, **New** to display the New Document task pane, and click **On My Computer**.

2. The Templates dialog box appears (see Figure 5.7). Click the tab that contains the template or wizard that you want to use.

FIGURE 5.7

Use the Templates dialog box to choose a template other than the Normal template.

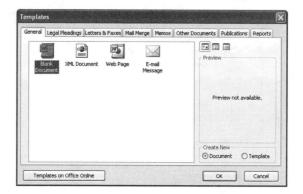

The Blank Document icon in the General tab is selected by default. If you leave this icon selected and click OK, Word creates a document based on the Normal template, just as if you had clicked the New Blank Document toolbar button. (Microsoft also refers to the Normal template as the Blank Document template, just to confuse you.)

You may see a different set of tabs than the ones shown here. As you'll learn in Hour 10, you can create your own tabs in the Templates dialog box to store custom templates. If you are missing some tabs, some templates may not have been included in your Word installation.

3. Click the icon for the template or wizard, and look at the Preview area on the right side of the dialog box. If you see the message "Click OK to install additional templates and create a new file," dig out your Office CD and insert it into your CD-ROM drive. (As soon as you click OK, Word will copy the necessary files from the CD to your hard drive.)

4. If the template is already installed, you might see a picture of it in the Preview area of the Templates dialog box, as shown in Figure 5.8. (Not all templates have previews.)

5. Click **OK** (or double-click the template or wizard).

In a moment, you'll see a new document based on the template or wizard you chose. You need to complete the document by adding all of your personalized text. In the next two sections, you practice using templates and wizards to create a fax cover sheet, a résumé, a memo, and a letter.

FIGURE 5.8

FIGURE 5.8

The Preview area of the Templates dialog box shows you what the currently selected template looks like.

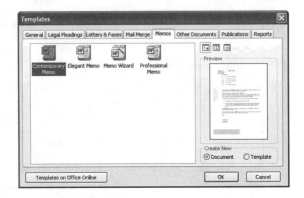

Creating a Document with a Template

Each template is unique, but there are a few characteristics that crop up in most of them. The Contemporary Fax and Professional Résumé templates are typical examples. After you've used both of them, you should feel comfortable trying the others.

The Contemporary Fax Template

It takes only a few moments to put together a nicely formatted fax cover sheet if you use a template or wizard.

To create a fax cover sheet by using the Contemporary Fax template, follow these steps:

1. Choose **File**, **New** to display the New Document task pane.

2. Click **On My Computer** to display the Templates dialog box.

3. Click the **Letters & Faxes** tab, and double-click **Contemporary Fax**.

4. If the template isn't already installed, Word installs it now (make sure to have your Office CD handy). A document based on the Contemporary Fax template then appears onscreen (see Figure 5.9).

5. In the upper-left corner, click the **[Click Here and Type Address]** text. Type your address, pressing Enter at the end of each line. The text you type replaces the dummy text.

Documents that you start from wizards or templates (other than Normal) display onscreen at a reduced magnification so that you can see the full width of the page. As a result, some of the text may be too small to read clearly. If you need to increase the magnification of the document to see what you're typing, increase the Zoom setting.

FIGURE 5.9

*A document based on
the Contemporary Fax
template, before it's
been filled in.*

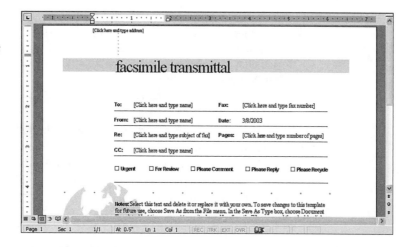

6. Continue to replace the other [Click Here and Type] prompts with the text that you want to include in the fax coversheet. If you want to leave an area blank (for example, you don't want to type a name after CC:), click the prompt text and press Delete.

7. Double-click any of the check boxes (Urgent, For Review, Please Comment, and so on) in which you want to place a check mark. (You can double-click when your I-beam mouse pointer is over the check box.)

8. In the body of the memo, select the text beginning with the word *Notes:*. Type over it with the text that you want in the body of the memo. The memo should now be completely filled in, as shown in Figure 5.10.

5

FIGURE 5.10

*A finished document
based on the
Contemporary Fax
template.*

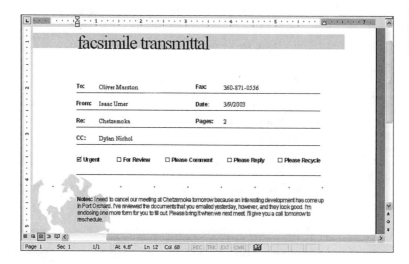

The "dummy" text after Notes includes instructions for modifying the template to include your personal information so that you don't have to type it each time you use the template. You'll learn how to do this in Hour 10, "Working with Templates."

9. Click the **Save** button in the Standard toolbar. In the Save As dialog box, notice that Word Document is selected in the Save As Type drop-down list (see Figure 5.11). This tells you that Word will save the file as a Word document, and not as a template, so it won't overwrite the template itself. (Templates have the file extension .dot instead of .doc, and they are stored in a special Templates folder.) Choose a name and location for the file, and click the **Save** button.

FIGURE 5.11

Save your document after you've filled it in.

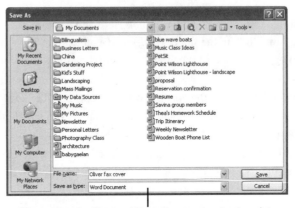

Word saves the file as a Word document, not a template

10. Choose **File**, **Close** to close the document.

The Professional Résumé Template

Designing a résumé can be quite time-consuming if you have to handle all of the formatting on top of drafting the text. If you use one of Word's résumé templates, you can use the built-in formatting in the template, which lets you focus on the writing.

To create a résumé using the Professional Résumé template, follow these steps:

1. Choose **File**, **New** to display the New Document task pane.

2. Click the **On My Computer** button to display the Templates dialog box.

3. Click the **Other Documents** tab, and double-click **Professional Résumé**.

4. If the template isn't already installed, Word installs it now (have your CD handy).

A document based on the Professional Résumé template then appears onscreen (see Figure 5.12).

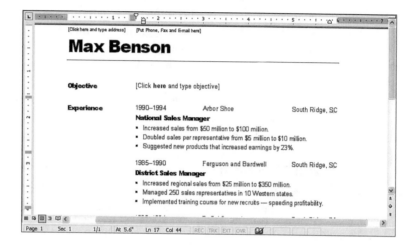

5. One by one, click the **[Click Here and Type Address]**, **[Put Phone, Fax, and E-mail Here]**, and **[Click Here and Type Objective]** prompts to select them, and type over them with your own personal information.

6. Notice that this template includes fictitious data about a person named Max Benson to show you where your text should go. Select all of this text, one piece of information at a time, and type over it with your own information. Figure 5.13 shows the document after the "dummy text" has been replaced.

7. Choose **File**, **Save As** to name and save the new document.

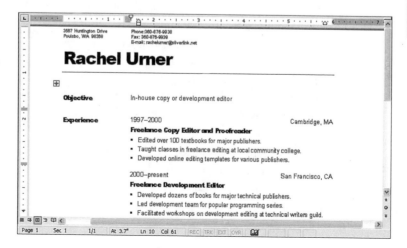

5

Creating a Document with a Wizard

Wizards give you as much hand-holding as possible, short of sending you the final document in the mail. Here, you practice using two kinds of wizards. The first one, the Memo Wizard, is an example of the standard type that you find in the Templates dialog box. You progress through a series of dialog boxes, answering a different set of questions in each one. When you click Finish at the end, Word generates the document. The second one, the Letter Wizard, is a bit atypical. You access it through the Tools menu, not the New dialog box, and instead of presenting a series of dialog boxes, it gives you only one dialog box, with all of the questions arranged in different tabs. After you've made your selections in each tab, you click OK to generate the document.

The Memo Wizard

When you need to dash off a quick memo, the Memo Wizard can be a great help. It fills in most of the details so that you need to do little more than type the memo text.

To create a memo by using the Memo Wizard, follow these steps:

1. Choose **File**, **New** to display the New Document task pane.
2. Click **On My Computer** to display the Templates dialog box.
3. Click the **Memos** tab, and double-click **Memo Wizard**.
4. If the wizard isn't already installed, Word installs it now (insert your Office CD if necessary).
5. The first of the wizard dialog boxes appears onscreen (see Figure 5.14). Along the left side of the dialog box is a "progress line" that shows you all of the steps you'll go through to get from start to finish. This progress line appears in all of the dialog boxes for the wizard. As you move through the wizard, the box next to the current step turns green so that you know where you are.
6. Click **Next** to move to the next dialog box, and choose the style for your memo. Continue clicking **Next** to move from one dialog box to the next, answering the wizard's questions about the memo title, heading fields, recipient, and so on. If you change your mind about the options you chose in a previous dialog box, click the **Back** button to move back to it and change your settings, and then click **Next** to get back to where you were.
7. When you get to the last step, click the **Finish** button. A memo that incorporates all of your instructions appears onscreen. Replace the [Click Here and Type Your Memo Text] prompt with the text you want in the memo (see Figure 5.15).
8. Save and close the document.

The progress line lets you keep track of where you are in the wizard.

FIGURE 5.14

The first dialog box of the Memo Wizard.

FIGURE 5.15

Type the body of the memo; the wizard has done everything else for you.

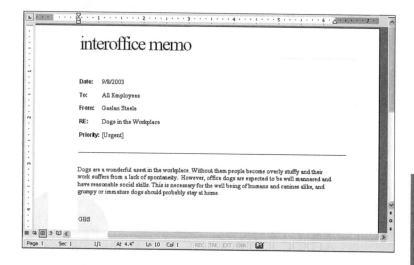

The Letter Wizard

The Letter Wizard, although different in its appearance, performs the same role as the Memo Wizard. If you don't have much time to compose a letter, you should find it helpful.

To create a letter by using the Letter Wizard, follow these steps:

1. Start a new document, and then choose **Tools**, **Letters and Mailings**, **Letter Wizard** to display the Letter Wizard dialog box, as shown in Figure 5.16.

FIGURE **5.16**

*Design your letter in
the Letter Wizard dia-
log box.*

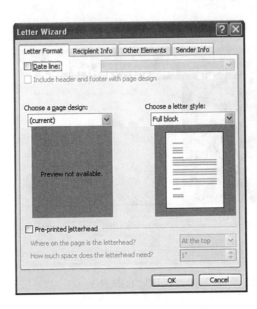

2. In the **Letter Format** tab, mark the **Date Line** check box if you want a date at the
   top of the letter, and choose the format for the date in the drop-down list to the
   right of the check box. Choose a page design and a letter style in the two drop-
   down lists in the middle of the dialog box. If you have preprinted letterhead, mark
   the **Pre-Printed Letterhead** check box, and specify where the letterhead is on the
   page and how much space it needs.

3. Click the **Recipient Info** tab and fill in the recipient's name and address and the
   salutation.

4. Click the **Other Elements** tab. If you want to include a reference line, mailing
   instructions, an attention line, or a subject line, mark the appropriate check boxes.
   For each check box you mark, choose the exact text from the associated drop-down
   list, or type your own text in the box at the top of the list. At the bottom of the dialog box, type the names of any people to whom you want to send courtesy copies.

5. Click the **Sender Info** tab, and fill in the sender's name and address. Mark the
   Omit check box if you are using letterhead that includes the return address. Under
   Closing at the bottom of the dialog box, choose standard text from the drop-down
   lists for the complimentary closing, your job title, and so on, or type your own text
   in the text boxes at the top of each list. The Preview area shows what your closing
   will look like.

6. After you've made your selections, click **OK**.

7. The letter appears onscreen. Type the body of the letter (see Figure 5.17) and then
   save and close it.

FIGURE 5.17

A letter written with the help of the Letter Wizard.

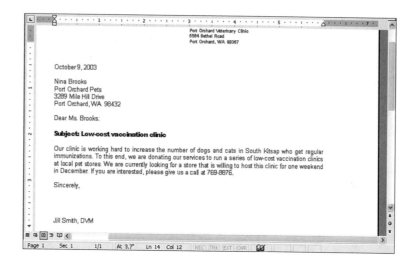

Summary

If your work requires you to write documents that are more similar than not, you can base your new documents on existing ones and then edit them without worrying about accidentally overwriting your originals. And when you need to dash off a letter, memo, or fax but don't have the time or inclination to fiddle with formatting, you can consider using a template or wizard. They can help you produce professional documents with a minimum of hassle. The next hour is the first of several on formatting; you will start by learning how to change the font of your text, as well as applying boldface, italic, underline, and other font attributes.

Q&A

Q I don't have the templates that you describe in my Templates dialog box. What is going on?

A When you install Office, you can choose which templates to include. Your company may not have installed all of the Word templates, or it may only have installed custom templates that someone designed specifically for your company. Check with your network administrator if you want to use a template that you don't see in your New dialog box. If you are using Word on a standalone computer, follow the instructions in Appendix A to add more templates to your installation.

Q When I use the Memo Wizard, I don't want to change any of the default choices. Do I still have to click Next repeatedly to go all the way to the last wizard dialog box before clicking Finish?

5

A No. If you want to keep all of the default options, just click Finish in the first wizard dialog box that appears. The Memo Wizard remembers the options that you chose the last time you ran the wizard. If you don't want to change them the next time you use the wizard, just click Finish in the first dialog box.

PART II

Formatting Documents

Hour

HOUR 6

Formatting Characters

Changing the appearance of characters is one of the parts of word processing that most people enjoy—even stodgy workaholics and high-octane business managers. The formatting that you can apply to individual characters—fonts, font sizes, bold, italic, underline, and so on—is referred to as *font formatting* or *character formatting*. You can apply font formatting to as little as one character, or as much as an entire document. In this hour, you learn how to apply a wide range of font-formatting techniques, and then you find out about a few more tricks for handling this type of formatting in your documents.

The highlights of this hour include

- Using other fonts and changing the font size
- Applying boldface, italic, and underline
- Changing font color
- Adjusting character spacing
- Applying text effects
- Choosing a different default font
- Copying and removing font formatting

Applying Font Formatting

By default, Word applies a Times New Roman, 12-point font to your text. To make any changes to this default setting, you use one of the font-formatting features described in this hour. As you're exploring the different formatting options, keep these three points in mind:

- In general, you need to select the text you want to format before issuing the formatting command. This is your way of telling Word exactly what text you want to format.

> There are two exceptions to the "select first" rule. First, if you're applying the font formatting to a single word, you can just click in the word without selecting it, and then issue the commands. The formatting is applied to the entire word. Second, if you haven't yet typed the text that you want to format, you can place your insertion point at the location where you want to type, turn on the font-formatting options, and then type your text. The text takes on the formatting you chose.

- The easiest way to tell what font, font size, font style (boldface, italic, underline), and font color has been applied to a block of text is to click in it. The options in the Formatting toolbar show you the formatting that is in effect wherever the insertion point is resting.
- If you want to apply the same font formatting to several blocks of text, a fast way to do it is to use the F4 key. F4, the *repeat* key, repeats whatever command you last issued. So if you used the Font dialog box to apply several types of font formatting to a heading, for example, you could then select the next heading, press F4, select the next heading, press F4, and so on. Each time you press F4, Word repeats the last command, which in this case is to apply all of the selections you made in the Font dialog box. (You can use F4 to repeat many other commands as well.)

Changing Fonts

In the world of personal computers, the term *font* is used to refer to the typeface of your text, which is basically the "look" of each character you type. Each computer has a different set of fonts, depending on what software is installed and what printer you're using. Office detects which fonts you have available and enables you to select them in Word.

As a general rule, it's best to use only one or two fonts in a document. If you apply more, your document is likely to look overly busy.

Selecting a Font Using the Font List

The quickest way to change a font is to use the Font drop-down list in the Formatting toolbar, although you can also change fonts in the Font dialog box, as you'll see in a moment.

To apply a font using the Font list, first select the text you want to change. Then click the down arrow to the right of the Font list in the Formatting toolbar. The list of fonts shows you what each font looks like (see Figure 6.1). Scroll down until you find the one you want to use, and click it.

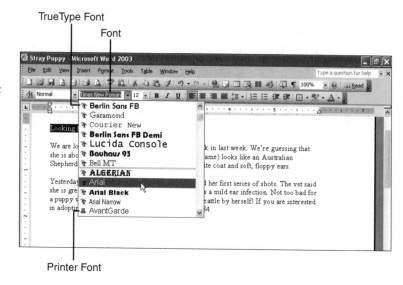

TrueType Font

Font

FIGURE 6.1

The Font list shows you what the fonts look like. Click the one you want to use.

Printer Font

6

Word applies the font to the selected text. To see the change more clearly, click once to deselect the text. In Figure 6.2, the title was changed to the Arial font.

Word places the fonts you use frequently above the double line in the Font list (refer back to Figure 6.1) so that you can get at them easily. Below the double line is an alphabetical list of all your fonts.

Arial Font

FIGURE 6.2
Word applies the font you chose to selected text.

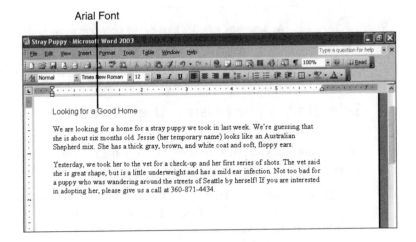

The symbols to the left of the fonts in the Font list indicate the font type. The TT icon represents a *TrueType* font. These fonts come with Windows or other Windows applications, and they are the best ones to use because they look the same onscreen as they do when printed. TrueType fonts are also scalable, meaning that they can be flexibly resized. The printer icon represents a *printer* font. These fonts come with your printer. They print just fine, but their onscreen appearance may not match the way they print.

Selecting a Font Using the Font Dialog Box

If you'd like to change other font formatting at the same time as you're changing the font, you may find it more convenient to use the Font dialog box. The dialog box gives you a "one-stop shopping" experience.

All of the font-formatting features described in this hour are accessible in the Font dialog box, although in many cases it's faster to use the Formatting toolbar or a keyboard shortcut.

To apply a font using the Font dialog box, follow these steps:

1. Select the text you want to change.
2. Choose **Format, Font** or press **Ctrl+D** to display the Font dialog box (see Figure 6.3).
3. Click the **Font** tab if it isn't already in front.
4. Scroll through the **Font** list and click the fonts that you're interested in to see what they look like in the Preview area at the bottom of the dialog box. (This is the same list as the one in the Font list in the Formatting toolbar.)

FIGURE 6.3
The Font dialog box provides access to all of the font-formatting commands.

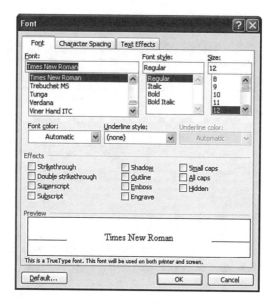

5. When you find the font that you want to use, select it and click **OK**. The new font is applied to your selected text.

Changing Font Size

Font size is measured in points. The larger the point size, the taller the font. There are approximately 72 points in an inch, so a 72-point font is about one inch tall. Typically, business documents are written in a 10- or 12-point font.

> If you use more than one font size in a document, it looks best if the sizes differ by at least 2 points.

6

As with changing font types, you can change font size by using either the Formatting toolbar or the Font dialog box, but there is no advantage to using the dialog box unless you want to make other font-formatting changes at the same time.

To change the font size by using the Font Size list, follow these steps:

1. Select the text you want to change.

2. Click the down arrow to the right of the **Font Size** list in the Formatting toolbar, scroll down the list, and click the size that you want to use (see Figure 6.4).

Font Size

FIGURE 6.4

Word includes commonly used font sizes in the Font Size list. Click the one you want to use.

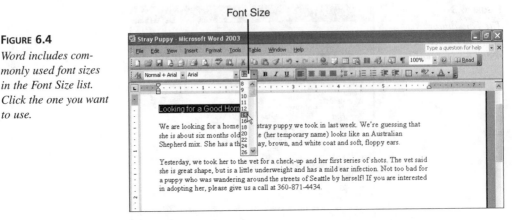

Word applies the font size to the selected text. To see the change more clearly, click to deselect. In Figure 6.5, the title was changed to a 14-point font.

14-point font

FIGURE 6.5

Word applies the chosen font size to selected text.

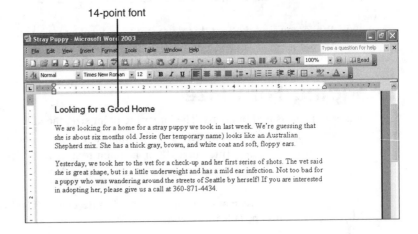

If you like, you can adjust font size one point at a time by pressing Ctrl+] to increase the size and Ctrl+[to decrease it.

You aren't limited to the point sizes in the Font Size list. If you want to use a size smaller than 8-point or larger than 72-point, click in the Font Size box to select the current size, type over it with the size that you want to use, and press Enter. (You can use this method to apply font sizes between 8 and 72 points as well.)

Applying Bold, Italic, and Underline

The most common type of font formatting other than font and font size is *font style*. This term refers collectively to boldface, italic, and underline. You can apply font styles individually, or you can apply two or more to the same block of text. For example, you could add boldface and italic to a sentence. Judicious use of font styles can add just the right emphasis to a document—overuse can make a document cluttered and difficult to read.

The easiest way to apply font styles is via the Formatting toolbar or a keyboard shortcut:

1. Select the text to which you want to apply a font style.
2. Click the **Bold**, **Italic**, or **Underline** button on the Formatting toolbar (see Figure 6.6). Alternatively, you can press Ctrl+B for bold, Ctrl+I for italic, or Ctrl+U for underline.

FIGURE 6.6

Click the Bold, Italic, or Underline button in the Formatting toolbar to apply a font style to the selected text.

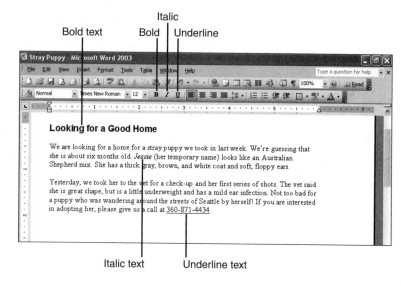

Word applies the font style. To see the change, click anywhere to deselect the text. Figure 6.6 shows a document that includes all three font styles.

Select the text and then click the toolbar button (or press the keyboard shortcut) again to remove a font style from the text.

The Underline button on the Formatting toolbar applies a single underline. However, Word provides a wide variety of other underlining options in the Font tab of the Font dialog box (words only, double, thick, dashed, and so on). Choose the style you want in the Underline Style list, and optionally select a color for the underline in the Underline Color list. To remove special underlining, select the text, choose Format, Font, and choose

None in the Underline Style list or Automatic in the Underline Color list. Another quick way to apply double underlining is to select the text and press Ctrl+Shift+D.

Changing Font Color

Changing the color of your text can brighten up a document and make key parts of it stand out. Remember that changing font color won't do much if you're printing on a black-and-white printer. (The colors print in shades of gray.) If, on the other hand, you have a color printer or your readers view the document onscreen, font colors can greatly enhance your document's appearance.

As usual, the easiest way to apply font color is to use the Formatting toolbar, as described in these steps:

1. Select the text to which you want to apply font color.

2. Click the down arrow to the right of the **Font Color** toolbar button at the right end of the Formatting toolbar. A palette appears with a large selection of colors (see Figure 6.7). Pointing to a color displays a ScreenTip with the color's name. Click the one you want to use.

FIGURE 6.7

Word gives you many colors to choose from. Click the one you want to use.

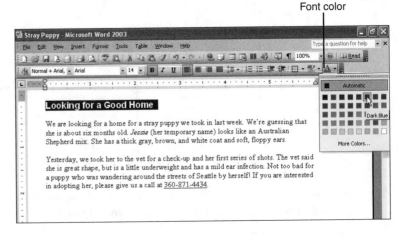

Word applies the color to the selected text. To see what it looks like, deselect the text. If you don't see a color that you want to use in the Font Color palette, click the More Colors button at the bottom of the palette to display the Colors dialog box. Choose a color you like, and click OK.

Font colors change the color of the text itself. You can also use the Highlighting feature to draw a transparent color over the selected text, just as you'd mark text with a highlighter pen. You learn how to apply highlighting in Hour 18, "Collaborating on Documents."

Adjusting Character Spacing

Word gives you several ways to adjust the amount of space between characters. In most documents, you won't need to adjust spacing, but once in a while you may want to change the spacing in a heading.

To adjust character spacing, follow these steps:

1. Select the text in which you want to change character spacing.
2. Choose **Format, Font** or press **Ctrl+D** to display the Font dialog box.
3. Click the **Character Spacing** tab (see Figure 6.8).
4. Select the desired options, and click **OK**.

FIGURE 6.8
The Character Spacing tab contains four options for adjusting spacing.

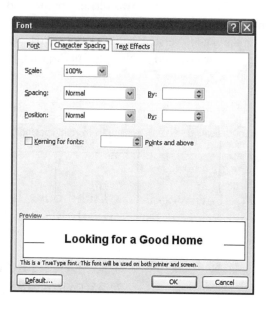

6

Here is an explanation of how to use the options in the Character Spacing tab:

- Scale—Use this list to expand or condense your text horizontally by a particular percentage. Any percentage over 100 percent expands the text; any percentage under 100 percent condenses it. If you like, you can click in the Scale box, type a percentage that doesn't appear in the list (120 percent, for example), and press Enter. In Figure 6.9, the top version of *Fernwood* is scaled at 100 percent. The lower one is scaled at 120 percent.

- Spacing—Use this list if you want to expand or condense your text by a number of points, and then type the number of points in the By text box. Figure 6.9 shows two versions of the heading *Lighthouse Times*. The first has normal character spacing; the second is expanded by 2 points.

- Position—Use this list to raise the text above the baseline or lower it beneath the baseline without decreasing its size (as you would if you applied superscript or subscript formatting, as described in the next section). Type the number of points by which you'd like to raise or lower the text in the By text box. In Figure 6.9, the word *fork* is lowered 6 points below *spoon* and *knife*.

- Kerning—Mark this check box if you want to adjust the amount of space between certain combinations of letters. When kerning is not turned on and you're using a large point size, large gaps appear between some letters. Kerning closes these gaps. In the Points and Above text box, type the smallest point size for which you want to adjust kerning. Figure 6.9 shows two versions of the heading *AVIARY NEWS*. Kerning is not turned on for the first one and there is a noticeable gap between the *A* and the *V*. In the second version, kerning is turned on and the gap between the *A* and the V is gone. Kerning works only with TrueType and Adobe Type Manager fonts.

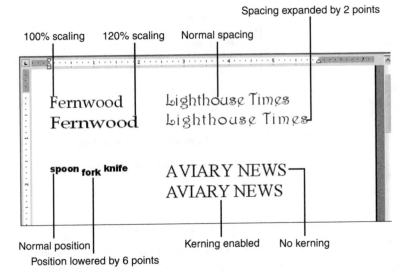

FIGURE 6.9
You may want to adjust character spacing and turn on kerning for large headings.

To return character spacing for a block of text to its default settings, select the text, choose Format, Font, click the Character Spacing tab, choose 100% in the Scale list, Normal in the Spacing and Position lists, clear the Kerning check box, and click OK.

Adding Effects

Depending on the kind of documents you create, you may need to use one or two of the effects available in the Font dialog box—superscript and subscript, perhaps—all the time. Other more specialized ones, such as emboss and engrave, you may never need, but just in case, Word puts them at your disposal.

To apply text effects, follow these steps:

1. Select the text to which you want to apply an effect.

2. Choose **Format**, **Font** or press **Ctrl+D** to display the Font dialog box.

3. Click the **Font** tab if it isn't already in front.

4. Mark the desired check boxes under **Effects** (refer to Figure 6.3). You can see what an effect does by marking its check box and looking at the Preview area at the bottom of the dialog box.

5. When you're done, click **OK**.

To remove any of these effects, select the text to which the effect is applied, choose Format, Font, and clear the appropriate check box under Effects.

One other effect you can apply to your text is animation. When you animate your text, it "comes alive" with neon lights, shimmers, or sparkles. This feature was probably designed with the junior high school set in mind, but even sober-minded adults may find it a good distraction during tax time. Note that animation can't be appreciated unless your readers view the document onscreen. To try it out, select some text, choose Format, Font, and click the Text Effects tab. Click a few options in the Animations list to see what they look like. When you find one that you like, click OK. (To later remove animation, select the text, display the Text Effects tab of the Font dialog box, choose None, and click OK.)

6

The Hidden option hides the selected text both onscreen and in the printed document. Word closes up the text around the hidden text so that you can't tell it's there unless you click the Show/Hide ¶ button in the Standard toolbar. When you turn on Show/Hide ¶, hidden text appears with a dotted line underneath it. This feature comes in handy in some documents. You could use it to hide confidential parts of a report before printing it, for example.

(If you want to see hidden text even when the Show/Hide ¶ button is turned off, choose Tools, Options. In the Options dialog box, click the View tab, mark the Hidden Text check box, and click OK.)

Some of the effects have convenient keyboard shortcuts. For example, you can select the text and then press Ctrl+Shift+A for all caps, Ctrl+Shift+K for small caps, Ctrl+equal sign for subscript, Ctrl+Shift+plus sign for superscript.

Changing the Case of Letters

If you realize after you type some text that you want to change its case, you don't have to retype it. Instead, just select the text, choose Format, Change Case to display the Change Case dialog box (see Figure 6.10), choose the option you want, and click OK.

FIGURE 6.10
Use the Change Case dialog box to change the case of text without retyping it.

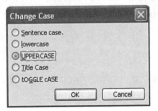

The Title Case option capitalizes articles and prepositions. So "a day at the beach" would become "A Day At The Beach." If you'd rather leave articles and prepositions lowercase (as in "A Day at the Beach"), you need to change their case manually.

The keyboard shortcut for changing case is Shift+F3. Select the text and then press Shift+F3 one or more times until you see the case you want.

Changing the Default Font Settings

If you use a different font than Times New Roman 12-point for most of your documents, you might want to change the default font. If you do, Word applies the new font in all new documents that are based on the Normal template. (The Normal template is what all new, blank documents are based on.)

To change the default font, follow these steps:

1. Choose **Format, Font** to display the Font dialog box.
2. Choose all of the font options that you want for the default font.
3. Click the **Default** button.
4. Word displays a message box asking whether you want to change the default font, and reminding you that this change affects all new documents based on the Normal template (see Figure 6.11). Click the **Yes** button.

FIGURE 6.11
Word confirms that you want to change the default font.

If you want to change the default font to something else in the future, repeat these steps.

Copying Font Formatting

If you have carefully applied several font formats to one block of text and then decide that you'd like to use the same combination of formats somewhere else in the document, you don't have to apply the formatting from scratch. Instead, you can use Word's Format Painter feature to copy the formatting of the original block of text and then "paint" it across the other text.

In "Checking the Formatting of Your Text" at the end of Hour 7, you will learn how to review the formatting of your text with the Reveal Formatting feature. This feature provides another method for copying all of the formatting from one selection to another.

6

Follow these steps to copy font formatting:

1. Click anywhere in the text that has the formatting you want to copy.
2. Click the **Format Painter** button on the Formatting toolbar (see Figure 6.12).

FIGURE **6.12**
Use the Format Painter button on the Standard toolbar to copy font formatting.

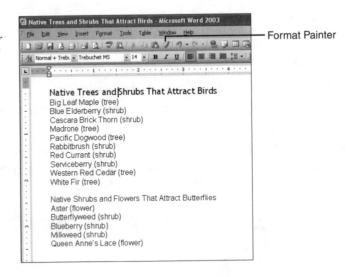

3. The mouse pointer becomes an I-beam with a paintbrush attached to it. Drag over the text to which you want to apply the formatting (see Figure 6.13).

FIGURE **6.13**
The Format Painter is a great way to copy font formatting quickly.

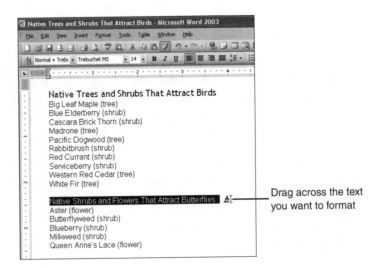

4. Release the mouse button. Word applies the formatting to the selected text (see Figure 6.14).

FIGURE 6.14

The formatting is copied as soon as you release the mouse button.

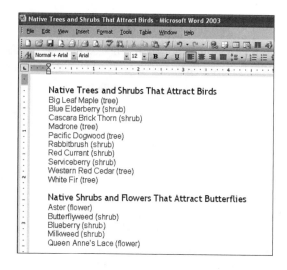

If you want to apply the same set of font formats to several blocks of text, double-click the Format Painter toolbar button in step 2. The Format Painter stays turned on while you drag over multiple blocks of text. When you're finished, click the button again to turn it off.

Removing Font Formatting

If you have applied several different font formats to a block of text and then decide you want to turn off all of them, you can, of course, select the text and then turn off each one individually. This method can be quite tedious, however, because you may have to use several dialog boxes, toolbar buttons, or keyboard shortcuts. A much faster method is to select the text and press the keyboard shortcut Ctrl+Spacebar, which removes all of the font formatting that has been manually applied.

This shortcut also comes in handy if you have to edit a document in which the font formatting is badly botched. To remove the font formatting from an entire document and start over, press Ctrl+A to select the document, and then press Ctrl+Spacebar.

6

Ctrl+Spacebar does not remove font formatting that is part of a *style* (a collection of formatting commands). It will, however, remove any font formatting that was added after the style was applied. (You'll learn about styles in Hour 9, "Working with Styles.")

Summary

Judicious use of font formatting can greatly enhance the appearance of your document. Experiment with different combinations of the font-formatting options you learned in this hour to see what is most effective for your documents. In the next hour, you learn how to apply paragraph formatting.

Q&A

Q **What is the difference between a *serif* and a *sans* serif font, and which type should I use where?**

A A serif font has "tails" at the ends of the letters. A good example of serif font is Times New Roman. Serif fonts are ideal for body text. A sans serif font is one that doesn't have the tails. Arial and Helvetica are examples of sans serif fonts. These fonts work well for headings and short blocks of text.

Q **When I click the down arrow to the right of the Font drop-down list on the Formatting toolbar, it takes forever for the list to appear. Is there any way to speed it up?**

A Yes. The Font drop-down list will display much more quickly if the font names aren't listed in the actual fonts. To turn this feature off, choose Tools, Customize. In the Customize dialog box, click the Options tab. Clear the List Font Names in Their Font check box, and click OK. This change affects the Font drop-down list in all Office applications.

Q **I tried to change a font format for some text in my document and nothing happened. What did I do wrong?**

A You probably forgot to select the text first.

HOUR 7

Formatting Paragraphs

Now that you know how to apply font formatting, you're ready to delve into *paragraph formatting*, the second of the three formatting categories. Paragraph formatting includes all of the formatting that can affect, at a minimum, a single paragraph. As you wend your way through this jam-packed hour, you'll learn about such paragraph formatting features as alignment, line spacing, custom tabs, and indentation.

The highlights of this hour include

- Changing alignment and line spacing
- Setting custom tabs and indents
- Adding space above and below paragraphs
- Controlling how paragraphs break across pages
- Creating bulleted and numbered lists
- Adding borders and shading
- Copying and removing paragraph formatting
- Checking the formatting of your text

Applying Paragraph Formatting

Just as Word makes some assumptions about font formatting, it also sets default paragraph formatting for you. The most obvious of these default settings are left alignment and single spacing. While you're exploring the different formatting options, keep these four points in mind:

- Paragraph formatting affects individual paragraphs. If you want to apply paragraph formatting to only one paragraph, you simply place the insertion point in that paragraph before applying the change. Word alters just that paragraph and no others.

- If you want to apply a paragraph formatting feature to more than one adjacent paragraph, you have to select them first. (Actually, you just have to make sure that at least a portion of each paragraph is included in the selection.) As you know, Word considers any text followed by a paragraph mark to be a paragraph. So, for example, a three-line title contains three paragraphs. If you want to center the title, you have to select all three lines first. By the same token, if you want to make an entire document double-spaced, you have to select the whole document first.

- Each new paragraph you begin takes on the paragraph formatting of the previous paragraph. So if you want to apply the same paragraph formatting to several paragraphs that you haven't yet typed, you can just type and format the first one, and then continue typing the remaining paragraphs. The formatting you applied to the first paragraph carries down to the others.

- As with font formatting, the options in the Formatting toolbar show you the paragraph formatting that's in effect for the paragraph containing the insertion point. The same is true with the settings on the horizontal ruler. To quickly see what paragraph formatting has been applied to a paragraph, you can simply click in it, and then look at the options that are turned on in the Formatting toolbar and the ruler. For another way to check both font and paragraph formatting, see "Checking the Formatting of Your Text" at the end of this hour.

Many paragraph features are accessible via the Formatting toolbar or keyboard shortcuts. If you use one of these methods for issuing a formatting command, you can save yourself a more time-consuming trip to a dialog box. In this hour, you learn the fastest way to issue each command, but also find out about alternatives where they are available.

If you find yourself applying a certain combination of font and paragraph formatting over and over, consider using a *style* to "collect" this set of formatting features into a group and apply them all at once to your paragraphs. (You'll learn about styles in Hour 9, "Working with Styles.")

Aligning Paragraphs

Alignment refers to the way the right and left edges of a paragraph line up along the right and left margins of your document. Word gives you four alignment choices—left, centered, right, and justified—as shown in Figure 7.1.

FIGURE 7.1

Word gives you four ways to align your paragraphs.

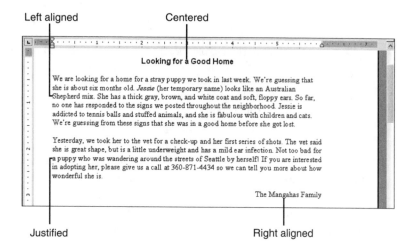

Left aligned   Centered

Justified   Right aligned

By default, Word uses left alignment, which produces a straight left edge and a ragged right edge. Left alignment is usually the best choice for body text in standard business documents such as letters, memos, reports, and so on. Center alignment centers your text horizontally between the right and left margins. You use centering for headings and other short lines of text. Right alignment lines up your text at the right margin and gives it a ragged left edge. This type of alignment works well for short lines of text that you want to appear on the far-right edge of the page. Finally, you may occasionally want to use justification. This type of alignment makes both the right and left edges of a paragraph straight. Word makes slight adjustments to the spacing between characters to produce the straight right edge. Justified text can be a little hard on the eyes because the spacing is uneven, but it is appropriate in some situations. For example, text that is indented from both sides or arranged in columns often looks better if it's justified.

To change alignment using the Formatting toolbar, follow these steps:

1. Click in the paragraph in which you want to change alignment (or select multiple adjacent paragraphs to change the alignment of all of them).

2. Click the **Align Left**, **Center**, **Align Right**, or **Justify** button on the Formatting toolbar (see Figure 7.2).

7

FIGURE 7.2

Click one of the alignment buttons to change alignment.

Justify

Align left   Align right

Align center

You can change paragraph alignment with these keyboard shortcuts: Press
Ctrl+L to left align, Ctrl+E to center, Ctrl+R to right align, or Ctrl+J to justify.
(Yes, using Ctrl+E for centering is a bit odd. Microsoft had to use the second
letter in the word *center* because the shortcut Ctrl+C is already taken by the
Copy command.)

The paragraph alignment options are also available in the Paragraph dialog box. Choose
Format, Paragraph, click the Indents and Spacing tab, choose the desired option in the
Alignment list, and click OK. The only reason to use this method is if you happen to be
in the Paragraph dialog box already to change some other setting. Otherwise, it's faster to
use the alignment toolbar buttons or the keyboard shortcuts.

Changing Line Spacing

Line spacing is the amount of space between lines in a paragraph. By default, paragraphs
are single-spaced. You might want to double-space a school paper or a rough draft of a
report (so that you have room to scribble edits between the lines). Some people like 1.5
line spacing better than single spacing because it can make the text a little easier to read.
In Figure 7.3, the document has been double-spaced.

To change line spacing using the Paragraph dialog box, follow these steps:

1. Click in the paragraph in which you want to change line spacing (or select multiple
   adjacent paragraphs to change the line spacing for all of them).

2. Click the down arrow to the right of the **Line Spacing** button on the Formatting
   toolbar to display a list of line spacing options. If you see the option you want,
   click it to apply the change (see Figure 7.4). Otherwise, click More at the bottom
   of the list.

FIGURE 7.3

This document is double-spaced.

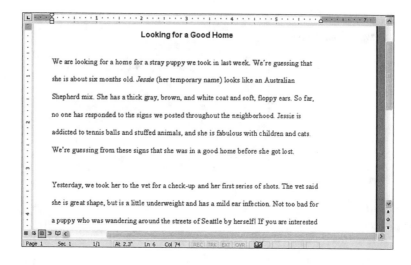

Line Spacing

FIGURE 7.4

The most common line spacing options are available in the Line Spacing list.

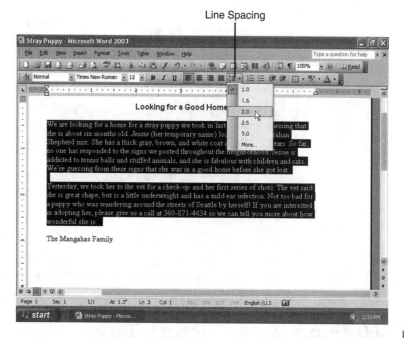

3. The Indents and Spacing tab of the Paragraph dialog box appears, as shown in Figure 7.5. Click the down arrow to the right of the **Line Spacing** list, and select the desired spacing. If you choose one of the last three options, **At Least**, **Exactly**, or **Multiple**, you need to type an amount (in points) in the **At** text box.

7

FIGURE 7.5

The Paragraph dialog box offers a wide range of line spacing options.

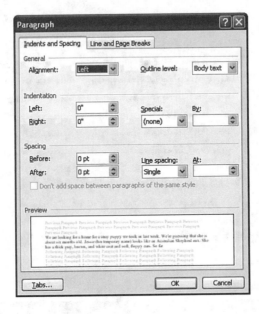

4. Click **OK**.

To change line spacing with keyboard shortcuts, press Ctrl+1 for single spacing, Ctrl+2 for double spacing, or Ctrl+5 for 1.5 line spacing.

If you change line spacing frequently, you might want to add buttons for single, double, and 1.5 line spacing to the Formatting toolbar (see "Adding or Removing Toolbar Buttons" in Hour 1, "Getting Acquainted with Word").

You can quickly display the Indents and Spacing tab of the Paragraph dialog box at any time by double-clicking one of the indent markers on the ruler.

Working with Custom Tabs

Word's default tabs are *left* tabs, meaning that they left-align text at the tab stops. The default tab stops are positioned every half-inch across the horizontal ruler. You can see them on the bottom edge of the ruler—they look like faint gray tick marks. Each time you press the Tab key, your insertion point moves to the next default tab stop, pushing over any text to the right of the insertion point.

In regular body text, the default tabs work just fine. In some situations, however, you may want to create a custom tab at the exact location on the horizontal ruler where you want to align your text. For example, if you wanted to line up several lines of text at the 3-inch mark, you would have to press the Tab key six times at the beginning of each line. A much more efficient solution is to create a custom tab at the 3-inch mark. When you insert the custom tab, all of the default tabs to its left disappear. You can then press the Tab key once to bring the insertion point directly to the spot where you want to type your text.

Another advantage of custom tabs is that in addition to creating custom left tabs, you can also create right, center, decimal, and bar tabs to align text in different ways. Figure 7.6 shows a document including all five types of custom tabs.

FIGURE 7.6

You can create five types of custom tabs in Word.

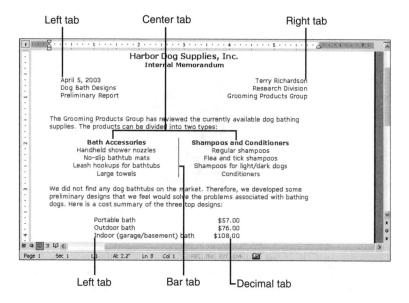

Left tab   Center tab   Right tab

Left tab   Bar tab   Decimal tab

Left tabs left-align text at the tab stop. *Right tabs* right-align text at the tab stop. *Center tabs* center text over the tab stop, and *decimal tabs* align numbers along the decimal point. *Bar tabs* create a vertical line at the tab stop. You can use a bar tab to add a vertical line between columns of text that you've aligned with the other types of custom tabs, or to put a vertical line along the right or left edge of a paragraph.

7

Custom tabs are great for creating simple lists in two or more columns. If your lists or charts require more complex formatting, however, the powerful table feature is a much better option (see Hour 15, "Columns and Tables").

Creating Custom Tabs

To create a custom tab using the ruler, follow these steps:

1. Click in the paragraph to which you want to add the tab (or select multiple adjacent paragraphs to add the tab to all of them). If you haven't yet typed the text in the paragraph, just click on the blank line where you want the custom tabs to begin.

2. Click the **Tab Stop Indicator** button at the left end of the ruler (see Figure 7.7) until you see the symbol for the tab that you want to insert. Each symbol is labeled with a ScreenTip so that you can easily tell which is which.

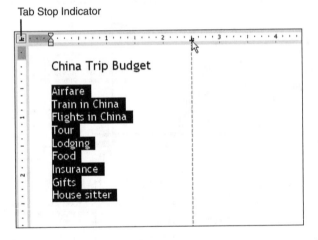

FIGURE 7.7

When you insert a custom tab, the default tabs to its left disappear.

The Tab Stop Indicator button also displays symbols for first line and hanging indents. It's probably easier to create these indents by dragging the indent markers on the ruler, as you'll learn later in this hour.

3. Click at the desired location on the ruler to insert the tab. In Figure 7.7, a decimal tab will be added at the 2.5-inch mark on the ruler for all of the paragraphs in the list of budget items (in preparation for typing a column of numbers). Note that all of the default tabs to the left of the custom tab will disappear as soon as the user clicks to place the tab on the ruler.

4. Repeat steps 2 and 3 to insert any additional custom tabs.

You can also create custom tabs from scratch in the Tabs dialog box (Format, Tabs). In the Tab Stop Position text box, type the position of the tab you want to add in inches, mark the desired option buttons under Alignment and Leader, and click the Set button (you'll learn about dot leaders in just a moment). Add any other custom tabs you like, and click OK. The tabs appear on the ruler just as if you had added them directly to the ruler.

Using Custom Tabs

To use your custom tabs, press Tab to move to the first custom tab stop, and type your text. Press Tab to get to the next tab stop (if any) and type your text. If you accidentally press the Tab key too many times, delete the extra tab characters by pressing Backspace (if the insertion point is just past the tabs) or Delete (if the insertion point is just before them). Press Enter after typing the last block of text on the line, and type the remaining paragraphs that use the custom tabs. Figure 7.8 shows the budget with all of the dollar amounts typed in and lined up on the decimal tab. The Show/Hide ¶ button in the Formatting toolbar is turned on so that you can see where the Tab and Enter keys were pressed.

FIGURE 7.8

Press the Tab key to move out to your custom tab stops, and type your text.

```
China·Trip·Budget¶
¶
Airfare           →      $1600.00¶
Train·in·China      →      $750.00¶
Flights·in·China    →      $800.00¶
Tour            →      $225.75¶
Lodging          →      $880.00¶
Food            →      $550.00¶
Insurance         →      $120.50¶
Gifts            →      $400.00¶
House·sitter       →      $100.00¶
¶
```

As a reminder, you can see what custom tabs are in effect for any paragraph by clicking anywhere in the paragraph, and then looking at the ruler.

7

Unlike the other custom tabs, the bar tab doesn't require you to press the Tab key. As soon as you add the bar tab to the ruler, a vertical line automatically appears at the location of the tab, running down the paragraph containing the insertion point (or the selected paragraphs).

Moving and Deleting Custom Tabs

When you work with custom tabs, you frequently need to adjust their positions on the horizontal ruler. To move a custom tab, follow these steps:

1. Click in the paragraph containing the tab (or select multiple adjacent paragraphs if they all contain the tab and you want the move to apply to all selected paragraphs).

2. Point to the tab on the ruler, drag it to the new position, and release the mouse button (see Figure 7.9). The text at that tab stop adjusts to the new position of the tab.

FIGURE 7.9

To move a custom tab, simply drag it along the ruler.

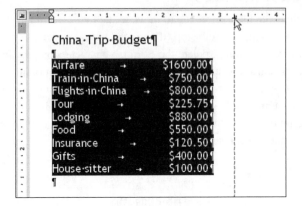

If you need to move the tab to a precise location on the ruler, hold down the Alt key as you drag. The ruler displays the exact location of the tab in inches as you drag it along the ruler.

If you select several adjacent paragraphs and notice that a custom tab on the ruler is gray instead of black, it means that the tab is set in some of the selected paragraphs, but not all. If you drag the tab, it creates the same tab in all of the selected paragraphs.

If you insert a custom tab by accident (easy enough to do), you need to know how to get rid of it. As soon as you delete a custom tab that does not have any other custom tabs to its right, all of the default tabs to its left automatically reappear. To delete custom tabs, follow these steps:

1. Click in the paragraph that contains the tab that you want to remove (or select several adjacent paragraphs if they contain the same tab and you want to delete it in all paragraphs). If you haven't yet typed the text in the paragraph, just click on the blank line.

2. Point to the tab on the ruler, drag straight down into the text area of the Word window, and then release the mouse button.

3. Repeat step 2 to delete any other custom tabs in the paragraph (or selected paragraphs).

If you want to restore all of the default tabs below a paragraph that contains custom tabs, click in the paragraph where you'd like the default tabs to begin, and simply drag all of the custom tabs off the ruler.

Adding a Dot Leader to a Tab

You can add a *dot leader*—a dotted line in the space created by the tab—to any type of custom tab. Figure 7.10 shows a phone list created with a custom left tab that has a dot leader.

FIGURE 7.10

Dot leaders are great for phone lists.

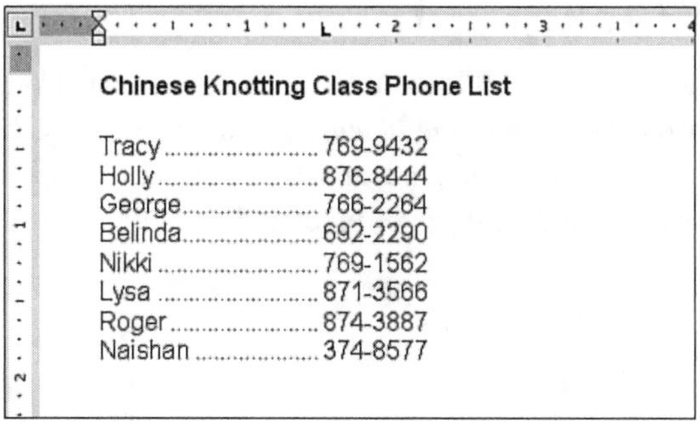

```
Chinese Knotting Class Phone List

Tracy ..................... 769-9432
Holly ..................... 876-8444
George .................... 766-2264
Belinda ................... 692-2290
Nikki ..................... 769-1562
Lysa ..................... 871-3566
Roger .................... 874-3887
Naishan ................. 374-8577
```

To add a dot leader to a tab, follow these steps:

1. Click in the paragraph that has the tab to which you want to add the dot leader (or select multiple adjacent paragraphs if they all contain the same tab).

2. Choose **Format, Tabs** to display the Tabs dialog box.

3. In the **Tab Stop Position** list, click the tab to which you want to add the leader (all of the custom tabs in the paragraph containing the insertion point or the selected paragraphs are listed). Mark the option button for the type of leader you want under **Leader**, and click the **Set** button. In Figure 7.11, a dot leader is added to the right tab at the 5-inch mark.

4. Click **OK**.

7

FIGURE **7.11**

You can use the Tabs dialog box to add a dot leader to a tab.

Indenting Paragraphs

Word's indentation feature enables you to indent paragraphs from the left and right margins. You can also create a *first line indent*, which indents only the first line of a paragraph, or a *hanging indent*, which indents all of the lines in a paragraph except the first. Figure 7.12 illustrates all four types of indentation.

First line Indent

Left Indent

Decrease Indent ─┐ ┌─Increase Indent

FIGURE **7.12**

You can indent paragraphs in four different ways.

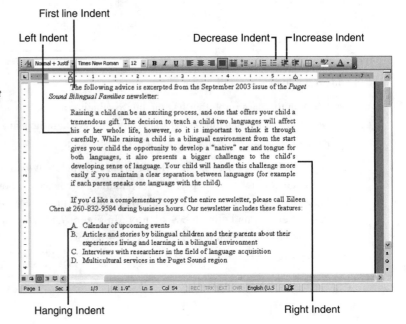

Hanging Indent   Right Indent

> By default, Word sets a first line indent of one-half inch when you press Tab at the beginning of a paragraph that you've already typed. It also sets a left indent of one-half inch when you press Tab at the beginning of any line of an existing paragraph other than the first. These indents carry down to additional paragraphs you type. If you don't like this behavior, choose Tools, AutoCorrect Options, click the AutoFormat As You Type tab, clear the Set Left-and First-indent with Tabs and Backspaces check box, and click OK.

Word provides several ways to set indents. If you want to set a left indent at a half-inch increment on the ruler, you can use the Decrease Indent and Increase Indent buttons on the Formatting toolbar (refer to Figure 7.12), as described in these steps:

1. Click in the paragraph you want to indent (or select multiple adjacent paragraphs to indent them all).

2. Click the **Increase Indent** button to indent the text one-half inch. If you want to indent the text further, continue clicking this button. To decrease the indentation, click the **Decrease Indent** button.

> The keyboard equivalent of clicking the Increase Indent toolbar button is Ctrl+M. The equivalent of the Decrease Indent button is Shift+Ctrl+M. You can also set a hanging indent by pressing Ctrl+T. To remove a hanging indent, press Ctrl+Shift+T.

The most efficient way of setting indents is to drag the indent markers on the ruler. When no indentation is set for a paragraph, the First Line Indent, Hanging Indent, and Left Indent markers are positioned at the left margin, and the Right Indent marker is positioned at the right margin, as shown in Figure 7.13.

FIGURE 7.13

When no indents are set, the indent markers appear at the margins.

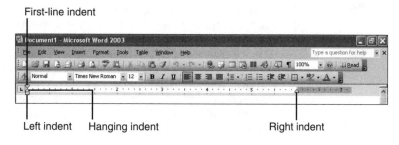

First-line indent

Left indent   Hanging indent   Right indent

7

Follow these steps to set an indent by dragging the indent markers:

1. Click in the paragraph you want to indent (or select multiple adjacent paragraphs to indent them all).

2. Point to the indent marker that you want to use (see Figure 7.13).

3. Drag the desired indent marker to the right spot on the ruler, and release the mouse button.

When you drag the Left Indent marker, the First Line Indent and Hanging Indent markers move too. And when you drag the Hanging Indent marker, the Left Indent marker moves with it.

If you like, you can drag more than one marker for the same paragraph. For example, you can drag both the Left Indent and Right Indent markers to indent a paragraph from both sides, or drag the First Line and Hanging Indent markers to create a hanging indent in which the first line in the paragraph is indented a little, and the remaining lines are indented further. In Figure 7.14, the insertion point is in a paragraph with this type of hanging indent. The position of the indent markers on the ruler shows where the indentation is set, and the tab characters show where the Tab key was pressed to make the text line up properly.

FIGURE 7.14

Hanging indents are useful for creating simple lists.

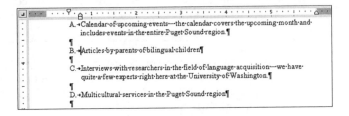

Another use for hanging indents is to create entries in a bibliography, in which the first line of each entry extends to the left of the remaining lines in the entry.

The Show/Hide ¶ button is turned on in Figure 7.14 so that you can see where the Tab key and Enter keys were pressed. To create a list like the one shown in the figure, set the hanging indent, and type the letter or number that begins the first item (*A.* in this example). Press the Tab key to move out to the hanging indent position, type the text in the item, press Enter once (or twice to create a blank line), and then continue with the remainder of the list. Note that if the automatic numbered lists feature is turned on (as it is by default), Word will recognize that you're creating a list after you type the first item in the list and will automatically help you format the remaining items in the list. See "Creating Bulleted and Numbered Lists" later in this hour for more information.

Finally, you can create indents in the Paragraph dialog box. If you and your mouse don't get along, this is probably the best method for you:

1. Click in the paragraph you want to indent (or select multiple adjacent paragraphs to indent all of them).
2. Choose **Format**, **Paragraph** to display the Paragraph dialog box (refer to Figure 7.5 earlier in this hour).
3. Click the **Indents and Spacing** tab if it isn't already in front.
4. Under **Indentation**, type the amount (in inches) that you want to indent the paragraph in the **Left** and/or **Right** text boxes. To create a first line or hanging indent, choose that option from the **Special** list, and type the desired amount for the special indentation (in inches) in the **By** text box.
5. Click the **OK** button.

To move an indent that you've set via any method, simply select the indented paragraphs and drag the appropriate marker on the ruler to its new position.

If you select several paragraphs and notice that an indent marker on the ruler is gray, not black, it means that the indentation is set for some of the selected paragraphs, but not all. If you drag the indent marker, it creates the same indentation in all of the selected paragraphs.

To remove an indent, select the indented paragraphs, and drag the appropriate marker back to the left or right margin on the ruler.

> Another quick way to remove all indents from the selected paragraphs is to choose Format, Paragraph. Click the Indents and Spacing tab and set the Left and Right text boxes to zero inches. Choose None in the Special list, and click OK.

Adding Paragraph Spacing

One way to add a blank line between paragraphs is to press Enter twice at the end of each paragraph. You can avoid having to press Enter a second time to create the blank line by adding *paragraph spacing* before and/or after your paragraphs. For example, if you are using a 12-point font, you can add 12 points of spacing below each paragraph to automatically get one blank line's worth of white space between each paragraph.

Paragraph spacing also enables you to fine-tune the amount of space above or below a paragraph to improve your document's appearance. In Figure 7.15, the paragraphs are separated by 6 points (one-half line) of space. The Show/Hide ¶ button is turned on so that you can see that no paragraph marks appear in the white spaces between paragraphs. These spaces were created with the paragraph spacing feature, not by pressing Enter.

7

FIGURE 7.15

Paragraph spacing enables you to control the amount of white space above and below paragraphs.

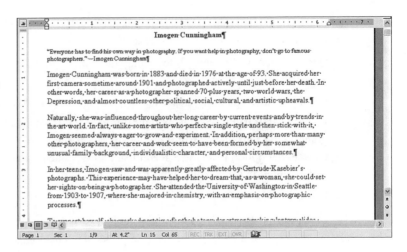

To add spacing before or after a paragraph, follow these steps:

1. Click in the paragraph to which you want to add spacing (or select multiple adjacent paragraphs to add the spacing to all of them).

2. Choose **Format**, **Paragraph** to display the Paragraph dialog box.

3. Click the **Indents and Spacing** tab.

4. Under **Spacing**, type a number in points in the **Before** and/or **After** text box (or use the spinner arrows to increment the spacing 6 points at a time).

5. Click **OK**.

If you select several adjacent paragraphs and add space before and after, you may end up with double the amount of white space between paragraphs that you expected. It's usually simpler to add spacing before or spacing after, but not both.

Adjusting Line and Page Breaks

Word enables you to control how paragraphs break across pages. You can, for example, prevent a paragraph from being split across pages, or instruct Word to insert a page break immediately before a paragraph so that it always appears at the top of a page.

To make these kinds of changes, click in the paragraph you want to affect (or select multiple adjacent paragraphs to affect all of them), choose Format, Paragraph, click the Line and Page Breaks tab (see Figure 7.16), mark the desired check boxes, and click OK.

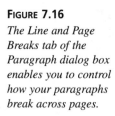

FIGURE 7.16
The Line and Page Breaks tab of the Paragraph dialog box enables you to control how your paragraphs break across pages.

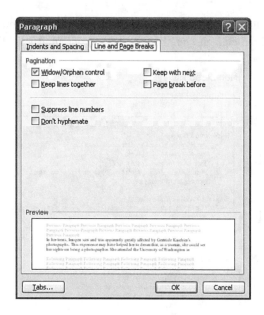

Here is a description of the options in the Line and Page Breaks tab:

- Widow/Orphan Control—This option, marked by default, prevents widows and orphans (single lines of text at the top or bottom of a page). When Word has to split a paragraph across a page break, it adjusts the position of the break to keep a minimum of two lines above or below the break.

- Keep Lines Together—If you mark this check box, the paragraph does not split across a page break. If the paragraph won't fit in its entirety at the bottom of a page, Word moves it to the top of the next page.

- Keep with Next—This option keeps the paragraph on the same page as the paragraph that follows it.

- Page Break Before—This option forces a page break immediately above the selected paragraph. You can mark this check box for a heading that you want to appear at the top of a page.

Creating Bulleted and Numbered Lists

Setting off items in a list with numbers or bullets is a great way to present information clearly. Word's bulleted and numbered list features add the bullets or numbers for you, and they create hanging indents so that when text in an item wraps to the next line, it doesn't wrap underneath the number or bullet. Also, when you use the numbered list feature to create a list and then add, delete, or move items in the list, Word keeps the numbering sequential.

7

Word enables you to create single-level lists, or lists with two or more levels. Figure 7.17 shows single-level bulleted and numbered lists, and one multilevel list.

FIGURE 7.17

You can create single-level and multilevel lists.

Numbered list

Bulleted list

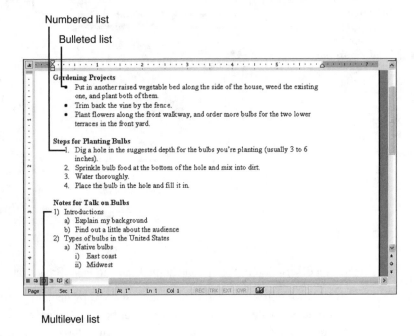

Multilevel list

Follow these steps to create a single-level bulleted or numbered list:

1. Click where you want the list to start.

2. Click the **Bullets** or **Numbering** button on the **Formatting** toolbar (see Figure 7.18).

FIGURE 7.18

The Bullets and Numbering buttons on the Formatting toolbar let you create lists quickly.

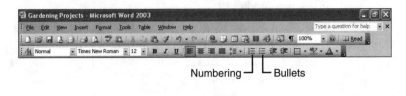

Numbering — └ Bullets

3. Type the first item in the list, and press Enter. Word inserts a bullet or number on the next line for you. Continue typing items in your list.

4. After the last item, press Enter twice to turn off the bullets or numbers.

You can also turn off the bullets or numbering by clicking in the paragraph where you don't want the bullets or numbers, and clicking the Bullets or Numbering toolbar button again.

To switch from numbers to bullets (or vice versa), select all of the items in the list, and then click the Bullets or Numbering button.

If you want two or more paragraphs within one item in a bulleted or numbered list, press Shift+Enter at the end of each paragraph but the last. Pressing Shift+Enter inserts a line-break character, which ends the line without ending the paragraph (a *soft return*), so you don't get a bullet or number on the next line. (Word inserts a bullet or number only at the beginning of a paragraph.) If you click the Show/Hide ¶ button on the Formatting toolbar, you'll see that the symbol for the line-break character looks like this: ↵. If you want to add a blank line in between the items in the list, select all but the first item in the list and press Ctrl+O to add one blank line above each of the selected paragraphs.

Instead of turning on the bulleted or numbered list feature and then typing the list, you can also type the list first, select it, and then click the Bullets or Numbering toolbar button.

You may notice that Word automatically turns on the bulleted or numbered list feature as soon as you type a line of text that begins with an asterisk (*), the number 1, or the letter A (followed by a space or a tab), and press Enter. If you like this behavior, great. If you don't, you can turn it off: Choose Tools, AutoCorrect Options, click the AutoFormat As You Type tab, clear the check boxes for Automatic Bulleted Lists and Automatic Numbered Lists, and then click OK.

If you want to insert a bullet or two but don't want to turn on the bulleted list feature, see "Inserting Symbols and Special Characters" in Hour 12, "Handy Editing Techniques."

7

If you have more than one numbered list in a document, Word starts each new list at number 1. If you want the numbering to continue from the previous list, right-click the first paragraph of the new list and choose Continue Numbering in the context menu that appears. By the same token, if Word assumes you want to continue the previous numbering and you want to restart it, choose Restart Numbering in the context menu. These options are also available in the Numbered tab of the Bullets and Numbering dialog box (Format, Bullets and Numbering).

Changing the Appearance of Your Bullets and Numbers

In many documents, the default bullets and numbers that Word uses will suit you. If you have a hankering for a different look, though, you can choose from a wide range of options.

Follow these steps to change the bullet used in your bulleted list:

1. Click where you want the bulleted list to start (or, if you've already typed your list, select the entire list).

2. Choose **Format**, **Bullets and Numbering** to display the Bullets and Numbering dialog box.

3. Click the **Bulleted** tab. This tab contains a *gallery* of different bullets (see Figure 7.19). The one you are currently using has a box around it. If you see a bullet that you want to use here, click it, and then click **OK**.

FIGURE 7.19

You may see the bullet you want to use in the Bulleted tab.

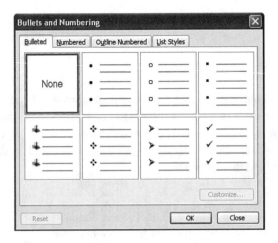

4. If you don't see a bullet you want to use, click one of the seven gallery positions that you don't mind replacing with another bullet (other than None), and click the **Customize** button to display the Customize Bulleted List dialog box (see Figure 7.20).

FIGURE 7.20

The Customize Bulleted List dialog box enables you to modify your bullet.

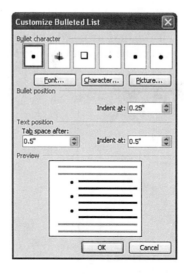

Some bullets look much better when they are larger. You can increase the size of your bullet by clicking the Font button in the Customize Bulleted List dialog box and then increasing the point size in the Font dialog box that appears. The Font button is dimmed out when the selected bullet is a graphic image and not a symbol from a character set. If you want to increase the size of a graphic bullet (called a *picture bullet*), after you insert it in your document, select it and increase its size.

5. If you want to use a symbol, click the **Character** button to display the Symbol dialog box (see Figure 7.21). Look for the symbol you want to use for your bullet. If you don't see the one you want, choose a different character set in the **Font** list. (The Webdings and Wingdings sets contain a lot of fun symbols.)

FIGURE 7.21

Hunt down the symbol you want to use in the Symbol dialog box.

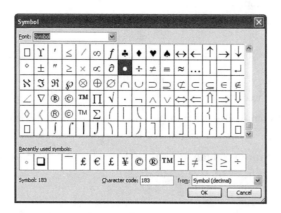

7

6. If you want to use a picture, click the **Picture** button to display the Picture Bullet dialog box (see Figure 7.22). If you have an image you want to use for your bullet stored on your own computer, click the **Import** button to locate it.

FIGURE 7.22

Browse the picture bullets until you find one you like.

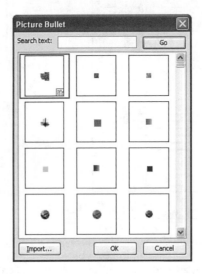

7. When you find the symbol or picture you want, click it and click **OK** twice to return to your document and insert the new bullet.

The new bullet is now the default, so clicking the Bullets toolbar button inserts this bullet until you repeat these steps to choose something else.

> If you choose a new bullet, it takes over a position in the Bulleted tab of the Bullets and Numbering dialog box. If you want to return that position to the bullet that appears there by default, click the position, and click the Reset button.

Follow these steps to change the numbering used in your numbered list:

1. Click where you want the numbered list to start (or, if you've already typed your list, select the entire list).

2. Choose **Format, Bullets and Numbering** to display the Bullets and Numbering dialog box.

3. Click the **Numbered** tab. If you see the numbering that you want to use here, click it, and then click **OK** (see Figure 7.23).

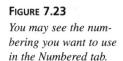

FIGURE 7.23

You may see the numbering you want to use in the Numbered tab.

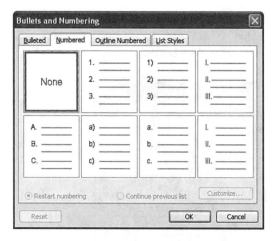

4. If you don't see the numbering you want to use, click one of the seven gallery positions that you don't mind replacing with another type of numbering (other than None), and click the **Customize** button to display the Customize Numbered List dialog box.

5. If you want to revise the format of the numbers, type the change in the **Number Format** text box. Leave the sample number in the box, but type any text you like before or after it or even remove the trailing period (see Figure 7.24). Use the **Number Style** list to change to another style, such as Roman numerals, ordinals, or letters. Use the **Number Position** and **Text Position** options to adjust the positioning of the numbers and text. Change the number in the **Start At** text box to begin the list at a number other than 1. The Preview area in the lower half of the dialog box shows you the effect of your changes. When you're finished, click **OK**.

The new numbering is now the default, so clicking the Numbering toolbar button inserts this numbering until you repeat these steps to change it to something else.

> If you modify your numbering, the new numbering takes over a position in the Numbered tab of the Bullets and Numbering dialog box. If you want to return that position to the numbering that appears there by default, click the position, click the Reset button, and click Yes.

7

Creating Multilevel Lists

Word enables you to turn any bulleted or numbered list into a multilevel list. When you want to create a sublist within your main list, click the Increase Indent button on the Formatting toolbar or press Alt+Shift+right arrow. Then type the first item in the sublist and press Enter. Word assumes you want to type another item in the sublist. If you do, continue typing sublist items. When you are ready to type another item one level up, click the Decrease Indent toolbar button or press Alt+Shift+left arrow.

FIGURE 7.24

The Customize Numbered List dialog box lets you modify your numbering.

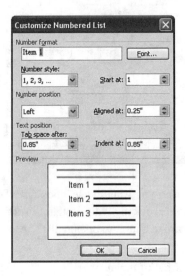

You can customize the numbering in a multilevel list by using the same method you use to customize bullets or numbers in a single-level list:

1. Click where you want the list to begin (or select the list if you've already typed it).

2. Choose **Format**, **Bullets and Numbering** to display the Bullets and Numbering dialog box.

3. Click the **Outline Numbered** tab (see Figure 7.25). If you see the numbering scheme you want to use in the top row of gallery positions, click it and click **OK**. (The lower row is used for creating outlines, which you'll learn about in Hour 13, "Working with Long Documents.")

4. If you don't see the outline numbering you want to use, click the scheme in the top row that most resembles the one you want to use, and click the **Customize** button to display the Customize Outline Numbered List dialog box (see Figure 7.26).

5. Under **Level** in the upper-left corner of the dialog box, click the list level that you want to change, and then select the desired options for that level. Repeat this process to adjust the appearance of any other levels, and then click **OK**.

As with the single-level lists, the new multilevel list takes a position in the Outline Numbered tab of the Bullets and Numbering dialog box. To reset the position to the default, click it and click the Reset button.

FIGURE 7.25

You may see the numbering you want to use in the Outline Numbered tab.

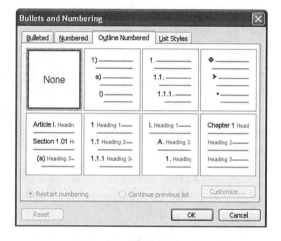

FIGURE 7.26

The Customize Outline Numbered List dialog box lets you modify your outline numbering.

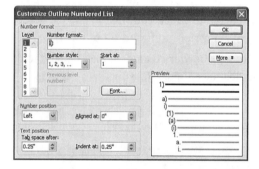

The List Styles tab in the Bullets and Numbering dialog allows you to select a style for your list. (You can also create, modify, or delete list styles from here.) A *style* is a collection of formatting codes, and a *list style* is a collection of formatting codes that is designed specifically for formatting lists. You will learn about styles in Hour 9, "Working with Styles."

Adding Borders and Shading

You don't have to know anything about graphics to set off paragraphs with attractive borders. You can also use the shading feature to add a background color to the paragraph. Figure 7.27 shows a little two-column list formatted with borders and shading.

7

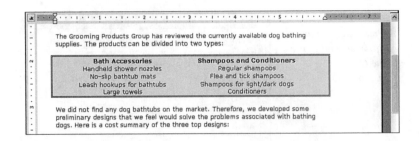

FIGURE 7.27
This list is enhanced by borders and shading.

You can apply borders and shading by using the Borders and Shading dialog box (Format, Borders and Shading) or the Tables and Borders toolbar. Here, you learn how to use the toolbar. You will work with this same toolbar extensively in Hour 15 when you learn how to create tables.

Follow these steps to add borders and shading to your text:

1. Click in the paragraph to which you want to add the borders and shading (or select multiple adjacent paragraphs to format all of them).

2. Click the **Tables and Borders** button on the Standard toolbar to display the Tables and Borders toolbar (see Figure 7.28).

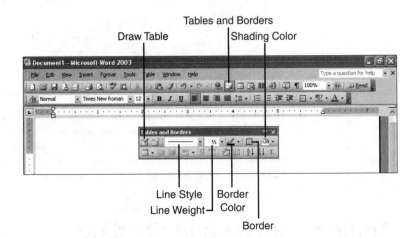

FIGURE 7.28
Clicking the Tables and Borders toolbar button displays the Tables and Borders toolbar.

3. Click the down arrow to the right of the **Line Weight** button, and select a thickness for your border in the list that appears.

4. If you want to create a color border, click the down arrow to the right of the **Border Color** button and select a color in the palette that appears.

5. Click the down arrow to the right of the **Border** button, and click the desired border in the palette that appears. (For example, to create a bottom border under the

paragraph containing the insertion point, click the **Bottom Border** option. To create a border around several selected paragraphs, click the **Outside Border** option.)

6. Finally, if you want to apply shading, click the down arrow to the right of the **Shading Color** button, and click a color in the palette that appears.

To remove borders from your text, select the paragraph, display the Tables and Borders toolbar, and choose the No Border option in the Border list. To remove shading, choose the No Fill option at the top of the Shading Color palette.

You can adjust the position of top and bottom borders by dragging them up or down with the mouse. You can also drag left and right borders out toward the margins. However, if you want to bring the left and right borders in toward the center of the page, you need to set left and right indents (the borders automatically move to the position of the indents).

If you like, you can add a border around your entire page. To learn how, see "Adding a Page Border" in Hour 8.

If you want to add a single horizontal border running from the left to the right margin, you don't need to use the Tables and Borders toolbar. Instead, click on the blank line where you want the border to go, type --- (three hyphens), and press Enter. To create a double line, type === (three equal signs) and press Enter. To get fancier borders, try using the ~ (tilde), # (pound), and * (asterisk) symbols. To disable these automatic borders, choose Tools, AutoCorrect Options, click the AutoFormat As You Type tab, clear the Border Lines check box, and click OK.

Copying Paragraph Formatting

In the last hour, you learned how to copy font formatting from one part of your document to another by using the Format Painter toolbar button. You can also use the Format Painter button to copy paragraph formatting—including all of the formatting you've learned about in this hour—from one paragraph to another.

The steps you use to copy paragraph formatting are the same general ones you used to copy font formatting in Hour 6:

1. Select the paragraph containing the formatting you want to copy. Word stores the paragraph-formatting information for a paragraph in the paragraph mark at the end of the paragraph, so you have to make sure to include it in the selection. (If you

7

aren't sure whether it's selected, turn on the Show/Hide ¶ button on the Standard toolbar.)

2. Click the **Format Painter** button on the Formatting toolbar.

3. A paintbrush is now attached to the I-beam mouse pointer. Click in the paragraph to which you want to apply the formatting.

The paragraph formatting is copied to the second paragraph. If you want to copy the formatting to several paragraphs, double-click the Format Painter button in step 2. It stays on while you click in multiple paragraphs. When you are finished using it, click it again to turn it off.

Removing Paragraph Formatting

You learned in the last hour that you can strip the manual formatting that's been applied to a block of text by selecting the text and then pressing Ctrl+Spacebar. The equivalent keyboard shortcut that removes paragraph formatting is Ctrl+Q. If you have applied several different paragraph formats to a paragraph and now want to turn all of them off, it's much faster to select the paragraph and press Ctrl+Q than to turn each one off individually.

This shortcut also comes in handy if you have to patch up a document with sloppy paragraph formatting. To strip the paragraph formatting from an entire document and start over, press Ctrl+A to select the document, and then press Ctrl+Q.

Ctrl+Q does not remove paragraph formatting that is part of a *style* (a collection of formatting commands). It does, however, remove any paragraph formatting that was added after the style was applied. (You'll learn about styles in Hour 9.)

Checking the Formatting of Your Text

At times, you may need to closely examine the formatting of some text. Perhaps you are finishing a document that was started by someone else and you want to see what formatting has already been applied. Or maybe you have been inconsistent in your formatting and now want to clean it up and finalize your document. Word's Reveal Formatting feature enables you to both examine the formatting of a single selected block of text and compare it to the formatting of another selection. Furthermore, Word can adjust the formatting of the second selection to match the first.

To check the formatting of some text and optionally copy it elsewhere in your document, follow these steps:

1. Choose **Format**, **Reveal Formatting** to display the Reveal Formatting task pane.

2. Select the text that you want to examine. A sample of the text appears in a box under **Selected Text** (see Figure 7.29). Under **Formatting of Selected Text**, scroll down the list and review the formatting. (If you have mixed formatting in your selection, the Reveal Formatting task pane lists the formatting at the beginning of the selection.)

FIGURE 7.29

The Reveal Formatting task pane lists all of the formatting that's been applied to the selected text.

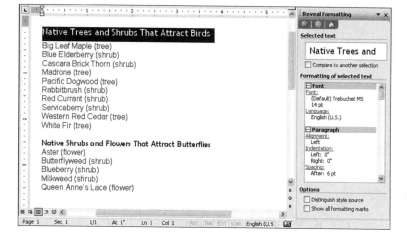

3. To compare to another selection, mark the **Compare to Another Selection** check box and select the second block of text. A sample of the selection appears in a second box under **Selected Text** (see Figure 7.30).

4. Review the differences under **Formatting Differences**. If there are no differences, *No formatting differences* appears in this list.

5. If there are differences (as shown in Figure 7.30), they will be listed. The formatting to the left of each arrow (->) is from the first block selection; the formatting to the right is from the second. If you want to make individual formatting changes to the selected block of text, you can click the blue, underlined links in the Reveal Formatting dialog box to take you to the appropriate dialog box to make the change. For example, in Figure 7.30, you could click the **Spacing** link to display the Indents and Spacing tab of the Paragraph dialog box, where you could change the paragraph spacing.

7

FIGURE 7.30

In this figure, there are differences between the first selection and the second in font, font size, and paragraph spacing.

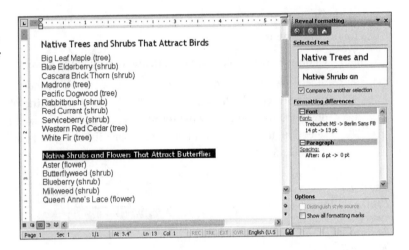

6. To format the second selection to match the first, point to the second sample box and click the down arrow that appears on its right, then choose **Apply Formatting of Original Selection.**

If you want to copy the formatting of the first selection to the second selection as well as any other text formatted like the second selection, in step 6, choose Select All Text with Similar Formatting before you choose Apply Formatting of Original Selection.

7. Close the **Reveal Formatting** task pane, and click to deselect the text. The second selection has been formatted to match the first.

The Formatting Differences list in the Reveal Formatting task pane organizes formatting differences into three categories: Font, Paragraph, and Section. The first two will probably prove to be the most useful to you. The third category, *Section*, refers to page formatting that's been applied to some, but not all of your document. You'll learn about sections in "Varying the Page Formatting in Your Document" in the next hour.

Summary

Of the three categories of formatting—font, paragraph, and page—paragraph formatting undoubtedly takes center stage. It includes a large number of features, some of which can require a little practice to master. You covered a lot of territory in this hour, so don't expect to retain everything! You can always return to specific sections when you need to apply particular paragraph-formatting features. In the next hour, you learn how to apply page formatting, the third and final category of formatting in Word.

Q&A

Q **I want two blocks of text on the same line—one on the left margin and one near the right. How do I do that?**

A Type the phrase on the left margin, and then add a custom right tab at the right margin. You can place it directly on top of the right indent marker. Press the Tab key to move out to the right tab, and type the text that you want flush against the right margin. (If you like, you can experiment with adding these tabs using the Click-and-Type feature, which was discussed in Hour 2, "Entering Text and Moving Around.")

Q **I notice there is a Border button in the Formatting toolbar as well as the Tables and Borders toolbar. Are they different?**

A No. They work in exactly the same way, so you can use either one.

Q **When I cut and pasted a paragraph, it lost all of its paragraph formatting. Why did that happen?**

A. You didn't include the paragraph mark at the end of the last sentence when you selected the paragraph before cutting it. Remember that all of the paragraph formatting is stored in the paragraph mark, so if you leave it behind when you cut and paste the paragraph, you'll leave behind the paragraph formatting as well.

7

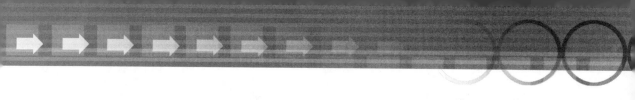

HOUR 8

Formatting Pages

In this last hour on formatting techniques, you learn about *page formatting.* This category includes all of the formatting that affects the entire page, including margins, paper size, page numbers, and so on. After you learn how to apply page formatting, you find out how to control where your pages break and how to vary the page formatting in different sections of your document. (You will learn about one other page formatting feature, columns, in Hour 15, "Columns and Tables.")

The highlights of this hour include

- Changing margins
- Page orientation and size
- Centering text vertically on the page
- Adding page numbers
- Working with headers and footers
- Adding page borders
- Inserting page breaks
- Inserting section breaks

Applying Page Formatting

Once again, Word decides what's best for you (in a well-intentioned sort of way). It makes two main assumptions about page formatting: You want 1-inch top and bottom margins and 1 1/4-inch left and right margins, and you are printing on 8 1/2x11-inch paper. To change these and other default page-formatting options, use the techniques described in this hour. You need to know two things up front to understand how page formatting works:

- Page formatting is automatically applied to every page in your document. Therefore, it doesn't matter where your insertion point is when you apply the formatting, or whether any text is selected.

- If you want to apply different page formatting to different portions of a document—for example, set different margins on one page of a multipage document—you need to insert *section breaks* to divide your document into two or more sections. You'll learn how to do this in "Varying the Page Formatting in Your Document" at the end of this hour.

You can't issue page-formatting commands via the Formatting toolbar, as you can with font and paragraph formatting. Word assumes that you won't need to apply page formatting as frequently, so it reserves the space on the Formatting toolbar for font- and paragraph-formatting commands. To apply page formatting, you'll use a combination of dialog boxes (primarily the Page Setup dialog box), the rulers, and keyboard shortcuts.

> As you practice applying the page formatting available in the Page Setup dialog box, you may discover that you make a particular change in almost every document you create. For example, if you're using preprinted letterhead, you may need to change the margins on all of your documents. In these situations, you can modify the Normal template to assume the page formatting you use. To do so, display the Page Setup dialog box (File, Page Setup), set the option that you want to use, click the Default button in the lower-left corner of the dialog box, and click the Yes button in the message box that appears.

Changing Margins

The default margins are a perfectly good starting point, but you frequently encounter situations in which you need to change them. For example, you might want to narrow the margins to fit more text on the page, increase the top or left margin to make room for a preprinted letterhead, or widen the inner margins for a document that will be bound.

To change the margins using the Page Setup dialog box, follow these steps:

1. Choose **File**, **Page Setup** to display the Page Setup dialog box.

As a shortcut, you can display the Page Setup dialog box by double-clicking in the shaded margin areas at the ends of the horizontal and vertical rulers.

2. Click the **Margins** tab if it isn't already in front (see Figure 8.1).

FIGURE 8.1

Use the Margins tab of the Page Setup dialog box to change your margins.

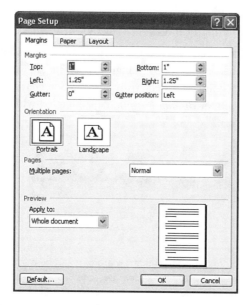

3. The value in the Top text box is highlighted. If you want to change the top margin, type a new value in inches to replace the selected value (you don't have to type the inch mark). Press the Tab key to move to the Bottom, Left, or Right text box, and type new values for any of these margins. (You can also use the spinner arrows to the right of any of these text boxes to increment the margins 1/10 inch at a time.)

4. Click the **OK** button.

You can see your new margins in Print Layout view (change the Zoom setting to Page Width or Whole Page) or in Print Preview.

If you are going to bind your document, you probably want to increase the margins that are to be bound. If the document will be bound on the top edge of the pages, display the Gutter Position drop-down list and choose Top. Otherwise, leave it set to Left. Type the amount by which you want to increase the bound margins in the Gutter text box. (For example, type .5 to increase the margins by one-half inch.) If you are binding the document on the left side of the pages and printing single-sided pages, leave the Multiple Pages drop-down list set to Normal. Word adds the amount of space you specify in the Gutter text box to the left margin of all of the pages. If you are printing double-sided pages, choose Mirror Margins in the Multiple Pages list. Word adds Inside and Outside text boxes at the top of the Margin tab to enable you to specify the margin width for the bound (inside) and outside edges of each page.

You can also change margins by using the horizontal and vertical rulers. To set margins this way, follow these steps:

1. Make sure you're using Print Layout view (**View**, **Print Layout**).

2. Point to the dividing line between the shaded margin area and the white part of the ruler, at the spot between the two triangle-shaped indent markers. The mouse pointer becomes a double-headed arrow, and the ScreenTip says *Left Margin, Right Margin, Top Margin,* or *Bottom Margin,* depending on which margin you're changing (see Figure 8.2).

FIGURE 8.2

Drag the inside edge of the margin on the ruler.

 When you're adjusting the left margin, it can be a little tricky to get the double-headed arrow to appear because Word may think you're pointing to one of the left indent markers. If you have trouble getting the Left Margin ScreenTip to appear, use the Page Setup dialog box to change the margin instead.

3. Drag in the desired direction. As you drag, a vertical dashed line shows you the width of the margin. When it's the right size, release the mouse button.

 If you start dragging and then press and hold down the Alt key, Word changes the display on the ruler to show you the precise width of the margin in inches.

Changing Paper Orientation

8

Word assumes that you want to use *portrait* orientation, which means that the top of the document prints across the short edge of the paper. Occasionally, you may need to change to *landscape* orientation, so that the top of the document prints across the long edge of the paper.

To change to landscape orientation, follow these steps:

1. Choose **File**, **Page Setup** to display the Page Setup dialog box.
2. Click the **Margins** tab (refer to Figure 8.1).
3. Under Orientation, mark the **Landscape** box.
4. Click **OK**.

To see the change in paper orientation, use either Print Layout view or Print Preview. Figure 8.3 shows a document in Print Layout view whose orientation was changed to landscape. (The Zoom box shows 47% because the user chose a Zoom setting of Whole Page.)

FIGURE 8.3

Landscape orientation enables you to fit more text across the width of your page.

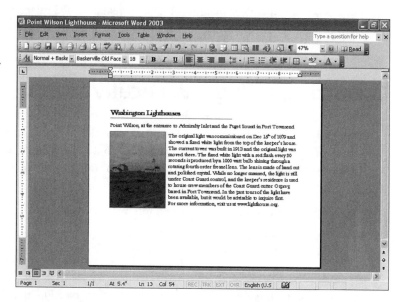

When you're using landscape orientation and the Zoom setting is 100 percent, you have to use the horizontal scrollbar to bring the entire width of the page into view. To avoid having to scroll horizontally, change the Zoom setting to Page Width.

Your rulers also reflect changes in paper orientation. If you switch to landscape mode and don't change the default margins, your horizontal ruler is 9 inches long with 1-inch margins and your vertical ruler is 6 inches long with 1 1/4-inch margins.

Changing Paper Size

Word assumes that you want to print on 8 1/2x11-inch paper, but it can adjust to most other standard sizes, and you can even set a custom size if you like.

To print on a different paper size, follow these steps:

1. Choose **File**, **Page Setup** to display the Page Setup dialog box.
2. Click the **Paper** tab if it isn't already in front.
3. Display the **Paper Size** drop-down list and choose the desired size. (If you are printing on a nonstandard paper size, choose the last option, **Custom Size**, and then type the width and height of your paper in the **Width** and **Height** text boxes.)
4. Click **OK**.

Just as when you change margins or paper orientation, the rulers change to reflect the new paper size. Depending on the size, you may need to change the Zoom setting to avoid having to scroll horizontally.

Centering a Page Vertically

Many people try to center text vertically on the page by moving the insertion point to the top of the page and then pressing Enter several times to force the text down. More often than not, you end up pressing Enter too many (or too few) times and then have to add or delete blank lines to position the text where you want it. A more straightforward method is to let Word center the page vertically for you.

To vertically center the text on a page, follow these steps:

1. Remove any blank lines from above and below the text you want to center vertically.
2. Choose **File**, **Page Setup** to display the Page Setup dialog box.
3. Click the **Layout** tab if it isn't already in front (see Figure 8.4).
4. Click the down arrow to the right of the **Vertical Alignment** drop-down list, and click **Center**.
5. Click the **OK** button.

FIGURE 8.4

Use the Layout tab of the Page Setup dialog box to center your text vertically.

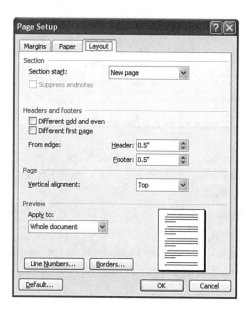

To see what the vertical centering looks like, use Print Preview or Print Layout view. If you decide not to use vertical centering, change the setting in the Vertical Alignment drop-down list back to Top.

Adding Page Numbers

Word offers two methods for adding page numbers to your document. First, you can use the Insert, Page Numbers command, as described here, to tell Word what type of page number you want and where it should appear. Word then adds the page number field to the header or footer for you. Second, you can enter the page number field by inserting it directly in the header or footer (see the next section). This second method gives you more control over the appearance of your page numbers, and you can add other text to the header or footer at the same time if you like. (A *field* is a "holding place" for information that can be updated. In this case, the page number field updates automatically to display the correct page number on each page. Later in this hour, you'll learn how to insert other fields in the header or footer, and in Hour 12, "Handy Editing Techniques," you learn about fields in more depth.)

To add the page number to your document using the Page Numbers dialog box, follow these steps:

1. Choose **Insert**, **Page Numbers** to display the Page Numbers dialog box (see Figure 8.5).

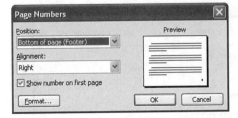

2. If you want the number at the bottom of the page, skip to the next step. To place the number at the top of the page, display the **Position** drop-down list and choose **Top of Page (Header)**.

3. Display the **Alignment** drop-down list and choose the alignment you prefer for your page numbers.

4. Clear the **Show Number on First Page** check box if you don't want the page number to print on the first page of your document.

5. Click the **OK** button.

> If you clear the Show Number on First Page check box, Word creates a *first page header* or *first page footer* and leaves it blank. (You'll learn more about this in "Creating a Different Header or Footer on First or Odd and Even Pages" later in this hour.)

> If you need the page numbering to start on a number other than 1, click the Format button in the Page Numbers dialog box to display the Page Number Format dialog box. Type the desired number in the Start At text box, and click OK.

You can view your page numbers—and any other text in the header or footer—in Print Layout view and Print Preview, among others. Page numbers are not visible in Normal view.

Removing a page number field that you inserted via the Page Numbers dialog box is easier said than done. First, display the header or footer and activate the footer area if necessary (see the next section). Depending on how Word is set to display fields on your computer, the page number may appear with a light gray background. (If it isn't gray now, it may turn gray when you click it.) Click the page number. A crosshatched box appears around it. Point to this box (your mouse pointer changes to a four-headed arrow)

8

and click it to select it—small black squares appear on all four sides of the box. At this point, you can press the Delete key to remove the field. Thankfully, when you insert the page number field using the Header and Footer toolbar, as described in "Inserting the Page Number or Date in the Header or Footer" later in this hour, the field is not enclosed in a crosshatched box. You can simply drag over it and press Delete to get rid of it.

Creating Headers and Footers

A *header* appears at the top of every page, and a *footer* appears at the bottom of every page. You might want to use headers and footers to display the document title, your name, the name of your organization, and so on. Figure 8.6 shows a document in Print Preview. The name of the organization and the date are entered in the header, so they print on every page.

FIGURE 8.6

By default, the text in headers and footers prints on every page of your document.

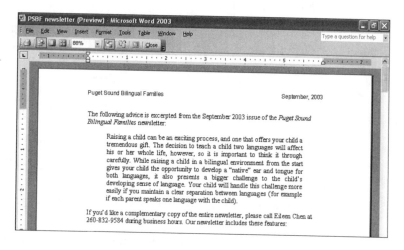

As you'll see, Word makes it easy to center and right-align header and footer text by providing a center tab in the middle of the header and footer and a right tab at the right edge of the header and footer.

To create a header and/or footer, follow these steps:

1. Choose **View**, **Header and Footer**.

When you have text in your header or footer, you can double-click it when you're in Print Layout view to activate it instead of choosing View, Header and Footer.

2. Word activates the header area and displays the Header and Footer toolbar (see Figure 8.7). Note the custom tabs in the center and on the right. If you want to create a footer, click the **Switch Between Header and Footer** toolbar button to activate the footer area. (Click the same button again when you want to switch back to the header area.)

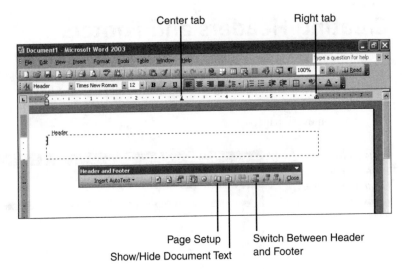

FIGURE 8.7
The View, Header and Footer command activates the header area of your document and displays the Header and Footer toolbar.

Center tab   Right tab

Page Setup | Switch Between Header
Show/Hide Document Text | and Footer

3. Type any text that you want to appear at the left margin.

4. If you want any text centered, press the **Tab** key to jump to the center tab and type the text.

5. If you want some text to be right-aligned at the right margin, press the **Tab** key twice to move to the right tab and type the text.

6. Apply any formatting that you like to text (and fields) in your header or footer by selecting it and using the standard formatting techniques, including the Formatting toolbar, the Font and Paragraph dialog boxes, keyboard shortcuts, and so on. To select all of the text in the header or footer, click when your mouse pointer is in the left margin, outside of the dashed-line that demarcates the header or footer area. Figure 8.8 shows a footer with text on the left and right margins, formatted in an Arial 10-point font.

It's common to make header and footer text a couple of point sizes smaller than your document text to set it apart from the text stream.

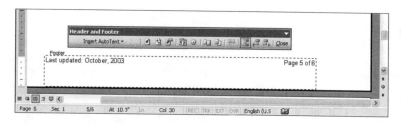

FIGURE 8.8
You type whatever text you want in the header and footer.

8

7. Click the **Close** button in the Header and Footer toolbar to return to viewing your document text.

> The Insert AutoText button at the left end of the Header and Footer toolbar displays a list of typical header and footer entries, such as the filename of the document, the date on which it was last printed, and so on. Most of the entries are a combination of regular text and fields. Clicking an entry in this list is faster than creating it yourself.

By default, the document text is dim but visible when you're working with headers and footers. If you like, you can hide it completely by clicking the Show/Hide Document Text button in the Header and Footer toolbar. To bring the document text back into view, click the toolbar button again. If you want to display the Page Setup dialog box to modify the header or footer (see "Creating a Different Header or Footer on the First or Odd and Even Pages"), click the Page Setup toolbar button.

To delete text in your header or footer, activate the header or footer area and then delete the text by using any of the usual methods. To delete a field, double-click it or drag over it and then press the Delete key. If you want to see clearly what text is a field and not normal text, choose Tools, Options. In the View tab of the Options dialog box, display the Field Shading drop-down list and choose Always (if you want your fields to always be light gray) or When Selected (if you only want your fields to appear light gray when you click them). Then click OK.

Inserting the Page Number or Date in the Header or Footer

The Header and Footer toolbar makes it easy to insert fields for the page number and the date or time (see Figure 8.9). As with the page number field, fields for the date and time automatically update to display the current date and time.

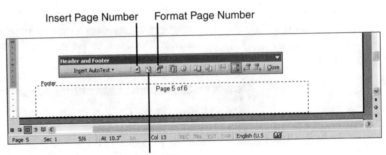

FIGURE 8.9
The Header and Footer toolbar has buttons that make it simple to add page numbering.

To insert the page number in the header or footer, follow these steps:

1. Choose **View, Header and Footer**.
2. Click the **Switch Between Header and Footer** button if you want to insert the page number in the footer.
3. Press **Tab** once or twice if you want to center or right-align the page number.
4. Click the **Insert Page Number** button on the Header and Footer toolbar (or press Alt+Shift+P).

> If you want to use the format *Page 1 of 8, Page 2 of 8, Page 3 of 8*, and so on, click the Insert AutoText button, and then click Page X of Y in the list that appears.

5. Format the header or footer however you like, and then click the **Close** button on the Header and Footer toolbar.

If you want to begin page numbering with a number other than 1, click the Format Page Number button on the Header and Footer toolbar to display the Page Number Format dialog box, type the desired number in the Start At text box, and click OK. If you have divided your document into multiple sections (see "Varying the Page Formatting in Your Document" later in this hour), Word automatically continues the page numbering from one section to the next. To restart the page numbering in each section, activate the header and footer in each section, as described in "Creating Different Headers and Footers in Different Sections of Your Document" later in this hour, display the Page Number Format dialog box, and enter **1** in the Start At text box.

To insert the date or time in the header or footer, follow these steps:

1. Choose **View, Header and Footer**.

2. Click the **Switch Between Header and Footer** button if you want to insert the date or time in the footer.

3. Press **Tab** once or twice if you want to center or right-align the date or time.

4. Click the **Insert Date** toolbar button (or press **Alt+Shift+D**) to insert the date. Click the **Insert Time** toolbar button (or press **Alt+Shift+T**) to insert the time. Figure 8.10 shows the date field inserted at the right edge of the header.

FIGURE 8.10

Use buttons in the Header and Footer toolbar to add date and time fields to your header or footer.

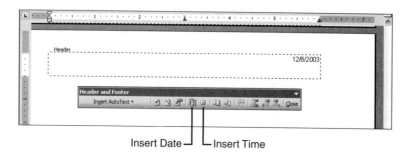

Insert Date ─┘ └─ Insert Time

5. Format the header or footer as you like, and then click the **Close** button.

Word inserts the date field in the default format. If you want to change the default to something else (from 11/18/03 to November 18, 2003, for example), choose Insert, Date and Time to display the Insert Date and Time dialog box, click the format you want in the Available Formats list, click the Default button, click Yes, and then click OK. You'll learn more about the Date and Time dialog box in Hour 12.

Creating a Different Header or Footer on the First or Odd and Even Pages

Word gives you a straightforward way to create a different header and footer for the first page of a multipage document. The most common reason to do this is to keep the header and footer from printing on the first page. And it is equally easy to create different headers and footers for your odd and even pages. You may want to do this if the document is to be double-sided and bound.

In many documents, you want to print the header and footer on every page but the first. For example, you probably don't want the page number to appear on the first page of a letter. To suppress the header and footer on the first page of a document, you tell Word that you want a different header and footer on the first page, and then you simply leave the first page header and footer blank:

1. Choose **File**, **Page Setup** to display the Page Setup dialog box. If you are viewing your headers and footers already, you can also click the **Page Setup** button on the Header and Footer toolbar (refer to Figure 8.7).

2. Click the **Layout** tab (refer to Figure 8.4).

3. Mark the **Different First Page** check box.

4. Click **OK**.

5. Choose **View**, **Header and Footer**.

6. When you are viewing the header or footer for the first page, the left side of the header or footer indicates *First Page Header* or *First Page Footer*, as shown in Figure 8.11. If you don't want any header or footer text on the first page, leave the first page header and footer blank.

Leave the first page header or footer blank if you like.

FIGURE 8.11

You can create a sepa-rate header and footer for the first page.

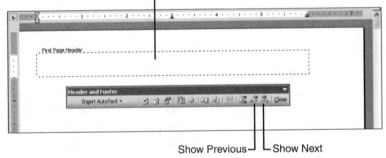

Show Previous ⎤ ⎡ Show Next

7. Click the **Show Next** button in the Header and Footer toolbar to move to the header and footer for the remainder of the document, and insert and format the desired text and fields. (If you want to move back to the first page header and footer, click the **Show Previous** toolbar button.)

8. Click the **Close** button in the Header and Footer toolbar.

To create different headers or footers for odd and even pages in your document, follow these steps:

1. Choose **File**, **Page Setup** to display the Page Setup dialog box.

2. Click the **Layout** tab (refer to Figure 8.4).

3. Mark the **Different Odd and Even** check box.

4. Click **OK**.

5. Choose **View**, **Header and Footer**.

6. When you are viewing the header and footer for odd pages, the left side of the header or footer indicates *Odd Page Header* or *Odd Page Footer*, as shown in

Figure 8.12. Type and format the text that you want to appear in the odd header and footer.

FIGURE 8.12

You can create different headers and footers for odd and even pages.

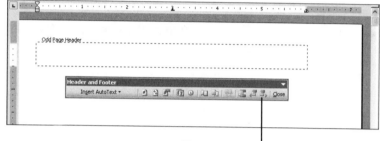

Click the Show Next button to move
to the next even page header.

7. Click the **Show Next** toolbar button to move to the header and footer for even pages (they are labeled *Even Page Header* and *Even Page Footer*), and type and format the header and footer text.

8. Click the **Close** button in the Header and Footer toolbar.

Creating Different Headers and Footers in Different Sections of Your Document

If you divide your document into sections, as described in "Varying the Page Formatting in Your Document" at the end of this hour, you can then create different headers and footers in each section. You might do this if you're printing a long document with multiple chapters and you want to include the chapter name and number in the header or footer, for example.

Word makes a less-than-intuitive assumption about headers and footers in documents that are divided into multiple sections. Unless you tell it otherwise, Word makes the header and footer text in each section the same as the previous section. You have to turn off this feature if you want to vary the header and footer text from section to section. Figure 8.13 shows the header in section 2 of a document. Note that the section number appears on the left side of the header and *Same As Previous* appears on the right side. To "unlink" the header and footer in the current section from the previous section, click the Link to Previous button in the Header and Footer toolbar to turn it off (it's turned on by default).

You have to do this in each section individually. After the sections are unlinked, you can click the Show Previous and Show Next buttons in the Header and Footer toolbar to move from section to section and type and format each one separately.

FIGURE **8.13**
Click the Link to
Previous button to
unlink the header and
footer from the previ-
ous section.

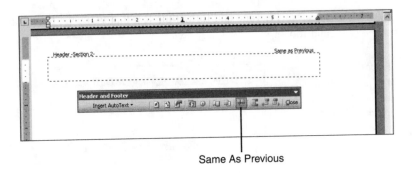

Same As Previous

You can specify different first page and/or different odd and even page
headers and footers within each section of a document, if you like.

Adding a Page Border

In the last hour, you learned how to add borders to individual paragraphs. Using a related
feature, you can add borders to entire pages. Page borders can snazz up documents such
as announcements, flyers, and title pages. Figure 8.14 shows a decorative border around
a flyer for a concert.

FIGURE **8.14**
Page borders can focus
the reader's attention
on your text.

To add a border around the page, follow these steps:

1. Choose **Format**, **Borders and Shading** to display the Borders and Shading dialog
   box.

2. Click the **Page Border** tab (see Figure 8.15).

FIGURE 8.15

Use the Page Border tab of the Borders and Shading dialog box to create your page border.

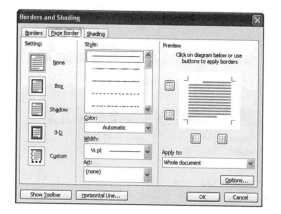

3. Click the option under **Setting** that most closely matches the border you want to create.

4. Using the **Style**, **Color**, **Width**, and **Art** lists in the middle of the dialog box, specify the type of border you want to use. The border shown in Figure 8.14 is one of the options in the Art list. As you choose options, the Preview area on the right side of the dialog box shows what the border looks like.

> Even if you have divided your document into multiple sections, Word automatically adds the page border to every page in the document. If you like, you can restrict the page border to the first page of the current section, to all pages except the first page in the current section, or to all pages in the current section. To choose one of these options, click the desired setting in the Apply To list in the Page Border tab.

5. When you've made all of your selections, click **OK**.

Choosing What Printer Paper Trays to Use

By default, Word pulls paper from the default paper tray in your printer. If your office uses preprinted letterhead, you probably want to use the letterhead for the first page of your documents and plain paper for the remaining pages. To do this, you need to instruct your printer to pull the paper for the first page from one paper tray and the paper for the remaining pages from another. (This assumes that your printer has more than one paper tray.)

Follow these steps to tell Word which paper trays to use for the first page and remaining pages of your document:

1. Choose **File**, **Page Setup** to display the Page Setup dialog box.

2. Click the **Paper** tab if it isn't already in front (see Figure 8.16).

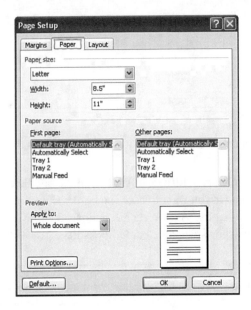

3. Choose the paper tray to use for the first page in the First Page list, and choose the tray for the remaining paper in the Other Pages list. (The names of the trays vary depending on your printer. If you aren't sure which trays to choose, check your printer manual.)

4. Click **OK**.

Controlling Page Breaks

As you know, Word inserts automatic page breaks when your pages are full of text. If you want to break a page that isn't full, you have to insert a manual (or hard) page break. You might want to insert a manual page break to end a section of a report or to separate a title page from the rest of the document.

The steps to insert a manual page break are extremely simple:

1. Move the insertion point to the location where you want to insert the break.

2. Press **Ctrl+Enter** (or choose **Insert**, **Break**; mark the **Page Break** option button; and click **OK**).

A manual page break looks just like an automatic page break in Print Layout view. In Normal view, however, it is labeled with *Page Break*, as shown in Figure 8.17.

FIGURE 8.17

A manual page break appears in Normal view as a dotted line with the words Page Break on it.

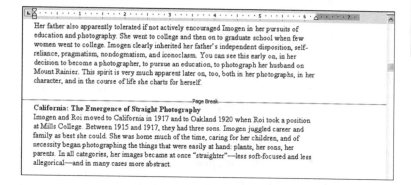

Her father also apparently tolerated if not actively encouraged Imogen in her pursuits of education and photography. She went to college and then on to graduate school when few women went to college. Imogen clearly inherited her father's independent disposition, self-reliance, pragmatism, nondogmatism, and iconoclasm. You can see this early on, in her decision to become a photographer, to pursue an education, to photograph her husband on Mount Rainier. This spirit is very much apparent later on, too, both in her photographs, in her character, and in the course of life she charts for herself.

------------------------------Page Break------------------------------

California: The Emergence of Straight Photography
Imogen and Roi moved to California in 1917 and to Oakland 1920 when Roi took a position at Mills College. Between 1915 and 1917, they had three sons. Imogen juggled career and family as best she could. She was home much of the time, caring for her children, and of necessity began photographing the things that were easily at hand: plants, her sons, her parents. In all categories, her images became at once "straighter"—less soft-focused and less allegorical—and in many cases more abstract.

If you revise text above a manual page break, you probably will end up bumping the break into the wrong place in your document. If this happens, just delete it and reinsert it in the desired location.

To delete a manual page break in Normal view, click on the break and press Delete, or, if your insertion point is just past the break, press Backspace. If you're in Print Layout view, press Delete if your insertion point is immediately above the break and press Backspace if your insertion point is just after it.

Varying the Page Formatting in Your Document

Word automatically applies all page formatting to your entire document. In many cases, you need to alter this behavior. For example, you may have a table in a long report that you have to print in landscape orientation to fit all of the columns on the page, but you want the other pages to print in portrait orientation. Or you might want to vertically center the text on your title page but not on the remaining pages. To make these kinds of changes, you have to divide your document into multiple *sections* by inserting *section breaks* at the appropriate spots. After you've done this, you can apply different page formatting in each section, independent of the others.

Word lets you create four kinds of section breaks:

- Next page—This section break is like a page break and a section break combined. It both breaks the page and starts a new section. An appropriate place to use a next page section break would be at the end of a title page.

- Continuous—This section break does not break the page. Once in a while, you may need to apply different page formatting on the same page. For example, if you want to format your document text in two columns but want the title to be centered in the middle of the page, you can insert a continuous section break directly under the title. This enables you to keep the title and document text on the same page but use the default single-column format for the title and a two-column format for the text.

- Even page—This type of section break is most useful for longer documents that are divided into multiple parts, especially those that are bound. It forces the text in the new section to begin on the next even page.

- Odd page—This is the same as an even page section break, but it forces the text in the new section to begin on the next odd page.

It's easiest to work with section breaks in Normal view because the breaks are labeled onscreen. To insert a section break, follow these steps:

1. Choose **View**, **Normal** if you aren't already using Normal view.

2. Move the insertion point to the location where you want to insert the section break.

3. Choose **Insert**, **Break** to display the Break dialog box (see Figure 8.18).

FIGURE 8.18

Use the Break dialog box to insert a section break.

4. Under **Section Break Types**, mark the desired option button.

5. Click **OK**.

If you want to apply different page formatting from the Page Setup dialog box to a particular block of text in your document, you can have Word create the section breaks for you automatically. To do so, select the text and then choose File, Page Setup. Choose the desired options in the dialog box, and then display the Apply To drop-down list and choose Selected Text. Click OK. Word will insert next page section breaks above and below the selected text and restrict the page formatting options you chose to the new section.

8

After you've inserted one or more section breaks in your document, you can use the status bar to keep track of which section you are in. Figure 8.19 shows a next page section break in Normal view. Note that the section break is labeled Section Break (Next Page), and the insertion point is below the break, so the status bar indicates Sec 2.

FIGURE 8.19

The status bar tells you in what the section the insertion point is located.

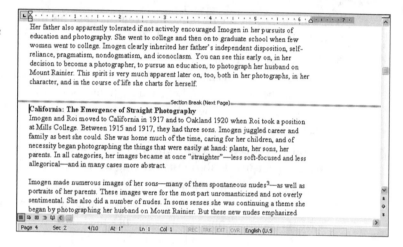

When your document has more than one section, all of the formatting options in the Page Setup dialog box are by default applied to the section containing the insertion point. To apply page formatting to the entire document, change the setting in the Apply To list from This Section to Whole Document.

To delete a section break, use the same methods as the ones you use to delete manual page breaks (see the preceding section). To change a section break from one type to another, delete the old break and then insert the new one.

When you delete a section break, the page formatting options that were applied to the section immediately above the break are removed from your document. Any text that was in that section then takes on the formatting of the next section. So, for example, if section 1 of your document is formatted to use landscape orientation and section 2 is formatted with portrait orientation and you remove the break between them, the pages in what had been section 1 take on the portrait orientation.

Summary

You now have a solid foundation in Word's formatting techniques. By mixing and matching the formatting options you learned in this hour and the two previous ones, you can create documents that are easy to read and pleasing to the eye. In the next hour, you learn to collect font and paragraph formatting into styles, which you can apply to your documents to give them a consistent look.

Q&A

Q I want to adjust the distance between the page border and the edge of the page. Does Word allow me to do this?

A Yes. In the Page Border tab of the Borders and Shading dialog box, click the Options button to display the Border and Shading Options dialog box. Change the values in the Top, Bottom, Left, and Right text boxes to adjust the distance. You can also clear the Surround Header and Surround Footer text boxes if you want the header and/or footer text to appear outside of the page border.

Q I want every section in my report to begin on a new page. Do I have to insert a manual page break above the heading for each section?

A That is one way to handle it. The other option is to format the headings with the Page Break Before option that you learned about in the last hour. (Click in the heading; choose Format, Paragraph; click the Line and Page Breaks tab; mark the Page Break Before option button; and click OK.)

HOUR 9

Working with Styles

A *style* is a collection of formatting options to which you assign a name. For example, you could create a style called *MyTitle* that contains all the formatting—font, font size, alignment, and so on—that you normally apply to the titles of your reports. When you apply a style to text, the text takes on all the formatting that the style contains. As you'll see, using styles can greatly speed up the formatting process. If you apply a lot of formatting in your documents, you will probably come away from this hour a true believer in the value of styles.

The highlights of this hour include

- Applying styles to your text
- Creating your own styles
- Modifying styles
- Chaining styles together
- Viewing styles onscreen
- Restricting the formatting allowed in your document to a certain set of styles

Understanding Styles

If you know a bit about how styles can benefit you, what kinds there are, and where they are stored, you will feel confident about creating and using them in your documents.

The Advantages of Using Styles

Styles are advantageous for several reasons:

- They enable you to apply formatting quickly. Instead of applying several different formatting options one at a time, you can apply them all at once by applying a style that contains all the options already set to your specifications.

- They enable you to modify your formatting quickly. If you decide to make a formatting change to some element of your document (for example, you decide that all your headings should be boldface instead of italic), you need to update only the style you applied to that element, and the affected text throughout your document reformats instantly.

- They enable you to create a consistent look for all the documents that you and your coworkers create.

- If you use *heading styles* (paragraph styles that are designed specifically for formatting headings) to format the different levels of headings in a document, you can take advantage of four handy features—the table of contents feature, the Document Map, Outline view, and cross-references. The table of contents feature generates a table of contents for your document automatically. The Document Map helps you to navigate in a lengthy document. Outline view helps you create and edit your document's heading structure, and the cross-reference feature lets Word update your cross-references automatically. (You'll learn about these features in Hour 13, "Working with Long Documents.")

The advantages of heading styles apply equally well to Word's built-in heading styles (Heading 1, Heading 2, Heading 3, and so on) as they do to heading styles that you create yourself.

Styles Come in Four Flavors

You can create four types of styles in Word:

- Character styles— Character styles can contain only font formatting, and for this reason, they are far less useful than paragraph styles. However, you might occasionally want to create a character style if a word or phrase crops up frequently in your documents and has to be formatted in a particular way. For example, company style might dictate that the name of your company always appear in an Arial, 12-point, bold font.

- Paragraph styles—Paragraph styles can contain both font formatting and paragraph formatting. This makes them much more versatile than character styles. As you might expect, paragraph styles must be applied, at a minimum, to a single paragraph. In this hour, you will focus on working with paragraph styles.

- List styles—List styles can contain any combination of font and paragraph formatting, including a broad range of formatting specific to lists. They are used for formatting bulleted, numbered, and multilevel lists.

- Table styles—Table styles can also contain any combination of font and paragraph formatting, as well as specialized formatting options specifically used in tables.

Because the steps for creating styles are quite similar for all four types of styles, this hour will focus on character and paragraph styles.

9

Applying Styles

The styles that are available in your document are listed in the Style list on the Formatting toolbar (see Figure 9.1).

Style list

FIGURE 9.1

The Style list gives you access to your available styles.

The style names appear with the font formatting that is specified in the style, as well as the alignment and indention paragraph formatting. To the right of all paragraph styles is a paragraph symbol (¶).

The styles in the Style list in Figure 9.1 come with the Normal template. Normal is the default paragraph style. Heading 1, Heading 2, and Heading 3 are paragraph styles that you can use to format your headings. (You'll learn more about them in "Creating Styles for Your Headings" later in this hour.) Clear Formatting strips all the formatting from the selected text—including formatting you've applied via a style and formatting you applied manually (*direct* formatting)—and reapplies the default Normal style. And the More command displays the Styles and Formatting task pane, which you'll use extensively in this hour.

By default, as you apply direct formatting to your text, entries for the direct formatting also appear in the Style list. Figure 9.2 shows the style list for a document in which some direct formatting has been applied. The Heading 1 style was used to format a paragraph, and then the user selected the paragraph and applied the Bookman font. Some text was italicized, and some text was indented and justified.

Styles and Formatting   Direct formatting entries

FIGURE 9.2

By default, the Style list also includes entries for direct formatting.

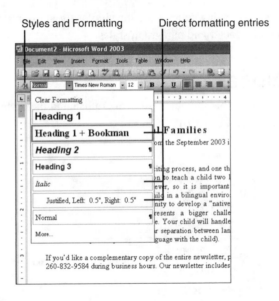

To apply a character or paragraph style using the Style list, follow these steps:

1. To apply a character style, select the text. To apply a paragraph style, click in the paragraph, or select multiple paragraphs to apply the style to all of them.

2. Click the **Style** list drop-down arrow in the Formatting toolbar, scroll down the list, and click the style that you want to apply.

To apply a style using the Styles and Formatting task pane, follow these steps:

1. Click the **Styles and Formatting** toolbar button in the Formatting toolbar to display the Styles and Formatting task pane.

2. Click the **Styles and Formatting** button on the Formatting toolbar to display the Styles and Formatting task pane.

3. Click the style in the **Pick Formatting to Apply** list in the task pane. (If you don't see the style you want, choose **All Styles** in the **Show** drop-down list at the bottom of the task pane.)

The other options in the Show drop-down list are as follows: Available Formatting (the default) lists all of the styles you've created and stored in the current template, some of the built-in styles that are available in the current template, as well as any direct formatting you've applied to your document. Formatting in Use displays only the styles and direct formatting actually in use in the current document. For a detailed description of Available Styles, All Styles, and Custom options, see "Customizing Your Style List" later in this hour.

9

In step 2 of the preceding steps, if you want to apply your style to all of the text in your document that's currently formatted with the same combination of direct formatting or with a particular style, simply click in one block of text that is formatted with the style or direct formatting you want to replace. Then click the Select All button in the Styles and Formatting task pane to select all instances of the same formatting/style in your document.

To check what style you've applied in a particular location, just click in the text. The Style list in the Formatting toolbar displays the style in effect at the location of the insertion point. In Figure 9.3, the insertion point is in a paragraph formatted with the Heading 1 style, so this style name appears in the Style list.

The paragraph containing the insertion point
is formatted with the Heading 1 style

FIGURE 9.3

To check what style you've applied, click in the text and look at the Style list.

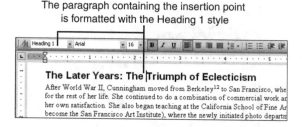

Customizing Your Style List

If you have a hard time finding your styles in the Styles list or the Styles and Formatting task pane amidst all of the direct formatting entries, you can hide the direct formatting entries, and even pick and choose what styles you'd like to see. To do so, follow these steps:

1. Click the **Styles and Formatting** button in the Formatting toolbar (refer back to Figure 9.2) to display the Styles and Formatting task pane (see Figure 9.4).

FIGURE 9.4
The Styles and Formatting task pane gives you ready access to all the tools you need to work with styles.

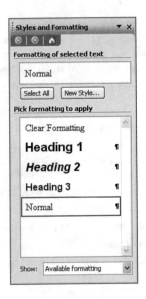

2. Display the **Show** drop-down list at the bottom of the task pane, and choose **Custom** to display the Format Settings dialog box (see Figure 9.5).

FIGURE 9.5
The Format Settings dialog box enables you to customize the Style list and the list in the Styles and Formatting task pane to suit your preferences.

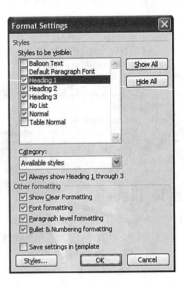

3. If you want to change what styles appear, first select a category of styles in the **Category** list. Here is an explanation of the categories:

- Available Styles—The most commonly used built-in styles and all user-defined styles in the current document and/or template.
- Styles in Use—All the styles that are actually in use in the current document.
- All Styles—All the built-in and user defined styles from the current document and/or template. Includes heading styles, list styles, table styles, as well as other specialized styles.
- User-Defined Styles—Styles that you or someone else has created.
- Do Not Show Styles—Use this option if you *only* want to see formatting options in your Style list.

Styles in the category you selected appear in the Styles to Be Visible list. Mark or clear check boxes as desired. You can also click **Show All** to mark all of the check boxes, or **Hide All** to clear all of them.

4. Under **Other Formatting**, clear check boxes for the types of formatting that you don't want to appear in the Style list.

5. If you don't want to repeat these steps with each document you create, mark the **Save Settings in Template** check box. Word will then remember the custom settings for all documents you create based on the current template and automatically use them in the Style list on the Formatting toolbar and in the Styles and Formatting task pane. When you're done, click **OK**.

To give you an idea of how you might use a custom view of styles, let's say you have created a set of your own styles and modified the built-in heading styles Heading 1, Heading 2, and Heading 3 to contain just the formatting you want in your headings. If these are the only styles you need, you can follow the preceding steps to customize your style list, choosing User-Defined Styles in step 3, and marking the Always Show Heading 1 through 3 and Save Settings in Template check boxes in step 4.

Creating Your Own Styles

To take full advantage of styles, you need to create your own. This way, you can include the exact formatting you need for the different elements in your documents. For example, if you have to type a weekly calendar of events, you might want to create one style for the names of the events, one for their descriptions, one for the date and time information, and so on. You can create new styles in two ways, as described in the next two sections.

Using the Style List in the Formatting Toolbar

The fastest way to create a style is to use the Style list in the Formatting toolbar (this technique is sometimes called *style by example*). However, using the Style list has a major limitation: Any styles you create this way will be stored only in the document, not in the underlying template, so they won't be available outside of the document. In addition, this method works to create only paragraph styles, not character styles.

To create a style by using the Style list, follow these steps:

1. Format a paragraph with all the options that you want to include in the style. For example, if you are creating a style for your body text, you might format the paragraph with a Verdana 10-point font, left alignment, and 12 points of paragraph spacing after the paragraph (so that you won't have to press Enter to create blank lines between the paragraphs).

2. Make sure your insertion point is in the paragraph, and click whatever style is currently showing in the Style list to select it.

3. Type over the selected style name with the name of your new style (it can include spaces). Figure 9.6 shows the insertion point in the formatted paragraph, and the name *Body* entered in the Style list.

FIGURE 9.6

Type a name for your new style in the Style list.

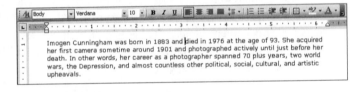

4. Press **Enter**.

Word creates a style that includes all the font and paragraph formatting in the paragraph. The new style is now included in the Style list and in the Styles and Formatting task pane.

Using the New Style Dialog Box

The most flexible way to create styles (either character or paragraph) is to use the New Style dialog box. When you use this method, you can instruct Word to save the style in the template so that it will be available to other documents.

To create a style by using the New Style dialog box, follow these steps:

1. If it's convenient, click in a paragraph that contains formatting similar to the style you want to create. This can save you a click or two selecting the desired formatting in a moment, but it is not necessary.

2. Click the **New Style** button in the Styles and Formatting task pane (refer back to Figure 9.4) to display the New Style dialog box (see Figure 9.7).

FIGURE 9.7

The New Style dialog box enables you to create styles.

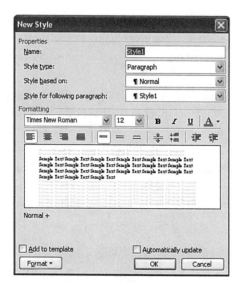

3. Type a name for your style in the **Name** text box (type over the default name *Style1*). Leave the **Style Type** option set to Paragraph, unless you want to create a character style. Look at the **Style Based On** text box, and choose **Normal** if it isn't already selected. Doing this ensures that your new style is based on the "plain-vanilla" Normal style. For now, don't worry about the Style for Following Paragraph text box. That is covered later in "Chaining Styles Together."

4. Mark the **Add to Template** check box if you want to add the style to the template underlying the current document. If you do this, the style will be available to other documents based on the template.

In general, it's best to leave the Automatically Update check box clear. When it's marked, you can modify a style by revising the formatting in a paragraph to which the style is applied. However, when you modify a style in this way, the modified version is saved in the document only, not in the template. Furthermore, you can easily end up modifying a style when you didn't mean to.

5. Buttons for the most commonly used font and paragraph formatting options appear under Formatting in the middle of the dialog box. If you see any options you want to include in your style here, select them now.

6. If there are other formatting options you want to add, click the **Format** button in the lower-left corner of the New Style dialog box to display a list of commands that lead to all the dialog boxes in which you can select font and paragraph formatting.

7. Click the command that leads to the dialog box that contains the formatting you want to add. For example, click Font to display the Font dialog box so that you can specify the font formatting for the style. Make your selections in the dialog box, and click **OK** to return to the New Style dialog box.

8. Repeat steps 6 and 7 to add all the formatting that you want to the style. It is based on the Normal style, and also contains a Garamond, italic, 12-point font, left and right indents of 1 inch, justification, and 12 points of paragraph spacing after the paragraph.

FIGURE 9.8

All the formatting that you've added to the style is listed at the bottom of the New Style dialog box.

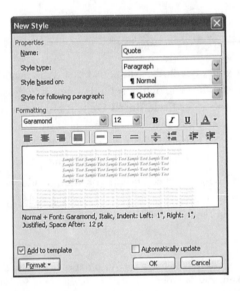

If you want to apply your style with a keyboard shortcut, click the Format button, and then choose the Shortcut Key command in the menu that appears. In the Customize Keyboard dialog box, press the keyboard shortcut you want to use so that it appears in the Press New Shortcut Key text box. If the shortcut is already assigned to a different command, Word displays a message to that effect in the dialog box. You may use that shortcut if you like, replacing the current command, or choose another one that's unassigned. When you have found the shortcut that you want to use, click the Assign button, and then click the Close button.

9. Click **OK** to close the New Style dialog box.

Your new style now appears in the Style list in the Formatting toolbar and in the Styles and Formatting task pane.

Creating Styles for Your Headings

If you want to take advantage of four key features for working with documents that contain headings and subheadings—the table of contents feature, the Document Map, Outline view, and cross-references—you have to apply styles to your headings that tell Word what level each heading should be. You have two options for doing this. The first option involves using (and optionally modifying) the default heading styles:

- Apply the default heading styles that come with the Normal template (Heading 1, Heading 2, and Heading 3). Use Heading 1 for your main headings, Heading 2 for your subheadings, and Heading 3 for your sub-subheadings. You can't change the names of these styles, but you can modify them to change the formatting they contain (see the next section). This is often the easiest method to use.

> To apply the built-in Heading 1, Heading 2, and Heading 3 styles with the keyboard, click in the desired paragraph and press Ctrl+Alt+1, Ctrl+Alt+2, or Ctrl+Alt+3 respectively. If you want convert any paragraph to which you've applied a heading style back to the Normal style, click in it and press to Ctrl+Shift+N.

The second option involves creating your own heading styles:

- Create your own heading styles with whatever names you choose. (You could use the names Chapter Heading, Section Heading, and Sub Heading, for example, though the style names do not even need to include the word *heading*.) Then include in each style an *outline level* setting that tells Word the style's heading level. See the next set of steps.

When you are adding the formatting to your custom heading styles (see steps 5–8 in the preceding section), use the Format button to set the outline levels for your styles, as described in these steps:

1. Click the **Format** button in the New Style dialog box.

2. Click the **Paragraph** command to display the Paragraph dialog box, and click the **Indents and Spacing** tab.

3. Display the **Outline Level** drop-down list in the upper-right corner of the dialog box, and choose an outline level (see Figure 9.9). Choose Level 1 as the outline level for your top-level heading style, Level 2 for your next-highest heading style, and so on.

Choose the appropriate outline level.

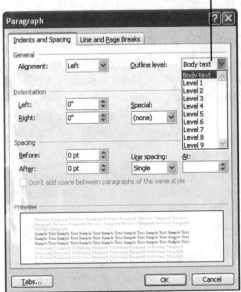

FIGURE 9.9

Assign an outline level to your style if you want to use it as one of your heading styles.

Modifying Existing Styles

Whether you modify a style that comes with Word or one you created yourself, as soon as you make the change, all the paragraphs formatted with that style in your document automatically update to reflect the new formatting in the style. (Any text formatted with the same style in other existing documents does not get reformatted.) Furthermore, you can save the modified style in the underlying template if you like so that the modified version will be available to new documents that you base on the same template.

To modify a style, follow these steps:

1. Click the **Styles and Formatting** button in the Formatting toolbar to display the Styles and Formatting task pane. (It doesn't matter where your insertion point is when you issue the command.)

2. Point to the style that you want to modify in the **Pick Formatting to Apply** list, click the down arrow that appears to its right, and choose **Modify** in the drop-down list (see Figure 9.10). (If you don't see the style, choose **All Styles** in the **Show** drop-down list.)

3. The Modify Style dialog box appears (see Figure 9.11). Notice that this dialog box is identical to the New Style dialog box shown in Figure 9.8, with the exception of the name in the title bar.

FIGURE 9.10

Choose Modify to make changes to your existing style.

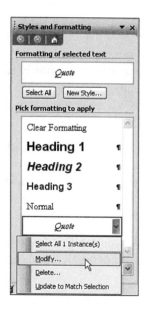

FIGURE 9.11

Use the Modify Style dialog box to modify an existing style.

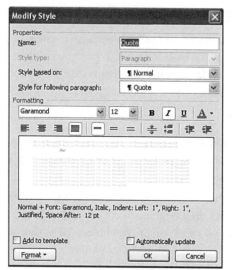

4. Make any changes that you want to the style (see steps 5–8 in "Using the New Style Dialog Box" earlier in this hour).

5. If you stored the original style in the template and want the modified style to replace the original in the template, mark the **Add to Template** check box. (Otherwise, the modified version is stored in the document only; the version in the template remains unchanged.)

6. Click **OK** to close the Modify Style dialog box.

Chaining Styles Together

If you create documents in which the various text elements always appear in a particular order, you can "chain" them together so that when you press Enter to end a paragraph formatted with one style, Word automatically applies the second style to the next paragraph. Linking styles in this way can save you many trips to the Style list in the Formatting toolbar.

For example, let's say you're creating an instruction manual in which each topic is composed of a heading, an introductory paragraph, and then a numbered list of steps. And let's say you've created styles named Topic, Intro, and Steps for these three elements. You can chain the styles together so that Topic leads to Intro, Intro leads to Steps, and Steps leads back to Topic.

When you're creating or modifying a style, you can specify a style to follow by choosing it from the Style for Following Paragraph list in the New Style or Modify Style dialog box.

Deleting Styles

You can delete any of the styles you or someone else created; however, Word does not allow you to delete any of the built-in styles. When you delete a style, all the text that was formatted with that style in your document reverts to the style on which the deleted style was based (this is most often the Normal style).

To delete a user-defined style, follow these steps:

1. Click the **Styles and Formatting** button in the Formatting toolbar to display the Styles and Formatting task pane. (It doesn't matter where your insertion point is when you issue the command.)

2. Point to the style that you want to delete in the **Pick Formatting to Apply** list, click the down arrow to its right, and choose **Delete** in the drop-down list. (If you don't see the style you want to delete, choose **All Styles** in the Show drop-down list.)

3. Click **Yes** in the dialog box that appears.

Basing One Style on Another

If you're creating a style that is similar to an existing one, you can base the new style on the existing one so that it gains all the formatting in the existing style. Then all you need to do is tweak the new style a little to get the formatting exactly as you want it. To base a style on another one, you select the "based on" style in the Style Based On list in the New Style or Modify Style dialog box.

Although you can create styles rather quickly with this method, it can cause two problems down the road. First, when you look at the description of a style that's based on another style (in the bottom half of the New Style or Modify Style dialog box), it lists the "based on" style plus whatever adjustments you've made to it. For example, in Figure 9.12, the Short Quote style is based on the Quote style, so the description lists *Quote* plus the one modification (the indentation was removed). If you want to see *all* the formatting in the new style, you need to track down the content of the "based on" style—a tedious task. And if the "based on" style is itself based on another style, reach for some coffee or chocolate to cheer yourself up.

9

FIGURE 9.12

Think carefully before basing one style on another.

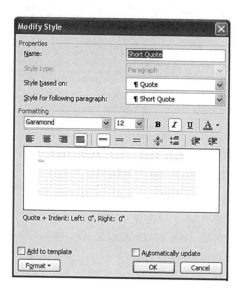

Second, if you base several styles on a style and then modify the "based on" style, all the other styles will change accordingly. This "ripple effect" can produce some unexpected (and often unwanted) results. This said, keep in mind that you can also turn this second potential problem into an advantage, if you think things through carefully. For example, if you have used several styles based on the same style and you decide to change the font of the entire document, you can change it in the "based on" style, and this change will update the font in all of the other styles as well.

The most straightforward route in most situations is to base each style on the Normal style, so you can see exactly what formatting it contains and modify it without affecting other styles.

Viewing the Styles in Your Document

If you work with styles frequently, you'll be glad to know that you can quickly see what styles are applied to your paragraphs as you work. The styles appear in a vertical bar on the left side of the Word window, known as the *style area* (see Figure 9.13). This feature is available only in Normal view.

FIGURE 9.13

The style area makes your styles visible at all times.

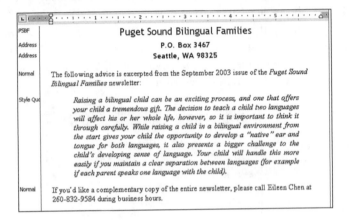

Follow these steps to open the style area:

1. If you aren't already using Normal view, switch to it now (choose **View**, **Normal**).
2. Choose **Tools**, **Options** to display the Options dialog box.
3. Click the **View** tab if it isn't already in front.
4. Set a value in the **Style Area Width** text box at the bottom of the View tab, such as **.5** inch. (You can always adjust it later.)
5. Click **OK**.

If you want to narrow or widen the style area, just drag the vertical line that separates it from your text. To remove it, drag the line all the way to the left, or repeat these steps and change the value in the Style Area Width text box back to 0.

Creating a Toolbar for Your Styles

Applying styles by clicking toolbar buttons is much faster than accessing them in the Style list in the Formatting toolbar or in the Styles and Formatting task pane. If you will be using styles extensively, work through this section to create a toolbar that contains buttons for your styles. If you don't think you'll use styles that frequently, feel free to pass by this topic and skip to the summary at the end of this hour.

Follow these steps to create a toolbar for your styles:

1. Open a document that contains the styles you want to put on the toolbar, and then choose **Tools, Customize** to display the Customize dialog box.

2. Click the **Toolbars** tab if it isn't already in front.

3. Click the **New** button to display the New Toolbar dialog box (see Figure 9.14).

4. Type a name for your toolbar (you might call it Styles) and specify the template in the **Make Toolbar Available To** drop-down list. You will most likely want to make the toolbar available to all documents, so choose Normal. Click **OK**.

FIGURE 9.14

Name your toolbar in the New Toolbar dialog box.

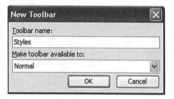

5. Word creates an empty toolbar floating over your document. Click the **Commands** tab in the Customize dialog box.

6. Scroll down the **Categories** list on the left side of the dialog box and click **Styles** to display a list of the styles in the current document in the Commands list on the right.

7. Drag the styles one by one from the Commands list, and drop them onto the new toolbar (see Figure 9.15).

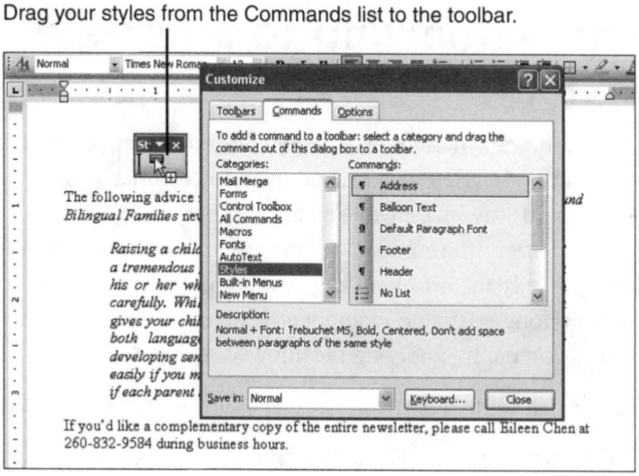

Drag your styles from the Commands list to the toolbar.

FIGURE 9.15

Drag styles from the Customize dialog box to create buttons for them on your new toolbar.

8. The default button names are rather long. To shorten them, right-click each button to display a context menu and edit its name in the **Name** text box (see Figure 9.16). You can use any name that reminds you which style the button will apply.

Edit the button name here.

FIGURE 9.16

*Shortening the button
names enables you to
fit more buttons on the
toolbar.*

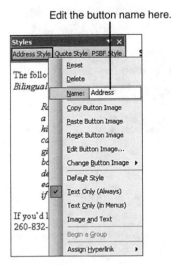

9. Click the **Close** button to close the Customize dialog box.

Try applying some styles with your new toolbar. You can move the toolbar wherever you like, and display and hide it as you do all the other toolbars (refer to "Working with Toolbars" in Hour 1, "Getting Acquainted with Word").

Limiting Formatting to a Certain Set of Styles

If your job requires you to create documents that other people have to revise (for example, you draft press releases and send them to coworkers for revision), you may have learned the hard way that a well-intentioned but not Word-savvy person can make mince-meat of your careful formatting. To prevent this unhappy state of affairs, you can restrict formatting to only the set of styles you want people to be able to use. If you do this, users will no longer be able to apply any direct formatting; they will only be able to format your document by applying the allowed styles.

To limit formatting to a particular set of styles, follow these steps:

1. Open the document whose formatting you want to restrict, and choose **Tools, Protect Document**.

2. In the Protect Document task pane that appears, mark the **Limit Formatting to a Selection of Styles** check box, and click the **Settings** link (see Figure 9.17).

FIGURE 9.17

Use the Protect Document task pane to restrict formatting to a particular set of styles.

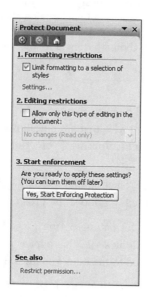

3. Word displays the Formatting Restrictions dialog box (see Figure 9.18). Click the **None** button to remove all of the check boxes from the **Checked Styles Are Currently Allowed** list, and then mark the check boxes for the styles that you want the user to be able to apply.

FIGURE 9.18

Mark the check boxes for the styles that you want the user to be able to apply.

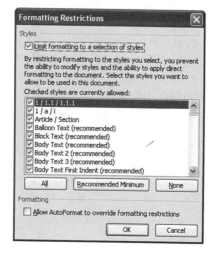

> You might think that clicking the Recommended Minimum button would be a fast way to select a small number of styles that you want the user to be able to apply, but it actually selects quite a large number—perhaps more than you'd expect. It seems to defeat the purpose of the tool. You're most likely going to be better off choosing None and then selectively clicking the ones you want.

4. When you're done, click **OK**. Word displays a message box asking whether you want to remove direct formatting or styles that are not allowed. Click **Yes** or **No** as desired, and then click the **Yes, Start Enforcing Protection** button in the Protect Document task pane.

5. Word displays the Start Enforcing Protection dialog box. Optionally enter and re-enter a password that will be required to remove the protection, and then click **OK**.

The protection is now in force. All of the formatting options, whether on toolbar buttons, in menus, or in dialog boxes, are dim, and the styles that appear in the Styles list and the Styles and Formatting toolbar are restricted to the ones you allowed.

To remove the protection, choose Tools, Unprotect Document. If you specified a password in step 5, you will be required to enter it now. After you've unprotected your document, you can modify the formatting restrictions by repeating these steps, or clear the Limit Formatting to a Selection of Styles check box to allow users to apply any type of formatting they like to your document.

Summary

Using styles can greatly reduce the time it takes to format (and reformat) your documents. If you work in an office, you can use styles to standardize the appearance of all the documents you and your coworkers generate. If you expect that styles will improve your quality of life, you will also benefit from the topic of the next hour, creating and modifying templates.

Q&A

Q **I created a set of styles that I'd like to share with my coworkers. How do I do that?**

A You have to store the styles in a template, not in a document. Then you have to make that template available to your coworkers. See the next hour to learn some strategies for doing this.

Q **I created a toolbar for my styles, but there are no lines visually separating the buttons. Can I add them?**

A Yes. To create separator lines between your toolbar buttons, start with the rightmost button in the toolbar. Hold down the Alt key as you drag the button slightly to the right, away from its neighbor. When you release the mouse button, the line appears. Working button by button to the left, continue this process to create the remaining separator lines.

Q **In this hour, I learned how to create a toolbar for my styles. Can I also create new toolbars for other commands?**

A Yes. You can certainly experiment with creating other toolbars for commands that you use frequently. In the Categories list in the Commands tab of the Customize dialog box, click the various categories to display the commands they contain on the right side of the dialog box. You can drag any of these commands to a toolbar to create a button for it.

9

HOUR 10

Working with Templates

In Hour 5, "Creating Documents from Existing Documents, Templates, and Wizards," you learned how to use the templates and wizards that come with Word to create documents with a minimum of fuss. In this hour, you gain more expertise in working with templates. To start with, you'll find out how to personalize Word's templates so that you have less typing and formatting to do in the documents you create with them. You then practice creating and modifying your own templates. Finally, you learn four "bonus point" techniques—changing the template that's attached to a document, copying items from one template to another, making items in one template available to all documents, and sharing your templates with others.

The highlights of this hour include

- Personalizing Word's templates
- Creating your own templates
- Modifying templates
- Attaching a template to the active document
- Copying items from one template to another
- Loading templates globally
- Sharing your templates with others

Understanding Templates

You can think of a template as a big bucket in which you store the things you need to work on a certain type of document. In addition to any formatting and text that you enter directly into a template, it can contain any combination of these items:

- Styles—You learned about styles in the last hour. They provide a convenient way of applying consistent formatting in your documents.

- AutoText entries— AutoText entries are covered in Hour 12, "Handy Editing Techniques." In a nutshell, AutoText entries are a way to enter blocks of text automatically. They are a great way to avoid typing the same text over and over in multiple documents.

- Toolbars—Toolbars, as you know, enable you to issue commands with a click of the mouse. In the preceding hour, you found out how to create a toolbar for your styles. If you've experimented a bit, you may have discovered that you can use the same basic steps to create toolbars for any commands you use frequently.

- Macros—In its simplest form, a macro is a recording of keystrokes that you can play back whenever you want. You typically create macros to perform repetitive tasks that would be time-consuming to perform "manually." They are also discussed in Hour 12.

The default template, Normal, is unlike other templates in that it is *loaded globally*. This is a geeky way of saying that the styles, AutoText entries, toolbars, and macros stored in the Normal template are available to *all* documents that you create, even if you base them on other templates. In "Loading a Template Globally" at the end of this hour, you learn how to load other templates globally so that you can use the items they contain with other documents.

Personalizing Word's Templates

If you have tried one of the templates that comes with Word and like the look of the finished document, it's probably worth taking a few minutes to make the template your own. Wherever possible, you can replace the "Click here and type" placeholder text with your personal information. For example, if you're revising a letter template, you might fill in your own return address, company name, and signature block. You can also remove any text you don't need and modify the formatting if desired.

After you've made these changes, creating letters based on the template will be a snap because you will need to fill in only the text that changes from one letter to the next.

To personalize one of Word's templates, you create a new template based on Word's template and then modify it. In these steps, you see how to modify a template stored on your own computer:

1. Choose **File**, **New** to display the New Document task pane.
2. Click **On My Computer** to display the Templates dialog box.
3. Click the tab that contains the template you want to modify, and click the template. Under **Create New** in the lower-right corner of the dialog box, mark the **Template** option button. This tells Word to start a new template (not a document) based on the selected template (see Figure 10.1). Then click the **OK** button.

FIGURE 10.1

Word will create a new template based on the Contemporary Fax template.

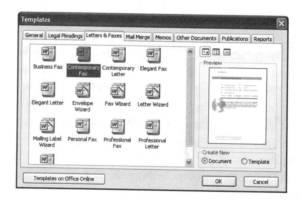

4. Word creates a new template based on the one you selected in the Templates dialog box. (Notice that the temporary name in the title bar begins with *Template*, not *Document*.) Fill in all the "Click here and type" prompts that should contain your own information, and leave the ones that you will need to change each time you use the template.
5. Delete or revise text in the template as needed, and make any changes to the formatting that you like. In Figure 10.2, the row of check boxes under the CC line was deleted, the words *facsimile transmittal* were changed to *fax*, and the return address was enlarged. (Refer to Figure 5.9 in Hour 5 to see the unmodified version of the Contemporary Fax template.)
6. Click the **Save** button in the Standard toolbar to display the Save As dialog box.
7. Because you're saving a template, Word automatically selects your Templates folder in the Save In list. (This folder is usually a subfolder of C:\Documents and Settings\[username]\Application Data\Microsoft.) If you save the template in the Templates folder itself, it appears in the General tab of the Templates dialog box. If this is what you want, skip to step 9.

FIGURE **10.2**

Delete, revise, and format the text in the template as needed.

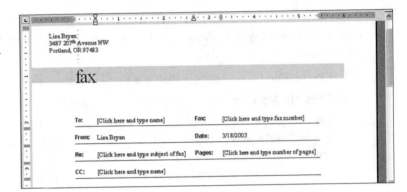

8. If you want your template to appear in one of the other existing tabs in the Templates dialog box, create a subfolder of that name under the Templates folder. For example, to make your template appear in the Letters and Faxes tab, create a Letters and Faxes subfolder. Word will list your template with the built-in templates in that tab. If your template doesn't belong in any of the existing tabs, you can create a new one. Create a subfolder of the Templates folder with the name that you want to appear on the tab (click the Create New Folder button on the toolbar at the top of the Save As dialog box). A tab corresponding to this subfolder appears in the Templates dialog box the next time you display it. (The Legal Pleadings tab visible in Figure 10.1 appears because the Templates folder contains a Legal Pleadings subfolder, as shown in Figure 10.3.)

9. Type a name for the template in the **File Name** text box (see Figure 10.3), and click the **Save** button.

FIGURE **10.3**

The Lisa's Fax template will appear in the General tab of the Templates dialog box because it's being saved in the Templates folder itself.

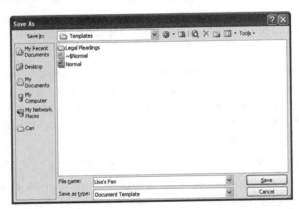

You can easily differentiate between Word documents and templates by looking at the extension at the end of the filename. Documents have an extension of .doc and templates have an extension of .dot.

Your new template now appears in the General tab of the New dialog box (or in another tab if you saved it in a subfolder of your Templates folder). Try using the template to see whether it works as you want it to. If you want to make further changes to it, see "Modifying Your Templates" later in this hour.

> An alternative method of personalizing one of Word's templates—either one on your computer or from Microsoft's Office Online Web site—is to start a new document based on the template and personalize the document. Then choose File, Save As to open the Save As dialog and select Document Template in the Save As Type list. Word automatically displays your Templates folder in the Save In list. Save template in your Templates folder or in one of its subfolders.

Creating Your Own Templates

If Word doesn't provide a ready-made template for the type of documents you create, or if you want more control over the appearance of your documents, you will probably want to create a template from scratch. You do this by basing the new template on the "plain-vanilla" Normal template.

To create a template based on the Normal template, follow these steps:

1. Choose **File**, **New** to display the New Document task pane.

2. In the **General** tab, make sure the Blank Document icon is selected (this is the Normal template). Under Create New in the lower-right corner of the dialog box, mark the **Template** option button, and click the **OK** button.

3. Word starts a new template based on the Normal template. Type and format the text that you want to appear in all documents based on this template. For example, if you're creating a template for business letters, you might include the letterhead, the beginning of the greeting line, and the signature block. To make the template easy to use, you might also add placeholders for text that needs to be filled in. Figure 10.4 shows a simple letter template.

4. If you want to include styles in the template, create them now (refer to the preceding hour if you need a refresher on creating styles). Because you're working with the template directly, not with a document based on the template, Word saves the styles in the template whether or not you mark the Add to Template check box in the New Style dialog box.

5. When you have completed the template, choose **File**, **Save As**, and save the file in the Templates folder or a subfolder of this folder.

FIGURE 10.4

Type and format the template as desired, and insert placeholders in the appropriate spots.

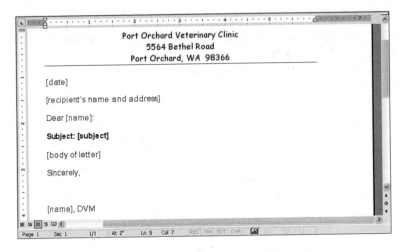

Instead of creating your template from scratch, as described in the preceding steps, you can also use one of your existing documents as a jump-off point. If you have a document that contains all the text and formatting you want in your template, you can simply save it as a template. First, remove the text that's specific to that document. (For example, if you're creating a memo template, delete the recipient's name, the body of the memo, and so on.) Then replace the text you deleted with placeholders, and choose File, Save As. Specify Document Template in the Save As Type list in the Save As dialog box, and save the template in the Templates folder or a subfolder.

Modifying Your Templates

No matter how carefully you originally design your templates, sooner or later you will want to make some improvements. Before you start, you will need to know where your templates are stored. To see where your user templates folder is located, choose Tools, Options, and click the File Locations tab. Double-click User Templates under File Types to display the Modify Location dialog box, and then display the Look In drop-down list to see the entire path to your user templates folder. (It is probably C:\Documents and Settings\[username]\Application Data\Microsoft\Templates.) You can then click Cancel to close the Modify Location dialog box and then close the Options dialog box.

Follow these steps to make changes to a template:

1. Click the **Open** button in the Standard toolbar.

2. In the **Files of Type** list at the bottom of the Open dialog box, select **Document Templates**. Then navigate to your user templates folder. When you find the template you want to revise, double-click it.

Remember to switch from Document Templates back to Word Documents or All Word Documents the next time you want to open a .doc file. Otherwise, you won't see your documents in the Open dialog box.

3. Revise your template as necessary.

4. Click the **Save** button in the Standard toolbar, and then close the template.

The preceding set of steps involves opening a template and making changes to it directly. These steps are necessary if you want to modify the text or formatting of the template. However, Word makes it simpler to save changes to your template that involve only adding, modifying, or deleting any of the four items you can store in templates (styles, toolbars, AutoText entries, and macros). When you close a document based on any template other than the Normal template after having made these types of changes, Word first asks whether you want to save changes to the document (if you have unsaved changes), and then it asks whether you want to save changes to the template. Click the Yes button to retain the changes.

In contrast, when you close a document based on the Normal template after you've added, modified, or deleted any of the items you can store in templates (styles, toolbars, AutoText entries, and macros), Word automatically saves these changes to the template.

If you want to be prompted to save changes to the Normal template, choose Tools, Options; click the Save tab; mark the Prompt to Save Normal Template button; and click OK.

Attaching a Template to the Active Document

You may encounter situations in which you need to change the template that's attached to a document. For example, you might click the New Blank Document button in the Standard toolbar and type for a while in the new document before realizing that you had meant to base the document on a template other than Normal. Or someone may give you a document that is based on an older version of a template, and you want to update the document to the current version. You can change the template that's attached to the active document with a few simple steps:

1. Open the document to which you want to attach a different template.

2. Choose **Tools**, **Templates and Add-ins** to display the Templates and Add-Ins dialog box (see Figure 10.5).

FIGURE 10.5

Use the Templates and Add-ins dialog box to attach a different template to the active document.

3. The currently attached template is listed in the Document Template text box. To change it, click the **Attach** button.

4. In the Attach Template dialog box that appears, navigate to the folder that contains the template you want to attach and then double-click it.

5. Back in the Templates and Add-ins dialog box, the template you selected is now listed in the Document Template text box. If you want the styles in the document to update to the ones in the newly attached template, mark the **Automatically Update Document Styles** check box.

6. Click **OK**.

The styles, toolbars, AutoText entries, and macros in the newly attached template are now available in the active document. However, if the template you attached contains any text, the text will not be copied into the document.

Copying Items from One Template to Another

If you created a style, AutoText entry, toolbar, or macro in one template and now realize that you need it in another, you can copy the item from the template in which it's currently stored to the other template.

To copy an item from one template to another, follow these steps:

1. Choose **Tools, Templates and Add-ins** to display the Templates and Add-ins dialog box.

2. Click the **Organizer** button to display the Organizer, as shown in Figure 10.6.

FIGURE 10.6

The Organizer enables you to copy items among your various templates.

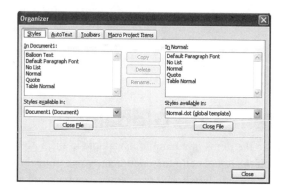

3. Click one of the two **Close File** buttons (it doesn't matter which one) to close the file whose contents are currently displayed on that side of the Organizer. The button name changes to **Open File**. Click this button to display the Open dialog box.

4. Navigate to the source template (the one that contains the item you want to copy) and double-click it.

5. Now click the second **Close File** button, and then click it when it becomes an **Open File** button. In the Open dialog box, navigate to and double-click the target template (the one to which you want to copy the item).

6. Now that you have the source and target templates displayed in the Organizer, click each of the four tabs (**Styles**, **AutoText**, **Toolbars**, and **Macro Project Items**) to see what items each template contains.

7. When you locate the item in the source template that you want to copy, select it and click the **Copy** button in the middle of the Organizer (see Figure 10.7).

8. The item is copied to the target template. If you want to copy any other items, do so now, and then click the **Close** button to close the Organizer.

You can also use the Organizer to copy styles from a document to a template, or from one document to another. Just select a document instead of a template in step 4 and/or step 5.

FIGURE 10.7

The Quote style will be copied from the PSBF template to the Normal template.

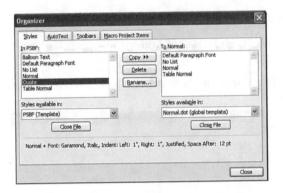

Loading a Template Globally

If you need to make the items in a template available in the active document, but you don't want to attach the template to the document, you can load the template globally. When a template is loaded globally, all the items it contains are available to all documents.

Follow these steps to load a template globally:

1. Choose **Tools, Templates and Add-ins**.

2. Click the **Add** button in the Templates and Add-ins dialog box to display the **Add Template** dialog box.

3. Navigate to the template that you want to add globally and double-click it.

4. In the Templates and Add-ins dialog box, the template now appears under Checked Items Are Currently Loaded (see Figure 10.8). (You can later clear the check box next to its name if you want to temporarily unload the template, or select it and click the **Remove** button to permanently unload it.)

5. Click the **OK** button.

If you want a template to load globally every time you start Word, copy the template to your Word Startup folder. To see where your Startup folder is located, choose Tools, Options, and click the File Locations tab. Double-click Startup under File Types to display the Modify Location dialog box, and then display the Look In drop-down list to see the entire path to your Startup folder. (It's likely to be C:\Documents and Settings\[username]\ Application Data\Microsoft\Word\Startup.) You can then click Cancel to close the Modify Location dialog box, and then close the Options dialog box.

FIGURE 10.8

The templates you selected appear in the Checked Items Are Currently Loaded list.

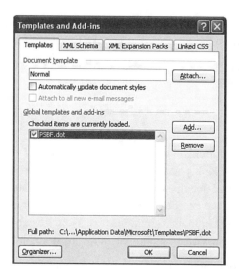

Sharing Your Template with Others

If you've invested a lot of time creating a spiffy new template, you may want to share this template with other people in your office so that they can use it as well. You can do this in a couple of different ways.

If you're on a network, you can give everyone access to it by copying it to the folder designated in Word as the workgroup templates folder. If you aren't sure which folder this is, choose Tools, Options, click the File Locations tab, and double-click Workgroup Templates. In the Modify Location dialog box, display the Look In drop-down list to see the entire path to this location. (Ask your network administrator for advice before proceeding.)

If you are not on a network, you can copy the template to the user templates folder (or one of its subfolders) on each of your co-workers' computers. If you use this method, you might want to require a password to modify the template, so people won't change it accidentally. To do so, follow these steps:

1. Open the template, and then choose **File**, **Save As**.

2. Click the **Tools** button at the top of the Save As dialog box, and choose **Security Options**.

3. In the Security dialog box that appears, enter a password in the **Password to Modify** text box.

4. Click **OK**.

5. In the Confirm Password dialog box that appears, type the password again, and click **OK** to return to the Save As dialog box. Then continue saving as usual.

People will be able to create documents based on the template, but they won't be able to modify the template itself.

Summary

Word provides templates for creating all kinds of documents. If you like one in particular, you can tweak it to make it your own. If you don't like Word's templates, or if none are designed for the type of documents you create, you can create a template from scratch so that it contains the exact text and formatting that you need. Templates can also store styles, AutoText entries, toolbars, and macros. Word gives you a variety of ways to access these items, regardless of what template they are stored in.

This is the last of the hours on formatting. In the next hour, you move on to spelling and grammar features.

Q&A

Q Can I store templates in any folder?

A No. Word expects to find templates in the user templates folder or one of its subfolders, or in the folder designated as the workgroup templates folder.

Q I don't see the file extensions .doc and .dot for my documents and templates in the Open, Save As, and Templates dialog boxes. Why is that?

A By default, Windows hides file extensions for common file types. To display them, choose Tools, Folder Options in My Computer or Windows Explorer; click the View tab; clear the Hide Extensions for Known File Types check box; and click OK.

Q I created my own template, and I want to see a preview of it in the Templates dialog box. Is this possible?

A Yes. Open your template and choose File, Properties. Mark the Save Preview Picture check box at the bottom of the Summary tab in the Properties dialog box, and click OK. The next time you select your template in the Templates dialog box, a preview of it will appear on the right side of the dialog box.

PART III

Working More Efficiently

Hour

HOUR 11

Checking Your Spelling and Grammar and Using the Thesaurus

For most people, writing is a bear. If you're not wondering whether *vicissitude* has one *s* or two, you're probably trying to recall what your high school English teacher said about split infinitives, or hunting down a more interesting word to substitute for *interesting*. Although Word can't turn a clunky phrase into elegant prose, it can help you fix most spelling and grammar errors, and it can assist you in tracking down alternative word choices.

The highlights of this hour include

- Fixing flagged spelling and grammar errors
- Using the spelling and grammar checker
- Using the thesaurus
- Using the Research tool

Correcting Spelling Errors Flagged by Word

Word's automatic spell checking monitors the characters you type and marks words that it doesn't find in its dictionary with red wavy lines (see Figure 11.1). This makes it easy to correct your spelling "on-the-fly" as you're typing.

FIGURE 11.1

When Word can't find a word in its dictionary, it marks it with a red wavy line.

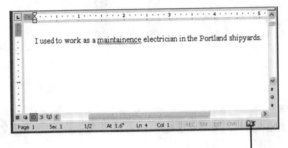

Spelling and Grammar status

You may discover that Word fixes some of your typos automatically. It does this with its AutoCorrect feature, which you'll learn about in "Correcting Text Automatically" in the next hour.

To correct the spelling of a word marked with a red wavy line, follow these steps:

1. Right-click the word.

2. A context menu appears with a list of possible spellings (see Figure 11.2). If you see the one you want, click it. Word makes the correction for you.

FIGURE 11.2

Click the correct spelling in the context menu.

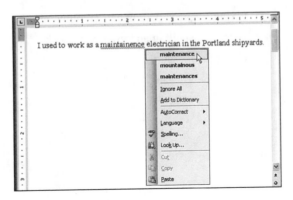

3. If the mistake is one that you make frequently, point to AutoCorrect, and click the correct spelling in the submenu that appears to create this AutoCorrect entry, as shown in Figure 11.3. If you do this, Word corrects the spelling automatically from now on.

FIGURE 11.3

Create an AutoCorrect entry for a misspelling so that you don't have to fix it in the future.

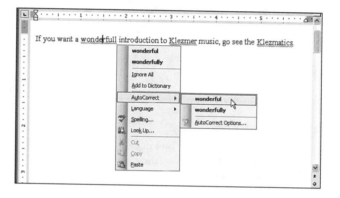

4. If a word is spelled correctly and you use it frequently, click **Add to Dictionary** to add it to the dictionary so that Word won't catch it in the future (see Figure 11.4).

11

FIGURE 11.4

Add a word to the dictionary if you don't want Word to think it's misspelled in the future.

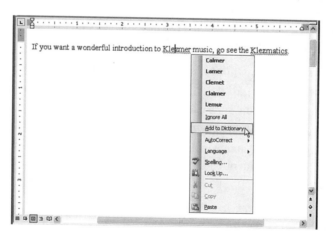

5. If a word is spelled correctly but you don't use it that often, choose **Ignore All** to prevent Word from marking it as a misspelling in this document only (see Figure 11.5).

FIGURE 11.5

*If you just want to hide
the red wavy line
under a word, you can
ask Word to ignore it.*

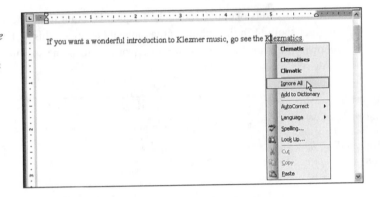

To move quickly from one possible spelling/grammar error to the next, double-click the Spelling and Grammar Error Status icon—the little book in the lower-right corner of the Word window (refer to Figure 11.1). Each time you double-click the icon, Word moves to the next mistake and displays the context menu you normally display by right-clicking the underlined word or phrase.

If you find the red wavy lines distracting, you can turn off automatic spell checking. To do so, follow these steps:

1. Choose **Tools, Options** to display the Options dialog box.

2. Click the **Spelling & Grammar** tab (see Figure 11.6), and clear the **Check Spelling As You Type** check box.

3. If you just want to hide all the red wavy lines in the current document without turning off the automatic spell checking altogether, mark the **Hide Spelling Errors in This Document** check box instead of clearing the Check Spelling As You Type check box.

4. Click **OK**.

FIGURE 11.6

If the red wavy lines drive you nuts, you can hide them temporarily or turn them off permanently.

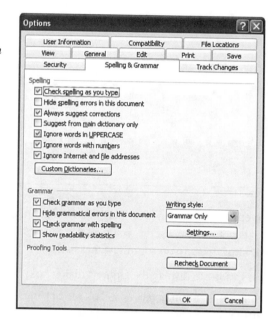

Correcting Grammar Errors Flagged by Word

11

When Word comes upon what it thinks is a possible grammar error in your document, it marks it with a green wavy line (see Figure 11.7). Depending on the error, it might complain about anything from a single space (it catches double spaces between words) to an entire paragraph.

FIGURE 11.7

When Word thinks it's found a grammar error, it marks it with a green wavy line.

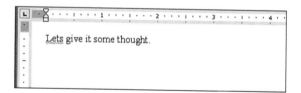

To correct the grammar of text marked with a green wavy line, follow these steps:

1. Right-click the underlined text.
2. Word displays a context menu with suggested corrections.
3. If you see a correction that makes sense, click it (see Figure 11.8).
4. If you want to leave your text as is, click **Ignore**.

FIGURE **11.8**
*Click the correction
that you want to use in
the context menu.*

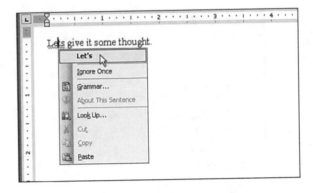

Word enables you to customize the kinds of things that the grammar checker looks for. If the grammar checker is not proving useful, you may want to first try tweaking its settings before you turn it off altogether. To do so, follow these steps:

1. Choose **Tools**, **Options** to display the Options dialog box.

2. Click the **Spelling & Grammar** tab, and click the **Settings** button to display the **Grammar Settings** dialog box (see Figure 11.9).

FIGURE **11.9**
*Select the grammar
checking options that
will work the best for
you.*

3. Scroll down the list of the types of grammar and style issues that Word can flag, and choose the options you want. (Note that by default, none of the style issues are flagged.)

4. When you are done, click **OK**.

Although the grammar checking feature is much better now than it was when Microsoft first introduced it, you may find that more often than not, you disagree with its suggestions or it misses obvious grammatical mistakes. If you want to turn off automatic grammar checking, follow these steps:

1. Choose **Tools**, **Options** to display the Options dialog box.

2. Click the **Spelling & Grammar** tab, and clear the **Check Grammar As You Type** check box (refer to Figure 11.6).

3. If you just want to hide the green wavy lines in the current document but keep automatic grammar checking enabled, mark the **Hide Grammatical Errors in This Document** check box instead of clearing the Check Grammar As You Type check box.

4. Click **OK**.

Using the Spelling and Grammar Checker

The spell checker lets you check the spelling (and grammar) of an entire document all at once. You won't really need to use it if you use automatic spelling checking to fix your spelling "on-the-fly." However, if you've disabled automatic spell checking, or if you're working on a rather large document, the spelling and grammar checker comes in handy.

11

1. Press **Ctrl+Home** to move the insertion point to the top of the document. (The spell check starts at the location of the insertion point.)

2. Click the **Spelling and Grammar** button on the Standard toolbar (or press **F7**, or choose **Tools**, **Spelling and Grammar**) to start checking your document (see Figure 11.10).

FIGURE 11.10

Click the Spelling and Grammar button in the Standard toolbar to start the spelling and grammar check.

Spelling and Grammar

3. Word displays the Spelling and Grammar dialog box (see Figure 11.11). As soon as you click a button in the dialog box to tell Word how to handle a possible misspelling or grammatical error, it goes on to the next error. When Word finds a spelling error, it highlights it in red in the top half of the dialog box. If you see the correct spelling, click it and click the **Change** button (or click **Change All** to change it throughout the document).

FIGURE **11.11**

The Spelling and Grammar dialog box enables you to check the spelling and grammar in your document all at once.

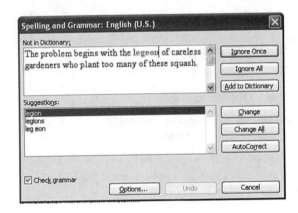

4. If you would like Word to correct the spelling of a particular word for you automatically every time you type it this way in the future, select the correct spelling in the bottom half of the dialog box and click the **AutoCorrect** button.

> If you don't want Word to look for grammatical problems during the spell check, clear the Check Grammar check box in the lower-left corner of the Spelling and Grammar dialog box.

5. Sometimes Word doesn't offer the correct spelling for a misspelled word. If this happens, select the word in the top half of the dialog box, type over it with the correct spelling, and click the **Change** button.

6. If the word is spelled correctly and you plan to use it often, click the **Add to Dictionary** button to add it to the dictionary.

7. To leave the word as is, click **Ignore Once** to ignore it this once or **Ignore All** to ignore it throughout the document.

8. If you have included grammar in your spell check, Word will highlight possible grammatical errors in green in the top half of the dialog box. If you see a correction you like in the bottom half of the dialog box, select it and click the **Change** button (see Figure 11.12).

FIGURE **11.12**

By default, Word includes grammar checking with your spell check.

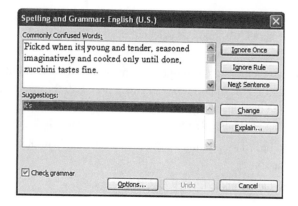

9. If you don't want Word to suggest fixes of this type in the rest of the document, click the **Ignore Rule** button. (Click **Explain** if you need to know more about the rule it is using.)

10. When Word has finished the spell check, it displays a message box to inform you of that fact. Click **OK**.

> If you want to exclude a section of your document from the spell check, select the text before running the spell check and choose Tools, Language, Set Language. In the Language dialog box, mark the Do Not Check Spelling or Grammar check box, and click OK.

11

Editing the Dictionary

If you add a word to the dictionary accidentally, you can remove it so that Word will start flagging it as a possible misspelling again.

By default, when you click the Add to a Dictionary command in the context menu that appears when you right-click a possible misspelling, or when you click the Add to the Dictionary button in the Spelling and Grammar dialog box, Word adds the word to a dictionary file called Custom.dic. You can open this file in a Word window and revise it to remove, edit, or add words.

To edit the contents of your custom dictionary, follow these steps:

1. Choose **Tools**, **Options**, and click the **Spelling & Grammar** tab in the Options dialog box.

2. Click the **Custom Dictionaries** button to display the Custom Dictionaries dialog box, make sure Custom.dic is selected if you have multiple dictionaries listed, and click the **Modify** button.

3. The custom dictionary Custom.dic opens in the CUSTOM.DIC dialog box (see Figure 11.13). This dialog box contains a list of all the words that you or Word has added to the dictionary, each one on a separate line. To delete a word that you want Word to flag as a possible misspelling, select it and click the **Delete** button.

4. To add a word in the dictionary, type your new entry in the Word text box and click the **Add** button.

5. When you have finished, click **OK** three times.

FIGURE 11.13
Use the CUSTOM.DIC dialog box to add or delete words in your dictionary.

Using the Thesaurus

If you find yourself overusing a particular word and want to find a good synonym for it, or if you want to get some ideas for livening up your text, Word's thesaurus can help.

To use the thesaurus, follow these steps:

1. Select the word that you want to look up, and press **Shift+F7** (or choose **Tools, Language, Thesaurus**). (You can also right-click the word and choose **Look Up** in the context menu.)

2. Word displays the Research task pane with the word you selected in the **Search For** text box and suggested meanings, synonyms, and sometimes even antonyms in the results list (meanings are in boldface), as shown in Figure 11.14.

FIGURE 11.14

The Research task pane lets you hunt for alternative word choices.

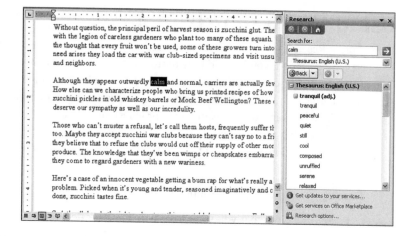

3. If the meaning at the top of the results list is not the one you need, scroll down the list to look for other meanings.

4. If you see a plus sign next to a meaning, click the meaning to display its synonyms. To hide the synonyms, click the meaning again.

5. If you want to see the synonyms of a synonym in the results list, click it. Word places the word in the **Search for** list and displays its synonyms in the results list. To go back to the previous contents of the results list, click the **Back** button immediately above the list.

6. When you see the word that you want to use, point to it, click the down arrow to its right, and click **Insert** in the list that drops down. Word replaces the selected word with the one you chose.

7. When you are finished, close the Research task pane.

> If you want to look up synonyms for a word that isn't in the results list, select the current entry in the Search for text box, type over it with the word whose synonyms you want to look up, and click the Start Searching button (the green arrow) or press Enter.

You can quickly look up the synonyms for a word without taking a trip to the Research task pane. Just right-click the word and point to Synonyms in the context menu to display a list of synonyms.

11

Using the Research Tool

Word's Research tool gives you handy access to a variety of research tools. In the preceding section, you learned how to use the thesaurus component of this feature. In addition, the Research tool also provides access to a host of online dictionaries, encyclopedias, translation services, and financial information. Keep in mind that the links provided here all point to Microsoft's own products and those of Microsoft's partner companies. That said, you might still find the Research tool to be very convenient at times. This section gives you a taste of the kinds of information you can access using the Research tool.

To access the Research tool, follow these steps:

1. Select a word that you want to research in your document.

2. Click the **Research** button on the Standard toolbar, or choose **Tools**, **Research** (see Figure 11.15).

FIGURE 11.15

Click the Research button in the Standard toolbar to open up the Research task pane.

You can also Alt+click a word in your document to open the Research task pane with the word you Alt+clicked entered in the Search For text box.

3. The Research task pane opens up (see Figure 11.16). If you selected a word, it will appear in the Search for text box, and the tool that was most recently used appears in the task pane. If you didn't select a word, type the one you want to research now.

4. Display the drop-down list under the **Search for** text box. The research services in the list are organized into three categories: reference books, research sites, and business and financial sites. Select the tool you'd like to use.

5. In a moment, the tool you selected appears in the task pane or in a browser window. In the example shown in Figure 11.16, the English (North America) version of the Encarta dictionary was selected and it has displayed the various definitions of the word *sponge*.

FIGURE **11.16**

The Research task pane gives you access to the Encarta dictionaries, among other tools.

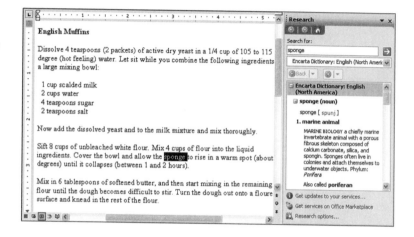

6. When you're finished using the Research tool, close the Research task pane.

Summary

Word's spelling, grammar, and thesaurus features are no substitute for careful writing and proofreading, but they can definitely help you produce clean and well-written documents. And when you need to look something up and don't have the right references at your fingertips, the Research tool will probably come through for you. In the next hour, you add to your bag of tricks with several time-saving editing features.

11

Q&A

Q I told Word to ignore some possible misspellings and now I'm not so sure I was right. How can I get Word to mark these words again?

A You can tell Word to reflag all possible spelling and grammar errors in the current document. Choose Tools, Options; click the Spelling & Grammar tab; click the Recheck Document button; click Yes in the message box that appears; and then click OK.

Q I have used a formal writing style in a document, and Word is suggesting all sorts of grammatical changes to make the prose more casual. Can I tell it that this document is supposed to be formal?

A Yes. You can set the writing style on which Word should base its grammar check. To do this, choose Tools, Options; click the Spelling & Grammar tab; and select the desired style in the Writing Style list. (To see what Word checks for this writing style—and optionally modify the list—click the Settings button to display the Grammar Settings dialog box and click OK when done.) Then click OK in the Options dialog box.

HOUR 12

Handy Editing Techniques

If you type only an occasional short document, you won't have much need for the features discussed in this hour. If, however, you generate a substantial number of documents, the shortcuts you learn here soon become an essential part of your repertoire. As an added benefit, facile use of these features is a surefire way to impress your co-workers or family members.

The highlights of this hour include

- Correcting text automatically
- Inserting standard blocks of text
- Finding and replacing text
- Inserting the date and other fields, symbols, and footnotes and endnotes
- Sorting lists
- Creating macros
- Creating keyboard shortcuts

Correcting Text Automatically

Word's AutoCorrect feature fixes spelling errors for you automatically. For example, if you type *hte*, AutoCorrect changes it to *the*. If you point to a word that AutoCorrect has revised, a little blue bar appears next to the word (see Figure 12.1).

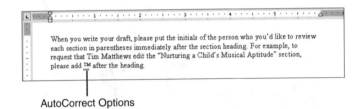

AutoCorrect Options

This bar is actually the "minimized" form of the AutoCorrect Options button. When you point to it, the full button appears. Click the button to highlight in gray the word that was changed and display a little drop-down list (see Figure 12.2).

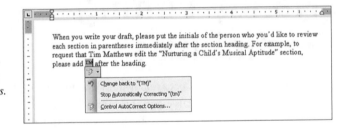

The first command in the list reverses the change this time only. The second command instructs Word to stop making the same change in the future, and the third command displays the AutoCorrect tab of the AutoCorrect Options dialog box, which you will use quite a bit in this hour.

> Another way to reverse an AutoCorrect change is to press Ctrl+Z to undo the change right after Word made it.

By default, AutoCorrect makes corrections based on suggestions from the spell checker. It also has its own list of many commonly misspelled words, and you can add your own favorite typos to the list. In addition, you can use AutoCorrect to automatically enter special symbols, long names, or phrases that you have to type frequently.

Follow these steps to add an entry to the list of words that AutoCorrect corrects automatically:

1. Choose **Tools, AutoCorrect Options** to display the AutoCorrect dialog box.

2. Scroll down the list at the bottom of the AutoCorrect tab to see what AutoCorrect knows how to fix. Word replaces the items in the left column with the items in the right column. At the top of the list are symbols, followed by a large number of commonly misspelled words.

3. To add an entry, click in the **Replace** text box and type the misspelling.

4. Click in the **With** text box and type the correct spelling (see Figure 12.3).

FIGURE 12.3

Type the misspelling in the Replace text box and the correct spelling in the With text box.

5. Click the **Add** button. The new entry appears in the list.

6. Click **OK**.

Try typing the misspelled word. As soon as you press the Spacebar or Enter, Word replaces the misspelled word with the correct spelling.

> If you add an AutoCorrect entry and later decide to delete it, choose Tools, AutoCorrect Options and click the AutoCorrect tab. Then click the entry in the list, click the Delete button, and click OK.

If you want to use AutoCorrect to insert a long name or phrase, type an abbreviation for the phrase in the Replace box and type the full spelling in the With box. For example, you could type *napf* in the Replace box and *National Association of Poodle Fanciers* in the With box.

If you enter an abbreviation for a long name or phrase in the Replace box, choose one that you don't ever want to leave "as is" in your document because Word changes it to

12

the full "correct" spelling every time you type it. (If AutoCorrect does make a change that you want to undo, however, you can always reverse it with the Undo command or the AutoCorrect Options button.)

Inserting Standard Blocks of Text Automatically

AutoText is an extremely handy feature enabling Word to "memorize" large blocks of text. After you've created an AutoText entry, you can insert it in your text by simply beginning to type the name of the entry. As soon as you've typed the first few characters, Word's AutoComplete feature takes over and inserts the entire block of text for you.

One of the advantages of using AutoText is that you only have to proofread the block of text once before you create the AutoText entry. From then on, each time you insert the entry in a document, you can rest assured that it is error-free.

Creating AutoText Entries

Creating an AutoText entry is relatively easy:

1. Type the text that you want Word to "memorize," and then select it.
2. Choose **Insert**, **AutoText**, **New** (or press **Alt+F3**) to display the Create AutoText dialog box.
3. Type over Word's suggested name with your own name for the entry. You can type a name of any length (and your name can include spaces), but choosing one that is at least four characters long will make it easier to insert in your document (see Figure 12.4).
4. Click **OK**.

FIGURE 12.4

Type a name for your AutoText entry in the Create AutoText dialog box.

Word comes with an AutoText toolbar (View, Toolbars, AutoText) that contains a New button. If the toolbar is displayed, you can click this button in step 2 to bring up the Create AutoText dialog box.

Inserting an AutoText Entry in Your Document

Word provides several ways of inserting AutoText entries into your document. The method described in these steps is the simplest.

Follow these steps to insert an AutoText entry in your document:

1. Click where you want to insert the entry.
2. Type the first four letters of the name. A ScreenTip appears for your entry (see Figure 12.5).

FIGURE 12.5

As soon as you type the first four letters of an AutoText entry's name, a ScreenTip appears.

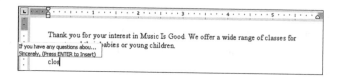

3. Press **Enter** to insert the entry in your document.

One other convenient way to insert an entry is to type the full name of the entry and press F3 when the insertion point is just past the name. This is the fastest method to use if your AutoCorrect entry's name is fewer than four letters long. For it to work, however, there must be a space, a paragraph mark (¶), or a line break (↵) immediately to the right of the insertion point.

Revising and Deleting AutoText Entries

If you want to revise the text for an AutoText entry but keep its name the same, follow these steps:

1. Type the new version of the text and select it.
2. Choose **Insert, AutoText, New**.
3. Type the entry's name in the **Create AutoText** dialog box.
4. Click **OK**.
5. When Word asks whether you want to redefine the AutoText entry, click the **Yes** button.

12

To delete an AutoText entry, follow these steps:

1. Choose **Insert**, **AutoText**, **AutoText** to display the AutoText tab of the AutoCorrect dialog box.

2. Click the entry in the middle of the dialog box. (You can start typing the entry's name in the **Enter AutoText Entries Here** text box to quickly jump to the entry in the list, and then click it.)

3. Click the **Delete** button, and click **OK**.

Finding and Replacing Text Automatically

Any time you find yourself about to embark on a time-consuming hunt through a long document for a word or phrase, or for certain formatting, see whether Word's Find and Replace features can do the work for you.

Finding Text

If you frequently type long documents, you have probably had the experience of scrolling through each page trying to find all of the places where you used a particular word or phrase. Word can help you with this process, searching for text much more quickly and accurately than we humans can. Follow these steps:

1. Choose **Edit**, **Find** (or press **Ctrl+F**) to display the Find tab of the Find and Replace dialog box (see Figure 12.6).

FIGURE 12.6

Use the Find tab of the Find and Replace dialog box to search for text.

2. Type the text that you want to find in the **Find What** text box.

3. Click the **Find Next** button. Word highlights the first occurrence of the word.

4. Continue to click the **Find Next** button to look for more matches.

5. Click **OK** when Word informs you that it has found all the matches.

6. Click the **Cancel** button in the Find and Replace dialog box to return to editing your document.

If you want to be more specific about what text you're looking for, click the More button to expand the dialog box and display more options (see Figure 12.7). To collapse the dialog box again, click the Less button.

Click the More button to expand the dialog box, and the Less button to collapse it.

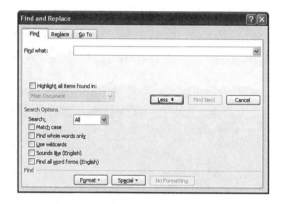

By default, Word searches the entire document for the Find What text, starting from the location of the insertion point down to the end of the document and then from the top of the document back down to the insertion point. If you only want to search up or down from the location of the insertion point, change the option in the Search list from All to Up or Down. (You can also select text first to search only within the selected text.) The five check boxes that appear when you click the More button work as described here:

- Match Case—Mark this check box if you want to find only occurrences of the word that have the same combination of upper- and lowercase letters that you typed in the Find What box.

- Find Whole Words Only—Use this option if you don't want Word to find the search text when it's part of another word. For example, you'd mark this check box if you wanted to find only the word *cat*, not *catch*, *decathlon*, or *scathing*.

- Use Wildcards—Mark this option if you want to use wildcard characters in the Find What text. You can enter wildcards by typing them directly or by clicking the Special button and choosing them from a list. (To learn more about wildcards, look up information on Find and Replace in Word's help system.)

- Sounds Like—This option finds words that sound like the text you're searching for; use it if you're not sure of the spelling.

- Find All Word Forms—Use this option to find all forms of the word. For example, if you search for *sing*, Word also finds *sings*, *sang*, *sung*, and *singing*.

12

Replacing Text

Sometimes you not only need to find text, but you also have to replace it with something else. Word's Replace feature takes the tedium out of making the same change in several places.

Follow these steps to search for text and replace it with something else:

1. Choose **Edit**, **Replace** (or press **Ctrl+H**) to display the Replace tab of the Find and Replace dialog box (see Figure 12.8).

FIGURE 12.8

Use the Replace tab of the Find and Replace dialog box to search for and replace text.

2. Type the text that you want to find in the **Find What** text box.

3. In the **Replace With** text box, type the text that you want to replace the Find What text. If you like, you can customize your find and replace operation by clicking the **More** button and then using the options in the expanded version of the Find and Replace dialog box (refer to Figure 12.7).

4. Click the **Find Next** button.

5. Word highlights the first occurrence of the word. To replace it, click the **Replace** button.

6. To skip this instance without making the change, click the **Find Next** button.

7. Continue this process. If you don't need to confirm every replacement, click the **Replace All** button.

8. Click **OK** when Word informs you that it has found all the matches.

9. Click the **Close** button in the Find and Replace dialog box.

If you change your mind about a replace operation after completing it, you can click the Undo button in the Standard toolbar to undo the replacements one by one if you used the Replace button, or all at once if you used the Replace All button.

Finding and Replacing Formatting

You can use Find and Replace as a quick way to search for and replace formatting in your document.

To modify formatting with Find and Replace, follow these steps:

1. Display the **Replace** tab of the Find and Replace dialog box, and click in the **Find What** text box. (If the dialog box isn't already expanded, click the **More** button.)

2. Click the **Format** button, and click the command that leads to the formatting option you want to search for. For example, if you want to search for boldface, click the Font command.

3. Select the desired formatting option in the dialog box that appears, and click **OK**.

4. The formatting is now listed beneath the **Find What** box.

5. Click in the **Replace With** text box and use the **Format** button to specify the formatting that you want to replace the Find What formatting (see Figure 12.9). If you want to strip off the Find What formatting without replacing it, choose the default formatting. For example, to remove boldface, you would choose **Not Bold** in the Font Style list in the Font dialog box.

FIGURE 12.9

Use the Format button to select the formatting to find and replace.

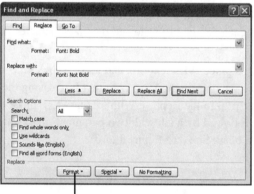

Click to select formatting

6. Continue with the usual replace procedure.

To remove formatting from the Find What or Replace With text boxes when you perform future find and replace operations, click in the appropriate text box and click the No Formatting button.

If you like, you can combine formatting and text in the Find and Replace dialog box. For example, you could type the words *Puget Sound* in the Find What text box and then type *Puget Sound* in the Replace With text box and specify a single underline. This would search for and underline every instance of Puget Sound in your document.

12

Finding and Replacing Special Characters

In addition to finding and replacing regular text and formatting, you can also work with special characters. This enables you to do such things as search for manual page breaks and fields, remove extra blank lines, and so on. As you'll see, Word uses a code that consists of the caret symbol (^) followed by a single letter to represent each special character. For example, the code for a paragraph mark is ^p. Fortunately, you don't have to memorize these—you can simply select the special characters from a list.

Follow these steps to search for and replace special characters:

1. Display the **Replace** tab of the Find and Replace dialog box, and click in the **Find What** text box. If the dialog box isn't already expanded, click the **More** button.

2. Click the **Special** button to display a list of special characters, and click the one you want. Depending on what you're doing, you may need to enter more than one symbol in the text box. For example, if your goal is to remove the tabs at the beginning of each paragraph and separate the paragraphs with blank lines instead, you would enter **^p^t** in the Find What text box to search for a paragraph mark (which ends each paragraph) followed by a tab character (which begins the next paragraph).

3. Click in the **Replace With** text box and use the **Special** button to insert the characters replacing the ones in the Find With text box. Using the same example, you would enter **^p^p** in the Replace With text box to replace each instance of a paragraph mark followed by a tab with two paragraph marks, thus removing the tab and adding a blank line (see Figure 12.10).

FIGURE 12.10

This find and replace operation will remove the tabs at the beginning of each paragraph and separate paragraphs with blank lines.

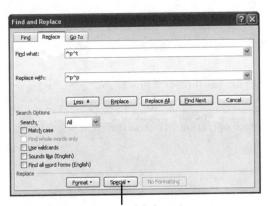

Click to select special characters

After you have learned the codes that Word uses for the various special characters, you can type them directly into the Find What and Replace With text boxes instead of using the Special button.

4. Continue with the usual replace procedure.

You can combine text and symbols in the Find What and Replace With text boxes if you like. For example, you could search for the word *Part* wherever it follows a manual page break by typing ^mPart in the Find What box. (The symbol for a manual page break is ^m.)

Using Find and Replace to Remove Breaks Within Paragraphs

It's not uncommon to receive a document—perhaps a text-only file or text that was copied from an e-mail message—that has paragraph marks (¶) or line-break characters (↵) at the end of each line within the paragraphs (see Figure 12.11). Before you edit the document in Word, you will want to remove all of these extra symbols and only leave the two paragraph marks (or two line-break characters) at the end of the paragraphs. Rather than tediously removing the rogue symbols one by one, you can ask Word to remove them for you by following these steps:

1. Make sure the **Show/Hide** ¶ button in the Standard toolbar is turned on so that you can see the paragraph marks or line-break characters. Press **Ctrl+Home** to move to the top of the document. (Or, if you only need to perform this operation on a particular block of text, select it now.)

2. Choose **Edit**, **Replace**. In the **Find What** text box, type two of Word's codes for the appropriate symbol. (Use ^p^p if you are removing paragraph marks, or ^l^l if you're removing line-break characters.)

12

FIGURE 12.11

You can use Find and Replace to strip out all of the paragraph marks or line-break characters within the paragraphs.

SOMEONE·THERE·IS·WHO·DOESN'T·LOVE·A·HEDGE¶
¶
Some·people·match·poorly·with·certain·plantings.·Take·me·and·hedges,·for·¶
example.¶
¶
Hedges,·I've·decided,·demand·orderly·sorts·of·owners,·people·keen·on·straight·¶
lines·and·neat·edges.·Someone·who·wouldn't·clip·a·poodle·if·he·owned·one·¶
isn't·likely·to·hack·it·as·a·hedge·keeper.·That·my·dogs·have·always·been·¶
shaggy·types·should·tell·you·something·about·my·affinity·for·things·formal.¶
¶
I·didn't·plant·our·hedge;·we·inherited·it·from·the·house's·previous·owners.·¶
When·we·moved·in,·there·it·was,·a·200-foot·wall·of·neatly·trimmed,·6-foot·¶
high·cedar.·Ann·noted·it·approvingly.·I·was·distracted·by·potential·garden·¶
sites·and·the·proximity·of·a·good·clamming·beach.¶
¶

3. In the **Replace With** text box, type two codes of your liking, such as [p][p] or [l][l]. Just make sure that your code does not appear anywhere in the text of the document because you will be replacing all of them momentarily. Perform the replace operation. Now the only ¶ or ↵ symbols left in the document will be the single ones at the end of lines within a paragraph, which you want to remove.

4. Replace all instances of the symbol with nothing. In other words, enter either a ^p or an ^l in the **Find What** text box and leave the **Replace With** text box empty.

> Depending on the document, you may need to type a single space in the Replace With text box instead. If leaving the Replace With text box empty results in a document where two words are run together at the end of each line, use Undo to reverse the find and replace procedure, and then repeat the steps with a space in the Replace With text box instead.

5. Replace all instances of your two codes ([p][p] or [l][l]) with two of Word's symbols (^p^p or ^l^l).

Figure 12.12 shows the same document after the errant symbols have been stripped out.

FIGURE 12.12

All of the extra symbols are now gone from the document.

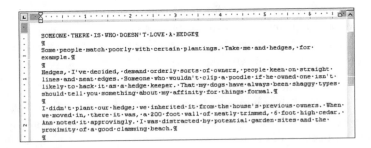

Inserting the Date

Your computer has a clock that keeps track of the date and the time. Instead of typing the entire date yourself, you can have Word take this information from the computer and insert it for you.

Begin typing today's date. After you type the month and a space after it, a ScreenTip containing the completed date appears (see Figure 12.13).

FIGURE 12.13

A ScreenTip appears after you type the month in the current date.

Press Enter to let Word fill in the rest of the date for you.

> As soon as you type the fourth letter in a month that is longer than five letters, a ScreenTip containing the completed month appears. Press Enter to insert the month quickly.

You can also insert the date as a *field*, which lets Word update it to the current date for you when you open the document in the future. Inserting a date as a field is useful in documents that you open frequently because the date is always current. This is a good technique to use when you don't need the date within the document to verify when the document was first created and saved. The previous date will always be replaced with the current date when the file is opened.

If you want to insert the date as a field, follow these steps:

1. Choose **Insert, Date and Time** to display the Date and Time dialog box (see Figure 12.14).

FIGURE 12.14

The Date and Time dialog box enables you to insert the date as a field.

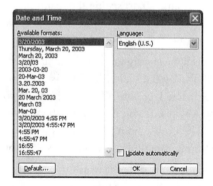

12

2. Mark the **Update Automatically** check box.

3. Click the date format that you want to use.

4. If you want to use this format all of the time, click the **Default** button and then click **Yes** in the message box that appears.

5. Click **OK** in the Date and Time dialog box.

To delete a date that you've inserted as a field, select it first and then press Delete or Backspace.

> If Word inserts the wrong date in your document, you have to correct your computer's clock. Double-click the time at the right end of the taskbar to display the Date and Time Properties dialog box. Specify the correct date in the Date & Time tab, and click OK.

Inserting Other Fields

You already know how to insert page number and date fields. Word lets you insert many other types of fields as well. For example, you can insert the FileName field in the footer so that the document's filename prints at the bottom of every page, or you can add the UserAddress field to the top of a letter to quickly insert your return address. You may not need to use any of these other fields, but it's worth poking around a bit to see if some of them might make your life easier. As you work with fields, these tips may come in handy:

- To force a field to update, select it and press F9. If you want to update all of the fields in your document, select the entire document and press F9.

- To see the underlying field code instead of the result of the code, select the field and press Shift+F9. To switch back to seeing the result of the code, press Shift+F9 again. If you want to display the underlying field codes for all of the fields in your document at once, press Alt+F9 (this shortcut is also a toggle).

- To control whether fields appear gray in your documents, choose Tools, Options; click the View tab; and display the Field Shading list. If you only want them to turn gray when they're selected, choose When Selected. If you want them to always be gray, choose Always. If you don't want them to ever appear gray, choose Never. Then click OK. The gray shading just makes it easier for you to differentiate between fields and regular text onscreen—it doesn't print.

- To convert a field to regular text so that it won't update automatically, select the field and press Shift+Ctrl+F9. If you do this, you can't convert it back to a field again.

- To delete any field, select it and then press Delete or Backspace.

Follow these steps to insert a field in your document:

1. Move the insertion point to the location where you want to insert the field. In many cases, you will want to insert the field in the header or footer. (See "Creating Headers and Footers" in Hour 8, "Formatting Pages," if you need help.)

2. Choose **Insert**, **Field** to display the Field dialog box (see Figure 12.15).

FIGURE 12.15

The Field dialog box enables you to insert all kinds of fields in your document.

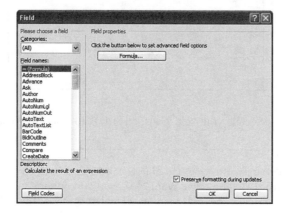

3. Click various categories in the **Categories** drop-down list in the upper-left corner of the dialog box. The fields in the selected category appear in the Field Names list.

> Some of the categories containing fields that are useful to the average Word user are Date and Time, Document Information, and User Information.

12

4. When you find the field that you want to insert, click it in the **Field Names** list. The right side of the Field dialog box updates to give you options for customizing the field (see Figure 12.16).

5. Customize the field by making selections under **Field Properties** and **Field Options** if you like. In the example shown here, the FileName field allows you to set the case in which the filename will appear in your document. It also has an option for including the path in the filename. If you mark this check box, the field not only displays the name of the document itself, such as resume.doc, but also displays the location of the file, as in C:\Documents and Settings\Sean Boulding\ My Documents\Job Search\resume.doc.

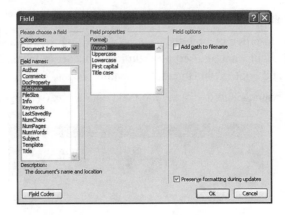

FIGURE 12.16

When you select a field name on the left, the right side of the dialog box displays options for customizing it.

6. When you've made your selections, click **OK** to insert the field in your document.

> If you liked the method of inserting fields used in versions of Word prior to Word XP (also called Word 2002), you can continue to use it. To do so, click the Field Codes button in the lower-left corner of the Field dialog box and then click the Options button to display the Field Options dialog box. If you want to return to the "new" interface for inserting fields, click the Hide Codes button.

Inserting Symbols and Special Characters

Many everyday documents, such as letters and memos, require special characters here and there. For example, you might need to use the trademark symbol (™), a long dash (—), or the ellipsis (…). Word inserts many of these symbols for you automatically as you type. If it doesn't insert the one you need, you can probably find it in the Symbol dialog box.

To see what symbols Word inserts automatically, first choose Tools, AutoCorrect Options to display the AutoCorrect dialog box, and click the AutoCorrect tab. As you saw in "Correcting Text Automatically" earlier in this hour, when you type the characters in the left column, Word replaces them with the symbols on the right. Next, click the AutoFormat As You Type tab. The Replace As You Type options at the top of the dialog box insert many symbols for you as well (see Figure 12.17). Click the Cancel button to close the AutoCorrect dialog box.

FIGURE **12.17**

The Replace As You Type options insert many symbols for you as you type.

To insert a less commonly used symbol, follow these steps:

1. Click where you want the symbol to go, and choose **Insert, Symbol** to display the Symbol dialog box (see Figure 12.18).

FIGURE **12.18**

The Symbol dialog box lets you insert all sorts of symbols.

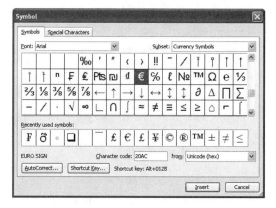

2. Click the **Symbols** tab if it isn't already in front.

3. Scroll through the grid to see what symbols are available. To navigate quickly to a particular subset of symbols, select the subset of interest in the **Subset** drop-down list.

4. If you don't see the symbol you are looking for, display the **Font** drop-down list and choose a different font set. To insert a symbol in the font of the text at the

12

location of the insertion point, choose **(Normal Text)** at the top of this list. (You may also want to check out the Webdings and Wingdings sets because they include some fun symbols.)

5. To insert a symbol, double-click it, and then click the **Close** button.

Word tracks the symbols you have used the most recently and displays them in the Symbols dialog box under Recently Used Symbols. If you see the one you want, just double-click it. Another quick way to insert a symbol is to use its keyboard shortcut. To find out what the keyboard shortcut for a symbol is, select the symbol in the Symbol dialog box and then refer to the bottom of the dialog box. In Figure 12.18, the Euro symbol is selected and the short-cut key listed at the bottom of the dialog box is 20AC, Alt+X. (You type **20AC**, and then hold down the Alt key as you press **X**.) These shortcut keys are not case sensitive (you could type 20ac, Alt+X as well).

Sorting Lists

Many people aren't aware that Word enables you to sort lists in alphabetical order, or by number or date. Remember this feature the next time you have to type a phone list!

To sort a list, follow these steps:

1. Select the entire list.

2. Choose **Table**, **Sort** to display the Sort Text dialog box (see Figure 12.19). Yes, it is a bit odd that the Sort command is in the Table menu, but there you have it.

3. By default, Word assumes you want to sort your paragraphs alphabetically, so Text is selected in the Type box. (If you want to sort by numbers or by date, display the Type list and choose Number or Date.)

You can also use the Sort Text dialog box to sort rows in a table. You'll learn how to do this in Hour 15, "Columns and Tables."

4. Click **OK** to sort the list.

Figure 12.19

Select all of the paragraphs you want to sort, and then display the Sort Text dialog box.

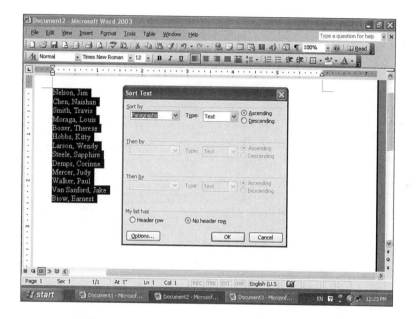

Inserting Footnotes and Endnotes

If you work in academia or are a researcher in the private sector, chances are you need to use footnotes and endnotes in your documents. Word's footnotes and endnotes feature is straightforward and easy to master. It handles all of the formatting for you and automatically numbers the footnotes/endnotes, renumbering as necessary when you insert new footnotes/endnotes in your document. Figure 12.20 shows a document with the Word window split to show you two footnote references at the top of the document, as well as the footnotes themselves at the bottom of the page. Endnotes are exactly like footnotes, except that they appear at the very end of the document instead of at the bottom of the page that contains the reference. You can have both footnotes and endnotes in the same document.

When you point to a footnote or endnote reference, a ScreenTip containing the footnote or endnote text pops up, as shown in Figure 12.21.

To insert a footnote or endnote, follow these steps:

1. Switch to Print Layout view, and move the insertion point to the location where you want to insert the footnote or endnote.

2. Choose **Insert**, **Reference**, **Footnote** to display the Footnote and Endnote dialog box (see Figure 12.22).

12

FIGURE **12.20**

*Word's footnote/
endnote reference
marks are automati-
cally numbered.*

Footnote references

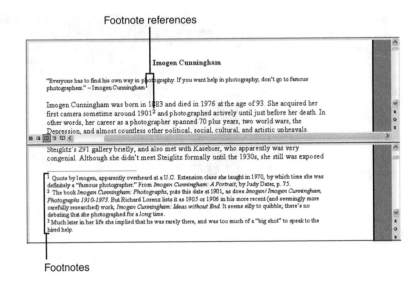

Footnotes

FIGURE **12.21**

*Word displays a
ScreenTip containing
the footnote or endnote
when you point to a
reference in the text.*

FIGURE **12.22**

*Word handles all of the
formatting and num-
bering of footnotes and
endnotes for you.*

3. Under Location at the top of the dialog box, mark the **Footnotes** or **Endnotes**
   option button, and use the associated drop-down list to specify where you want the
   footnote or endnote to appear. (Footnotes can appear at the bottom of each page or

immediately below the text if the text doesn't fill the page. Endnotes can appear at the end of the entire document, or, if the document is divided into sections, at the end of each section.)

4. Under **Format**, specify the number format you want to use, as well as the starting number and the numbering style (continuous, restart in each section, or restart on each page).

5. If you have used section breaks to divide your document, use the **Apply Changes To** drop-down list to specify whether you want the settings you're choosing in this dialog box to apply to the entire document or the current section.

6. Click the **Insert** button.

7. Word inserts the footnote/endnote reference at the location of the insertion point in step 1 and brings your insertion point to the bottom of the page (for footnotes) or document (for endnotes) so you can type your footnote or endnote text. Note that Word inserts a *separator line* above the footnote/endnote (refer to Figure 12.20).

8. Type the text of your footnote/endnote. When you're done, press **Shift+F5** to jump back to the location where you inserted the reference in the text.

After you've followed the preceding steps to establish your footnote or endnote settings and insert your first footnote or endnote, you can insert subsequent footnotes by pressing Alt+Ctrl+F, and endnotes by pressing Alt+Ctrl+D.

12

To delete a footnote or endnote, select the reference number in the text and press Delete. If you want to move or copy a footnote or endnote, select the reference mark in the text and use any of the standard cutting and pasting techniques. The note will move to reflect the new location of the reference mark, and the mark and note will be renumbered.

If at some point you decide you'd like to convert all of your footnotes to endnotes, or vice versa, follow these steps:

1. Choose **Insert**, **Reference**, **Footnote**.

2. In the Footnote and Endnote dialog box, click the **Convert** button.

3. In the Convert Notes dialog box that appears (see Figure 12.23), choose one of the three options and click **OK**. (Two out of the three options will be dim if your document contains only footnotes or endnotes, but not both.)

4. Click **Close** to close the Footnote and Endnote dialog box.

FIGURE 12.23

You can convert foot-
notes to endnotes, and
vice versa.

You can change the footnote or endnote separator line if you like. To do so, switch to Normal view and choose View, Footnotes. If you have both footnotes and endnotes in your document, the View Footnotes dialog box appears. Select View Footnote Area or View Endnote Area, select Footnote Separator or Endnote Separator in the Footnotes or Endnotes drop-down list, and then select and delete the existing separator line. You can then insert a new line by typing it by hand (entering a row of asterisks, for example) or by using the keyboard techniques for adding different types of borders described in the tip at the end of the "Adding Borders and Shading" section of Hour 7, "Formatting Paragraphs."

Automating Tasks with Macros

The term *macro* refers to a piece of programming code that accomplishes a particular task in Word. (Word macros were formerly written in WordBasic, but starting with Word 97 they have been written in Visual Basic for Applications.) Back when word processing programs were truly designed to help you process words and not much more, macros were well worth learning about. Now, however, Word has expanded to include many features that perform tasks we once used macros for. For example, macros were once useful for inserting large blocks of "boilerplate" text, but we now can use the AutoText feature to accomplish this task. Furthermore, to create complex macros, you need to understand a fair amount about programming in general and Visual Basic in particular.

Nonetheless, there are two aspects of working with macros that you might want to understand:

- How to use existing macros—If you know this, then if your company or someone else gives you a macro, you'll know what to do with it.
- How to record a keyboard macro—To create a complex macro, you have to write the VB code from scratch. However, you can create keyboard macros by simply recording the keystrokes you want the macro to automate. Word creates the Visual Basic for Applications code for you.

Macros are so versatile that there is no "representative" example of an existing one that you might want to use. However, it might still be helpful to "see" one in action: A macro called AddTones, available for download on the Web, inserts diacritic marks over roman-ized Chinese words (words written using *pinyin* instead of characters) to indicate tones. For example, if the user writes the text shown in Figure 12.24 and then selects it and runs the AddTones macro, it results in the text shown in Figure 12.25.

FIGURE 12.24

The user types num-bers to represent the four tones in Mandarin Chinese.

FIGURE 12.25

The AddTones macro converts the numbers to diacritic marks over each word.

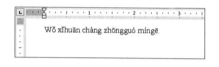

Using Existing Macros

As you learned in Hour 10, "Working with Templates," macros are stored in templates (along with styles, AutoText entries, and toolbars). When someone gives you a macro, it will arrive in a Word template (a file with a `.dot` extension). If you only need to use a macro when you're working with a document based on the template that contains the macro, you can store the template in the Templates folder. However, if you'd like the macro to be available whenever you are using Word, you need to store the template in Word's Startup folder or use the Organizer to copy the macro into the Normal template (see "Copying Items from One Template to Another" in Hour 10).

12

To locate either the Templates folder or the Startup folder, follow these steps:

1. Choose **Tools**, **Options**, and click the **File Locations** tab in the Options dialog box.

2. Double-click **User Templates** or **Startup**.

3. Display the **Look In** drop-down list in the Modify Locations dialog box and note the location of the folder.

4. Click the **Cancel** buttons to back out of this dialog box, and then click **Close** to close the Options dialog box.

After you've stored the Word template that contains the macro in the right folder, you need to know how to run it. To run a macro, follow these steps:

1. Start a new document based on the template that contains the macro.

2. Choose **Tools**, **Macro**, **Macros** (or press **Alt+F8**) to display the Macros dialog box. See Figure 12.26.

FIGURE **12.26**

The Macros dialog box lists your available macros.

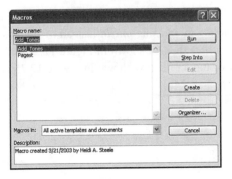

3. Double-click the macro you want to run.

Word templates containing macros can and often do carry viruses. You need to be extremely cautious about using macros that you find on the Web. If you want to check your macro security settings, choose Tools, Options; click the Security tab; and click the Macro Security button. For most people, the Medium option is a good one to use.

To delete a macro, display the Macros dialog box (Tools, Macro, Macros), select the macro, and press the Delete key.

Recording Your Own Macro

If you find yourself frequently repeating the same procedure on multiple documents—whether it involves typing, editing, formatting, or a combination of all three—it might be worth recording the keystrokes in a macro. For example, if you frequently have to remove paragraph marks or line-break characters from with paragraphs (as described in "Using Find and Replace to Remove Breaks Within Paragraphs" earlier in this hour), you can record the steps outlined in that section in a macro.

Keep in mind that a recorded macro works best if all of the documents you run it on are consistent. If they differ so much that the exact same set of keystrokes won't work on all of them, you won't be able to use this type of simple recorded macro. For example, a macro that removes breaks within paragraphs using the steps described earlier in this hour won't work if the document contains some single-line paragraphs that don't have blank lines in between them, and you need to keep those paragraphs as is (the macro would run them together).

The general steps for recording a macro are as follows: You choose a name for your macro, optionally create a toolbar button or keyboard shortcut for it, and then start recording your keystrokes. After the "tape recorder" is turned on, Word will record your every keystroke and menu command, whether you performed it accidentally or not. Consequently, it's wise to run through your keystrokes with a sample document first to make sure they work as intended before you create the macro. The last step is to turn off the tape recorder after you've recorded all of the keystrokes and menu commands.

If you do make a mistake recording your macro, the easiest way to fix it is to rerecord the macro, keeping the same macro name so that you overwrite the original. To edit the macro, you have to know something about Visual Basic.

While you're recording a macro, you can use the mouse to issue menu commands and select options in dialog boxes, but you must use the keyboard to select text. See Hour 2, "Entering Text and Moving Around," if you need help with this.

Here are the specific steps for recording a macro:

1. If you want to create a toolbar button for the macro, make sure the toolbar is displayed in your Word window. And if you want to store the macro in a template other than the Normal template, start a document based on that template now.

2. Choose **Tools**, **Macro**, **Record New Macro** to display the Record Macro dialog box (see Figure 12.27).

12

FIGURE 12.27

The Record Macro dialog box lets you define basic information about your macro.

2. Type a name for your macro in the **Macro Name** text box, and optionally type a description for it in the **Description** text box.

Here are the naming conventions for macros: The first character in the name cannot be a number. The name cannot include a space; period; exclamation point; or the characters @, &, $, or #. (You can use underscores.) Finally, the names cannot exceed 255 characters in length.

3. If you want to store the macro in a template other than the Normal template, select it in the **Store Macro In** drop-down list.

4. Optionally, click the **Toolbars** or **Keyboard** button to create a toolbar button or keyboard shortcut for the macro. If you don't want to do this, click **OK** and skip to step 7.

5. If you clicked the Toolbars button, the Commands tab of the Customize dialog box appears. Under Commands on the right side of the dialog box, a temporary name for your macro, such as Normal.NewMacros.MyMacro, appears. Drag this name out of the dialog box and onto the toolbar where you want the macro's toolbar button to go. Then right-click the button in the toolbar, select the temporary name to the right of the **Name** command in the context menu, type the name you want to appear on the button, and press **Enter**. Finally, click **Close** to close the Customize dialog box.

6. If you clicked the Keyboard button, the Customize Keyboard dialog box appears with the name for the macro listed under Commands. With the insertion point in the **Press New Shortcut Key** text box, press the key combination that you would like to use for your macro (actually press the keys; don't type the names of the keys). The dialog box refreshes and tells you whether the keyboard shortcut you pressed is assigned. When you find a key combination that's currently unassigned (or one that you don't mind overwriting), click the **Assign** button, and then click **Close**.

7. The dialog box you were using disappears, a small Stop Recording toolbar appears, and your mouse pointer changes to show a tape recorder (see Figure 12.28). At this point, the "tape recorder" is now turned on. Enter all of the keystrokes that you want to record.

8. When you are finished, click the **Stop Recording** button on the Stop Recording toolbar.

Word automatically stores the macro in the template you specified, and it will appear in the Macros dialog box the next time you choose Tools, Macro, Macros.

FIGURE 12.28

A special mouse pointer indicates that Word is recording your keystrokes.

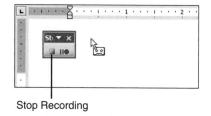

Stop Recording

Creating Custom Keyboard Shortcuts

In the preceding section, you learned how to create a keyboard shortcut for a macro. You can also create keyboard shortcuts for AutoText entries, styles, fonts, common symbols, or any Word command that you use frequently. To do so, follow these steps:

1. Choose **Tools**, **Customize** to display the Customize dialog box.

2. Click the **Keyboard** button to display the Customize Keyboard dialog box (see Figure 12.29).

FIGURE 12.29

Use the Customize Keyboard dialog box to add keyboard shortcuts for tasks you perform frequently.

3. On the left side of the dialog box, click the category that contains the command for which you want to assign a keyboard shortcut. (Scroll to the end of the **Categories** list to find categories for macros, fonts, AutoText, styles, and common symbols.)

4. On the right side of the dialog box, click the command. If it already has a keyboard shortcut assigned to it, the shortcut will appear in the **Current Keys** text box.

5. With the insertion point in the **Press New Shortcut Key** text box, press the key combination that you would like to use for your command (actually press the keys; don't type the names of the keys). The dialog box refreshes and tells you whether the keyboard shortcut you pressed is already assigned.

12

6. When you find a key combination that's currently unassigned (or one that you don't mind overwriting), click the **Assign** button, optionally create more keyboard shortcuts, and then click **Close** twice.

Summary

You can create perfectly respectable documents without using anything that you learned about in this hour. But if you do use even a few of these editing shortcuts, you can greatly reduce, or even eliminate, the tedious and repetitive typing that often goes along with word processing. In the next hour, you learn a variety of techniques for working with long documents.

Q&A

Q **I created some AutoText entries that I want to share with my co-workers. How do I do that?**

A AutoText entries are stored in templates, so you need to give your co-workers access to the template containing the entries you created. Refer to "Copying Items from One Template to Another" in Hour 10 if you have to move your AutoText entries to the template that you want to share. Review "Sharing Your Template with Others" in Hour 10 if you need suggestions for ways to share your template.

Q **The Insert, AutoText menu contains categories such as Attention Line, Closing, and Header/Footer. What are these?**

A Each of these menu items leads to a submenu of "prefabricated" AutoText entries that come with Word. To use one of these entries, simply click in the desired location and choose it from the submenu. If the entries you have created are formatted with the Normal paragraph style, they will appear in the Insert, AutoText menu under the category Normal. If they aren't, Word is inconsistent about how it lists them in the menu, so it is simplest to create your entries using the Normal style and then apply other styles to the text after you've inserted entries in your document.

Q **When I'm using the Find and Replace dialog box, I frequently spot things in my text that I want to edit. Do I have to close the dialog box before making these changes?**

A No. The Find and Replace dialog box is one of the few dialog boxes that can remain open while you edit your text. Just drag the dialog box's title bar to move it out of the way, and then click in your text to deactivate the dialog box and activate your document. When you want to go back to using the dialog box, click its title bar to activate it again.

Hour 13

Working with Long Documents

If you have to type long documents—reports, proposals, school papers, journal articles, and manuals—you will probably appreciate the features discussed in this hour. Although you can use all these features with documents of any length, they come into play most frequently with documents that are at least several pages long.

The highlights of this hour include

- Using the Document Map to navigate among headings
- Modifying the heading structure of your document
- Creating a table of contents
- Creating an index
- Inserting cross-references
- Bookmarking specific locations in your document
- Adding hyperlinks to your text

Navigating with the Document Map

Word comes with a feature called Document Map, which lets you view an outline of your document onscreen as you work and quickly navigate among headings. This feature only works properly if you have formatted your headings in one of these ways:

- You have applied built-in heading styles.
- You have applied your own heading styles that contain outline levels. This process is described in "Creating Styles for Your Headings" in Hour 9.
- You have applied outline levels to the individual paragraphs that you want to use as headings in your document (using the Outline Level drop-down list in the Paragraph dialog box).

> If you haven't formatted your headings using one of these three approaches and you turn on the Document Map, Word scans through your document looking for short lines of text that "look" like headings, formats them with an outline level of 1 (on par with level-1 headings), and then populates the Document Map with these paragraphs. Depending on the content of your document, you may get a list of actual headings, or you may get a pile of clutter. If you see a mess in the Document Map, close the document without saving, use one of the approaches above to format your headings properly, and then turn on the Document Map again.

Follow these steps to use the Document Map:

1. Click the **Document Map** button in the Standard toolbar (or choose View, Document Map).

2. An outline of your document appears in a pane on the left side of the Word window, as shown in Figure 13.1. The document in the figure contains two heading levels, formatted with the Heading 1 and Heading 2 styles. To navigate to another section of your document, click the desired heading in the Document Map. (If the Document Map is not wide enough to display a heading, the full heading will appear in a ScreenTip when you point to it.)

3. You can expand and collapse the outline in the Document Map by right-clicking anywhere in the Document Map and clicking the heading level that you want to view in the context menu. In Figure 13.2, the Document Map has been collapsed to show only the top-level headings, and the context menu is displayed.

4. To expand an individual heading in the Document Map to display its subheadings, click the plus sign next to its name. The plus sign changes to a minus sign. To collapse the heading again (thus hiding its subheadings), click the minus sign.

Document Map

FIGURE 13.1

Click the Document Map button in the Standard toolbar to display the Document Map to the left of your document.

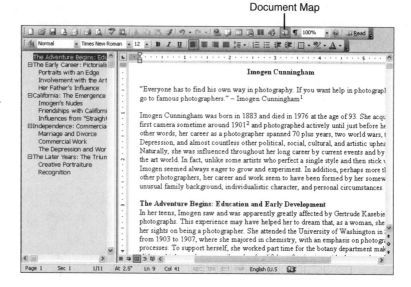

FIGURE 13.2

Click the heading level that you want to display in the context menu.

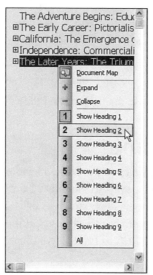

13

5. To alter the width of the document map, drag the right edge of the Document Map to the right or left.

6. To close the Document Map, click the **Document Map** toolbar button again.

If you find that the font used in the Document Map is larger than you'd like, you can reduce its size by changing the Document Map paragraph style. By default, the Document Map style is not displayed in the Styles and Formatting task pane, so you have to first display it, and then modify it to change its font. To do so, follow these steps:

1. Click the **Document Map** button on the Standard toolbar to display the Document Map.

2. Click the **Styles and Formatting** button on the Formatting toolbar to display the Styles and Formatting task pane.

3. Display the Show drop-down list at the bottom of the task pane and choose **Custom**.

4. In the Format Settings dialog box, display the Category list and choose **All Styles**. Then mark the **Document Map** check box in the Styles to Be Visible list, and click **OK**.

5. The Document Map style now appears in the list of styles shown in the task pane. Point to it and click its down arrow to display a drop-down list, and choose **Modify**.

6. In the Modify Style dialog box, mark the **Add to Template** check box to save this style change for all documents based on the current template, and then click the **Format** button and choose **Font**.

7. In the Font dialog box, choose the desired font settings, and click **OK**.

8. Click **OK** to close the Modify Style dialog box, and then close the task pane.

Organizing Your Outline

If you have applied built-in heading styles or user-defined heading styles that contain outline levels (or simply applied outline levels to individual paragraphs), you can use Outline view to examine and modify the heading structure of your document. Or, if you haven't started your document yet, you might want to use Outline view to sketch out the structure of your document, and then switch to Print Layout or Normal view to fill in the body text.

To use Outline view to review or edit headings that you've already typed in your document, follow these steps:

1. Choose **View**, **Outline**, or click the Outline View button in the lower-left corner of the Word window.

2. Word switches to Outline view and displays the Outlining toolbar. Headings that contain subheadings and/or body text have plus signs to the left of their names.

Those that are currently empty have minus signs. To collapse the outline down to your top-level headings, display the **Show Level** drop-down list in the Outlining toolbar, and choose **Show Level 1** (see Figure 13.3).

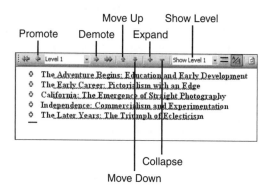

FIGURE 13.3

Click the heading level that you want to display in the Show Level drop-down list on the Outlining toolbar.

3. To further expand the view of your outline, click the desired option in the Show Level drop-down list. (For example, to display the top three heading levels in your document, choose **Show Level 3**.) If you want to display all headings, as well as the body text within each heading, choose **Show All Levels**.

4. To expand an individual heading to see all of its subheadings, click the plus sign to its left to select it (the mouse pointer changes to a four-headed arrow when you point to the plus sign), and then click the **Expand** button in the Outlining toolbar. To collapse the view of a heading, select it and click the **Collapse** toolbar button. (If you double-click a plus sign, you completely expand or collapse the associated heading. When a heading is completely expanded, the body text within it also is displayed.)

5. To restyle a heading to demote it one level or promote it one level, select it and then click the **Promote** or **Demote** buttons in the Outlining toolbar. Word applies the appropriate heading style. For example, if you demote a heading formatted with the Heading 2 style, Word reformats it with the Heading 3 style.

6. To move a heading (along with all the subheadings and body text it contains) to a new location in the document, drag its plus sign. As you drag, a horizontal line indicates where the heading will appear. When the line is in the right place, release the mouse button. (You can also click the plus sign next to the heading and then click the **Move Up** and **Move Down** buttons in the Outlining toolbar.)

7. When you're finished using Outline view, use the View menu or the View buttons to go to another view.

13

If you want to use Outline view to sketch out your outline at the start of working on a document, follow these steps:

1. Start a new Word document, and then choose **View**, **Outline**, or click the Outline View button in the lower-left corner of the Word window.

2. Word switches to Outline view and automatically turns on the Heading 1 style for the current paragraph. Type your first level-1 heading, and press **Enter**.

> Remember that you can modify the formatting of the built-in heading styles (Heading 1, Heading 2, and so on) to suit your preferences. Refer to Hour 9, "Working with Styles," if you need a reminder of how to do this.

3. Word brings you to a new paragraph formatted with the Heading 1 style. If you like, you can continue to enter all of your level-1 headings. Alternatively, you can click the **Demote** button to apply the Heading 2 style to the current paragraph, and then type a subheading.

4. You can start typing body text under any of your headings. Press Enter at the end of the heading to begin a new paragraph, and click **Body Text** in the Outline Level drop-down list. (A little square appears at the beginning of each paragraph of body text.) If you type quite a bit of body text and don't want it to clutter up the view of your outline, you can click the **Show First Line Only** toolbar button. Word hides all of the body text except the first line of each paragraph (see Figure 13.4). To bring all of the body text back into view, click the **Show First Line Only** toolbar button again.

FIGURE 13.4
You can hide all of the body text but the first line of each paragraph.

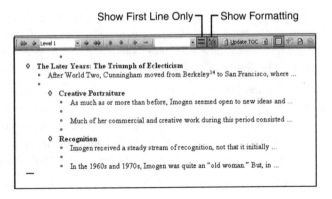

By default, Word displays the font formatting of your document in Outline view. If you'd prefer a very plain view of your text, click the Show Formatting button in the Outlining toolbar to turn it off. You can always click it again to turn it on at any time.

Remember that you can switch in and out of Outline view whenever you like. You might create some of your outline in Outline view, switch to Print Layout view to type some of the text of your document, and then switch back to Outline view when you want to make more modifications to your document's structure.

Generating a Table of Contents

Rather than painstakingly typing a table of contents yourself, and then retyping it whenever the page numbers or headings change, you can have Word handle this for you.

As with the Document Map and Outline view, you have to apply heading styles (or outline levels) before creating a table of contents. Word uses heading styles (or outline levels) to locate your headings and decide how to format them in the table of contents it generates. Asking Word to create a table of contents for you has three advantages:

- The table of contents is actually a field, so you can update it at any time to reflect changes in your document. Word can update both the headings and page numbers or just the page numbers.

- Each heading in the table of contents is a hyperlink that leads to that heading in the document text. The hyperlinks let your table of contents double as a navigation tool.

- Most importantly, you don't have to type the whole thing yourself.

To create a table of contents, follow these steps:

1. Click at the location where you want the table of contents to appear. If you want it to be on a separate page, insert manual page breaks before and/or after it as necessary.

2. Choose **Insert**, **Reference**, **Index and Tables** to display the Index and Tables dialog box, and click the Table of Contents tab (see Figure 13.5).

3. Experiment with different "looks" in the **Formats** drop-down list (Classic, Fancy, Modern, and so on) to find one that you like. If you want the table of contents to use the formatting of the heading styles that are stored in the template attached to your document, choose **From Template**.

13

FIGURE **13.5**

Use the Table of Contents tab in the Index and Tables dialog box to generate your table of contents.

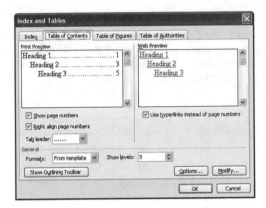

4. Specify the number of heading levels that you want in the table of contents in the **Show Levels** text box.

5. When you've made your selections, click the **OK** button.

6. In a moment, the table of contents appears (see Figure 13.6). When you click it, the table of contents may turn light gray to indicate that it's a field. This depends on the Field Shading setting you've chosen in the View tab of the Options dialog box (Tools, Options).

FIGURE **13.6**

This table of contents was created by using the Formal format, with two heading levels showing.

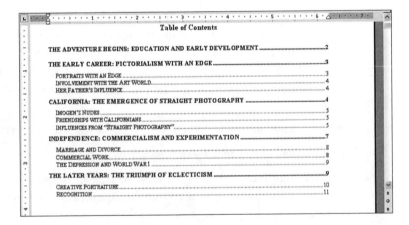

7. The table of contents also works as a navigation tool because the headings are formatted as hyperlinks. Hold down the **Ctrl** key as you point to a heading in the table of contents. The mouse pointer becomes a pointing hand. When you **Ctrl+click**, Word jumps to the associated heading in the text.

If you want to be able to follow hyperlinks with a click instead of a Ctrl+click, choose Tools, Options. Click the Edit tab, clear the Use Ctrl+Click to Follow Hyperlink check box, and click OK.)

After you revise your headings or if the pagination changes, you need to update the table of contents. To do so, right-click anywhere in it and choose Update Field in the context menu. (You can also click to the left of the table to select it and then press F9.) Word displays the Update Table of Contents dialog box (see Figure 13.7) to ask whether you want to update only the page numbers or the entire table. Mark the desired option button, and click OK. (Remember to update the table of contents right before you print.)

If you don't want to have to remember to update your table of contents each time you print, you can ask Word to do it for you. Choose Tools, Options. Click the Print tab, mark the Update Fields check box, and click OK. Word will now update the table of contents fields—as well as any other fields it finds—every time it sends a document to the printer.

Figure 13.7

The Update Table of Contents dialog box asks how you want to perform the update.

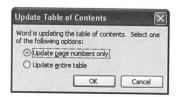

To delete a table of contents, click just to the left of the first character in the table of contents to select it, and then press Delete.

Creating an Index

13

Creating an index in Word involves two steps. The first step is the time-consuming one—marking entries for indexing. After you've marked all of your entries, generating the index takes only a moment.

You can mark all of the words that you want to include in the index in one of three ways:

- Insert an index entry field just after a word.
- Bookmark a block of text, and then insert an index entry field just after the book-marked text. If you use this technique, the index will list a range of pages for the index entry if the bookmarked text spans multiple pages.

- Create a *concordance file*, which is a list of words that you want indexed. Word will then use this file to automatically mark all of the index entries in your document. (For information on this method, search the Microsoft Word help system for the word *concordance file*.)

Regardless of which method you use to insert index entry fields in your text, the fields are formatted as hidden text, which means they are only visible when you have the Show/Hide ¶ button in the Standard toolbar turned on. Figure 13.8 shows two index entry fields in a paragraph, one for the word *street photos*, and the other for the word *pictorialism*. The fields are enclosed in curly brackets and lead with *XE* (for *index entry*). The words that will appear in the index itself are displayed in double quotes inside the fields. (In the example shown here, the words that will appear in the index match those they are marking in the text exactly, but as you'll find out in a moment, you can use a different word for the index entry if you like.) The dotted underline under the entries indicates that the fields are formatted as hidden text.

Index entry fields

FIGURE 13.8

This paragraph contains two index entry fields.

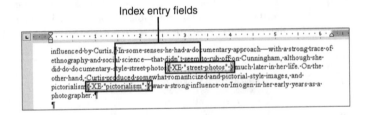

After you've marked your entries, you can generate the index. This process is similar to generating a table of contents. You click where you want the index to appear and select the desired formatting options for the index. Word then finds all of the entries and creates the index for you.

The next two sections describe this process in more detail.

Marking Your Index Entries

To mark a word in your document as an index entry, follow these steps:

1. Select the word that you want to add to the index.

If you want the index entry to point to the page number the word appears on, but want to use a different word for the entry itself, you can click just past the word in step 1 instead of selecting it.

2. Choose **Insert**, **Reference**, **Index and Tables**, click the **Index** tab, and click the **Mark Entry** button to display the Mark Index Entry dialog box, shown in Figure 13.9 (The keyboard shortcut for displaying this dialog box is **Alt+Shift+X**.)

FIGURE 13.9

The Mark Index Entry dialog box lets you specify the details of your index entry.

3. If you want the index entry to point to the page containing the insertion point, mark the **Current Page** option button. If you want the index entry to instead just refer the reader to a different entry in the index, mark the **Cross-reference** option button and type the index entry to which you want to refer the reader after *See* in the Cross-reference text box.

4. Optionally edit the text in the **Main Entry** text box, and type any index entries in the **Subentry** text box that you want to appear under this main entry. (To include a third-level entry, type the subentry followed by a colon (:) and then type the third-level entry.)

If you want to include multiple subentries, you have to insert a separate index entry field for each one, using the same word in the Main Entry text box. By the same token, if you want to include multiple third-level entries under the same subentry, you need to insert an index entry field for each one, using the same word in the Main Entry field and the same word to the left of the colon in the Subentry field.

13

If you want to apply any special formatting to the text for the main entry or subentry, right-click the text box and choose Font to display the Font dialog box. Make your changes and click OK.

5. Mark the **Bold** and/or **Italic** check boxes if you want to apply those formatting options to the index entry.

6. Click the **Mark** button to mark just this one entry, or click **Mark All** to mark all instances of this word in your document.

7. If you like, you can leave this dialog box open as you repeat steps 3 to 6 to mark other entries. Click outside of the dialog box to activate the document. Select another word or click in another location, and then click the title bar of the dialog box again. When you are finished, click the **Close** button.

Follow these steps to add an index entry field for a block of text that spans a range of pages:

1. Create a bookmark for the text now (see "Bookmarking Locations in Your Document" later in this hour). Then click just past the bookmarked text.

2. Press **Alt+Shift+X** to display the Mark Index Entry dialog box.

3. Under Options, mark the **Page Range Bookmark** option button, and select a bookmark from the drop-down list.

4. Continue with step 4 of the previous set of steps. (In step 6, the Mark All button will be dim because you are only marking the one bookmarked block of text.)

After you've added an index entry field to your document, you can edit it directly. For example, if you want to change the word that will appear in the index, you can edit the word in the double quotes in the field (refer back to Figure 13.8). If you want to delete an entry, select the field, including the curly brackets, and press Delete. If you make these kinds of changes, be sure to update your index, as described in the next section.

Generating the Index

After you have marked all of your entries, follow these steps to generate your index:

1. Click at the location where you want your index to appear. You'll probably want to insert a manual page break (**Ctrl+Enter**) at the end of your document and place the index on a new, final page.

2. If the Show/Hide ¶ button is turned on, click it again to turn it off. The index will not display the correct pagination if the index entry fields are visible at the time the index is generated.

3. Choose **Insert**, **Reference**, **Index and Tables** to display the Index and Tables dialog box, and click the Index tab (see Figure 13.10).

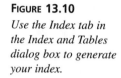

FIGURE 13.10

Use the Index tab in the Index and Tables dialog box to generate your index.

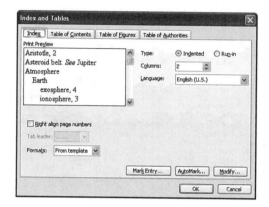

4. Try out different "looks" in the **Formats** drop-down list (Classic, Fancy, Modern, and so on) to find one that you like. If you want to use the formatting of the index styles stored in the template attached to your document, choose From Template. (If you choose this option, you can click the Modify button to display the Style dialog box, where you can modify the formatting of these styles.)

5. Under Type, mark the **Indented** option button if you want subentries to be on separate lines, indented from the main entry. Mark **Run-in** if you want subentries to be listed to the right of their main entry with no line breaks. To see how these options look, click them and then view the Print Preview area of the dialog box.

6. Use the **Columns** text box to specify the number of columns you want to use for your index.

7. Mark the **Right Align Page Numbers** check box if you want the numbers to be aligned at the right edge of the column. If you mark this check box, the **Tab Leader** drop-down list becomes active so that you can specify what type of tab leader you'd like to use.

8. Click the **OK** button to generate the index.

Figure 13.11 shows an index created using the index styles in the current template. It has two columns, and the page numbers are right-aligned. This index has examples of all three types of index entries: ones that reference the page(s) the word appears on, ones that reference a range of pages for a block of text, and ones that reference other index entries. It also includes one main entry (double images) that contains subentries.

After you add or delete index entry fields, you need to update the index. To do so, right-click anywhere in it and choose Update Field in the context menu. (You can also click to the left of the index to highlight it and then press F9.) If you haven't configured Word to update fields before printing (Tools, Options, click the Print tab, mark the Update Fields check box), be sure to update the index right before you print.

13

FIGURE 13.11
This two-column index includes all three types of index entries.

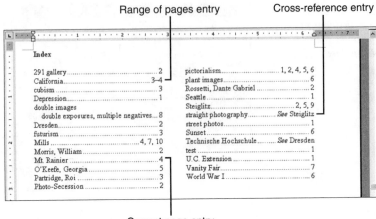

Range of pages entry

Cross-reference entry

Current page entry

Inserting Cross-References

If you are writing a manual or another type of reference document, you may want to include cross-references within the text to refer the reader from one part of your document to another. You could, of course, type these cross-references manually. As you revise your document, however, there is a good chance that the pagination, section headings, figure numbers, and so on will change, requiring you to update all of your cross-references. You can avoid this quagmire altogether if you insert the parts of your cross-references that will need updating as fields. This way, Word can update them for you as needed.

Furthermore, Word by default inserts cross-reference fields as hyperlinks, so if you're editing a document that contains cross-reference fields, you can Ctrl+click them to jump to their targets.

> If you want to insert cross-references to headings, you need to format your headings with heading styles or outline levels first.

To insert a cross-reference field, follow these steps:

1. Click at the spot where you want the cross-reference to go.

2. Choose **Insert**, **Reference**, **Cross-reference** to display the Cross-reference dialog box (see Figure 13.12).

FIGURE 13.12

The Cross-reference dialog box allows you to specify the type of item you want to reference and the information you want to appear in your document.

3. Display the **Reference Type** drop-down list and select the type of item you want the cross-reference to point to. If you want to refer to a heading in your document, for example, choose Heading. The Insert Reference To and For Which [Reference Type] lists in the dialog box change dynamically to present the options available for the reference type you choose.

To insert cross-references to figures, tables, and equations, you need to use Word's caption feature. For more information, search Word's help system for the word *caption.*

4. In the **Insert Reference To** list, select the type of information that you want to appear in the text. Using the preceding example, if you chose Heading as the reference type, you would select **Heading Text** in this list to insert the heading name as a field, or you would select **Page Number** to insert the page number on which the heading appears as a field.

5. In the **For Which [Reference Type]** list, select the specific item that you want to reference.

Mark the Include Above/Below check box if you want to insert the word *above* or *below* at the end of the field, depending on whether the target of the cross-reference is above or below the reference itself in the document.

6. Click the **Insert** button to insert the field in your document.

13

7. If you have more cross-reference fields you'd like to insert now, click outside of the dialog box to activate your document, click at the next location where you want to insert a cross-reference field, click the title bar of the Cross-reference dialog box to activate it again, and then repeat steps 3 to 6. When you're done, click the **Cancel** button.

Figure 13.13 shows a cross-reference in which both the heading and the page number are fields. (The user actually created two cross-references, one for the heading and one for the page number, and manually typed the words *see* and *on page* as well as the quotes.) This cross-reference will stay current even if you edit the heading or the heading moves to a different page.

FIGURE 13.13

If you use cross-reference fields, your cross-references update automatically.

To update a cross-reference field, click it and press F9. If you want to update all of the fields in your document, press Ctrl+A to select the entire document before pressing F9.

To delete a cross-reference field, drag over it and press the Delete key.

Bookmarking Locations in Your Document

If you're working on a long document, you might find it handy to "bookmark" a particular spot so that you can get back to it easily, just as you'd use a paper bookmark to mark a page in a book. You could bookmark a section that still needs work or one that's missing information, for example. In addition, you can use a bookmark as the target of a cross-reference or hyperlink, or to define a range of pages to an index.

Follow these steps to insert a bookmark:

1. Click at the location where you want to insert the bookmark.

2. Choose **Insert**, **Bookmark** (or press Shift+Ctrl+F5).

3. In the Bookmark dialog box, type a name for the bookmark (see Figure 13.14). Bookmark names cannot include spaces.

4. Click the **Add** button to add the bookmark and close the dialog box.

To navigate to a bookmark, display the Bookmark dialog box and double-click the bookmark in the list in the middle of the dialog box. When you're finished using the Bookmark dialog box, click its Close button.

FIGURE 13.14

Type a name for your bookmark in the Bookmark Name text box.

You can also navigate to bookmarks by using the Go To tab of the Find and Replace dialog box. Choose Edit, Go To (or press F5) to display the dialog box, choose Bookmark in the Go to What list, select the desired bookmark in the Enter Bookmark Name list, and click Go To.

To delete a bookmark, select it in the Bookmark dialog box and click the Delete button.

Inserting Hyperlinks

A *hyperlink* is a "clickable" piece of text or a graphic that leads to another location (the *target* of the hyperlink). With Word's Hyperlink feature, you can create links to other documents on your computer or network, to specific locations within a document, or to Web pages. Keep in mind that hyperlinks are useful only if your readers will view the document onscreen.

Figure 13.15 shows a hyperlink that points to an Excel spreadsheet. Note that when you point to a hyperlink, its target appears in a ScreenTip.

13

FIGURE 13.15

You can see where a hyperlink will take you by pointing to it.

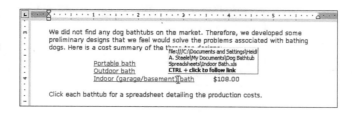

If you create a hyperlink to a document on your own computer network, make sure the document is in a folder that your readers can access.

Linking to Another Document

If you add hyperlinks to other documents, you can lead your readers to associated information without cluttering up your own document. If you want people to review several documents stored in different locations on your network, you can make it easy for them by giving them a short Word document that contains only hyperlinks to these documents. In this case, the Word document would function as a sort of table of contents. (This particular use of hyperlinks only works if the people who will be reading your document are also on your network.)

Follow these steps to insert a hyperlink to a document on your own computer or network:

1. Select the word or phrase in your document that you want to become the hyperlink text.

2. Click the **Insert Hyperlink** button in the Standard toolbar or press Ctrl+K (see Figure 13.16).

FIGURE 13.16

Click the Insert Hyperlink button in the Standard toolbar to insert a hyperlink in your document.

Insert Hyperlink

3. In the Insert Hyperlink dialog box, use the **Look In** drop-down list (and the **Up One Level** button to its right) to navigate to the folder that contains the document you want to link to (see Figure 13.17).

FIGURE 13.17

Use the Insert Hyperlink dialog box to specify the target of your hyperlink.

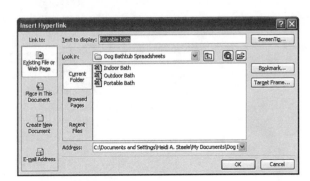

4. Select the document. Its location now appears in the Address text box. Click **OK**.

The hyperlink text is now colored and underlined. When you point to it, the address of the target document appears in a ScreenTip. Ctrl+click the hyperlink. Word may display a warning about clicking hyperlinks. If it does, click the Yes button. (This assumes that you trust the document you hyperlinked to does not contain any viruses.) In a moment, Word displays the document. If the document was created in another application, it launches that application and opens the document within it. When you're finished viewing the document, close it.

> Whenever you Ctrl+click a hyperlink in a Word document, the Web toolbar appears. This toolbar has buttons similar to those in a browser window. If you find it distracting, choose View, Toolbars, Web to hide it.

Linking to a Specific Location in a Document

If you've written a long Word document that people will view onscreen, consider adding some hyperlinks at the top of it that point to the main sections within the document. (You can also create hyperlinks in the main sections that lead back to the top of the document.)

Follow these steps to insert a hyperlink to a heading or a bookmark in the current document:

1. Select the word or phrase in your document that you want to become the hyperlink text.

2. Click the **Insert Hyperlink** button in the Standard toolbar or press Ctrl+K.

3. In the Insert Hyperlink dialog box, click the **Bookmark** button.

4. In the Select Place in Document dialog box that appears, you can specify the top of the document, a heading, or a bookmark as the target of the hyperlink. Click the plus signs next to Headings and Bookmarks to display the headings and bookmarks in the document. Select the desired location (see Figure 13.18), and click **OK**.

5. The location now appears in the Address text box in the Insert Hyperlink dialog box, preceded by a pound (#) sign. Click **OK**.

13

Word creates the colored and underlined hyperlink. When you point to it, the ScreenTip lists the specific location in the document. Ctrl+click the hyperlink to test it.

FIGURE **13.18**

Use the Select Place in Document dialog box to specify a heading or bookmark as the target of the link.

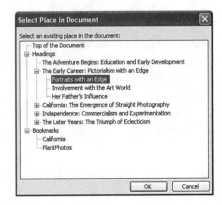

You can also create a link to a bookmark in another document. (You can't create a link to a heading in another document. If you want the link to point to a heading, insert a bookmark at that heading.) To do so, navigate to and select the file from the Insert Hyperlink dialog box, and then use the Bookmark button to select the bookmark in that file.

Linking to a Web Page

If you like, you can create hyperlinks that lead to Web pages. You might, for example, want to point your readers toward Web sites (or Web pages on your company intranet) that contain information related to topics in your document.

To add a hyperlink to a Web page, follow these steps:

1. Select the word or phrase in your document that you want to become the hyperlink text.

2. Click the **Insert Hyperlink** button in the Standard toolbar or press Ctrl+K.

3. Click the **Browse the Web** toolbar button in the Insert Hyperlink dialog box. Alternatively, you can type the full address of the target Web page (including the http://) in the Address text box) and skip to step 5.

4. Your browser window opens, and you are prompted to connect to the Internet if you aren't already online. Navigate to the target Web page, and then click the Word document's taskbar button to switch back to it.

5. The address of the document or Web page now appears in the Address text box. Click **OK**.

The hyperlink text is now colored and underlined. When you point to it, the address of the target Web page appears in a ScreenTip. Try Ctrl+clicking the hyperlink. In a moment, Word displays the target Web page. (You may be prompted to connect to the Internet if you disconnected after following steps 3 and 4 in the previous list.)

Modifying or Deleting a Hyperlink

If you want to modify a hyperlink, right-click it and choose Edit Hyperlink in the context menu to display the Edit Hyperlink dialog box. This dialog box looks just like the Insert Hyperlink dialog box. Make any changes you like to the hyperlink, and click OK.

To remove a hyperlink (thus converting the hyperlink text to regular text), right-click it and choose Remove Hyperlink in the context menu.

> If you have cleared the Use Ctrl+Click to Follow Hyperlink option in the Edit tab of the Options dialog box (Tools, Options), you may find it difficult to select a hyperlink without actually clicking it and jumping to its target. If this is the case, you can select it by right-clicking the hyperlink and choosing Select Hyperlink in the context menu.

Summary

Tasks that used to be complex and cumbersome—such as reorganizing your outline, creating a table of contents, and generating an index—are now a breeze. And in addition to these more prosaic features, you can take advantage of slick navigation features such as the Document Map, bookmarks, cross-references, and hyperlinks to jump from one location to another with a click (or Ctrl+click) of the mouse.

Q&A

Q Is it possible to change the ScreenTip that appears when you point to a hyperlink?

A Yes. Click the ScreenTip button in the upper-right corner of the Insert Hyperlink or Edit Hyperlink dialog box, edit the ScreenTip text in the Set Hyperlink ScreenTip dialog box, and click OK.

Q I want the page numbering to begin on the page after the table of contents. How should I do that?

A Insert a *next page* section break after the table of contents to start the text following the table of contents on a new page, and in a new section. Then add the page number field to the header or footer in the new section. When you do, click the Page Number Format button in the Header and Footer toolbar, and set the starting page number to 1. Also, make sure the Link to Previous button in the Header and Footer toolbar is turned off. Then select the table of contents and press F9 to update its page numbers. If you have questions about section breaks or headers and footers, refer back to Hour 8, "Formatting Pages."

13

HOUR **14**

Generating a Mail Merge

When you want to send a letter to a large number of people, Word's mail merge feature lets you sidestep the mind-numbing task of personalizing the document for each recipient. You prepare two documents: the form letter and a list of the recipients' names and addresses. Word then "merges" the information from the list into the form letter to generate the mass mailing. In this hour, you step through the standard mail merge procedure from start to finish to produce a form letter, and then you learn how to merge four other types of documents: envelopes, labels, directories, and e-mail messages. You also explore a few other options for customizing a mail merge.

The highlights of this hour include

- Understanding mail merge terminology
- Performing a standard mail merge to create a form letter
- Merging envelopes, labels, directories, and e-mail messages
- Merging records in a particular order
- Merging only selected records

Understanding Mail Merges

Before you start your "training run" through the mail merge process, you need to understand the two documents that make up a mail merge:

- Main document—This is the actual document that you are producing. It can be a form letter, e-mail message, envelope, label, or directory. The main document contains the text and formatting that stays the same for each copy of the letter, as well as *merge fields*, which are "placeholders" that tell Word where to insert individual pieces of information from the *data source*.

- Data source—This is the file that contains the data you will merge into the main document. It is organized into *records*, one for each recipient. Each record is composed of individual fields for specific pieces of information, such as first name, last name, address, and so on. If you create your data source during the mail merge process, Word will save it in the Office Address List format. This format, which is actually saved as an Access (.mdb) file, is good for simple address lists that are relatively small (a few hundred addresses or fewer). Word can also use data sources in many other formats, including Access, Excel, other database programs, Word tables, text files, and more. To learn what's possible, search in Word's help system for the keywords *data source mail merge* and click the link "Data sources you can use for a mail merge."

It's easiest to learn how to do a mail merge if you work through the next seven sections in one sitting (go all the way through the "Running the Merge" section). So make sure you have a full hour, grab your coffee, and plow in.

Starting the Main Document

In this phase of the mail merge process, you tell Word which document you want to use as the main document.

Follow these steps to start your main document:

1. If you have an existing letter that you want to use for your form letter, open it now, and delete any parts of it (such as the name and address) that you don't want to include in the form letter. If you want to start a letter from scratch, start a new, blank document.

2. Save the document (use **File**, **Save As** if you've opened an existing document) with a name like *Form Letter - Main* to remind you that it is a main document.

If you perform a lot of mail merges, you might want to create a separate folder for all your main documents to store these specialized documents separately from your other files. You could name this folder something like *Mail Merge Documents*. Word automatically uses a default folder named My Data Sources for your data source files.

3. Choose **Tools, Letters and Mailings, Mail Merge** to display the Mail Merge Wizard in the Mail Merge task pane.

4. In step 1 of the wizard (Select Document Type), mark the **Letters** button to indicate that you want to create a form letter (see Figure 14.1). (The remaining steps of the mail merge will differ depending on what type of document you choose here.)

FIGURE 14.1

The Mail Merge Wizard guides you through the mail merge process.

5. Click **Next: Starting Document** at the bottom of the task pane.

6. In step 2 of the wizard (Select Starting Document), mark the **Use the Current Document** button (see Figure 14.2).

7. Click **Next: Select Recipients** at the bottom of the task pane.

Continue this process by defining the data source for the merge document in the section that follows.

14

FIGURE 14.2

Select your starting document in the Mail Merge task pane.

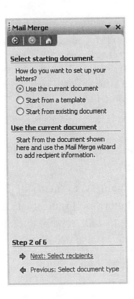

Choosing the Fields in Your Data Source

In this part of the mail merge process, you tell Word which document you want to use as your data source. You can either create a new data source or open an existing one.

The key step in creating a new data source is telling Word which fields you want to use. Typical fields are first name, last name, company, address, city, state, ZIP code, and so on. Include a field for any piece of information that you might want to use in your main document. For example, if you want to refer to the recipient's job title in your form letters, be sure to include a job title field. (When you are entering your records, as described in the next section, you can always leave a field blank if you don't have that piece of data for a particular recipient.)

> You can store other types of information in your data source than people's names and addresses. In the example used in this hour, a field called *Customer Since* is created to store the year that the customer first did business with the store. You can use merge fields anywhere you like in your main document. The Customer Since field will be used in the body of the letter to personalize it.

If you already have a data source you want to use, mark Use an Existing List instead of Type a New List in step 1 of the following steps and click the Browse link to display the Select Data Source dialog box (see Figure 14.3). If your data source is in a file format other than an Access database (.mdb) file, be sure that All Data Sources is selected in the Files of Type drop-down list. Locate and select your data source—there is a good chance it will be stored in the My Data Sources folder, which is Word's default location for data sources—and then click the Open button. You can then skip the remainder of these steps and the next section, "Entering Records and Saving Your Data Source," and go directly to "Sorting and Editing the Data Source."

FIGURE 14.3

Use the Select Data Source dialog box to select an existing data source.

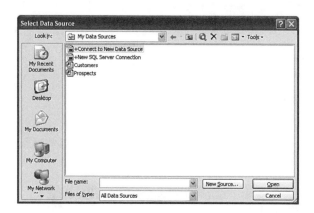

 The My Data Sources folder also contains some specialized tools for connecting to other types of data sources. Your network administrator may ask you to use one of them to access your data source.

Follow these steps to create your data source and specify the fields you want to use:

1. In step 3 of the wizard (Select Recipients), mark the **Type a New List** option button (see Figure 14.4).

2. Click **Create** to display the New Address List dialog box (see Figure 14.5).

3. Each line represents a field. To add or remove fields, click the **Customize** button.

4. In the Customize Address List dialog box that appears (see Figure 14.6), delete any fields you won't use by selecting them one by one, clicking the **Delete** button, and clicking **Yes** to confirm the deletion.

 If your mailing list contains a lot of addresses with building or department names, suite numbers, and so on, keep the Address2 field to use for this information.

14

FIGURE **14.4**

*Choose Type a New
List to start a new data
source.*

FIGURE **14.5**

*The New Address List
dialog box provides a
form for entering
addresses in your new
data source.*

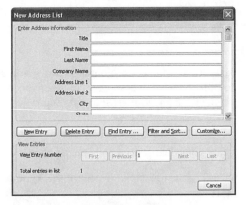

FIGURE **14.6**

*The Customize Address
List dialog box lets you
specify the exact fields
you want to use.*

5. To add a field you'd like to use, click the **Add** button.

6. In the Add Field dialog box that appears, type a name for your field and click the
   OK button (see Figure 14.7). In this example, Customer Since is added as a new
   field.

FIGURE 14.7

*You can add as many
fields as you like to
your data source.*

7. To change the order of the fields as they appear in the New Address List dialog
   box, click the field you want to move and then click the **Move Up** or **Move Down**
   button.

8. When you are done customizing your fields, click **OK**, and then continue with the
   next section. In Figure 14.8, several fields have been removed, and the Customer
   Since field has been added.

FIGURE 14.8

*When your list of fields
is customized to your
liking, continue with
the mail merge
process. Continue this
process by entering
records for the data
source in the section
that follows.*

Entering Records and Saving Your Data Source

In this phase, you enter the records in your data source. Luckily, you have to do this only
once—in the future, you can use the same data source with other main documents.
Before you start working through this section, gather together all of your names and
addresses so you have them in one place.

1. Enter the information for the first person in your list in the **New Address List** dialog box, using the **Tab** key to move from field to field (see Figure 14.9).

14

Figure 14.9

Enter your first address in the New Address List dialog box.

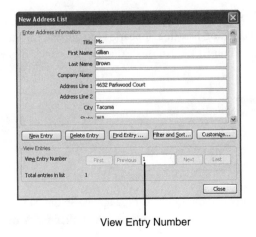

View Entry Number

2. When you are ready to add the next entry, click the **New Entry** button.

3. Word presents a set of blank fields to enable you to enter another person's address. The number in the **View Entry Number** text box lists the current record number.

4. Repeat steps 1 through 3 to enter all of the addresses in your list. Use the **First**, **Previous**, **Next**, and **Last** buttons if you need to review entries you've already typed.

5. To go to a particular record, type the number in the **View Entry Number** text box and press **Enter**. (The total number of records appears in the lower-left corner of the dialog box.)

6. When you've finished entering all the records, click the **Close** button.

7. The Save Address List dialog box opens and automatically navigates to the My Data Sources folder, which Word creates for you. (This folder is a handy place to store your data sources, although you can save them in another folder if you like.) Type a name for your data source in the **File Name** field (see Figure 14.10).

8. Click the **Save** button.

Continue this process by sorting and editing the data source for the merge document in the section that follows.

FIGURE 14.10

Use the Save Address List dialog box to specify a name and location for your data source.

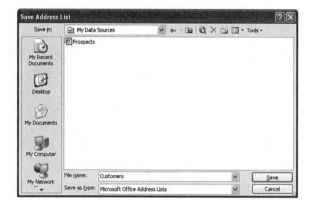

Sorting and Editing the Data Source

After you have entered all of the records in a data source (or opened an existing data source), Word gives you an opportunity to sort the list by any one of its fields or to remove people from the mail merge. (To sort by more than one field—for example, to sort by ZIP code, and then sort by last name within each ZIP code—use the method described in "Sorting Records in a Merge" later in this hour.)

To sort and edit your recipient list, follow the previous set of steps, and then continue with these:

1. After you've created and saved your data source, the Mail Merge Recipients dialog box opens (see Figure 14.11). Each row is one record, and the fields are arranged in columns across the top of the dialog box.

FIGURE 14.11

Use the Mail Merge Recipients dialog box to sort and edit your address list.

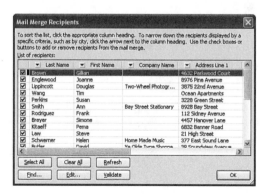

14

2. To sort the records by one particular field, click the gray column label. If you sort your list, Word remembers the sort order the next time you run the merge, and any new records you add are automatically sorted into the proper place in the list. (If

you want to sort by two or three fields instead, see "Sorting Records in a Merge" later in this hour.)

3. Clear the check boxes for any people you do not want included in the merge.

4. If you see any records that are incorrect, click the **Edit** button in the Mail Merge Recipients dialog box to display a dialog box where you can edit the record. (This dialog box looks like the New Address List dialog box shown in Figure 14.9 except for its title bar.) When you have made your changes, click the **Close** button in the dialog box to return to the Mail Merge Recipients dialog box.

5. When you are done, click **OK**.

6. In the Mail Merge task pane, click **Next: Write Your Letter.**

You are now ready to complete the merge document by adding text and inserting fields from the data source. This is completed in the section that follows.

Completing the Main Document

In this phase, you finish the main document. This entails typing and formatting the text (if you started your main document from scratch) and inserting the merge fields that tell Word where to insert the data from your data source.

Follow these steps to complete the main document:

1. You have reached step 4 of the wizard (Write Your Letter). Type and format the letter, leaving blank lines for the recipient's address block and the greeting line (see Figure 14.12).

FIGURE 14.12

Type and format your letter, leaving room for the merge fields.

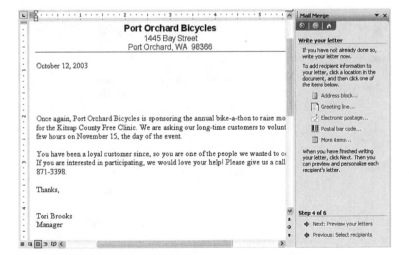

2. Place the insertion point on the blank line for the recipient's address block, and click **Address Block**.

3. In the Insert Address Block dialog box, make the desired selections to specify how the address block will look (see Figure 14.13). When the preview looks right, click **OK**.

FIGURE 14.13

Use the Insert Address Block dialog box to define how you want your address block to look.

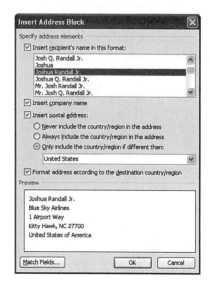

4. Word inserts the Address Block merge field in your document (see Figure 14.14). Click where you want to insert the greeting line, and then click **Greeting Line**.

Address Block merge field

FIGURE 14.14

Word inserts the Address Block merge field in your letter.

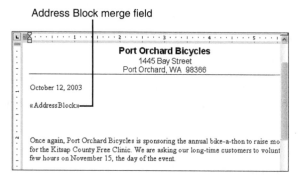

14

5. In the Greeting Line dialog box (see Figure 14.15), specify the appearance of your greeting line, and click **OK**.

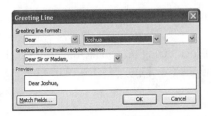

FIGURE 14.15

Use the Greeting Line dialog box to define how you want your greeting line to look.

6. The greeting line field is inserted. Use the remaining links under Write Your Letter in the Mail Merge task pane to insert any other fields you want to use. In Figure 14.16, a Customer Since field was inserted in the body of the letter using the More Items link.

FIGURE 14.16

Insert any additional links you like.

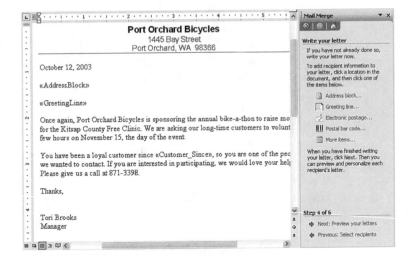

If you insert a merge field such as Address Block or Greeting Line and later want to revise the options you chose for that field, right-click the field in your document and choose Edit [merge field] to display the appropriate dialog box (the Insert Address Block or Insert Greeting Line dialog box, for example).

7. Save your main document. Then click **Next: Preview Your Letters** at the bottom of the task pane.

The next step in the process is to preview the merged letters in the section that follows.

Previewing Your Merged Letters

At this phase in the mail merge process, Word allows you to see what your letters will look like when they are merged. You can browse through the previewed letters, or use the Find feature to jump to a particular merged letter you want to view. In addition, you can exclude particular records from your merge. If you find problems when previewing the letters, you can fix them before you actually run the merge.

1. In step 5 of the wizard (Preview Your Letters), Word displays a preview of the first merged letter for you to examine. The merge fields are replaced with data from your data source (see Figure 14.17).

FIGURE 14.17

The merge fields are replaced with actual data from your data source.

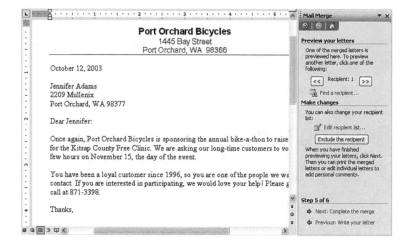

2. Click the chevron arrow buttons in the Mail Merge task pane to view your letters one by one. If you see any letter that you want to exclude from the mail merge, click the **Exclude This Recipient** button.

3. Click **Find a Recipient** if there is a particular person whose merged information you want to review.

4. In the Find Entry dialog box (see Figure 14.18), enter the contents of a field. (If you know which field the text is in, select the field in the **This Field** list to speed the search.) Click **Find Next**. When you are finished searching for particular recipients, click **Cancel**.

5. If you see incorrect data in one of your letters or want to change the sort order, click **Edit Recipient List** to display the Mail Merge Recipients dialog box. Make any changes in this dialog box (refer to "Sorting and Editing the Data Source" earlier in this hour). When you're done, click **OK**.

14

FIGURE 14.18

The Find Entry dialog box lets you quickly locate a particular letter.

If you see the same problem in every letter—for example, a field is in the wrong location, or the letter contains a typo—go back to step 4 of the wizard (Write Your Letter), fix the main document, and then return to this step.

6. When you are finished previewing your letters, click **Next: Complete the Merge** at the bottom of the task pane.

You are now ready to produce the final merged documents in the section that follows.

Running the Merge

In this final phase of the mail merge process, you merge the main document with the data source to produce your form letters. In these steps, you can choose to print the merge letters as they are merged without displaying them onscreen (steps 1 through 4), or merge all of them to a new document so that you can make any further edits before printing (steps 5 through 8).

Usually, there's usually no need to save the letters you generate in a mail merge, because you can always merge the same main document and data source to regenerate them.

1. In step 6 of the wizard (Complete the Merge), click the **Print** link if you are sure that all of your letters are ready to be printed. They will be sent to the printer without appearing onscreen.

The Print option is a good option to use if your data source contains hundreds of addresses. The document containing all of your merged letters would be hundreds of pages long (or more if your form letter is more than one page long), and if your computer is short on memory, it may balk at the task of displaying this document onscreen.

2. In the Merge to Printer dialog box that appears, mark the **All** option button if you want to print all of your records (see Figure 14.19).

FIGURE 14.19

Use the Merge to Printer dialog box if you want to send all of your merged letters directly to the printer without displaying them onscreen.

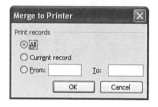

3. If you only want to print the letter that's onscreen now, mark the **Current Record** option.

4. If you want to print a particular set of letters, enter the beginning and ending record numbers in the **From** and **To** boxes. Then click **OK** to merge the letters and send them to the printer.

5. To instead create a document containing the merged letters and display it onscreen, click **Edit Individual Letters**.

6. The Merge to New Document dialog box appears with options exactly like the Merge to Printer dialog box (see Figure 14.20). When you've made your selections, click **OK**.

FIGURE 14.20

Use the Merge to New Document dialog box if you want to see your merged letters on screen and optionally edit them before printing.

7. Word performs the merge and displays the merged letters onscreen in a document titled *Letters1* (see Figure 14.21). The letters print on separate pages because Word separates them with next-page section breaks. (If your main document is a multiple-page letter, the section break comes at the bottom of the last page of each letter.) The document shown in Figure 14.21 is 26 pages long because it contains a one-page letter for each of the 26 people in the data source.

14

FIGURE **14.21**

*Use the Merge to New
Document dialog box
if you want to see
your merged letters on
screen and optionally
edit them before
printing.*

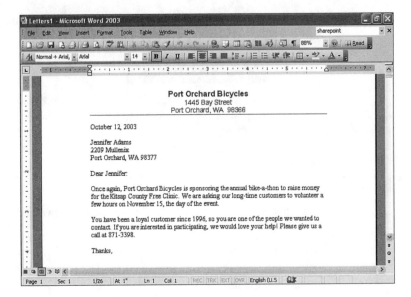

8. Edit any letters that need fine-tuning, and then click the **Print** button on the
   Standard toolbar to print the letters.

9. Close the Letters1 document. Assuming you didn't do extensive editing in the previous step that you want to save, you don't need to save the merged letters because
   you can always run the merge again.

That's it! Everything else you can do with mail merge builds on the procedure you've
just completed.

Merging Envelopes and Labels

Chances are that you usually need to print labels or envelopes to go with your form letters. When you merge addresses onto labels or envelopes, the six basic steps of the Mail
Merge wizard stay the same. However, you will see different options as you run through
the wizard that are specific to envelopes or labels as opposed to letters.

Merging Envelopes

Because the general steps for merging envelopes are the same as for merging letters,
you'll find it helpful to practice a few mail merges with letters before proceeding with
this section and the next. Also note that this section assumes you already have a data
source, so you'll open an existing one rather than creating a new one.

If you have an envelope tray on your printer that holds a stack of envelopes, it will be much simpler for you to print a merge file for envelopes. To print a merge file of envelopes without an envelope tray, you have to feed each envelope manually.

To merge your envelopes, follow these steps:

1. Start a new, blank document and save it with a name that ends with *Main* to remind you that it's a main document used in mail merges.

2. Choose **Tools, Letters and Mailings, Mail Merge** to display the Mail Merge task pane.

3. Click **Envelopes** in the Mail Merge task pane (refer to Figure 14.1), and then click **Next: Starting Document** at the bottom of the task pane.

4. Keep **Change Document Layout** marked in the task pane, and click the **Envelope Options** link.

5. In the Envelope Options tab of the Envelope Options dialog box (see Figure 14.22), choose a different envelope size if desired (the default is a standard business envelope).

FIGURE 14.22

Use the Envelope Options dialog box to specify the style of envelopes you are using.

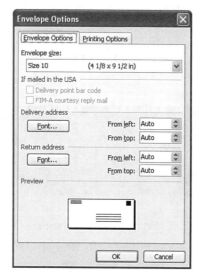

6. Click the **Printing Options** tab, make any changes and click **OK**.

7. Your document is reformatted as an envelope, and a return address appears if you have one in the User Information tab of the Options dialog box (Tools, Options). If

14

no return address appears, type it on your envelope now. (You might want to increase the Zoom setting on the Standard toolbar to see what you type more clearly.) You can also add it to the User Information tab so you don't have to type it again in the future. Then click **Next: Select Recipients**.

> If you have preprinted return addresses on your envelopes, just select the return address if one appears and delete it.

8. Leave **Use an Existing List** marked, and click **Browse**. In the **Select Data Source** dialog box, navigate to and select your data source, and click **Open**.

9. The Mail Merge Recipient dialog box appears. Sort and edit your address list (see "Sorting and Editing the Data Source" earlier in this hour), and then click **OK**.

10. Click **Next: Arrange Your Envelope** at the bottom of the task pane.

11. Click in the area of the envelope where the recipient's address will be printed. The text box in which the address block will go will become visible, and your insertion point will appear inside of it (see Figure 14.23).

FIGURE 14.23

Click roughly in the middle of the envelope to activate the text box in which the address block will appear.

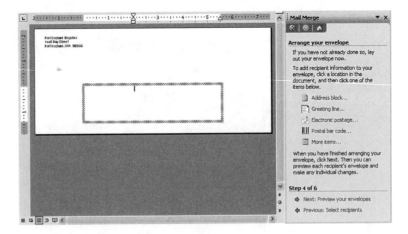

12. Click the **Address Block** link in the task pane. Make the desired selections in the Insert Address Block dialog box that appears, and click **OK**. The Address Block field is inserted in your envelope.

13. If you want to change the look of the text, select the Address Block field on your envelope and apply whatever font or paragraph formatting you like to it, using the standard methods. (The merged addresses will take on the formatting of the

Address Block field.) If the text is too small to see clearly, increase the Zoom setting on the Standard toolbar.

> If you want to use the Electronic Postage link (see Figure 14.23), you must first install electronic postage software. If you click this link, Word presents a dialog box asking if you want to visit Microsoft's Web site to find out about this type of software. You can use the Postal Bar Code link to insert the postal bar code. (Word determines what the code will be based on the ZIP code and street address of each address in your recipient list.)

14. Save your main document, click the **Next: Preview Your Envelopes** link, and then follow the same steps as those described in "Previewing Your Merged Letters" and "Running the Merge" earlier in this hour. If you merge to a new document, the merged envelopes will be called *Envelopes1* (or *Envelopes2* and so on, depending on how many other merges you have completed in this Word session).

Merging Labels

As with merging envelopes, it's easiest to merge labels if you practice a few mail merges with form letters first. And remember that this section assumes that you already have a data source, so you'll open an existing one rather than creating a new one.

Follow these steps to merge labels:

1. Start a new, blank document and save it with a name that ends with *Main* to remind you that it's a main document used in mail merges.

2. Choose **Tools, Letters and Mailings, Mail Merge** to display the Mail Merge task pane.

3. Click **Labels** in the Mail Merge task pane, and then **Next: Starting Document** at the bottom of the task pane

4. Keep **Change Document Layout** marked, and click **Label Options**. Select the product number for your labels, and click **OK**.

> If you are not using Avery labels, display the Label products drop-down list in the Label Options dialog box and look for the product line that includes your labels. When you select a different product, the Product number list updates to reflect that company's labels. If you still can't find your labels, click the New Label button, manually enter your label's measurements, and click OK.

14

6. Your document is reformatted as a sheet of labels. Click **Next: Select Recipients**.

> Word uses its table feature to format labels. The gridlines that divide the rows and columns of a table can be visible onscreen or hidden. If they are hidden, you won't see much of a change in the appearance of your document in step 6. To bring the gridlines into view, choose Table, Show Gridlines.

7. Leave **Use an Existing List** marked, and click **Browse**. Then select your data source in the **Select Data Source** dialog box, and click **Open**.

8. The **Mail Merge Recipient** dialog box appears. Sort and edit your address list (see "Sorting and Editing the Recipient List" earlier in this hour), and then click **OK**.

9. Click **Next: Arrange Your Labels** at the bottom of the task pane.

10. The insertion point appears in the upper-left label where your address block field should go, and Next Record merge fields appear in all of the other labels (see Figure 14.24). Click the **Address Block** link in the task pane**.**

FIGURE 14.24
Your insertion point appears in the upper-left label, where you need to insert the Address Block field.

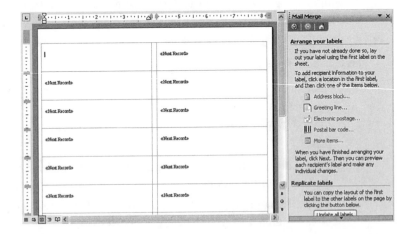

11. Make the desired selections in the Insert Address Block dialog box, and click **OK**.

12. The Address Block merge field is inserted in the upper-left label on your sheet of labels. At this point you can select the field and apply whatever font or paragraph formatting you like to it, using the standard methods. (The merged addresses will take on the formatting of the Address Block field.) If the text is too small to see clearly, increase the Zoom setting in the Standard toolbar.

13. Click the **Update All Labels** button near the bottom of the task pane to copy the Address Block field from the upper-left label to the remaining labels on the page. (It will appear immediately after the Next Record field in each label.)

14. Save your main document, click the **Next: Preview Your Labels** link, and then follow the same steps as those described in "Previewing Your Merged Letters" and "Running the Merge" earlier in this hour. If you merge to a new document, the merged labels will be called *Labels1*.

If you haven't printed on the particular labels you're using before, you might want to merge to a new document, and then print only one page of labels first to check how the addresses line up on the labels. If you need to adjust their position, see the "Q&A" section at the end of this hour.

Creating a Directory Using the Merge Feature

In step 1 of the Mail Merge Wizard (Select Document Type), you choose the type of main document you want to create. In addition to letters, envelopes, and labels, you can also choose to create a *directory*. A directory is different from a letter in that it places information from multiple records in your data source on the same page. This type of main document is very useful for printing a nicely formatted list of the names and addresses in your data source. Depending on the kinds of information you have in your data source, you might also use it to print a phone list, a catalog, a list of people and their job titles and occupations, and so on. Figure 14.25 shows a merged directory of names and addresses.

FIGURE 14.25

The directory main document is quite handy for simply printing out the records in your data source.

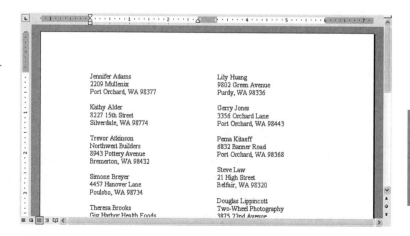

14

The steps for performing a directory mail merge are quite similar to the ones you've already practiced for letters, envelopes, and labels; here are some tips to keep in mind before you get started.

- In step 4 of the wizard (Arrange Your Directory), you may want to format your document into multiple columns or into a table. (The directory shown in Figure 14.25 uses a two-column format.) A table is useful for placing labels to the left of the pieces of information in each record. Figure 14.26 shows a directory created using a table (the table borders are hidden). You will learn how to create columns and tables in Hour 15.

FIGURE 14.26

You can place the merge fields in a table if you want to label the information.

- In step 4 of the wizard, you only need to insert merge fields for one person. Word automatically repeats the set of fields for each person in your database. Figure 14.27 shows the main document that produced the directory shown in Figure 14.25. You can tell that the document is formatted to display text in two columns by looking at the ruler along the top of the text area.

FIGURE 14.27

This simple main document is all you need to generate a directory of names and addresses.

Figure 14.28 shows the main document that produced the directory shown in Figure 14.26.

- If you use the columns feature and don't want an individual person's information to be split across columns, select the set of fields in your main document in step 4 of the wizard and choose **Format, Paragraph**. In the Paragraph dialog box, click the **Line and Page Breaks** tab, and mark the **Keep Lines Together** and **Keep with**

Next check boxes. Also, you'll probably want to add a blank line after the merge fields (or a blank row if you're using a table) to separate each person's information.

FIGURE 14.28

This main document uses a table to label the individual pieces of information in the directory.

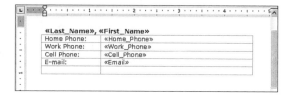

- When you enter your merge fields in step 4 of the wizard, you may want to insert individual pieces of the Address Block field (such as First Name, Last Name, and so on) individually. To do this, use the More Items link in the task pane. (This method was used for the main document shown in Figure 14.26.)

- When you merge to a table, you may see table borders and want to remove them. To do so, select the table (Table, Select, Table), and choose Format, Borders and Shading. Click the Borders tab, click None, and click OK. If you do this, you might want to choose Table, Show Gridlines to display nonprinting gridlines in your table.

- In step 5 of the wizard (Preview Your Directory), you will still only see one person's information. You won't see multiple records on the same page until you actually run the merge.

- The option to send the merged document directly to the printer is not available for a directory. You must merge to a new document first, and then print it as you would any other document in Word.

Merging E-mail Messages

The final type of main document you can create is e-mail messages. As with the directory main documents, the process of merging e-mail messages is quite similar to merging letters, envelopes, and labels. Here are two points to keep in mind:

- If you use Outlook for e-mail, you can select an Outlook contacts folder to use for your data source in step 3 of the wizard (Select Recipients). However, you cannot edit the recipient information from the Mail Merge Recipients dialog box; you must edit it in Outlook. (If you don't use Outlook for e-mail, just make sure your data source includes a field for the recipient's e-mail address.)

14

- In step 6 of the wizard (Complete the Merge), you will click the Electronic Mail link instead of a link to merge to the printer or a new document. This link displays the Merge to E-mail dialog box. In this dialog box, use the To drop-down list to choose the field from your data source that contains the recipient's e-mail address. Use the Subject Line text box to type the subject of your e-mail message. Use the Mail Format drop-down list to indicate whether you want to send the document as a plain text or HTML e-mail message, or as a Word document attachment to an e-mail message.

Sorting Records in a Merge

You can sort your records by one particular field by clicking the column heading button for the desired field in the Mail Merge Recipients dialog box (see step 2 in "Sorting and Editing the Data Source" earlier in this hour). However, there may be times when a more complex sort is in order. Let's say, for example, that you want to sort your records in ZIP code order, within ZIP code by last name, and within last name by first name. Word lets you sort your data source on up to three fields, but you need to do so in the Filter and Sort dialog box, as described in these steps:

1. If you're creating a new data source for your mail merge, stop when you have finished entering new addresses in the New Address List dialog box (see "Entering Records and Saving Your Data Source" earlier in this hour), and skip to step 3.

2. If you're using an existing data source for your mail merge, when you reach the step where the Mail Merge Recipients dialog box appears, click the **Edit** button. A dialog box that looks exactly like the New Address List dialog box appears (see Figure 14.29). The dialog box title bar displays the path and filename of your data source.

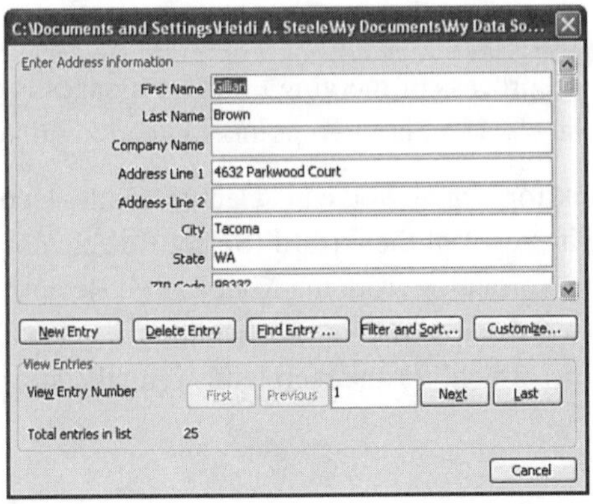

FIGURE 14.29

This dialog box is identical to the New Address List dialog box, except for the title bar.

3. Click the **Filter and Sort** button to display the Filter and Sort dialog box, and click the **Sort Records** tab if it isn't already in front.

4. Display the **Sort By** list, and click the field you want to use for the sort. To further refine the sort, display the first **Then By** list, and select the field you want to sort on when Word finds more than one record containing the same value in the first sort field. Then use the second **Then By** list to define a third field to sort on. In the example shown in Figure 14.30, Word will sort all the records by city, within the same city by last name, and within the same last name by first name. When you've defined the sort order, click the **OK** button to return to the previous dialog box.

FIGURE 14.30

Use the Sort Records tab to define up to three levels on which to sort your records.

Your records will now be sorted in the order you specified. Continue with the mail merge process to run the merge.

> The options you set in the Filter and Sort dialog box remain in effect until you clear them. So if you establish a particular sort order and then add records to the data source, Word automatically sorts the new records into the existing sort order when you next run a merge. To clear the sort order so that new records are not automatically sorted, display the Filter and Sort dialog box and click the Clear All button in the Sort tab. (A sort order that you set in the Mail Merge Recipients dialog box is automatically entered in the Filter and Sort dialog box, so you can clear it there as well.)

Filtering Records in a Merge

At times you may want to print form letters, labels, or envelopes for some of the people in your data source, but not others. If you want to send a form letter to clients who live in Seattle, for example, you can tell Word to merge only those addresses that contain *Seattle* in the City field. You indicate which group of records you want to merge by defining a *filter*.

14

Follow these steps to merge only some of the records in your data source:

1. If you're creating a new data source for your mail merge, stop when you have finished entering new addresses in the New Address List dialog box (see "Entering Records and Saving Your Data Source" earlier in this hour), and skip to step 3.

2. If you're using an existing data source for your mail merge, when you reach the step where the Mail Merge Recipients dialog box appears, click the **Edit** button. A dialog box that looks exactly like the New Address List dialog box except for its title bar appears. The dialog box title bar displays the path and filename of your data source.

3. Click the **Filter and Sort** button to display the Filter and Sort dialog box, and click the **Filter Records** tab if it isn't already in front.

4. Display the first **Field** list, and click the field that you want to use to filter the records.

5. If necessary, display the list of choices under **Comparison**. If you want to look for records that contain one particular value in a field (*94367* in the ZIP Code field or *Port Orchard* in the City field, for example), you can leave this option set to Equal To.

> Many of the choices in the Comparison list are useful only for number or date fields. For example, if you have a Salary field and you want to send a letter to only those employees who earn more than a particular amount, you would first select the Salary field in step 4. Then select Greater Than in the Comparison list, and type the cut-off salary in the Compare To box.

6. In the **Compare To** box, enter the value you are looking for. In Figure 14.31, Word will merge only records that contain *Port Orchard* in the City field. Click the **OK** button to return to the previous dialog box.

Your records will now be filtered with the rules that you defined. Continue with the mail merge process to run the merge.

> If you like, you can use additional rows in the Filter tab of the Filter and Sort dialog box to set up a more complex filter. You have to connect multiple rules by selecting *And* or *Or* from the list at the left edge of the dialog box. (The *And* operator will include only those records for which *both* rules connected by the *And* operator are true. The *Or* operator will include any record for which *at least one* of the two rules connected by the *Or* operator is true.)

FIGURE 14.31
Define your filter in the Filter Records tab.

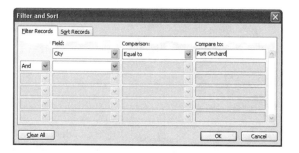

Opening a Main Document Whose Data Source Has Filter and/or Sort Options Set

Remember that filter and sort options remain in effect until you clear them. (This is true whether you set the options in the Mail Merge Recipients dialog box or in the Filter and Sort dialog box.) It is especially important to remember this fact if you've set filter options, because until you clear the options (by clicking the Clear All button in the Filter tab of the Filter and Sort dialog box), you won't be able to merge all the records. When you open a main document that uses the data source, Word displays a rather cryptic message like the one shown in Figure 14.32 to remind you that filter and/or sort options have been set. Click Yes to open the data source with the filter and/or sort options still in effect. Click No to open the data source with all of the filter and/or sort information cleared.

FIGURE 14.32
Word informs you that the data source you're opening has filter and/or sort options set.

Running Future Merges

When you want to run a merge using the same main document in the future, just open the main document with the usual File, Open command, and display the Mail Merge task pane (Tools, Letters and Mailings, Mail Merge). The Mail Merge Wizard begins at the third step (in which you specify your recipient list), and the data source you used with this main document the last time is listed under Use an Existing List (see Figure 14.33).

14

FIGURE **14.33**

When you use the same main document for a future mail merge, Word remembers which data source you used.

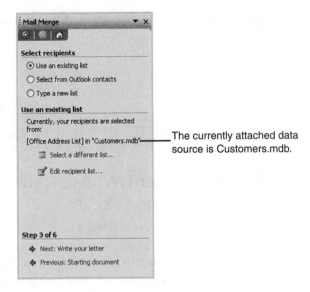

The currently attached data source is Customers.mdb.

If you want to keep the same data source, just continue through the wizard. Edit the main document if needed, preview your merged documents, and run the merge. (Make sure to save the main document if you make changes to it.)

To use a different data source, click Select a Different List to display the Select Data Source dialog box. Navigate to and select your data source, click Open, and then continue with the wizard.

If you attach a data source that has different field names than the ones referenced in the merge fields in your main document, the Invalid Merge Field dialog box will appear when you preview your merged documents. This dialog box gives you options for removing merge fields from your main document that don't exist in your data source, or choosing fields in the data source to use for merge fields in your main document (even if they have different names).

If you accidentally used the wrong document for your main document and want to restore it to a normal Word document, choose Tools, Letters and Mailings, Show Mail Merge Toolbar. Click the Main Document Setup button on the Mail Merge toolbar, choose Normal Word document in the Main Document Type dialog box, and click OK.

Summary

You should now have a good overall feel for how to run a merge, although it will probably take a little practice to feel completely comfortable with the process. If you veer off the beaten path and get perplexed, come back to the procedure described here to solidify your understanding of the basic steps.

Q&A

Q I put a merge field in the wrong place in my main document. How do I get rid of it?

A Delete a merge field just as you delete all other fields: Select it and press the Delete key.

Q I used the Print link in the Mail Merge task pane to merge a data source with hundreds of records, only to realize that the main document contained a typo. I wasted more paper than I want to admit before I managed to delete the print job. How can I avoid this in the future?

A One option if you're planning to use the Print link to print a large number of letters is to specify in the Merge to Printer dialog box that you only want to print the first five records or so. If those documents look good, use the Merge to Printer option to print the remainder of the records.

Q The addresses on my merged labels are printing too close to the left edge of each label, and I want to adjust their vertical position as well. How can I do this?

A The easiest way to move the addresses in from the left is to increase the left indentation of your labels. Open the main document (your page of labels), choose Table, Select, Table to select the entire table, and then choose Format, Paragraph, and click the Indents and Spacing tab. Increase the setting in the Left text box, and click OK. To adjust the vertical position of the addresses on each label, select the entire table again, and choose Table, Table Properties. In the Table Properties dialog box, click the Cell tab. You can choose Top, Center, or Bottom to change the vertical alignment of each address within each cell. Or, if you just need to move the addresses down a little, click the Options button in the Cell tab. In the Cell Options dialog box, increase the value in the Top text box, and click OK twice.

Q I miss the Mail Merge toolbar that I used in previous versions of Word. Is it still available?

A Yes. If you would rather use the Mail Merge toolbar instead of the Mail Merge task pane, choose View, Toolbars, Mail Merge. The toolbar buttons give you access to all of the key mail merge tasks.

14

Q **I'm using an Access table for my data source. If I want to sort my merged documents, do I sort the records in Access or follow the steps under "Sorting Records in a Merge"?**

A If you're using an Access table, it's easiest to sort the records in Access before running the merge in Word, but either way works.

Q **Can I use an Access query as my data source instead of filtering the records in Word?**

A Yes. When you select an Access database (an .mdb file) that contains multiple tables and/or queries in the Open Data Source dialog box and click Open, Word displays the Select Table dialog box to enable you to select the table or query in the database that you want to use as your data source. (Word refers to Access queries as *views.*)

PART IV

Adding Columns, Tables, and Images

Hour

HOUR 15

Columns and Tables

You already know all the basic formatting techniques, and now you're ready to add some flair to your documents. In this hour, you learn how to format text in columns and tables. Then in the following two hours, you get the rundown on graphics. If you combine the skills you learn in these three hours, you will be equipped to produce anything from professional reports to eye-catching flyers and brochures.

The highlights of this hour include

- Creating columns
- Modifying columns
- Creating tables
- Typing, navigating, and selecting in tables
- Changing the structure of a table
- Formatting a table
- Sorting text within a table

Creating Columns

If you plan to produce newsletters, bulletins, journal articles, and so on with relatively simple formatting, you'll appreciate Word's capability to format text in multiple columns. When you use this feature, the text snakes from column to column (see Figure 15.1). After you've formatted your text in columns, changing the number of columns is a breeze. (For highly formatted documents that use columns, you will probably want to use a layout program such as Publisher, which comes with several editions of Microsoft Office 2003.)

FIGURE 15.1

This document is formatted in two columns.

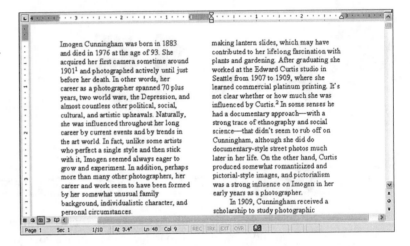

Columns fall into the page formatting category. As with other page formatting, columns apply to your entire document unless you insert *section breaks* around the text that you want in columns. For example, you might do this if you want a title above the columns that is centered in the middle of the page (see Figure 15.2). To do this, you need to insert a continuous section break between the title and the remainder of the document.

Column Width Marker

FIGURE 15.2

A continuous section break separates the title from the rest of the text.

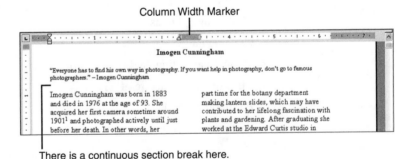

There is a continuous section break here.

You can then leave the default (single) column formatting in the first section, and apply two or more columns to the rest of the text. If you need help with section breaks, see the section "Varying the Page Formatting in Your Document" in Hour 8, "Formatting Pages."

Follow these steps to format your text in columns:

1. Make sure you're using Print Layout view (choose **View**, **Print Layout**). Columns don't display accurately in Normal view.

2. If you have inserted section breaks, make sure your insertion point is in the section where you want to apply the columns. If you're applying columns to the entire document, your insertion point can be anywhere in the document.

3. Click the **Columns** button on the Formatting toolbar, and click the number of columns that you want in the grid that drops down (see Figure 15.3).

15

Columns

FIGURE 15.3

Click the number of columns that you want in the grid attached to the Columns button in the Formatting toolbar.

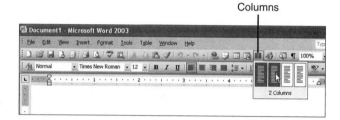

Word creates the number of columns that you specified. If you decide to change the number of columns in your document, follow these steps again. To remove columns, click the leftmost column in the grid in step 3.

If you want your entire document formatted in columns and your document does not already include section breaks, you can simply click anywhere in your document, choose Format, Columns, click the number of columns you want under Presets, and click OK. If you want some but not all of your document formatted in columns, it is also possible to select the text that you want formatted in columns first and then define your columns in the Columns dialog box. Word will insert section breaks around the selected text for you. If you use this approach, however, Word may not insert the type of section breaks around your selected text that you wanted. If it inserted next-page section breaks and you wanted continuous ones, or vice versa, you need to switch to Normal view, delete the breaks, and insert the ones you want.

Improving the Appearance of Text in Columns

In addition to the standard font and paragraph formatting you learned about in Hour 6, "Formatting Characters," and Hour 7, "Formatting Paragraphs," Word gives you a few other choices for formatting text in multiple columns.

Follow these steps if your columns need to be a specific width or if you want to add a vertical line between the columns:

1. Click anywhere in the multiple-column text, and choose **Format**, **Columns** to display the Columns dialog box (see Figure 15.4).

FIGURE 15.4

You can make changes to your column formatting in the Columns dialog box.

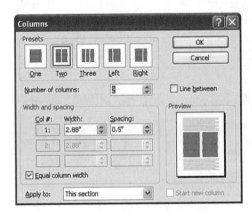

2. If you see a format under Presets at the top of the dialog box that matches what you want, click it.

3. If you have specific requirements for column widths, first clear the **Equal Column Width** check box. Then enter the desired settings for each column under **Width** and **Spacing**. (*Spacing* refers to the amount of space between columns.)

4. To add vertical lines between your columns, mark the **Line Between** check box.

5. When you have made all your selections, click **OK**.

> To quickly adjust column width, drag the Column Width marker (see Figure 15.2). If you want to see the precise widths of the columns, hold down the Alt key as you drag.

Columns sometimes look better if the text is justified so that it has a straight right edge. If you do justify your text, it will probably look best if you hyphenate it as well to reduce gaps between words. To apply hyphenation, choose Tools, Language, Hyphenation, mark the Automatically Hyphenate Document check box, and click OK.

If you need to force a column to break in a particular place, move the insertion point there, choose Insert, Break, mark the Column Break option button, and click OK. Word shifts the text beneath the break to the top of the next column.

To balance the length of your columns on the last page of a document, insert a continuous section break at the very end of the document. Press Ctrl+End to move to the end of the document, choose Insert, Break, mark the Continuous option button, and click OK.

15

Creating Tables

Word's table feature gives you a wonderfully flexible way of aligning text in a grid of rows and columns. You enter text into the individual boxes in the grid, which are referred to as *cells*. The text in each cell wraps independently of the text in neighboring cells. This makes it possible to format and edit documents in which certain blocks of text have to be aligned alongside one another. You can create a table that looks table-ish, like the one shown in Figure 15.5.

FIGURE 15.5

This table doesn't disguise its true nature.

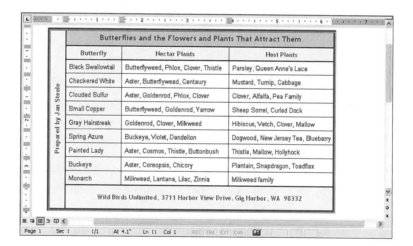

But you can also create tables that are "invisible" by hiding the gridlines between cells. The résumé shown in Figure 15.6 is actually typed in a table, but the gridlines have been hidden so that it's not obvious.

Word gives you two methods for creating tables. With the standard method, you tell Word to create a table with a particular number of rows and columns, and then revise it from there. With the second method, you "draw" the table with your mouse. The first method is a little faster and you have the option of setting AutoFit options, but the second is better for creating a more complex table such as the one shown earlier in Figure 15.5.

FIGURE **15.6**

Tables don't have to look as if they belong in a scientific paper.

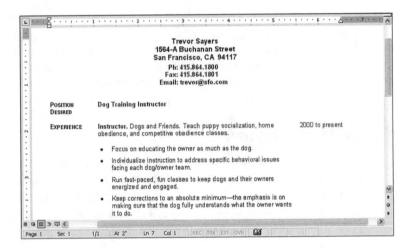

Using the Standard Method

create a table using the standard method, you can either use the Insert Table button on the Standard toolbar or the Insert Table dialog box; the end result is the same. The one catch to using the Insert Table toolbar button is that you can start with a table that's no more than five columns wide by four rows tall. This is a minor limitation, however, because you can add rows and columns later on.

In these steps, you use the Insert Table toolbar button, which is the faster of the two techniques:

1. Move the insertion point to the place where you want to insert the table.

2. Click the **Insert Table** button on the Standard toolbar.

3. The squares in the grid that drops down represent cells. Drag through the approximate number of rows and columns that you want (see Figure 15.7), and then release the mouse button.

A table appears in your document (see Figure 15.8). When the Show/Hide ¶ setting is turned on, as it is in Figure 15.8, an *end of cell marker* appears in each cell. When you type text in a table cell, it will be inserted to the left of the marker. To change the number of rows and columns in your table, see "Adding and Deleting Rows and Columns" later in this hour.

Insert Table

FIGURE 15.7
Drag through the number of rows and columns that you want to start with.

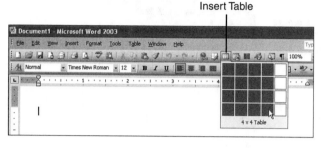

FIGURE 15.8
A blank table is inserted in your document.

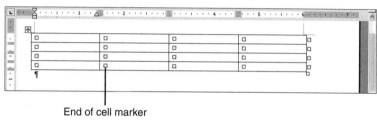

End of cell marker

> If you start a table at the very top of a document and then decide that you want to insert text above the table, click at the far-left edge of the upper-left cell in the table and press Enter. Word inserts a blank line above the table; you can now click in the blank line and type your text. (If the table isn't at the top of the document, pressing Enter adds a blank line to the cell.)

There are advantages to using the Insert Table dialog box instead of the Insert Table toolbar button. The Insert Table dialog box has AutoFit options that let you control how Word adjusts column widths in the table. It also provides access to the AutoFormat feature (which you'll learn about later in this hour), which enables you to tell Word to "remember" the settings you choose for new tables. To see these options, choose Table, Insert, Table. The dialog box shown in Figure 15.9 appears.

You specify the number of columns and rows you'd like to start with under Table Size at the top of the dialog box. Under AutoFit Behavior, select one of these options:

- Fixed Column Width—When this option is set to Auto (the default choice), the table starts with columns of equal width, and it fills the space between the left and right margins. If you know the exact width you'd like your columns to be (in inches), enter that amount in the text box.

FIGURE 15.9
The Insert Table dialog box contains AutoFit options for controlling column width.

- AutoFit to Contents—The column widths automatically expand to fit the text you type. Word does not permit the overall table width to exceed the left and right margins of the page, so it wraps text within columns and narrows columns as necessary to prevent this from happening. (Even if you use this option, however, you can still widen a table to the point that it does not fit on the page if you widen the columns manually. You'll learn how to adjust column width later in this hour.)

- AutoFit to Window—This option is only useful if you're creating a document (either a Word document or a Web page) that will be displayed in a browser window. Choosing this option will permit the table to resize so that as the user resizes the browser window, the full width of the table is always visible.

If you don't choose an AutoFit option now, you can always select one using the Table, AutoFit command after you've inserted your table in the document.

To ask Word to remember all of your selections in the Insert Table dialog box (except for any AutoFormat option you choose) the next time you create a table using the Insert Table dialog box, mark the check box labeled Remember Dimensions for New Tables. Marking this check box does not affect the tables that you create with the Insert Table toolbar button.

Drawing a Table

To draw a table, you use the Draw Table button on the Tables and Borders toolbar. (You can't use this tool in Normal view. If you click it in Normal view, Word automatically switches to Print Layout view.) Although you can start by drawing a single cell and then add on, it's usually more straightforward to draw the outline of a table and then fill in the rows and columns. This method of creating a table is extremely flexible; if you can envision a design for your table, you can almost certainly create it.

To draw a table, follow these steps:

1. Click the **Tables and Borders** button on the Standard toolbar (see Figure 15.10) to display the Tables and Borders toolbar. (If you weren't already using Print Layout view, Word switches to it automatically.)

Table and Borders

FIGURE 15.10

Click the Tables and Borders toolbar button to display the Tables and Borders toolbar.

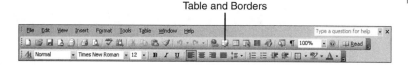

2. Click the **Draw Table** button if it isn't already selected (highlighted). Your mouse pointer now looks like a small pencil when it's over your document.

3. Display the **Line Style** list and choose a line style for the outside border of your table.

4. Display the **Line Weight** list and choose a line weight for the outside border of your table.

5. Click the **Border Color** button and click a color for the outside border of your table in the drop-down palette.

6. Starting in the upper-left corner, drag diagonally down and to the right, releasing the mouse button when the outline is the right size (see Figure 15.11). Word creates the outside border of your table.

Eraser   Line Weight

Draw   Line
Table   Style   Border Color

FIGURE 15.11

Drag until the outline of your table is approximately the right size.

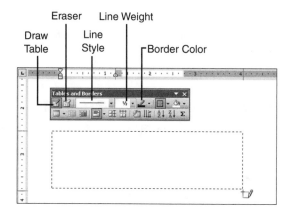

7. Now repeat steps 3–5 to choose what kind of inside lines you want, and draw them with the **Draw Table** tool (see Figure 15.12). If you want to remove a line, click the **Eraser** toolbar button and then draw over the line. When you release the mouse button, the line disappears. (Don't worry if your rows or columns are not even now. You'll learn how to fix that later in this hour.)

FIGURE 15.12

Draw the inside lines in your table.

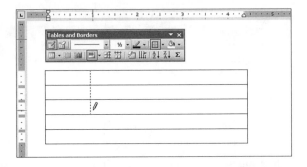

You can draw lines to divide up the inside of the table however you like. You are not restricted to a standard grid. You can create cells of different sizes depending on what you're using the table for. Word even lets you draw diagonal lines.

8. Click the **Draw Table** button to turn it off, and enter the text in the table (see the next section).

If you inserted a table accidentally and want to start over, make sure that the insertion point is in the table, and choose Table, Delete, Table.

Typing, Navigating, and Selecting in a Table

Typing, navigating, and selecting in a table works much as you might expect, with a few twists.

Typing Text in a Table

When you type text in a cell, if the entry is too wide to fit in the cell, Word automatically wraps the text to the next line and increases the row height. In Figure 15.13, the text was allowed to wrap within cells, and the row height adjusted accordingly.

FIGURE 15.13

Unlike a spreadsheet program, Word wraps text in cells automatically.

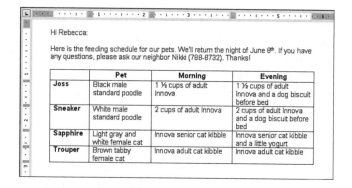

Pressing Enter in a cell ends the paragraph and adds a blank line to that row. (If you accidentally press Enter, press Backspace to remove the blank line.)

> If you want to insert a tab within a cell, press Ctrl+Tab instead of Tab. (Pressing the Tab key by itself just selects the contents of the cell to the right.)

Navigating in a Table

Navigating in a table with the mouse is just a matter of clicking in the cell you want to move to. To navigate with the keyboard, refer to Table 15.1.

TABLE 15.1   Keyboard Techniques for Moving the Insertion Point in a Table

Navigation Technique	Moves the Insertion Point
↓	Down one row.
↑	Up one row.
→	One cell to the right, or character by character to the right if the cell contains text.
←	One cell to the left, or character by character to the left if the cell contains text.
Tab	One cell to the right; if the cell to the right contains text, it will be selected. If you press Tab when the insertion point is in the last (lower-right) cell in the table, Word adds a new row to the bottom of the table.
Shift+Tab	One cell to the left; if the cell to the left contains text, it will be selected.

Selecting Parts of a Table

Selecting is a big deal in a table. In many cases, you have to select the part of the table that you want to affect before issuing a command. For this reason, it's worth taking a few moments to practice the various selection techniques outlined in Table 15.2. Before you do, check to make sure the Draw Table and Eraser buttons in the Tables and Borders toolbar are turned off.

TABLE 15.2 Selection Shortcuts in a Table

Amount Selected	Technique
One cell	Point just inside the left edge of the cell. When the mouse pointer becomes a black arrow (see Figure 15.14), click once.
A group of cells	Select the first cell and then drag over the additional adjacent cells.
One row	Rest the mouse pointer outside the left border of the table—it should be a white arrow angled toward the table, as shown in Figure 15.15. Click once. (If you've increased the row height or you drew your table, only the top of each cell in the row becomes highlighted. Don't worry; the row is selected.)
Multiple rows	Select the first row and then drag straight up or down to add rows to the selection.
One column	Rest the mouse pointer on the top border of the column. When it changes to a small downward-pointing arrow (see Figure 15.16), click once. You can also Shift+right-click anywhere in the column.
Multiple columns	Select the first column and then continue dragging to the right or left to add columns to the selection.
Entire table	Click the four-headed arrow icon just outside the upper-left corner of the table (see Figure 15.17). (This icon appears only when the Draw Table and Eraser tools are turned off.)

Double-clicking the four-headed arrow icon selects the table and displays the Table Properties dialog box, where you can set a variety of options for your table.

Figure 15.14

Click at the left edge of a cell to select the cell.

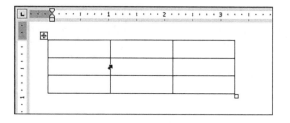

15

Figure 15.15

Click to the left of a row to select the row.

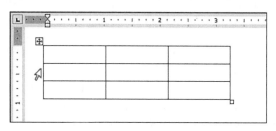

Figure 15.16

Click the top edge of a column to select the column.

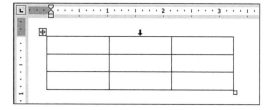

Figure 15.17

Click the four-headed arrow icon to select the table.

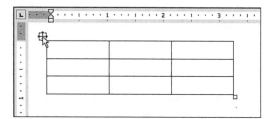

Changing the Structure of a Table

As you enter text in a table, you will almost certainly need to change its structure. Here you learn the most common adjustments that you'll need to make. As you experiment with these techniques, keep in mind that Word does not prevent you from making a table too wide to fit on the page. If you're adding columns and increasing column widths, check periodically to make sure that the table isn't running off the page. (You have to check in Print Layout view or Print Preview—Normal view won't do the trick.)

Most of the commands in the Table menu are active only when the insertion point is in a table. If you notice that the commands are dim, it's a sign that you accidentally clicked outside the table. Click inside the table and then display the Table menu again.

Adding and Deleting Rows and Columns

You can add or delete rows and columns in a table using the following steps:

1. If you want to add a row at the end of the table, click anywhere in the lower-right cell in the table, and press the **Tab** key.

2. To add a row in the middle of the table, select the row below the desired location of the new one, and click the **Insert Rows** button on the Standard toolbar. (The Insert Table button turns into Insert Rows when a row is selected.) If you want to add two or more rows, select that number of rows before clicking the Insert Rows button.

3. To insert a column, select the column to the right of where the new one will go, and click the **Insert Columns** button on the Standard toolbar. (The Insert Table button turns into Insert Columns when a column is selected.) Again, you can add two or more columns at once by selecting that number before clicking the Insert Columns button.

4. If you want to delete a row or column, select it first, and then choose **Table**, **Delete**, **Rows** or **Table**, **Delete**, **Columns** (or right-click the selected row or column and choose **Delete Rows** or **Delete Columns**).

Merging and Splitting Cells

When you merge cells, they become one larger cell. You might, for example, merge all the cells in the top row of a table to create a large cell in which to type a centered title. You can merge cells that are horizontally or vertically adjacent to one another. To merge cells, first select them, and then click the Merge Cells button in the Tables and Borders toolbar (see Figure 15.18).

Merging cells is not the same as hiding the lines that separate them. When you merge cells, they become one single cell. When you hide the lines, the individual cells remain separate even though they appear to be a single cell.

You can also split a cell into two cells. To do so, click in the cell and then click the Split Cells toolbar button.

FIGURE **15.18**

The Merge Cells and Split Cells buttons in the Tables and Borders toolbar give you a quick way to merge and split cells.

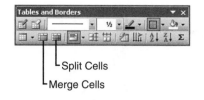

└ Split Cells
└ Merge Cells

Another way to merge cells is to erase the lines between them with the Eraser tool in the Tables and Borders toolbar. And you can split a cell by drawing a line through it with the Draw Table tool. This approach gives you more flexibility in choosing where the cell should be split.

Formatting a Table

Formatting a table can take far longer than creating it in the first place. Try not to overdo it. If your table is plastered with wild colors, fancy lines, and flamboyant fonts, the text it contains will be almost impossible to read. Also, be careful to select the exact cells that you want to format before issuing a command, and remember that you can always use Undo if you make a change that you don't like.

At the risk of stating the obvious, you can apply all the regular font and paragraph formatting in a table. Select the part of the table that you want to affect, and then use the familiar options in the Formatting toolbar, Font and Paragraph dialog boxes, and so on. The next five sections describe formatting that's specific to tables.

Changing the Appearance of Lines and Adding Shading

To change the appearance of the lines in your table, choose the desired options in the Line Style, Line Weight, and Border Color lists in the Tables and Borders toolbar. If you want to hide the lines, choose No Border in the Line Style list. Then turn on the Draw Table tool, if necessary, and draw over the lines you want to affect.

To apply shading, select the desired part of the table, display the Shading Color list in the Tables and Borders toolbar (see Figure 15.19), and click the desired color.

Shading Color

FIGURE 15.19

Click a color in the Shading Color palette to shade the selected cells.

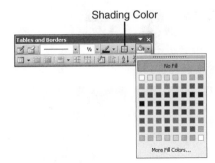

> The most recently selected color appears on the face of the Shading Color button. If you want to apply this color, just click the button itself instead of choosing a color from the palette.

Resizing Columns, Rows, and the Entire Table

To adjust a column's width, drag its right border. To adjust a row's height, drag its bottom border. When you point to any line in a table, the mouse pointer changes to a double-headed arrow to remind you that you can drag to resize (see Figure 15.20).

FIGURE 15.20

Drag the right border of a column to resize it.

> Be careful not to drag a column boundary when you have individual cells on either side of the boundary selected. You'll end up moving the boundary for only the selected cells, not the entire column.

You can be more precise about column width and row height if you like. If you hold the Alt key down as you drag the column or row boundary, the horizontal or vertical ruler shows you the exact width/height of the columns or rows.

If it's easier for you to just enter the exact measurements instead of dragging, you can do so in the Table Properties dialog box.

Follow these steps to resize columns:

1. Select the columns you want to adjust.

2. Choose **Table**, **Table Properties**, and click the **Column** tab (see Figure 15.21).

FIGURE 15.21

Use the Column tab of the Table Properties dialog box to specify exact column widths.

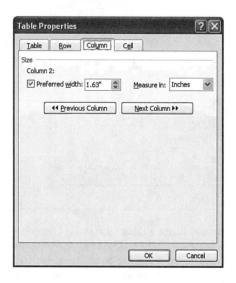

3. Enter the desired width in the **Preferred Width** text box. By default, you enter the width in inches, but if you like you can select **Percentage** in the Measure In drop-down list, and then type a percentage in the Preferred Width text box instead.

4. Click **OK**.

Follow these steps to resize rows:

1. Select the rows you want to adjust.

2. Choose **Table**, **Table Properties**, and click the **Row** tab (see Figure 15.22).

3. Mark the **Specify Height** check box, and enter the height in the **Specify Height** text box.

4. In the Row Height Is drop-down list, choose either **At Least** or **Exactly**. If you choose At Least, Word will not let the row height get smaller than the height you specify, but it will let the row height get bigger if it needs to do so to fit the text.

5. Click **OK**.

FIGURE 15.22

Use the Row tab of the Table Properties dialog box to specify exact row heights.

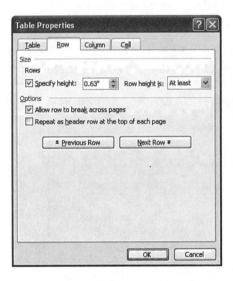

If you accidentally resize a table so that its right edge runs off the edge of the page, here's a way to bring the edge back into view: Choose Table, Table Properties. In the Table tab of the Table Properties dialog box, type a width narrower than the distance between your margins in the Preferred Width text box, and click OK.

To make multiple rows the same height, or multiple columns the same width, select the rows or columns, and then click the Distribute Rows Evenly or Distribute Columns Evenly button on the Tables and Borders toolbar (see Figure 15.23).

FIGURE 15.23

The Distribute Rows Evenly and Distribute Columns Evenly buttons enable you to quickly even out your rows and columns.

Distribute Rows Evenly

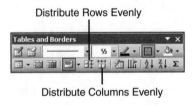

Distribute Columns Evenly

To proportionally resize the entire table, make sure the Draw Table and Eraser tools are turned off, and point to the small square just outside the lower-right corner (refer to Figure 15.20). Then drag diagonally up and to the left to shrink the table, or down and to the right to enlarge it. If you don't see this square, make sure the Draw Table and Eraser tools are turned off, and rest the mouse pointer inside the table.

Adjusting the Position of the Table on the Page

To move your table around on the page, drag the four-headed arrow icon located just outside the upper-left corner of the table (refer to Figure 15.20). If you need to position the table more precisely, you can also click in it and choose Table, Table Properties to display the Table Properties dialog box (see Figure 15.24).

FIGURE 15.24

Use the Table tab of the Table Properties dialog box to position your table more precisely.

If you want your table to be left-aligned, right-aligned, or centered on the page, select the desired option under Alignment. You can also use the Indent from Left text box to indent the table a specific amount from the left margin. Finally, click the Around box if you want the text surrounding your table to be able to wrap around it.

Aligning Text and Changing Its Direction

To change the vertical/horizontal alignment of text in your table, select the cells whose alignment you want to change, display the Align list (see Figure 15.25), and click the desired option. To change the direction of text from the default left-to-right to either bottom-to-top or top-to-bottom, select the cell and then click the Change Text Direction button one or more times. The bottom-to-top option was used to align the text in the leftmost cell in Figure 15.5 (shown earlier in this hour).

FIGURE 15.25
Use the Align and Change Text Direction tools to play with the appearance of text in a table.

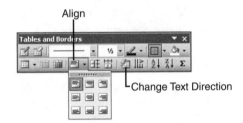

Using the Table AutoFormat Feature

If you want your table to look beautiful but are lacking inspiration, you might check out the Table AutoFormat feature. Word offers a wide variety of built-in table styles that you can choose from to apply a facelift to your table. Not surprisingly, this feature is also useful if creativity does come knocking because it enables you to create your own table styles or modify the built-in ones. This would be a useful approach if your job requires you to create many similar tables and you want them to have a consistent look.

The default "plain vanilla" table style that Word applies to tables is called Table Grid. To apply any of the other built-in table styles to your table, follow these steps:

1. Click anywhere in the table and choose **Table**, **Table AutoFormat**.

2. In the Table AutoFormat dialog box, shown in Figure 15.26, click the various table styles to display previews of them in the bottom half of the dialog box.

FIGURE 15.26
Use the Table AutoFormat dialog box to spruce up your table.

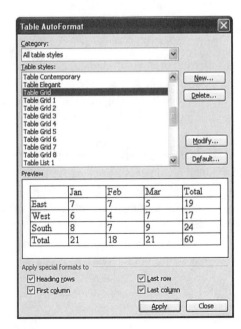

3. When you find one you like, you can clear any of the check boxes under Apply Special Formats To if you want to change the style so as to remove the formatting from the heading rows, first column, last row, or last column of the table. Then click the Apply button.

15

If you want to remove a built-in style from your table and return it to its default state, just repeat these steps and select the Table Grid style in step 3.

To modify a table style, select it and click the Modify Style button. The Modify Style dialog box that appears is almost exactly like the Modify Style dialog box you used in Hour 9, "Working with Styles." The only difference is that it contains some table-related formatting options. Remember that you can mark the Add to Template check box if you want the modified version of the style to be available to other documents that you base on the current template. After you've modified the style, you can click the OK button to apply the modified style to the whole table. If you'd rather apply it to only a particular part of the table, select that part in the Apply Formatting To drop-down list, and then click OK.

If you want to create a new style, click the New button in the Table AutoFormat dialog box to display the New Style dialog box. This dialog box is also very similar to the New Style dialog box you worked with in Hour 9, except that it has some special formatting options that are specific to tables. Again, make sure to mark the Add to Template check box if you want to use the style outside of the current document, and select a particular part of the table in the Apply Formatting To drop-down list to apply the new style to that part only.

To delete a table style, select it in the Table AutoFormat dialog box, click the Delete button, and then click Yes in the message box that appears.

Finally, if you are so taken with one of the table styles that you want to make it the default for either the current document or all documents based on the current template, select the style in the Table AutoFormat dialog box and click the Default button. In the Default Table Style dialog box, mark either of the two option buttons to indicate whether you want the style to be the default in the current document only or for all documents based on the current template.

Sorting Rows in a Table

The fastest way to sort rows in a table is to use the Tables and Borders toolbar. Click in the column that you want to sort by, and click the Sort Ascending or Sort Descending button (see Figure 15.27). Word assumes that you want to sort all rows but the first. (In Figure 15.27, the last row was added after sorting by the Name column to prevent it from being included in the sort.) If you want to include the first row, click in the column to sort by, choose Table, Sort, mark the No Header Row option button, and click OK. You can also specify which rows should be included in a sort by selecting them first and then choosing Table, Sort, specifying the column to sort by in the Sort By drop-down list, and clicking OK.

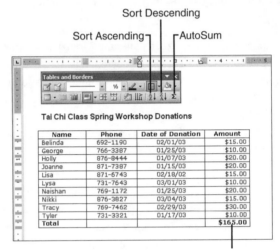

FIGURE 15.27

Click the Sort Ascending or Sort Descending button in the Tables and Borders toolbar to sort by the column containing the insertion point.

This field was inserted with the AutoSum tool.

If you have entered numbers in a column, you can have Word total them automatically. Click in the last cell in the column and then click the AutoSum toolbar button to insert a field that sums the numbers above. If you later change some of the numbers, remember to press F9 to update the field. (It won't update automatically.)

Summary

The Columns feature is the way to go if you want your text to wrap from one column to the next. For all other documents in which you want text to line up in columns, use custom tabs (described in Hour 9) or tables.

Q&A

Q I have a table that takes up five pages and I want the first row, which contains labels, to repeat at the top of each page. How can I do this?

A Select the first row, and choose Table, Heading Rows Repeat.

Q **I don't want to let some of the rows in my table break across page breaks.
How do I prevent that from happening?**

A Select the rows and then choose Table, Table Properties to display the Table
Properties dialog box. Click the Row tab, and clear the Allow Row to Break Across
Pages check box.

Q **I have a list of products and their descriptions that is currently formatted in
regular paragraphs, but I think it would look better as a table with the products listed on the left and their descriptions on the right. Can I convert the
whole list into a table?**

A Yes. You can convert regular text to a table, or vice versa. To convert text to a table,
select the text and then choose Table, Convert, Text to Table. In the Convert Text to
Table dialog box, specify the details of how you want the text to be converted, and
click OK. (You will probably get better results if you remove blank lines from the
text before performing the conversion.) To convert a table to text, click anywhere in
the table and choose Table, Convert, Table to Text. In the Convert Table to Text
dialog box, specify how you want the text that had been in individual table cells
separated, and click OK.

15

HOUR 16

Inserting Images, Drawing Shapes, and Creating Text Effects with WordArt

One of the perks of using a powerful word processing program is that you get to put pictures in your documents. Images help break up the text, convey meaning, and grab the reader's attention. Plus they are just plain fun to work with. In this hour, you start by learning how to insert an image in your document. Word lets you insert images from a variety of sources. You can pull them from any folder on your own computer or network, or from Microsoft's clip art collections. And if you have a scanner or digital camera, you also have the option of importing images directly from the scanner or camera software into Word without first saving them to disk. You then learn how to draw shapes (this isn't as boring as it sounds) and use WordArt to create special effects with text. In this hour, you will focus on inserting images into your document. In the next hour, you will learn all manner of techniques for manipulating images that you've already placed in your document, including moving them, resizing them, and so on.

The highlights of this hour include

- Inserting images from your disk or network
- Inserting images directly from a digital camera or scanner
- Inserting images from the Clip Gallery
- Drawing shapes with the drawing tools
- Dressing up your text with WordArt

Inserting Images from Your Disk or Network

If the image you want to insert in your document is sitting in a folder on your computer or network, chances are you can use it. Word can handle image files in all sorts of formats, including (but not limited to) BMP, EMF, EPS, PNG, GIF, JPG, PCX, PICT, PING, TIFF, and WMF. (If these formats don't mean anything to you, don't worry about it. Word will most likely be able to use your image file without a problem.) The image may be a digital photograph, a scanned image, or another piece of digital artwork. You may have received it as an attachment to an e-mail message or downloaded it from the Web. Regardless of how it arrived at your doorstep, after it's saved to your own disk or your network, you can probably insert it in your Word document.

It's a good idea to check the copyright of any image that you haven't created yourself to make sure that you have permission to use it.

To insert an image from a folder on your hard disk or network, follow these steps:

1. Move the insertion point to the approximate place where you want to insert the graphic.
2. Choose **Insert**, **Picture**, **From File** to display the Insert Picture dialog box.

By default, Office 2003 creates a My Pictures subfolder of My Documents to give you a handy place to store images. The Insert Picture dialog box automatically points to this folder, but you can navigate to any other folder that you like.

3. Navigate to the drive and folder that contains the image you want to insert.

4. Word displays thumbnails of your image files, as shown in Figure 16.1. (To switch views, click the down arrow to the right of the **Views** button, and select the desired option.)

Views

16

FIGURE 16.1

Select the image file that you want to insert in the Insert Picture dialog box.

5. Click the image you want to insert, and then click the **Insert** button.

6. The image is inserted in your document. Don't worry if it is not the right size or in exactly the right place. You'll learn how to make these changes in the next hour.

7. Click the image. The Picture toolbar may appear automatically (see Figure 16.2). If it doesn't, right-click the image and choose **Show Picture Toolbar**. You will use this toolbar in the remainder of this hour and in the next.

FIGURE 16.2

The Picture toolbar gives you a set of tools for working with images.

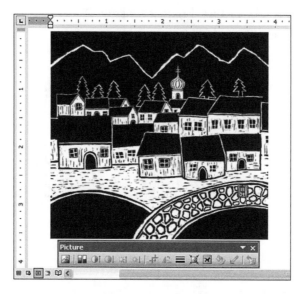

Inserting Images Directly from Your Digital Camera or Scanner

Word knows how to "talk" to the software that manages scanners and digital cameras. If you have one of these gadgets, you can easily insert a scanned image or digital photograph into your Word document without first saving it as a separate image file on disk. If you want to insert an image directly from your digital camera or scanner, first make sure you've installed the software that came with the camera or scanner, and connect the device to your computer. Depending on the device, you may also need to turn it on. Then follow the steps in one of the next two sections.

If you don't have a scanner or digital camera (or if you haven't installed the software or connected the scanner or camera to your computer) don't even bother with these steps. If you try to issue the Insert, Picture, From Scanner or Camera command, Word displays an error message telling you that it can't connect to a scanner or camera.

Inserting a Photograph Directly from a Digital Camera

To retrieve a photograph from your digital camera's memory card and insert it in your document, follow these steps:

1. Move the insertion point to the approximate place where you want to insert the image.

2. Choose **Insert**, **Picture**, **From Scanner or Camera**.

3. In the Insert Picture from Scanner or Camera dialog box (see Figure 16.3), select your camera.

FIGURE 16.3

Select your digital camera in the Device list.

If you're using the Clip Organizer (discussed later in this hour), you may want to mark the Add Pictures to Clip Organizer check box so that you'll be able to access the image more easily in the future, either via the Clip Art task pane or in the Clip Organizer window. If you mark the check box, the Clip Organizer stores a copy of the image in the Microsoft Clip Organizer folder, which is a subfolder of the My Pictures folder.

16

4. Click the **Custom Insert** button.
5. Follow the directions in the next dialog box that appears (these will vary with the device). In Figure 16.4, the software for the digital camera displays a dialog box that enables you to browse the photographs stored in the camera's memory card and select the one you want to retrieve.

FIGURE 16.4

Use your camera's software to select the photograph you want to insert.

As soon as you issue the command in your camera's software to retrieve a photograph, the image appears in your document (see Figure 16.5).

Some cameras appear to Windows as additional disk drives. If you have one of these, it will not appear in the Device list in the Insert Picture from Scanner or Camera dialog box. To insert images from this type of camera, simply follow the steps in "Inserting Images from Your Disk or Network" earlier in this hour.

FIGURE 16.5

When you select a photograph from your camera's memory card, it appears in your document.

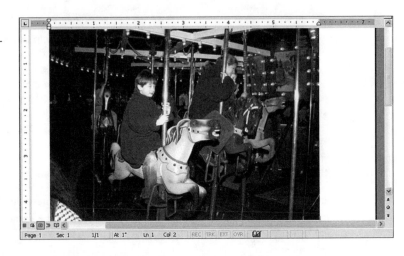

Inserting an Image Directly from a Scanner

To insert an image from your scanner, place the image in your scanner, and follow these steps:

1. Move your insertion point to the location where you want the image to appear in your document.
2. Choose **Insert**, **Picture**, **From Scanner or Camera**.
3. In the Insert Picture from Scanner or Camera dialog box (see Figure 16.6), select your scanner.

FIGURE 16.6

Select your scanner in the device list.

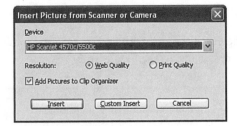

4. Depending on the software that runs your scanner, the Insert button and the associated Web Quality and Print Quality option buttons may be active or dim. (If these buttons are dim, skip to steps 5 and 6.) If they're active, as they are in Figure 16.6, the software knows how to send an image to Word with no more participation from you after this dialog box. Select **Web Quality** (poorer quality and smaller file

size—good for images you'll send via e-mail or include in Web pages) or **Print Quality** (better quality and larger file size—better for documents that you will print). (See Figure 16.7.)

5. Click the **Custom Insert** button to launch the software you use for your scanner.

6. Issue the command to scan the image. After a moment, the image appears in your document.

FIGURE 16.7

The image appears in your document as soon as it's scanned.

16

Inserting Clip Art Images

Microsoft Office comes with a collection of stock clip art images, and many more are available at the Microsoft Office Online Web site. When you search for a clip art image, Word automatically includes the Office Online Web site in its search if you have an Internet connection. Even if you don't often use clip art, you may find the Microsoft Clip Organizer useful, because you can use it to catalog other images you created yourself or gathered from various sources (see the next section), and you will be able to access these images in the Clip Art task pane.

To insert a piece of clip art into your document, follow these steps:

1. Move the insertion point to the approximate place where you want to insert the image.

2. Choose **Insert**, **Picture**, **Clip Art** to display the Clip Art task pane (see Figure 16.8). (If the Drawing toolbar is displayed, you can click its Insert Clip Art button instead.)

FIGURE **16.8**

The Clip Art task pane lets you browse clip art images and insert them into your document.

3. Enter the type of image you want to search for in the **Search For** text box.

4. Display the **Search In** drop-down list and, if needed, revise the list of locations in which Word will search for the clip art. In Figure 16.9, the My Collections check box is marked and shows cascading check boxes underneath it, which indicates that it and all of its subfolders will be searched. (To make the cascading check boxes appear, click once to mark a check box, and then click it again.) The Office Locations check box is marked, which indicates that it will be searched, but its subfolders will not be included. The Web Collections check box is cleared, so it will not be searched, but you can still mark any of its subfolders to include them.

You might want to include My Collections in the search if you have used the Clip Organizer to create your own collections (see "Using the Clip Organizer" later in this hour). Office Collections are collections of clip art that come on the Office CD. Web Collections are collections of clip art on the Web. By default, this category only includes the Microsoft Office Online Web site, although you can add more with the Clip Organizer.

5. By default the Clip Art task pane searches for photographs, movies, and sounds in addition to clip art. If you don't want to search for all types of media, display the **Results Should Be** drop-down list and clear the check boxes of the types you don't want to include.

FIGURE 16.9

Use the Search In list to specify the locations in which you want to search for clip art.

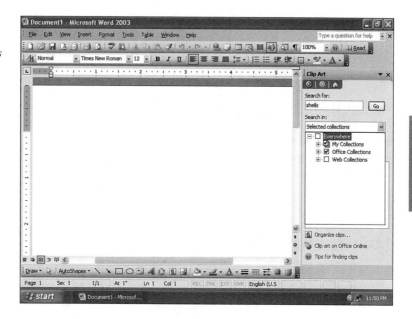

6. Click the **Go** button to perform the search.

7. Scan the thumbnails of the images in the results list (see Figure 16.10).

FIGURE 16.10

Scroll through the results of the search.

8. When you find an image that you want, click it to insert it in your document. (You can also point to it, click the **down arrow** to its right, and choose **Insert** in the menu that appears.)

The image is inserted in your document (see Figure 16.11). Don't worry if the image is not the right size or in the right place. You'll learn how to resize it and move it in the next hour. You'll also learn how to use the Picture toolbar, which appears when you click the image to select it.

FIGURE 16.11

Clicking a thumbnail in the Clip Art results list inserts the image in your document.

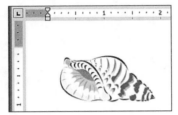

Using the Clip Organizer

The Clip Organizer, shown in Figure 16.12, comes with Microsoft Office. It is accessible from Word's Clip Art task pane, but it is not specific to Word. You can open it at any time by choosing Start, All Programs, pointing to Microsoft Office, then Microsoft Office Tools, and then clicking Microsoft Clip Organizer. You can use the Clip Organizer as a "binder" of sorts to collect all your images in one place. For example, if you have a corporate logo, or a scanned image of your signature that you typically place at the end of your letters, you might add these images to the Clip Organizer so that they are readily available in the Clip Art task pane.

FIGURE 16.12

You can use the Clip Organizer to catalog all of your clip art, as well as other types of media files.

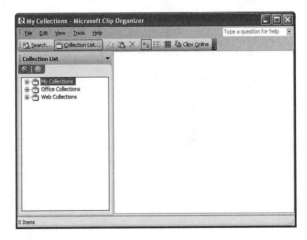

To display the Clip Organizer, click the Organize Clips link at the bottom of the Clip Art task pane. The first time you do this, the Add Clips to Organizer dialog box appears to ask whether you want it to catalog all of the media files it finds on your computer. It won't move or rename them; it will just catalog the ones it finds under the My Collections folder. In addition, it will use their filenames to generate a list of keywords you can use to search for the clips in the Clip Art task pane. If you'd like to go ahead and catalog your clips, click the Now button. (Even if you don't catalog existing clips, you can still use the Clip Organizer to create new collections, add images to existing collections, and so on.)

Because the Clip Organizer isn't a part of Word, it is not covered here in detail. To learn more about the Clip Organizer, choose Help, Clip Organizer Help in the Clip Organizer, and search for help on *new collections* or *add clips*.

16

Deleting Images

To delete an image from your Word document, click it to select it and then press the Delete key. When an image is selected, small black squares or white circles (called *selection handles*) appear around its edges (see Figure 16.13). The color and shape of the selection handles vary depending on whether the image is in the same layer of the document as the text, or floating above the text. (You'll learn more about this in the next hour.)

FIGURE 16.13

To delete an image, select it and then press Delete.

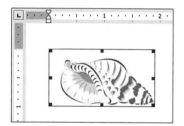

Drawing Shapes

Sometimes you don't need a complex image in your document—you just need something simple, such as an arrow or a box. Word's Drawing toolbar lets you quickly draw all manner of arrows, rectangles, ovals, callouts, banners, and so on. (You can also create text boxes, which are discussed at the end of this section.) Figure 16.14 shows one example of a drawing you can create with Word's drawing tools. After you have inserted a drawing object, you can modify the image in a variety of ways, as you'll see in the next hour.

FIGURE **16.14**

*This software architec-
ture drawing is an
example of what you
can create with Word's
drawing tools.*

FIGURE **16.14**

*This software architec-
ture drawing is an
example of what you
can create with Word's
drawing tools.*

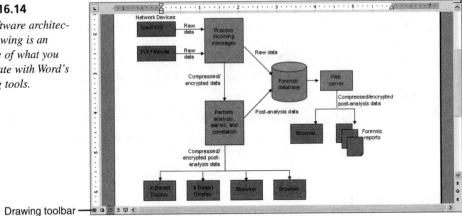

Drawing toolbar

1. Click the **Drawing** button on the Standard toolbar (see Figure 16.15).

2. The Drawing toolbar appears docked at the bottom of the Word window by default. In Figure 16.15, it has been moved and is floating over the Word window.

FIGURE **16.15**

*The Drawing toolbar
contains a wide variety
of tools for creating
and manipulating
drawing objects.*

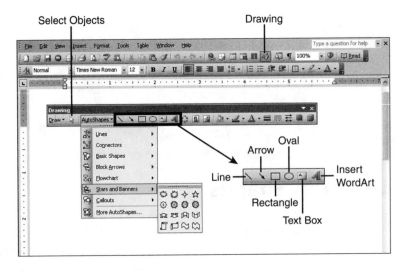

3. Click the drawing tool that you want to use. The tools for basic shapes (lines, arrows, boxes, and so on) are available directly on the toolbar. If you want a more unusual shape, click the **AutoShapes** button, point to the category that you want to use, and click the shape in the submenu. (In Figure 16.15, the Stars and Banners submenu is displayed.)

4. As soon as you click a drawing tool, an empty *drawing canvas* appears, along with the Drawing Canvas toolbar. The drawing canvas, which you'll learn more about in the next hour, can help you keep all of the shapes in your drawing together. (Don't worry, you'll also learn how to turn off the drawing canvas if you're used to earlier versions of Word that didn't use it.) Point with the crosshair mouse pointer to the upper-left corner of the spot where you want the shape to go, and drag diagonally down and to the right (see Figure 16.16). Or, in the case of lines and arrows, simply point to the location where you want the line or arrow to begin and drag to the location where you want it to end. (If you or someone else has already turned off the drawing canvas, you will draw your shape on the document itself.)

16

FIGURE 16.16

Drag over an area within the drawing canvas to create the shape.

5. Release the mouse button to finish drawing the shape (see Figure 16.17). The shape will be surrounded by two or more *selection* handles (white circles) and, in the case of two- or three-dimensional shapes, with one *rotate* handle (a green circle).

FIGURE 16.17

The object you drew is automatically selected.

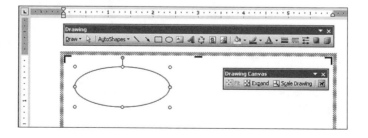

If you plan on drawing several objects using the same tool (for example, you want to draw several lines), *double-click* the button in step 3. It will stay turned on as long as you want to use it. When you're finished, click it again to turn it off. (This does not work for the tools in the AutoShapes menu.)

If you are using the Rectangle tool and want to draw a perfect square, hold down the Shift key as you drag. This also works with the Oval tool to get a perfect circle, the Star tool to get a perfectly proportioned star, and so on.

To delete a drawing object, click it to select it. When you see the selection handles, press the Delete key.

One drawing object that deserves special attention is the text box. The Text Box tool on the Drawing toolbar lets you draw a rectangular box in which you can type text. Putting text in a text box gives you control over the position of the text in your document because you can drag the text box around just as you do other drawing objects (see the next hour). In Figure 16.14 earlier in this hour, the text labels in the diagram were all created with text boxes. (Their borders were removed, and some of them were placed on top of other drawing objects.)

To create a text box, click the Text Box tool, drag to create a rectangle of about the right size, and then release the mouse button. An insertion point appears in the box to let you type text, and the Text Box toolbar appears in your Word window (see Figure 16.18).

FIGURE 16.18
When a text box is selected, an insertion point appears in it to let you type.

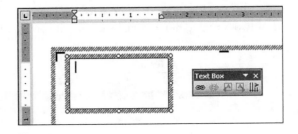

After you've typed your text, you can apply all the usual font and paragraph formatting to it. In addition, you can format the box itself, adjusting the appearance of the borders, changing the fill color, and so on. (You'll learn these techniques in the next hour.)

In addition to creating text boxes with the Text Box tool, you can type text into any drawing object (with the exception of lines and arrows) by right-clicking it and choosing Add Text in the context menu. An insertion point appears in the object. Type the text as you would in a text box.

Creating Special Effects with WordArt

16

When you add images to a document, you aren't limited to working with images separate from your text. WordArt lets you add flair to your text itself. It's perfect for creating splashy headings and titles. You start with a basic "look" for your word or phrase, and then tweak it to get the exact effect you want. After you've added a WordArt image, you can resize it, add borders, and so on (see the next hour). Figure 16.19 shows a heading created with WordArt.

FIGURE 16.19

You can create a variety of effects with WordArt.

To create a WordArt image, follow these steps:

1. Click where you want the WordArt image to go.

2. Choose **Insert**, **Picture**, **WordArt**. (If your Drawing toolbar is displayed, you can also click the Insert WordArt button on this toolbar.)

3. The WordArt Gallery dialog box opens (see Figure 16.20). Click the look that you want to start with, and click the **OK** button. The Edit WordArt Text window appears (see Figure 16.21).

4. Type the text for your WordArt image, replacing the dummy text. Your text won't take on the look you chose in step 3 until it's inserted in the document.

5. Use the **Font** and **Size** lists and the **Bold** and **Italic** buttons to make additional adjustments to the text.

6. Click the **OK** button.

FIGURE 16.20
Choose the WordArt style that most closely matches what you want.

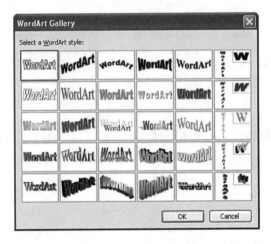

FIGURE 16.21
Type the text that you want to use in the Edit WordArt Text window.

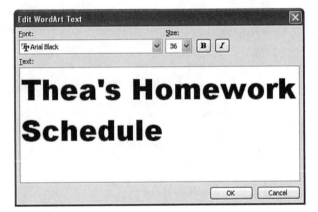

The WordArt image appears in your document. To revise the WordArt text or change its appearance after you've created the image, use the WordArt toolbar. This toolbar appears as soon as you insert a WordArt image. If you don't see it, choose View, Toolbars, WordArt. (You'll learn more about this in the next hour.)

Summary

You can insert existing images into your documents—from your digital camera or scanner, your own hard disk or network, or via the Clip Art task pane—or you can create new images with the drawing tools or WordArt. After an image is in your document, you have to adjust its size, position, and relationship to the surrounding text, and otherwise alter its appearance. You'll learn how to make these kinds of changes in the next hour.

Q&A

Q **Are there other places to find clip art on the Internet? I'm not enthralled with what I see at the Microsoft's Office Online site.**

A Yes. There are literally hundreds of sites on the Internet that offer free clip-art images. A good way to start looking is to visit Google (`www.google.com`) and search for the keyword *clip art*.

Q **I need to create several identical drawing objects. Do I have to draw each one separately?**

A No. Draw the first one, click it to select it, and click the Copy button in the Standard toolbar (or press Ctrl+C). Then click the Paste button in the Standard toolbar (or press Ctrl+V) to paste a duplicate of the image. The copy appears on top of the original image. Continue with the next hour to learn how to move it to a new location.

16

HOUR 17

Manipulating Images

Putting an image in your document is a bit like bringing home a new piece of furniture. After you get it in the door, you have to play around a bit to make it blend in with its surroundings. Word lets you modify images (photographs, artwork, drawing objects and the drawing canvas, and WordArt) in a myriad of ways. In this hour, you'll try out quite a few techniques for manipulating images. You should also feel free to experiment more on your own, and remember that if you botch something badly, you can always click the Undo button.

The highlights of this hour include

- Resizing and moving images
- Controlling the way that text wraps around an image
- Cropping out part of an image
- Making your image look good
- Working with multiple images

Exploring the Format Dialog Box

In this hour, you will learn a whole host of methods for manipulating images, many of which involve toolbar buttons and mouse techniques. If you forget some of these details, just remember that for every image in your documenst, regardless of its type, you can display a dialog box that contains options specific to that particular object type.

To display the dialog box, simply double-click the image. The name of the dialog box
will be Format *[object]*. The exact name of the dialog box varies depending on the type
of object you double-click. For example, if you double-click a drawing object, the dialog
box will be labeled Format AutoShape, and if you double-click a photograph, it will be
Format Picture. Figure 17.1 shows the Format AutoShape dialog box.

FIGURE 17.1

*If you're curious about
how you can modify an
image, simply double-
click it to display its
Format dialog box and
see what options are
available.*

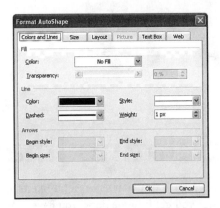

You can learn a lot about the possibilities for formatting an image by clicking the various
tabs in this dialog box. (Some tabs may be grayed out depending on the options available
for the selected object.)

Resizing an Image

After you've placed an image in your document (or placed a drawing object on the drawing canvas), one of the first adjustments you'll probably want to make is to change its
size.

To resize an image, follow these steps:

1. Click the image to select it. As you learned in the last hour, when an image is
   selected, sizing handles appear around it. (These handles may be black squares or
   white circles. You can resize the image with either one.)

2. Point to a sizing handle. The mouse pointer becomes a double-headed arrow.

3. Drag to enlarge or shrink the image (see Figure 17.2). As you drag, you'll see the
   sizing pointer (a crosshair) and an outline that indicates how big the image will be.
   Release the mouse button when the image is the right size.

When you are resizing a picture, you can keep the height and width proportional by
dragging a corner sizing handle (as shown in Figure 17.2). If you drag a side sizing handle, you will skew the image. Drawing objects and WordArt images work a little differently. By default, when you drag a corner sizing handle of one of these image types, the

height/width ratio is not maintained. If you want to preserve the image's proportions, hold down the Shift key as you drag a corner sizing handle.

FIGURE **17.2**

As you drag, an outline shows how large the image will be when you release the mouse button.

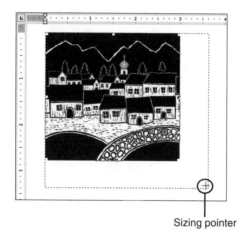

Sizing pointer

 To keep an image's center "pinned" to the same spot as you resize the image, hold down the Ctrl key as you drag a sizing handle.

If you know the exact dimensions that you want your image to be, double-click the image to display the Format dialog box. Click the Size tab and type the desired measurements in the Height and Width text boxes under Size and Rotate. Or, if you want to resize the image relative to its original or current size, mark or clear the Relative to Original Picture Size check box as you like, and then enter the desired percentages in the Height and Width boxes under Scale.

For some images such as photographs or screen captures, you might want to indicate their size in the Height and Width text boxes using pixels instead of inches. As one example of when this might be useful, when you insert an image that is larger than can fit on the page, Word automatically shrinks it to get it to fit. Depending on the type of image, this may reduce its quality, and you might prefer to resize the image back to its original size (which was probably measured in pixels in your graphics program) and then crop it as necessary to get it to fit. If you want to enter your image's dimensions in pixels, choose Tools, Options. In the Options dialog box, click the General tab, and mark the Show Pixels for HTML Features check box. (Yes, it's an odd name for the check box because you may want to use pixels to enter measurements for images that have nothing to do with HTML.) This change will take effect for all objects. If you want to enter measurements using inches again, clear the check box.

17

Moving an Image

By default, Word places images *inline*. (Word documents use two layers, which you can think of as transparency sheets. The document text is on the lower sheet, and images can either be placed on the lower sheet along with the text, in which case they are inline, or on the upper sheet, in which case they are *floating*.) As you saw in the previous section, you can resize an image when it's inline. However, if you want to move an image, it's much easier if you first set a *text-wrapping option*, which takes the image out of the text layer. You'll learn more about text-wrapping options in the next section. For now, note that you can choose any text-wrapping option you like before moving the image—you can always change it later.

You can tell when an image is inline because it has black square sizing handles. As soon as you remove it from the text layer, it gets white circle sizing handles.

Drawing objects and WordArt images, unlike pictures, have a text-wrapping option (In Front of Text) turned on by default. So if you're moving one of these image types, you can skip step 1.

Follow these steps to move an image:

1. Select the image. If it is inline (has black sizing handles), click the **Text Wrapping** button in the Picture toolbar and click **Square**, as shown in Figure 17.3. (If you don't see the Picture toolbar, choose **View**, **Toolbars**, **Picture**.)

2. The image's sizing handles are now white circles, and any text that had been below the image has now moved up alongside it. Point to the middle of the image and drag the image to the desired location (see Figure 17.4). As you drag, you'll see the moving pointer, which looks like a four-headed arrow, and an outline of the image.

3. Release the mouse button when the outline is in the right place.

In Figure 17.5, the photograph has been moved to the right side of the page, and the text is wrapping on its left.

Text Wrapping

FIGURE **17.3**
*Choose the Square
text-wrapping option
for now (you can
always change it
later).*

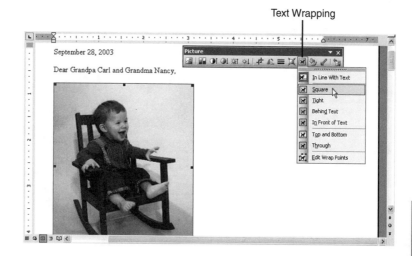

17

Moving pointer

FIGURE **17.4**
*Drag your image to the
desired location.*

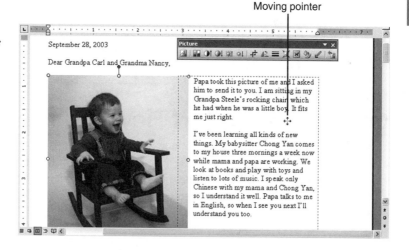

To position a image precisely on the left margin, in the horizontal center of the page, or
at the right margin, follow these steps:

1. Make sure the image has a text-wrapping option turned on, and then double-click
   the image.

2. In the **Format** dialog box that appears, click the **Layout** tab.

3. Mark the **Left**, **Center**, or **Right** option button under Horizontal Alignment.

4. Click **OK**.

FIGURE 17.5

*The photograph is now
on the right side of the
page.*

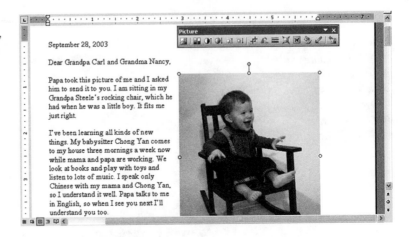

When an image is selected, you can use the four arrow keys on your keyboard to move it around a small amount at a time. The image will move in increments based on invisible gridlines in your document. If you want finer control than you get this way, hold down the Ctrl key as you press the arrow keys. (See the Q&A section at the end of this hour for more information about this.)

Controlling the Text Flow Around an Image

When an image is inline—in the same layer as your text—text cannot flow around it. In Figure 17.6, the insertion point was just before the first character in the document when the image was inserted inline. The image is selected in the figure so you can see that the baseline of the image is positioned in the actual line of text.

FIGURE 17.6

This image is inline.

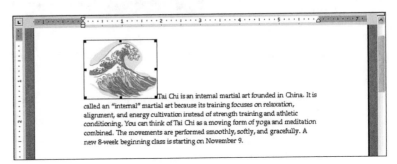

Word gives you six options for taking the image out of the text layer and enabling text to flow around it. The same options are available for all images. To set one of these text-wrapping options, select the image, click the Text Wrapping button on the Picture toolbar (or the WordArt toolbar), and click one of following six wrapping options. Here is a description of what each option does:

- Square—Wraps the text in a square shape around the image.
- Tight—Wraps the text right up to the outside edges of the image. This option only works with images that have irregular boundaries, such as the clip art image shown in Figure 17.7.
- Through—Same as Tight, but text also flows through any open areas inside the image. If there are no open areas, it will look the same as Tight.
- Behind Text—Doesn't wrap the text at all; the image is sent behind the text so that the text flows over the image.
- In Front of Text—Doesn't wrap the text; the image appears in front of the text so that the text is not visible behind it.
- Top and Bottom—Wraps the text above and below the image, but not along its sides.

With the Tight and Through options, you can control exactly how close the text wraps to the image. Select the image, click the Draw button on the Drawing toolbar, point to Text Wrapping, and click Edit Wrap Points. (You can also display the Text Wrapping drop-down list in the Picture toolbar and choose Edit Wrap Points at the bottom of the list.) A dashed red line appears around the image to indicate the wrapping boundary. Drag any of the small black squares on the red line to adjust the boundary. When you're finished, click outside the image.

Figure 17.7 shows an example of each text-wrapping option. Note that the Through option looks similar to Tight because the wave clip art doesn't contain any open areas.

By default, images are inserted inline, but you can change this setting so that images are automatically inserted with a specific wrapping option. To do so, follow these steps:

1. Choose **Tools**, **Options** to display the Options dialog box.
2. Click the **Edit** tab.
3. Display the **Insert/Paste Pictures As** drop-down list, and select the wrapping option you'd like to use as the default.
4. Click **OK**.

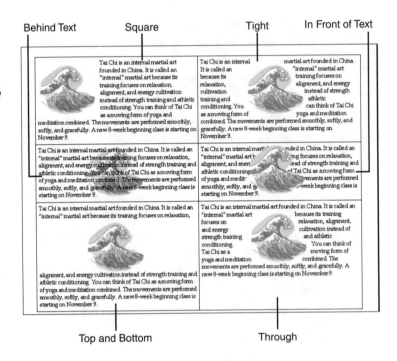

FIGURE 17.7

Word gives you six options for controlling the flow of text around a image.

The text-wrapping options are not available for objects you have placed on a drawing canvas because text doesn't flow within a canvas. You can, however, set a text-wrapping option for the entire canvas, as described in "Using a Drawing Canvas" later in this hour.

Cropping a Picture

You can crop a picture to remove a portion of it. Cropping doesn't resize the image or change its proportions—it just cuts off part of it as though you cut it out with scissors. You can't crop drawing objects or WordArt images.

Follow these steps to crop a picture:

1. Select your picture.

2. Click the **Crop** button on the Picture toolbar. (If you don't see the Picture toolbar, choose View, Toolbars, Picture, or right-click the picture and choose Show Picture Toolbar in the context menu.)

3. You will see a special cropping pointer, and the sizing handles around the image will be replaced with black cropping handles. Point to a cropping handle, start

dragging, and release the mouse button when the desired portion is cropped out (see Figure 17.8). (If you want to crop one side only, drag a side cropping handle. To drag two sides at once, drag a corner cropping handle.)

FIGURE 17.8

Drag a sizing handle with the cropping pointer to cut out a part of the image.

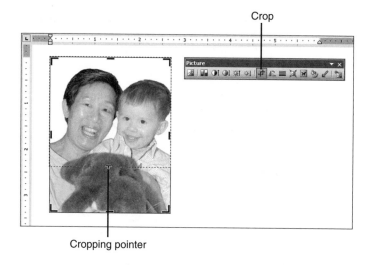

Crop

Cropping pointer

17

If you want to crop equally on two opposite sides of a picture, hold the Ctrl key down as you drag the center sizing handle on either side. If you want to crop all four sides of a picture equally, hold down the Ctrl key as you drag one of the corner sizing handles.

4. Click the **Crop** button again to turn it off.

If you crop a picture and then change your mind, you can use the cropping pointer to "uncrop" the image (drag outward from the center of the picture) and Word will fill in the portion of the picture that you had cropped out.

Changing the Appearance of an Image

Modifying how an image looks is the part of working with images that can gobble up as much time as surfing the Web. As you're fiddling with an image, save frequently, be patient, and don't be obsessed with getting it perfect.

In general, the Picture, Drawing, and WordArt toolbars are designed to work with their respective image types. However, you can "mix and match" in many cases. For example, you can use the Text Wrapping button on the Picture toolbar to set a text-wrapping option for a drawing object, or use the Line Color button on the Drawing toolbar to add a colored border around a picture. If you aren't sure whether a particular toolbar button works with the selected image, try it out. The worst thing that will happen is nothing.

Adding or Modifying the Borders of an Image

Adding borders around the edge of an image gives it definition, and removing borders makes it blend into the surrounding text. You can add borders around pictures, drawing objects, and WordArt images. (With WordArt images, the border appears around the outside edge of each letter.)

To add or modify a border, follow these steps:

1. Select the image.
2. If you haven't yet done so, set a text-wrapping option. (You can't add borders to inline images.)
3. Display the **Line Style** menu in the Drawing (or Picture) toolbar, and choose the desired line style.
4. If you want a colored border, keep the image selected, display the **Line Color** menu in the Drawing toolbar, and choose the desired color (see Figure 17.9).

FIGURE 17.9

The border around this clip art was added with the Line Style and Line Color tools.

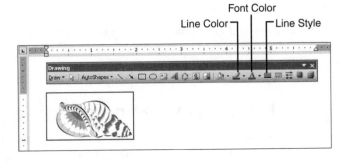

Word adds a border to the image. You may want to click outside of the image to deselect it so that you can see the border more clearly.

To remove a border, select the image, click the Line Color button in the Drawing (or Picture) toolbar, and choose No Line.

Adding or Modifying the Fill Color of an Image

If an image has a background, you can fill it in with color. You can also use fill color to color drawing objects such as rectangles and ovals. When you apply a fill color to a WordArt image, it colors the inside portion of each letter. If your image doesn't have any background areas, nothing will happen when you apply a fill color.

To add or modify the fill color of an image, follow these steps:

1. Select the image.
2. Click the **Fill Color** button in the Drawing toolbar (see Figure 17.10) and click the desired color in the menu that appears.

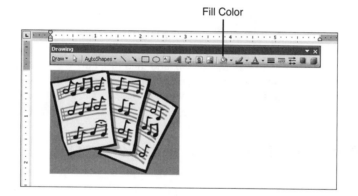

FIGURE 17.10
The fill color is the background color behind the sheets of music.

Fill Color

Rotating a Drawing Object or a WordArt Image

You can rotate a picture, drawing object, or WordArt image. The image stays the same—you just adjust its angle on the page.

Follow these steps to rotate a drawing object or WordArt image:

1. If you haven't already applied a text-wrapping option, do so now (see "Controlling the Text Flow Around an Image" earlier in this hour).
2. Select the image, and point to the **green rotate handle**. The mouse pointer changes shape when it's resting on top of the handle.
3. Drag the image. As you drag, the mouse pointer changes shape to become a rotate pointer (see Figure 17.11). When you've rotated the image the right amount, release the mouse button. (If you want to rotate the image in 15° increments, hold down the Shift key as you drag the rotate handle.)

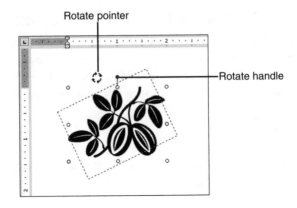

FIGURE 17.11
Drag the rotate handle to rotate the image.

If you want to rotate the image in 90° increments, select the image, and click the Draw button on the Drawing toolbar. In the menu that appears, point to Rotate or Flip, and then click Rotate Left 90°, Rotate Right 90°, Flip Horizontal, or Flip Vertical. (The Picture toolbar also contains a button called Rotate Left 90° that you can use.)

Adjusting Brightness and Contrast

If you have a picture with brightness or contrast problems—maybe it looks washed out or it's too dark—try using the More Contrast, Less Contrast, More Brightness, and Less Brightness buttons on the Picture toolbar (see Figure 17.12). Select the image and then click the desired button one or more times until you see the desired effect. These tools are especially useful for photographs.

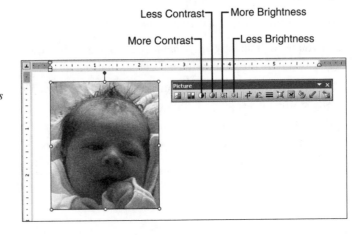

FIGURE 17.12
This photograph was lightened with the Less Brightness tool.

Modifying a WordArt Image

As you've seen, many of the tools you can use with pictures and drawing objects also work with WordArt images. However, the WordArt toolbar also contains five tools that are specific to modifying WordArt images (see Figure 17.13). The WordArt toolbar appears automatically when a WordArt image is selected, but you can display it at any time by choosing View, Toolbars, WordArt.

FIGURE 17.13
WordArt comes with some special tools.

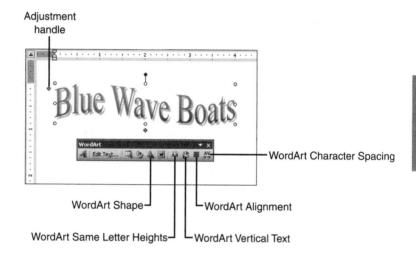

Adjustment handle

WordArt Character Spacing

WordArt Shape

WordArt Alignment

WordArt Same Letter Heights

WordArt Vertical Text

17

The names of the WordArt tools give you a good idea of what they do:

- WordArt Shape—Use this tool to change the overall shape formed by the letters in your WordArt.

- WordArt Same Letter Heights—Use this tool if you want the lower- and uppercase letters in your WordArt text to be the same height.

- WordArt Vertical Text—Use this tool to stack the letters in your WordArt image vertically.

- WordArt Alignment—Use this tool if your WordArt image has two or more lines of text and you want to change their alignment.

- WordArt Character Spacing—Use this tool to adjust the amount of space between the letters.

You may have noticed the two small yellow diamonds that appear when a WordArt image that is formatted with a text-wrapping option is selected. These are adjustment handles; you can drag either one of them to skew the image.

Adding a Watermark to Your Document

If you want an image to appear behind your text, you might want to format it as a watermark. When you do this, Word washes out the colors in the image to make the text on top of it legible. Word provides two options for creating a watermark: You can use tools on the Picture toolbar to turn an image that's already in your document into a watermark, or you can use the Printed Watermark dialog box. One advantage of the first option is that it lets you put the watermark on some pages of a multiple-page document, but not on others. (In contrast, the second option automatically places the watermark on all pages of a multiple-page document.) An advantage of the second option is that it allows you to create a text watermark.

Formatting an Image Already In Your Document As a Watermark

If you just use the Behind Text text-wrapping option to send an image behind the text of your document but don't alter the colors of the image, the text on top of it may be hard to read. Figure 17.14 shows an announcement that's overlaid on top of a leaf image. The image was originally black and white, but formatting it as a watermark turned the black to a light gray.

FIGURE 17.14

The text over the watermark is easy to read.

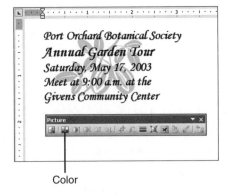

Color

Follow these steps to create a watermark:

1. Select the image, click the **Text Wrapping** button in the Picture toolbar (or Drawing toolbar), and choose **Behind Text**.

2. Click the **Color** button in the Picture toolbar (refer to Figure 17.14), and click **Washout**.

When an image is behind text, it can be hard to select. If you're having trouble, click the Select Objects button on the Drawing toolbar (the white mouse pointer). The mouse pointer changes to a white arrow. Click the image to select it. When you're finished using the Select Objects button, click it again to turn it off and return to your regular I-beam mouse pointer.

If you want a watermark to appear on every page of a multiple-page document (or on some pages, but not others), follow the previous steps, but insert the image in the header or footer. (Choose View, Header and Footer and click in the header or footer area before inserting the image.) The image can be much bigger than the default header or footer area. In fact, you can drag it out of the header or footer area so that it appears over the document text. In Figure 17.15, the selected clip art is formatted with the Behind Text and Washout options. The image is still inserted in the header, even though it has been dragged down underneath the header area.

Figure 17.16 shows the same document in Print Layout view so that you can see how the watermark will look when the document is printed.

17

FIGURE 17.15

Put the watermark in the header or footer if you want it to print on more than one page.

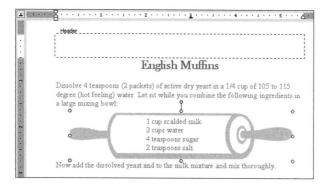

FIGURE 17.16

The watermark in this figure was placed in the header.

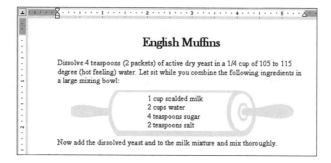

If you want the watermark to appear on some but not all pages of your document, divide your document into sections and only insert the watermark in the header or footer of the sections in which you want it to appear. For more information about creating section breaks and varying your headers and footers, refer to Hour 8, "Formatting Pages."

Adding a New Watermark

If you want a text watermark, or if you haven't yet inserted the image that you want to format as a watermark, you can use the Printed Watermark dialog box. This method automatically adds the watermark to every page, and it allows you to insert text watermarks as well as an image. To use this approach, follow these steps:

1. Choose **Format**, **Background**, **Printed Watermark** to display the Printed Watermark dialog box (see Figure 17.17). The options in the dialog box are dim until you mark the Picture Watermark or Text Watermark option button.

FIGURE 17.17

Use the Printed Watermark dialog box to insert an image or a text watermark.

2. To insert a picture watermark, mark the **Picture Watermark** option button, and then click the **Select Picture** button.

3. In the Insert Picture dialog box that appears, navigate to and select the image you want to use, and click the **Insert** button.

4. The path and name of the image now appear to the right of the Select Picture button. If you want to control how Word scales the image, select a setting other than Auto in the **Scale** drop-down list. By default, Word will wash out the image so that any text on top of it is easy to read. If you don't want to wash it out, clear the **Washout** check box.

5. If you want to insert a text watermark, mark the **Text Watermark** option button, and choose the desired text, font, size, color, and layout options.

6. When you've made your choices, click **OK**.

Figure 17.18 shows a document in Print Preview that includes the word *DRAFT* as a text watermark.

FIGURE 17.18

Word handles the formatting of text or image watermarks for you.

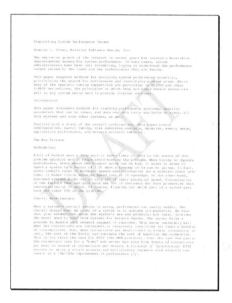

Working with Text Boxes

Text boxes provide a great deal of flexibility in arranging text on a page. You can use them for sidebars, pull quotes in newspaper or magazine-style articles, and text labels in a drawing, among other things. In addition to formatting both the text boxes and the text they contain, you can also link text boxes together so that text flows from one text box into the next.

Formatting the Text in a Text Box

As you learned earlier in this hour, you can format a text box in the same way you can other drawing objects—applying a fill color, border colors, and so on. You can also format the text in a text box with any standard font and paragraph option in the Formatting toolbar. This includes changing the font color with the Font Color button, which appears in both the Formatting toolbar and the Drawing toolbar (refer to Figure 17.9). Finally, you can change the text direction. When a text box is selected, a small Text Box toolbar appears. This toolbar contains a Change Text Direction button (refer to Figure 17.19). Click the button one or more times to change the orientation of your text.

If you don't see the Text Box toolbar, you can also choose Format, Text Direction. This menu command becomes active when a text box is selected.

Before issuing a command to format a text box, select the entire text box to format all the text it contains, or drag over a portion of the text to format just that amount.

You can select the text box itself by clicking anywhere on its border, or activate the area inside the text box by clicking anywhere inside it. When the text box itself is selected, the insertion point inside the text box disappears, and the borders of the text box are made up of tiny dots. When the area inside a text box is activated, an insertion point appears inside the text box, and the borders are made up of slash marks. Sometimes this distinction makes a difference. For example, if you want to move or copy a text box, you need to select the entire box before issuing the Cut or Copy command; otherwise, Word will think you want to cut or copy text within the box.

Linking Text Boxes

If you want text to flow from one text box to another, you can link them together. To do so, follow these steps:

1. Create at least the first two text boxes (you can add more later).
2. Select the first text box, and then click the **Create Text Box Link** button on the Text Box toolbar. (If you don't see the toolbar, choose View, Toolbars, Text Box.)
3. The mouse pointer changes to look like a measuring cup from which you "pour" text into the next text box (see Figure 17.19). Click the text box to which you want to create your link.
4. Type your text in the first text box. When the text box is full, the text spills into the second text box (see Figure 17.20).
5. To move from one linked text box to another, click the **Previous Text Box** and **Next Text Box** buttons on the Text Box toolbar.
6. If you want to break the link between two text boxes, select the first text box and then click the **Break Forward Link** button in the Text Box toolbar. All of the text returns to the first text box. If you break the links between text boxes and then go back and revise the text, it will no longer flow correctly from one text box to the next.

Formatting and linking text boxes works the same whether or not they are in a drawing canvas. In Figures 17.19 and 17.20, the text boxes were created without a drawing canvas.

Previous Text Box

Break Forward Link

Next Text Box

Create Text Box Link

Change Text Direction

FIGURE 17.19

When you see the special Text Box Link mouse pointer, click the text box to which you want to link.

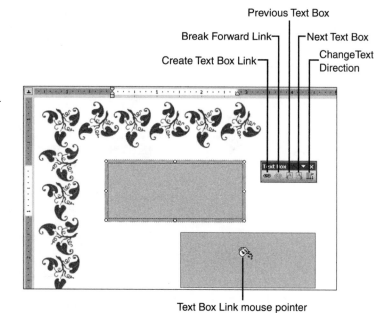

Text Box Link mouse pointer

FIGURE 17.20

When text boxes are linked, text spills from one to the next.

Spring is here and it's time to start thinking about what to plant. We are thought it would be nice to

go in on a seed order together, and it seems a pleasant way to do this would be to have a brunch

Using a Drawing Canvas

The drawing canvas provides an area on which you can draw multiple objects—including WordArt images—and keep them together as you manipulate them. If you place your drawing objects on a drawing canvas, you can treat them as a unit without having to group them together (see "Grouping Images" later in this hour).

As you learned in the last hour, when you draw shapes using drawing tools on the Drawing toolbar, Word automatically places them within a drawing canvas, as shown in

Figure 17.21. (Note the black sizing handles on the drawing canvas.) If you haven't yet
drawn any shapes but want to start with an empty canvas, you can choose Insert, Picture,
New Drawing to insert an empty drawing canvas in your document, and then draw
objects on top of it.

FIGURE 17.21

*The drawing canvas
keeps multiple objects
together.*

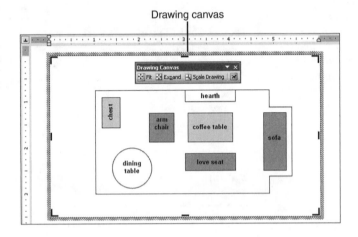

Word places your drawing canvas inline. If you want to apply a text-wrapping option to
your canvas, you can do so using the same steps as described in "Controlling the Text
Flow Around an Image" earlier in this hour.

You can resize a drawing canvas by dragging its handles on the sides and corners. When
you do this, the objects within the canvas stay the same size, and Word does not allow
you to shrink the canvas smaller than the size required to hold the objects it contains.

To delete a drawing canvas and all of the objects it contains, select it (click anywhere on
its border) and press the Delete key.

If you'd rather not have a drawing canvas appear automatically when you draw a shape
with a drawing tool, follow these steps to turn it off:

1. Choose **Tools**, **Options**, and click the **General** tab.

2. Clear the **Automatically Create Drawing Canvas When Inserting AutoShapes**
   check box.

3. Click **OK**.

If you clear this check box, your drawing objects will automatically be formatted with
the In Front of Text text-wrapping option when you add them to your document.

If you don't want to use the drawing canvas but forget to turn it off before clicking a drawing tool in the Drawing toolbar, you can make the drawing canvas go away by deliberately drawing your shape outside the borders of the canvas.

If you want to take an object off the drawing canvas, simply drag it off with the mouse. You can now manipulate it independently. To move an existing object onto the drawing canvas, apply a text-wrapping option if the object is inline, and then drag it onto the canvas.

The drawing canvas automatically appears with the Drawing Canvas toolbar (refer back to Figure 17.21), which contains three tools designed specifically for manipulating a drawing canvas:

- Fit—Click this button to shrink the drawing canvas so that it fits tightly around the objects it contains.

- Expand—Click this button to slightly expand the drawing canvas. The objects within it do not change size.

- Scale Drawing—Click this button to put white circle sizing handles around the canvas. You can now drag any of the handles to enlarge or shrink the canvas. Word resizes all of the objects contained in the canvas proportionately. When you're finished, click the button again to turn it off.

If you don't see the Drawing Canvas toolbar, right-click a blank part of the drawing canvas and choose Show Drawing Canvas Toolbar.

Working with Multiple Images

When you are creating a drawing made up of multiple drawing objects, or if you have more than one picture on a page, you may need to stack images on top of one another, align them, or group them together to treat them as a unit. As you learned in the previous section, if you're working with drawing objects or WordArt, some of these tasks are easier to accomplish if you place the objects in a drawing canvas. In the remainder of this hour, you'll learn a variety of techniques for working with multiple images.

Ordering Images

If you have moved images on top of one another, you can reorder them however you like. Select the image in the stack that you want to move, click the Draw button on the Drawing toolbar, point to Order, and choose one of these commands:

17

- Bring to Front—Brings the image to the top of the stack.
- Send to Back—Sends the image to the bottom of the stack.
- Bring Forward—Moves the image up one level at a time.
- Send Backward—Moves the image down one level at a time.
- Bring in Front of Text—Brings image in front of text if the text-wrapping option is currently set to Behind Text.
- Send Behind Text—Sends image behind text if the text-wrapping option is currently set to In Front of Text.

Figure 17.22 shows two copies of a stork and frog pair. On the left, the frog image is in front. On the right, it has been sent to the back.

FIGURE 17.22

You can order stacked images however you like.

This frog is hiding.

Selecting Multiple Images

When you're working with multiple images, it helps to be able to select more than one at a time. When multiple images are selected, you can then move them as a unit, apply the same formatting to all of them, copy or delete all of them at once, and so on.

To select multiple images, click the first one, and then Shift+click the additional ones. If you need to select a large number of images, click the Select Objects button in the Drawing toolbar (the white arrow toward the left end of the toolbar), and then drag to draw a large rectangle around all the images. When you release the mouse button, they will all be selected. To remove one image from a selection, Shift+click it again. If you want to deselect all the images, click anywhere else in the document.

If you frequently handle the same set of images together, consider putting them on a drawing canvas.

Grouping Images

When you group two or more images, Word treats them as a single object. This makes it possible to maintain the same spatial relationships between them when you move them around. To group images, select them all, click the Draw button in the Drawing toolbar, and click Group. When the images are grouped, you will see only one set of sizing handles around all of them, as shown in Figure 17.23.

FIGURE 17.23

These three photographs are grouped together.

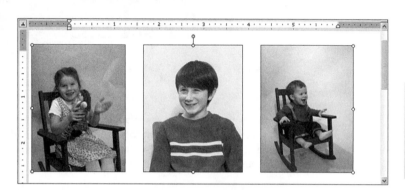

17

To ungroup images, select the group and choose Ungroup in the Draw menu. As soon as they are ungrouped, they all get their own sizing handles. If you ungroup a set of images to manipulate one of the images in the group independently and then want to group them again, make sure one of the members of the group is selected and choose Regroup in the Draw menu. Word remembers which objects were originally in the group and includes them again.

You can group a set of images and then set a text-wrapping option for the entire group. However, if you later ungroup the images so that you can manipulate one of the images individually, and then regroup them, Word does not automatically restore the text-wrapping option that you originally applied to the grouped objects. To avoid this annoying behavior, place multiple objects in a drawing canvas and then set a text-wrapping option on the canvas instead.

Aligning and Distributing Images

If you want to align two or more images with each other, select them all, click the Draw button, point to Align or Distribute, and choose any of the alignment options in the submenu that appears. (The commands Distribute Horizontally and Distribute Vertically put an even amount of space between the selected images.) In Figure 17.24, the two photographs have been aligned in the middle.

FIGURE 17.24

These two photographs are aligned on the middle.

> If you want to align objects relative to the page instead of to each other, click the Draw button, point to Align or Distribute, and then click Relative to Page at the bottom of the submenu. When you want to turn off this feature, just click the command again.

Summary

If you're at all visually oriented, you'll get a kick out of working with images. In addition to adjusting the size and position of an image, you can also crop portions out, change the way text flows around the image, and tweak its appearance in many other ways. And if you have several images overlapping or in close proximity to one another, you can change the way they are arranged and aligned, either with or without a drawing canvas. In the next hour, you switch gears and start learning how to collaborate on documents and integrate Word with other Office products.

Q&A

Q I've aligned several drawing objects along their top edges, and now I want to shift one to the right. How can I drag it without accidentally moving it out of vertical alignment with the other images?

A If you hold down the Shift key as you drag an image, Word lets you move it only vertically or horizontally, but not both. This lets you maintain an image's alignment with other images as you drag.

Q I want to have finer control over resizing, moving, cropping, and images. Is this possible?

A Yes. When you drag to resize, move, or crop an image, Word uses invisible grid-lines to respond to your mouse movements. By default, the gridlines are 0.13 inch apart. If you reduce this amount to, say, 0.02 to 0.05 inch, you will have much finer control. To do this, click the Draw button in the Drawing toolbar, and click Grid to display the Drawing Grid dialog box. Under Grid Settings, decrease the values in the Horizontal Spacing and Vertical Spacing text boxes, and then click OK. (You can also hold down the Ctrl key as you drag to crop all four sides of a picture equally.)

Q **I rotated a drawing object and now I want to get it back to its original orientation. How do I do this?**

A Double-click the object to display the Format dialog box. Then click the Size tab, change the setting in the Rotation text box back to 0, and click OK.

Q **I resized and cropped an image, and now I want to get it back to its original state. What do I do?**

A Double-click the image to display the Format dialog box. To reset the size, click the Size tab, and then click the Reset button. To reset cropping and any changes you made to the image's brightness and contrast, click the Picture tab and click the Reset button. Then click OK.

17

PART V

Collaboration and Integration

Hour

HOUR 18

Collaborating on Documents

In today's office environments, people are increasingly abandoning red ink pens, highlighters, and post-it slips in favor of software tools that enable them to collaborate on documents without printing them out. For example, you can write the rough draft of a document in Word and send it to a colleague for review. Your colleague edits the document onscreen and then sends it to a second person, who adds more revisions before e-mailing the document back to you. After you receive the edited copy, you incorporate your colleagues' suggestions and finalize the document. In this hour, you learn how to use Word's collaboration tools and a few related features that come in handy when working on documents with other people. When you arrive at the sections on inserting comments and tracking changes to a document, keep in mind that Word uses the term markup to refer collectively to both of these features.

The highlights of this hour include

- Using the highlighter to call attention to text
- Inserting comments in a document
- Tracking the changes made to a document
- Protecting your document from revisions
- Saving multiple versions of a document
- Ensuring that your Word documents are compatible with older versions of Word

Using the Highlighter

Word's highlight feature lets you mark up your document onscreen just as you would use a highlighter pen to mark up a printed document. Highlighting is designed for use on documents that you'll edit onscreen, but it will also print out. If you don't have a color printer, highlighting prints in a shade of gray.

To use the highlighter, follow these steps:

1. Click the down arrow to the right of the Highlight button on the Formatting toolbar, and click the color that you want to use in the palette that appears (see Figure 18.1).

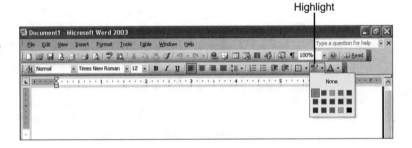

FIGURE 18.1

You can choose among many highlighter colors.

2. The I-beam takes on the shape of a highlighter pen. Drag across the text that you want to highlight, and then release the mouse button.

3. The text is now highlighted with the color you chose (see Figure 18.2). Highlight any other text you like, and then click the Highlight button again to turn the feature off.

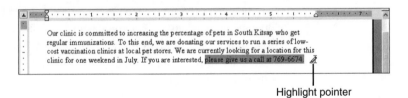

FIGURE 18.2

Highlight text to call attention to it.

The Highlight button shows the color that you most recently selected from the palette. If you want to use that color, click the button itself in step 1 instead of choosing a color in the palette.

Another way to apply highlighting is to select the text and then click the Highlight button (or display the palette and choose a different highlight color).

To remove highlighting, select the text, display the Highlight palette, and choose None.

Working with Comments

You may, at times, want to write notes in a document (either to yourself or to other people) that don't print out. Word's Comment feature lets you add comments that reference particular blocks of text and track comments from multiple people. Furthermore, each person's comments appear in a different color, which makes them easy to differentiate onscreen.

If you work extensively with comments, you'll appreciate the buttons in the Reviewing toolbar (choose View, Toolbars, Reviewing), shown in Figure 18.3.

FIGURE 18.3

The Reviewing toolbar contains buttons for working with comments.

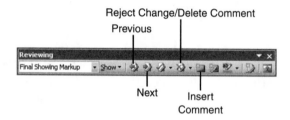

Using Print Layout View

The comments feature behaves differently depending on whether you're in Print Layout or Normal view. These steps for inserting a comment assume you are using Print Layout view:

1. Select the text that you want to comment on.
2. Click the **Insert Comment** button in the Reviewing toolbar. (You can also choose Insert, Comment or press Alt+Ctrl+M.)
3. Word highlights the text you selected and creates a balloon to the right of the document text that includes a reference mark. The reference mark is made up of the word *Comment*, your initials, and a sequential number (each person's comments are numbered sequentially). Type your comment in the balloon (see Figure 18.4).

FIGURE 18.4

Type your comment in the balloon.

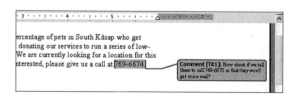

18

4. Click in the document text when you are done. You may also need to use the horizontal scroll bar to scroll the left edge of your document back into view.

After you finish the comment, the text you selected remains highlighted and enclosed in thin colored brackets to indicate that there is a comment about it. A dotted line runs from the highlighted text to the balloon. To read the comment, you can read the contents of the balloon or simply rest the mouse pointer over the highlighted text. In a moment, a ScreenTip appears with the name of the person who wrote the comment and the comment itself (see Figure 18.5).

FIGURE 18.5

Rest your mouse pointer over highlighted text to read the associated comment.

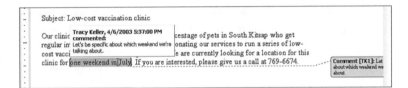

To move from one comment to the next in a document, click the Next and Previous buttons in the Reviewing toolbar. If your document also includes tracked changes and you don't want to stop at each tracked change, click the Show button in the Reviewing toolbar and clear the check mark next to Insertions and Deletions to temporarily hide tracked changes from view.

To edit a comment, click in the balloon and revise the text. (If you right-click the highlighted text of any comment and choose Edit Comment in the context menu, Word places the insertion point in the associated balloon.)

To delete a comment, click either the highlighted text or the balloon and click the Reject Change/Delete Comment button on the Reviewing toolbar (or right-click the highlighted text or balloon and choose Delete Comment from the context menu). If you want to delete all the comments in your document, click the down arrow to the right of the Reject Change/Delete Comment button and choose Delete All Comments in Document.

If you want to temporarily hide the highlights in the text and the balloons from view to get a clean view of your document, click the Show button in the Reviewing toolbar and click Comments in the menu that appears to clear its check mark.

Using Normal View

If you are using Normal view, clicking the Insert Comment button on the Reviewing toolbar opens the Reviewing pane at the bottom of the Word window (see Figure 18.6) and inserts a header for your comment. After you've typed your text, click the Reviewing Pane button in the Reviewing toolbar to close the pane. By the same token, when you right-click highlighted text and choose Edit Comment in the context menu, Word opens the Reviewing pane and places your insertion point in the appropriate comment text. You'll also notice that in Normal view the reference mark appears in the document text immediately after the highlighted text.

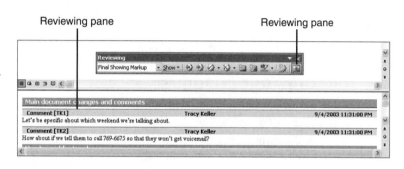

FIGURE 18.6
When you're using Normal view, you enter comments in the Reviewing pane.

Reviewing pane   Reviewing pane

Some people find the balloons distracting. If you would prefer to always use the Reviewing pane instead of balloons, even when you're using Print Layout view, click the Show button in the Reviewing toolbar and point to Balloons. In the submenu that appears, choose Never.

18

Tracking Changes to a Document

The cornerstone of Word's collaboration features is *track changes*. This feature lets you track the revisions (insertions, deletions, and some formatting changes) that are made to a document. When the feature is turned on, any text you insert in the document is displayed in color with an underline, or off to the side in a "balloon," depending on the view you're using. Text you delete is shown in color with strikethrough, or off to the side in a balloon. If more than one person edits a document, each person's changes show up in a different color. When you are ready to finalize a document, you can go through and accept or reject each tracked change. Accepting changes will remove any deleted text and incorporate any additions into the original document. Rejecting changes reverts your document to the original text. You can accept and reject each change independently or all changes at one time with or without reviewing each one individually.

As you work with tracked changes, you will use the buttons in the Reviewing toolbar, shown in Figure 18.7.

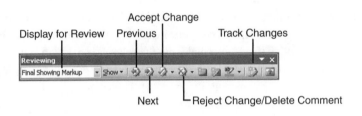

FIGURE 18.7

The Reviewing toolbar contains buttons for working with tracked changes.

Tracking Your Changes

To turn track changes on or off, click the Track Changes button in the Reviewing toolbar (or Tools, Track Changes). The TRK indicator in the status bar at the bottom of the Word window is dark when track changes is turned on. (You can also double-click the TRK indicator to toggle this feature on and off.)

After you've turned on track changes, revise your text as you normally do. If you're using Print Layout view, inserted text will be colored and underlined, and deleted text will be removed from the text stream and placed in a balloon to the right of the document. (This description assumes you have selected the default setting for displaying markup—Final Showing Markup. You'll learn more about this setting later in this section.) If more than one person has edited a document and you want to see who made a particular change, rest your mouse pointer over the revision (either inserted text in the text stream or deleted text in a balloon). A ScreenTip appears that lists the name of the person who made the edit and the date on which it was made (see Figure 18.8).

FIGURE 18.8

When you rest your mouse pointer over a tracked change, Word tells you who made the change and when.

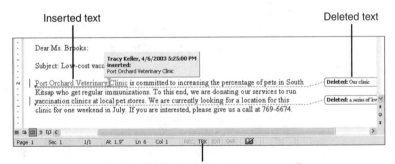

One of the most useful parts of the track changes feature is the Display for Review drop-down list in the Reviewing toolbar, which provides four different views of the revisions that have been made to your document:

- Final Showing Markup—Shows tracked changes and comments. Puts the insertions in the text stream and the deletions in balloons. This option (the default) is a good one for editors to use because it shows you the document in its revised state.

- Final—Hides tracked changes and comments. Shows the document as it will appear if you accept all the changes. This option is a good one to use when you're ready to proofread your document before finalizing it.

- Original Showing Markup—Shows tracked changes and comments. Puts the deletions in the text stream and the insertions in balloons. This option is a good one for authors because it enables them to focus on what changes people have made to their original text.

- Original—Hides tracked changes and comments. Shows the document as it was before it was edited.

Figure 18.9 shows the same text as you saw in Figure 18.8, but the Final option is chosen instead of Final Showing Markup. Choosing Final (or Original) does not turn off the track changes feature; it merely hides the changes. If you like, you can edit the document while changes are hidden, and Word continues to track your edits. When you next choose Final Showing Markup or Original Showing Markup, you will see all the revisions you have made, both those you made when changes were visible and those you made when they were hidden.

18

FIGURE 18.9

Hiding tracked changes by choosing Final is a great way to see how the text would read if the changes were all accepted.

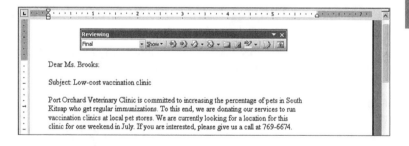

As with comments, you can temporarily hide all insertions and deletions from view by clicking the Show button and then clicking Insertions and Deletions in the menu that appears. If you do this while Final Showing Markup is selected in the Display While Reviewing drop-down list, the text will appear as it would if you chose Final. By the same token, Original and Original Showing Markup would appear the same. (Of course, if your document also contains comments and Comments is still marked in the Show menu, you will see your comments when you choose Final Showing Markup or Original Showing Markup.)

If you are using Normal view, or if you have turned off the balloons feature, both your insertions and deletions will appear in the text stream (see Figure 18.10).

FIGURE 18.10

When you're using Normal view or have turned off the balloon feature, insertions and deletions both appear in the text.

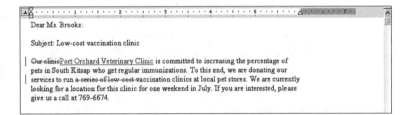

Dear Ms. Brooks:

Subject: Low-cost vaccination clinic

~~Our clinic~~Port Orchard Veterinary Clinic is committed to increasing the percentage of pets in South Kitsap who get regular immunizations. To this end, we are donating our services to run ~~a series of low-cost~~ vaccination clinics at local pet stores. We are currently looking for a location for this clinic for one weekend in July. If you are interested, please give us a call at 769-6674.

In this situation, the Final Showing Markup and Original Showing Markup display options are identical.

When you turn track changes on, Word tracks who made what formatting changes as well as changes to the document text, but by default it hides the markup for formatting changes from view. To display formatting change markup, click the Show button in the Reviewing toolbar and choose Formatting.

Understanding the Colors of Tracked Changes

By default, Word assigns a different color to each person (*author*) who edits a document. To see how this works, choose Tools, Options to display the Options dialog box and click the Track Changes tab (see Figure 18.11).

FIGURE 18.11

The Track Changes tab of the Options dialog box lets you change the settings for track changes.

For the colors to work properly, you have to use the default setting of By Author in the Color lists for Insertions and Deletions. You can't choose a particular color for your revisions; when you edit a document with track changes turned on, Word assigns you the next available color in its color palette. If you choose a specific color in the Color lists, all authors' edits will appear in that color, which pretty much defeats the purpose of using track changes.

Helping Word Recognize Different Authors

Word recognizes the different authors who work on a document by checking the name that's listed in the Name text box in the User Information tab of the Options dialog box (Tools, Options), as shown in Figure 18.12.

FIGURE 18.12

Make sure your user information is current before using track changes.

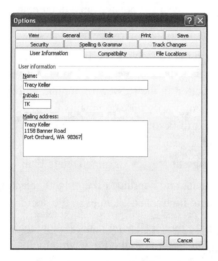

18

Before you use track changes, you should check the User Information tab and make sure that your name is entered correctly. If it isn't and you revise a document with track changes turned on, other people who review the document after you will assume that your edits were made by whoever happens to be listed in the User Information tab.

If you edit a document on a computer where you don't have an account, Word will assume the changes were made by the person whose account you were borrowing. To avoid this situation, you need to update the User Information tab before editing the document. But don't forget to set it back when you are done!

In some cases, you may need to edit a document twice. If you want your edits on separate passes to appear in different colors, change the name in the User Information tab before you begin your second pass. For example, you could enter *Tina Larson (first pass)* in the User Information tab before beginning your first pass and then change it to *Tina Larson (second pass)* before beginning your second pass.

Accepting and Rejecting Tracked Changes

When you have finished editing a document with track changes, you need to go through and decide whether to accept or reject each of the revisions. If you accept an insertion, the inserted text becomes part of the document. If you accept a deletion, the text is removed.

Follow these steps to accept or reject the changes in a document:

1. Press **Ctrl+Home** to move to the top of the document.
2. Click the **Next** button in the Reviewing toolbar to find and select the next change. If your document also includes comments and you don't want to stop at each comment, click the Show button in the Reviewing toolbar and clear the check mark next to Comments to temporarily hide comments from view. Similarly, you should clear the check box next to Formatting in the Show menu if you don't want Word to stop at formatting changes.
3. Click the **Accept Change** or **Reject Change/Delete Comment** toolbar button.
4. Click **Next Change** again, and continue accepting or rejecting changes until Word informs you that it found no tracked changes in the document.

You can also review changes in the Reviewing pane. Follow the preceding steps, but after step 1, click the Reviewing Pane button in the Reviewing toolbar and click in the Reviewing pane to activate it. Then continue with the remaining steps. An advantage of using the Reviewing pane is that it lists the author and date of each change.

You can accept all the changes in the document by clicking the down arrow to the right of the Accept Change button and choosing Accept All Changes in Document. Or, if you've used the Show button to hide formatting changes or insertions and deletions, you can choose Accept All Changes Shown to accept only those changes that are currently shown. To use the two equivalent options for rejecting changes, click the down arrow to the right of the Reject Change/Delete Comment button and choose Reject All Changes in Document or Reject All Changes Shown.

Remembering to Finalize Your Document

If you have hidden tracked changes or comments, it's pretty easy to forget that they are there and assume that your document has already been finalized. Sending out a document that contains markup when you thought it was finalized can cause great embarrassment or, in the worse cases, breaches in confidentiality or security. Word helps prevent these problems in two ways.

First, by default Word shows hidden markup every time you open a document to remind you that it's there. Second, Word can warn you before you print, save, or send a file that contains markup. (This option is turned off by default.) Note that Word only warns you when you save if you have edited or formatted the document since your last save. And it only warns you about e-mailing the document if you send it from within Word (see Hour 22, "Using Word for E-mail"). (At the time of this writing, if you marked the check box labeled Make Hidden Markup Visible When Opening or Saving, Word only made hidden markup visible when you opened a document, not when you saved it.)

If you want enable or disable either of these features, choose Tools, Options to display the Options dialog box. Click the Security tab, and mark or clear the check box labeled Make Hidden Markup Visible When Opening or Saving or the check box labeled Warn Before Printing, Saving or Sending a File That Contains Tracked Changes or Comments.

Protecting Documents from Being Opened or Modified

18

You might want to require a password to enable people to open and/or modify your document (or template). For example, there may be a group of people that you want to be able to open and read your document, and within that group, a few people that you want to be able to actually modify the document. If you require a password to open your document, Word encrypts the file and decrypts it only when the user enters the correct password. If you require a password to modify your document, anyone can open and edit your document, but they can't overwrite the original document with their revised version. Instead, they are required to save the edited document under a different name and/or location. Only users who enter the correct password can overwrite the original with a modified version. You can use just one of these types of passwords on a document or use them both together.

To protect your document from being opened and/or modified, follow these steps:

1. With the document onscreen, choose **File**, **Save As**.

2. Click the **Tools** button at the top of the Save As dialog box, and click **Security Options**.

3. In the Security dialog box (see Figure 18.13), type a password in the **Password to Open** and/or **Password to Modify** text box. Passwords can be up to 15 characters long, and they are case sensitive. If you are requiring a password to open the document, you can select among a range of encryption types. To do so, click the

Advanced button. If you aren't sure what type of encryption to use, check with your system administrator.

You can display the same security settings by choosing Tools, Options and clicking the Security tab. It doesn't matter which route you take to get to these settings; both methods will apply the settings to the current document only.

4. Click **OK**.

5. Retype the password in the Confirm Password dialog box, and click **OK** again to return to the Save As dialog box. If you entered passwords for both opening and modifying the document, you will see two Confirm Password dialog boxes. Enter the password for opening the file in the first dialog box and the password for modifying the file in the second.

6. Finish saving the document.

If you required a password to open the document, the next time you issue the command to open the document, the Password dialog box shown in Figure 18.14 appears.

If you required a password to modify the document, you will see the dialog box shown in Figure 18.15. (If you required both types of passwords, Word will only display the dialog box for modifying the document if you entered a correct password for opening the document.)

FIGURE 18.15

Type the password and click OK to modify the document.

If you know the password to modify the document, you can enter it and click OK. Otherwise, you have to click the Read Only button to open the document. When you open a document as a read-only file, the label [Read-Only] appears in the title bar to remind you that if you revise the document, you will have to save the edited document under a new name.

> The Read-Only Recommended check box in the Security dialog box gives you the lightest level of protection. If you mark it, Word suggests that the user open the document as a read-only file, but doesn't require him/her to do so. If you don't need a high level of protection and just want to give a user the option of opening the document as a read-only file, use this technique.

18

Saving Different Versions of a Document

If you want to keep track of multiple versions of the same document as you're working on it, you might want to store them all in one place under the same filename instead of saving them as separate documents. Word's versioning feature lets you save "snapshots" of a document at its various stages of development so that you can refer back to previous versions if need be. For each version, Word stores information about who created it, when it was created, and a brief description of it.

To save a version of a document, follow these steps:

1. Open the document and revise it if desired to create the version that you want to save.

2. Choose **File**, **Save As**.

3. Click the **Tools** button at the top of the Save As dialog box, and click **Save Version**.

4. In the Save Version dialog box, type a brief comment about the version that's onscreen (see Figure 18.16).

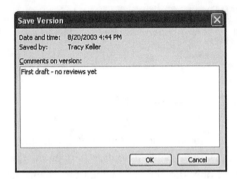

5. Click **OK**.

You can repeat these steps to continue saving "snapshots" of the document during your editing process.

When you want to open the most recent version of the document, just open it as you would open any other file. If you want to open a previous version, first open the document, and then choose File, Versions to display the Versions dialog box (see Figure 18.17). This dialog box lists any versions of the document that you have saved with the versioning feature. Select the one that you want to review, and click the Open button.

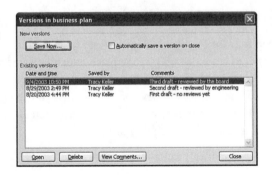

Word arranges the current version in a Word window across the top half of your screen and the previous version in a separate Word window beneath it. This enables you to review both versions at the same time. If you decide to modify a previous version, you are required to save the modified version as a separate file so that the record of versions in the original file isn't altered.

Making Your Word Documents Compatible with Earlier Versions of Word

Word 2003 saves files in the same format as Word 2000, Word 2002 (XP), and Word 97, so someone who is using these older versions of Word can open your Word 2003 documents without converting them. You can also open older Word documents in Word 2003 without a conversion process. However, Word 2003 does have some features that are not supported by earlier versions of Word. If you want to create documents specifically for use in Word 97 or Word 6.0/95—perhaps most of the people in your office are still using Word 97 or Word 6.0 (95)—you can tell Word 2003 to disable all the features that Word 97 or Word 6.0/95 does not support. Follow these steps:

1. Choose **Tools**, **Options**.
2. Click the **Save** tab (see Figure 18.18).

FIGURE 18.18

Use the Save tab to disable features not supported by Word 97.

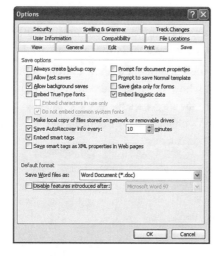

18

3. Mark the **Disable Features Introduced After** check box, and choose Word 97 or Word 6.0/95 in the drop-down list.
4. Click **OK**.

Word 2003 does not save files in the same format as Word 6.0 or Word 95. If you want to give a document to someone who is using one of these versions of Word, you need to save it in a format that he or she can open. To do so, choose Word 97-2003 & 6.0/95 – RTF in the Save As Type list at the bottom of the Save As dialog box. When you open a Word 6.0/95 file in Word 2003, it automatically converts it to Word 2003 format for you.

Summary

Collaborating on documents with other people has plenty of rewards, but it can be frustrating if you lose track of who made what changes when. Word's collaboration features can bring some semblance of order to an essentially messy process. Now that you know some of the key collaboration features Word has to offer, you'll be better able to decide whether and how you and your colleagues might work on Word documents as a team.

Q&A

Q I need to send a document to someone, but don't want to include any information about the name of the author, and so on. I know this information is usually available when you choose File, Properties. Is there any way to strip this out?

A Yes. When the document is open, choose Tools, Options. In the Options dialog box, click the Security tab and mark the check box labeled Remove Personal Information from File Properties on Save.

Q Several people have reviewed my document and I want to review their changes and comments one by one. Is there a way to do this?

A Yes. In the Reviewing toolbar, click the Show button, point to Reviewers, and click the name of the person whose changes and comments you want to view. When you're ready to go on to the next person, repeat these steps. You can always go back to seeing everyone's changes and comments at once by choosing Reviewers, All Reviewers in the Show menu.

HOUR 19

Electronic Forms

If you or your coworkers often fill out simple forms by hand, or fill in the same small pieces of information in a Word document over and over, you may find it easier to create a *form* in Word that you and your officemates can use. A Word form is a document that contains *form fields*, such as text fields, check boxes, and drop-down lists. Users press the Tab key to move from field to field, filling in information as they go. Outside of the fields, forms are protected, so users can't format the document or change it other than by filling in fields. In this hour, you will learn the basics of creating and using forms. Keep in mind that if you are familiar with Visual Basic for Applications (VBA), you can greatly extend the power of forms with VBA macros and ActiveX controls.

The highlights of this hour include

- Creating forms for use in Word or as printed documents
- Filling in forms
- Making changes to forms
- Exploring options for extending the functionality of forms

Creating a Form

Before you begin the actual process of creating your form, think about how you want your form to look. Do you want to use a table so that the form can be arranged in rows and columns? If so, do you want the table gridlines to be showing or not? Or perhaps you want your form to look like a standard document containing paragraphs of text? Will your form only be filled out in Word, or do you want to print it out and have users fill out hard copies as well?

When you have a general layout in mind, you're ready to sit down at the computer. The process of creating a form involves four general steps:

1. Add all of the text and formatting to your document.
2. Insert the form fields and define how they will behave.
3. Protect the form.
4. Save the form as a template.

The next four sections describe these steps in more detail.

> Word's form fields do not allow you to specify *tab order*—that is, you can't specify the order in which the fields are activated when the user presses the Tab key. Rather, the Tab key activates form fields in the order in which they appear in the document. It's a good idea to keep this limitation in mind when you're designing your form.

Adding Text and Formatting to Your Form

The first step to laying out your form is to enter all of the text that you want to include in the form. This can include paragraphs of text, as well as labels for the form fields. You can also include any images you like to spruce up the appearance of the form. For now, don't worry about getting all of the text and formatting just right—you can modify it at any time. Figure 19.1 shows the beginnings of a form used by the administrators of a summer music camp to confirm registrations. The form is created so that it can be filled out in Word by camp staff and then sent to the camp participants. Note that it uses a Word table to align the content of the form. Tables work very well in this capacity.

FIGURE 19.1

This as-yet-unfinished form was created using a Word table. The form fields will go in the second and fourth columns.

Inserting Form Fields

When you've got the text of your form roughed in, you are ready to insert your form fields. Word provides these three types of form fields:

- Text—Use this form field if you want the user to enter text. You can use text form fields for data of the following types:

  Regular text—Use this type if it's okay for the user to type any combination of text, numbers, symbols, and spaces.

  Number—Use this type if you want to require the user to type a number.

  Date—Use this type if you want to require the user to type a date.

  Current date—Use this type if you want to display the current date in your form. The user cannot edit this field.

  Current time—Use this type if you want to display the current time in your form. The user cannot edit this field.

  Calculation—Use this type if you want to insert a formula in the form (using the syntax =(formula)) to calculate numbers. For example, you could use it to total a column of numbers, or to calculate the sales tax. The user cannot edit this field.

If you want Word to check the values that the user enters more carefully than the rudimentary checking of dates and numbers described in the preceding list, you need to write VBA code for entry or exit macros (see "Where to Go from Here" later in this hour) or to use with ActiveX controls. These

> tools would enable you to check whether a social security number was entered in the proper syntax, for example, or whether an employee ID number is indeed one that's found in your employee database. (You may be able to find VBA code that other people have written on the Web.)

- Drop-down list—Use this form field to create a drop-down list from which the user can select one item.
- Check box—Use this form field if you want to add one or more check boxes that the user can mark or clear. If you have multiple check boxes, the user will be able to mark more than one of them.

To add form fields to your form, you use the Forms toolbar, shown in Figure 19.2.

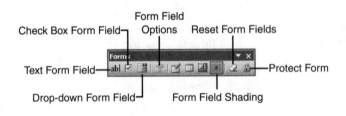

FIGURE 19.2
The Forms toolbar contains tools for inserting form fields and working with forms.

Follow the steps in the next three sections to add the different types of form fields to your form and tell Word how you want them to function.

Adding a Text Form Field

Follow these steps to insert a text form field:

1. Move your insertion point to the location where you want the text form field to go.
2. Choose **View**, **Toolbars**, **Forms** to display the Forms toolbar.
3. Click the **Text Form Field** button.
4. A blank text form field appears in your form. In Figure 19.3, the field is shaded to make it easy to see (the shading doesn't print). If you want to turn off field shading, click the **Field Shading** button in the Forms toolbar.
5. Double-click the text form field (or click it and then click the Form Field Options button in the Forms toolbar) to display the Text Form Field Options dialog box (see Figure 19.4).

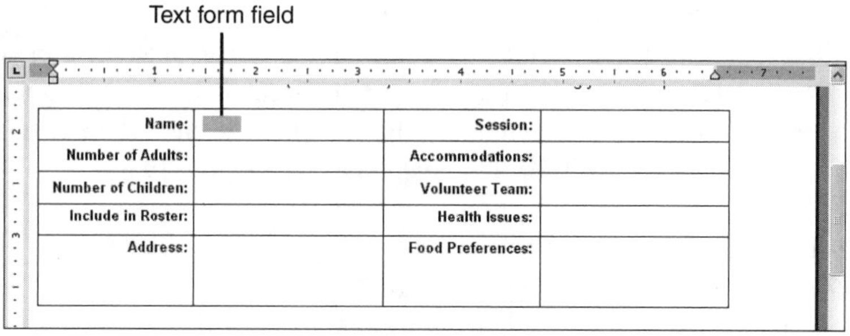

Text form field

FIGURE **19.3**

You can shade your form fields to make them easy to see.

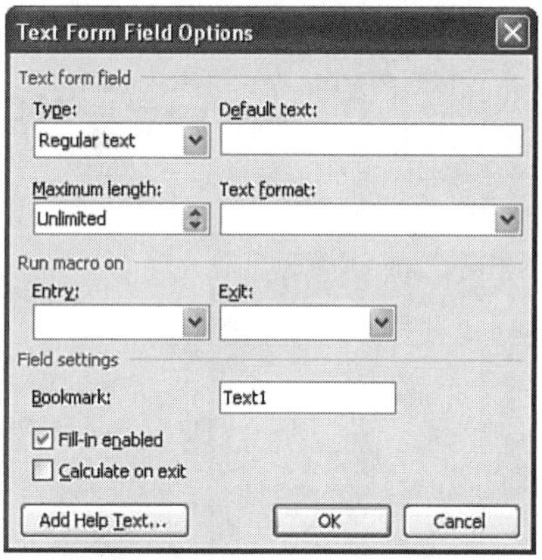

FIGURE **19.4**

Use the Text Form Field Options dialog box to define how you want your text form field to behave.

6. Use the **Type** drop-down list to specify the type of data that the user will enter in the text form field.

7. If you chose the Regular Text, Number, or Date type in the previous step and want a default entry to appear in the text field, type it in the **Default [type]** text box. (The text box will be labeled *Default Text*, *Default Number*, or *Default Date*.) If you chose the Current Date or Current Time type, this field will be dim. If you chose the Calculation type, this field will be labeled Expression. Use it to enter your formula.

8. Select an option from the **[type] Format** drop-down list. Depending on the type you selected in step 5, this field will be labeled *Text Format*, *Number Format*, *Date Format*, or *Time Format*. Use it to specify how you want the data to appear in the field.

9. Use the **Maximum Length** field to specify the maximum number of characters that you want the user to be able to enter in the text field. For text form fields of the Regular Text type, users will be able to press Enter to move to a new line, so you can use it for address fields.

19

10. You can, if you like, add *help text*—text that assists the user in filling out the field. This text can either appear in the status bar when the user activates the field (see Figure 19.5), or it can appear in a Help dialog box when the user activates the field and presses F1. To add help text, click the **Add Help Text** button to display the Form Field Help Text dialog box (see Figure 19.6).

FIGURE 19.5

The help text for the Include in Roster field appears in the status bar when the user tabs into the field.

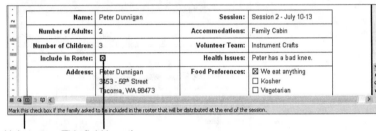

Help text   This field is active.

FIGURE 19.6

Use the Form Field Help Text dialog box to add text that will help the user fill in the field correctly.

11. Click the **Status Bar** or **Help Key (F1)** tab, depending on which type of help text you want to provide. The options in both tabs are identical.

12. If you or someone else has already created an AutoText entry that contains the text you want to use, mark the **AutoText Entry** option button and select the entry from the drop-down list. Otherwise, mark the **Type Your Own** option button and type the help text in the text box below the option button. When you're done, click **OK**.

13. See the "Automating Your Form" section later in this hour for information about the remaining fields in this dialog box. Then click **OK** to close the dialog box.

You have now inserted the text form field and defined how it will behave. Note that if your fields are shaded, Word does not change the length of the shaded text form field based on the maximum number of allowable characters, but when the user fills in the field, the field will expand to accommodate the allowable amount of text.

Adding a Check Box Form Field

Adding a check box form field to your document is a simple process. Follow these steps:

1. Move your insertion point to the location where you want the check box form field to go.

2. Choose **View**, **Toolbars**, **Forms** to display the Forms toolbar.

3. Click the **Check Box Form Field** button.

4. A blank check box form field appears in your form. Double-click it (or click it and then click the Form Field Options button in the Forms toolbar) to display the Check Box Form Field Options dialog box (see Figure 19.7).

FIGURE 19.7

Use the Check Box Form Field Options dialog box to define how you want your check box form field to behave.

5. To set a specific point size for the check box, mark the **Exactly** option button and specify the point size in the drop-down list. Otherwise, leave the Auto button selected and Word will automatically size the check box.

6. Under Default Value, mark the **Checked** option button if you want the check box to be marked by default.

7. Optionally add help text (see steps 10–12 in the previous section).

8. Select from the remaining options (refer to the "Automating Your Form" section later in this hour). When you're done, click **OK**.

You have now inserted the check box and defined how it will behave.

Adding a Drop-Down List Form Field

Follow these steps to create a drop-down list in your form:

1. Move your insertion point to the location where you want the drop-down list form field to go.

19

2. Choose **View, Toolbars, Forms** to display the Forms toolbar.

3. Click the **Drop-Down Form Field** button.

4. A blank drop-down form field appears in your form. Double-click it (or click it and then click the Form Field Options button in the Forms toolbar) to display the Drop-Down Form Field Options dialog box (see Figure 19.8).

5. To add an item to your drop-down list, type it in the **Drop-down Item** text box and click the **Add** button to add it to the Items in Drop-down List box. Continue to add items until the list is complete. Use the **Move** arrows to change the order of the items in the list. If you have one entry that you want to use as the default, move it to the top of the list.

6. To edit an item in the list, select it and then click the **Remove** button. It will appear in the Drop-down Item text box. Edit it there, and then click the **Add** button again to return it to the list. To remove an item, select it and click the **Remove** button. In Figure 19.9, the **Items in Drop-down List** box has been completed.

7. Optionally add help text (see steps 10–12 in the "Adding a Text Form Field" section earlier in this hour).

8. Select from the remaining options (see the next section, "Automating Your Form"). When you're done, click **OK**.

You have now inserted a drop-down form field in your form and told Word what it should contain.

Automating Your Form

The Form Field Options dialog boxes shown in Figures 19.4, 19.7, and 19.8 all contain the same set of options under Run Macro On and Field Settings. These options are only useful if you want to automate certain parts of your form. Here is how you use them:

- Entry and Exit drop-down lists—Use these drop-down lists to specify macros that run when the user activates the form field (Entry) or moves somewhere else in the form (Exit). (See "Where to Go from Here" at the end of this hour.)

- Bookmark text box—Use this text box to assign a bookmark to the field (or accept the default bookmark name). You can then use the bookmark in formulas and macros that refer to this field, or to retrieve the content of this field in another location in the form.

- Enabled check box—This check box is labeled Fill-in Enabled, Check Box Enabled, and Drop-down Enabled in the three Form Field Options dialog boxes. Clear this check box if you don't want the user to be able to fill in the field. You might do this if you are using an entry macro to fill in the field automatically.

- Calculate on Exit check box—Mark this check box if you want Word to update any other form fields in the document that are dependent on this field as soon as the user leaves the field. You have to mark this check box if the user will type a number in the field that you use in a formula somewhere else in the form.

To see some of these features in action, refer to Figure 19.10. This revised reservation confirmation form contains three new fields in the lower-right corner: Total, Deposit, and Balance Due.

19

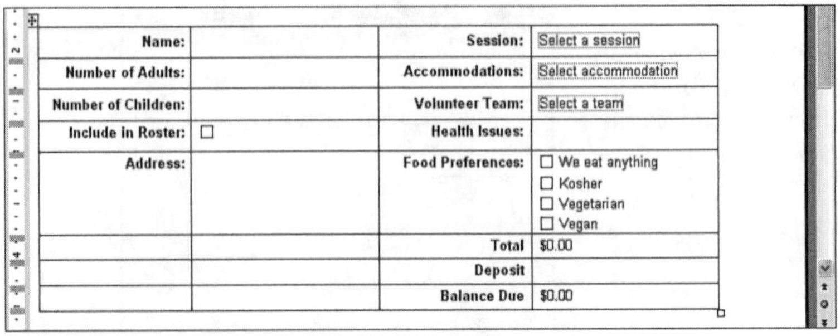

FIGURE **19.10**

The reservation confirmation form now contains Total, Deposit, and Balance Due fields.

The Total field is a formula that refers to the numbers the user entered in the Number of Adults and Number of Children fields. It multiplies each of these numbers by the tuition for adults and children and adds them together to get the total tuition due. Figure 19.11 shows the Text Form Field Options dialog box for this field.

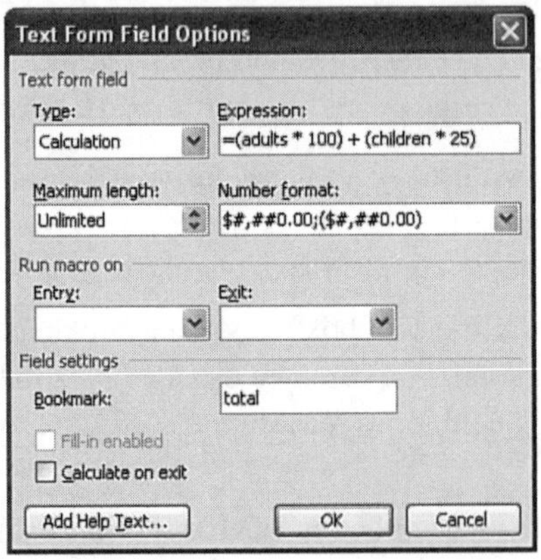

FIGURE **19.11**

Text Form Field Options dialog box for the Total field.

Note that this text field is defined as a Calculation type, and its formula is entered in the Expression text box. Because the bookmark names *adults* and *children* were assigned to the Number of Adults and Number of Children fields in their Text Form Field Options dialog boxes, they can be used in the formula here. Notice also that a currency format has been selected in the Number Format drop-down list.

The Deposit field is a text form field of the Number type. The user fills in this field. The Balance Due field is also a Calculation type field. Its formula, =(total-deposit), uses the bookmarks assigned to the Total and Deposit fields to calculate the balance due amount.

In order for the values entered by the user in the Number of Adults, Number of Children, and Deposit fields to be used in the Total and Balance Due formulas, their Calculate on Exit check boxes were marked.

Protecting a Form

After you have inserted all of the form fields into your form, you're ready to finalize it. The form fields in a form don't become active and ready to receive input from the user until you *protect* the form. When you protect a form, you restrict the user from modifying anything in the document other than the form fields themselves. Furthermore, when a form is protected, the user can press the Tab key to move from field to field (or press Shift+Tab to move to the previous field).

To protect a form without requiring a password to unprotect it, first choose View, Toolbars, Forms if the Forms toolbar is not already visible. Then click the Protect Form button on the Forms toolbar (refer to Figure 19.2).

Notice that most of the toolbar buttons and menu commands in the Word window are now dim because the user can't make changes to the text or formatting of the document. When you want to make changes to the form, click the Protect Form button again to unprotect the document.

If you want to require a password to unprotect the document, use this method of protecting the document instead:

1. Open the document whose formatting you want to restrict, and choose **Tools, Protect Document**.

2. In the Protect Document task pane that appears, mark the **Allow Only This Type of Editing in the Document** check box, and then choose **Filling in Forms** in the list box under Editing Restrictions (see Figure 19.12).

19

FIGURE 19.12

Select Filling in Forms to restrict people to filling in forms as opposed to modifying them.

4. Click the **Yes, Start Enforcing Protection** button in the Protect Document task pane.

5. Word displays the Start Enforcing Protection dialog box. Enter and re-enter a password that will be required to remove the protection, and then click **OK**.

The document is now protected. To remove the protection, you can either choose Tools, Unprotect Document or click the Protect Form button in the Forms toolbar. If you required a password in step 5 in the preceding step sequence, you will be required to enter it now.

When you've protected your form, you're ready to save it as a template, as described in the next section.

If you want some parts of a document to remain unprotected after you have protected the part that contains the form fields, you need to divide the document into sections (see "Varying the Page Formatting in Your Document" in Hour 8 if you need help with this), and then protect only the section(s) that contains form fields. When your document has multiple sections, a Select Sections link appears under Editing Restrictions in the Protect Document task pane. Click this link to display the Select Protection dialog box, clear the check boxes for the sections that you don't want to protect, and click OK.

Saving a Form As a Template

As you learned in Hour 10, "Working with Templates," the advantage of using templates (.dot files) is that you can use them over and over to create documents without ever overwriting the template itself. Furthermore, if you have macros that you or someone else wrote to use with the form, you can (and should) save them in the template so that they are always available with the form (see "Where to Go from Here" later in this hour.)

To save your form as a template, follow these steps:

1. With your completed and protected form onscreen, choose **File, Save As**.

2. In the Save As dialog box, display the Save As Type drop-down list and choose **Document Template (*.dot)**.

3. Save the file in the Templates folder or one of its subfolders.

> Hour 10 covered a lot of information that you might want to review at this point. In particular, it would be a good idea to review steps 6–8 in the "Personalizing Word's Templates" section.

4. Click the **Save** button.

Filling in a Form

To use a form that you or someone else has created, follow these steps:

1. Choose **File**, **New**, and click **On My Computer** in the New Document task pane.

2. In the Templates dialog box, select the form template, and click **OK**.

3. Fill in the form fields. You can either click in each field or press Tab to move from field to field. Figure 19.13 shows the form used in the examples earlier in this hour after a user has filled in the fields. One of the drop-down lists is displayed so that you can see what it looks like.

FIGURE 19.13

This form has been filled out.

4. Save the document. Word will save it as a Word document (`.doc` file) so that it doesn't overwrite your template. (You might want to think of a naming convention to use for all of the filled-in forms you base on this template so that you can store them in an organized way.)

If you position your form fields carefully, you can use a Word form to fill in the information in preprinted forms. For example, if you have preprinted invoices, you could create a Word form that matches the appearance of your printed form, with the form fields arranged in the positions they need to be in to print in the boxes in the printed form. When you are ready to print, load the preprinted forms in your printer, and choose File, Print. In the Print dialog box, click the Options button to display a second Print dialog box. Mark the Print Data Only for Forms check box, click OK, and then click OK again. Word will only print the contents of the form fields onto your preprinted forms.

Modifying a Form

You can go back at any time and modify your form. To do so, follow these steps:

1. Open the template that contains the form you want to modify (see "Modifying Your Templates" in Hour 10 if you need a little coaching).

2. Choose **View**, **Toolbars**, **Forms** if you don't see the Forms toolbar.

3. Click the **Protect Form** button on the Forms toolbar to unprotect the form (or choose Tools, Unprotect). If you required a password to unprotect the document, you will need to enter it now.

4. Make whatever changes you like to the text, formatting, and form fields.

5. Click the **Protect Form** button again to turn protection on. If you had previously assigned a password to unprotect and want to continue to require a password, use the Tools, Protect Document method to assign the password again (Word will not retain the password from the last time you assigned it).

6. You might want to fill in some test data to see how the modified form behaves. If you are happy with the results, continue to the next step. Otherwise, repeat steps 3 through 5 again. If you want to clear out the test data after you unprotect the form to modify it further, click the **Reset Form Fields** button in the Forms toolbar (refer to Figure 19.2).

7. Save and close the template.

Summary

In this hour, you just scratched the surface of Word's forms. If you are not interested in writing VBA macros, you will probably never delve any deeper into this feature. However, if you know VBA or are planning on studying it, you might want to keep poking around the forms feature to learn more. Furthermore, knowing a little about what advanced forms can do for you will also be helpful if you work with programmers in the future. Here are just a few of the possibilities:

- You can create forms that populate fields with information retrieved from a database or store user input into a database.

- You can validate input data to make sure it has been entered correctly and corresponds to data in your database.

- You can create forms that have a far broader range of input controls, including option buttons, list boxes, and so on.

- You can also use forms to create interactive documents. For example, you might create a vacation request form that contains a calendar showing dates that would conflict with vacations already approved for other coworkers.

To create forms with more sophisticated user interfaces and/or forms that communicate with databases and execute VBA code, you will need to use some combination of entry and exit macros and ActiveX controls.

Entry and Exit Macros

An advantage of using entry and exit macros is that the macros run code that interacts with the standard Word form fields (as opposed to fields created with ActiveX controls). Word's text form fields can blend right into the text stream, so you can create documents that don't look like forms at all but execute code in the background. Entry macros are used to set default content in form fields, and are especially handy when the defaults are contingent on one or more other fields. So, for example, you could use an entry macro in a bed-and-breakfast reservation form to set the default departure date for one day after the arrival date. Exit macros are commonly used to validate data and may also be used to update other fields. In many cases, you can perform the same tasks using entry or exit macros—there are pros and cons to each method, and the one you choose is a judgment call.

ActiveX Controls

Microsoft developed ActiveX controls to provide tools you can use in all of the Office applications to design user interfaces, including forms and dialog boxes, and attach VBA code to them. ActiveX controls are much more extensive than Word's form fields. They include option buttons, list boxes, spinner arrows, and so on. (To see what controls are available, choose View, Toolbars, Control Toolbox. The Control Toolbox toolbar is designed for working with ActiveX controls.) Unlike Word's text form fields, ActiveX

19

controls are not designed to be able to blend into the text stream; they look like the user-interface elements that they are, both onscreen and when printed.

Q&A

Q Can I control the formatting of the text that a user enters in a form field?

A Yes. Select the field by dragging over it (double-clicking a form field displays the dialog box for defining its behavior) and apply the formatting using all of the standard methods.

Q I want to create an employment application to be filled out in Word, and I'm guessing it's probably already been done before. Is there a repository of Word forms on the Web that I can access?

A Yes. Choose File, New. In the New Document task pane, click the Templates on Office Online link to go to Microsoft's Office Online Web site. Search the Templates category for the type of form you're looking for. When you find one that looks interesting, click its link to preview it, and then follow the onscreen instructions to download it and open it in Word.

HOUR **20**

Integrating with Other Office Products

Chances are that you acquired Word as a part of Office 2003. If Word is the only Office application you use, no problem—there's nothing wrong with ignoring Word's siblings. If, however, you do use other Office applications and want to use data from them in your Word documents, you'll learn some useful techniques in this hour. (Even if you're only using Word 2003, you may still want to skim this hour to learn general principles related to integrating Windows applications.) Keep in mind that you can integrate Office applications in many ways—this hour does not discuss all of them. Rather, it introduces a few methods that you can use as a jump-off point for further exploration.

The highlights of this hour include

- Inserting linked data from an Excel worksheet in your Word document
- Embedding data from Excel in your Word document
- Exporting a PowerPoint presentation to a Word document
- Adding an individual PowerPoint slide to a Word document
- Using data from Outlook in your Word documents
- Importing data from an Access table or query into a Word table

Inserting Data from Excel Worksheets

If you want to insert data from an Excel worksheet, you can, of course, copy it into a Word document with the Copy and Paste commands. (Select the desired cells in Excel, issue the Copy command, switch to the Word document, click at the desired location, and issue the Paste command.)

When you use this method, Word puts the Excel data in a table, which you can format and modify with the techniques you learned in Hour 15, "Columns and Tables." In Figure 20.1, the data in the table was pasted from an Excel worksheet.

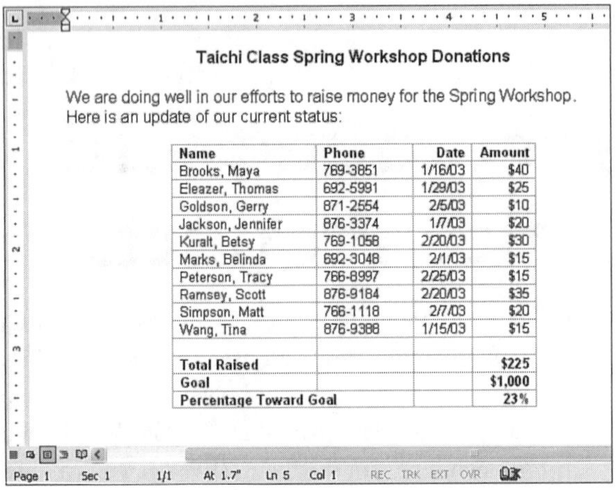

Taichi Class Spring Workshop Donations

We are doing well in our efforts to raise money for the Spring Workshop. Here is an update of our current status:

Name	Phone	Date	Amount
Brooks, Maya	769-3851	1/16/03	$40
Eleazer, Thomas	692-5991	1/29/03	$25
Goldson, Gerry	871-2554	2/5/03	$10
Jackson, Jennifer	876-3374	1/7/03	$20
Kuralt, Betsy	769-1058	2/20/03	$30
Marks, Belinda	692-3048	2/1/03	$15
Peterson, Tracy	766-8997	2/25/03	$15
Ramsey, Scott	876-9184	2/20/03	$35
Simpson, Matt	766-1118	2/7/03	$20
Wang, Tina	876-9388	1/15/03	$15
Total Raised			$225
Goal			$1,000
Percentage Toward Goal			23%

FIGURE 20.1
Excel data that you insert with the Copy and Paste commands appears in a Word table.

This method has two drawbacks. First, the Excel formulas are converted to plain numbers, so they won't update if you revise any of the numbers in the table. Second, no link exists between the pasted data in the Word document and the original data in the Excel worksheet, so revising the data in Excel does not update it in Word.

Linking to an Excel Worksheet

One way to avoid these shortcomings is to link the pasted data in Word to the original data in the Excel worksheet. Then whenever you update the data in Excel, it is automatically updated in the Word document.

To insert linked data from Excel into your Word document, follow these steps:

1. In Excel, select the cells that you want to copy to Word and issue the **Copy** command.
2. Switch to the Word document, move the insertion point to the desired location, and choose **Edit**, **Paste Special** to display the Paste Special dialog box.

3. Mark the **Paste Link** option button, choose **Microsoft Office Excel Worksheet Object** in the list in the middle of the dialog box (see Figure 20.2), and click **OK**.

FIGURE 20.2

Choose Paste Link in the Paste Special dialog box to link the pasted data with the original data in Excel.

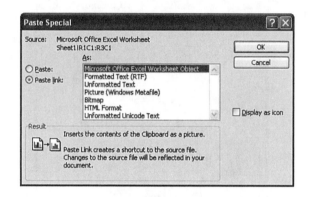

4. Switch back to Excel, press the **Esc** key to turn off the marquee around the copied data, save, and then close the workbook.

The data is pasted into Word as an object, as shown in Figure 20.3 (the object may be pasted in as an inline or floating object, depending on your settings). You can use techniques you learned in Hour 17, "Manipulating Images," for working with pictures, drawing objects, and WordArt to position the Excel object in your document and format its appearance.

FIGURE 20.3

Your Excel data appears as an object in Word.

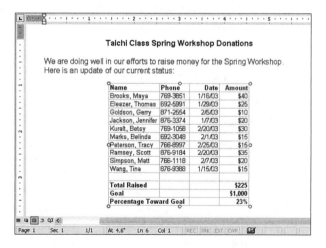

20

To edit the data in Excel, double-click the linked object in your Word document. In a moment, the associated worksheet opens in Excel with the linked cells selected (see Figure 20.4). When you revise the data in Excel, it is instantly updated in the Word document. (You can't edit the linked data in the Word document.)

FIGURE 20.4

With the Paste Link option, any changes you make to the data in Excel are immediately reflected in your Word document.

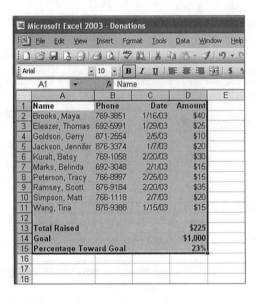

If the Word document isn't open when you revise the data in Excel, it's updated the next time you open the document. If you are ever unsure whether the Excel data in your Word document has been updated with the most recent changes to the linked data in Excel, you can always click the Excel object in your Word document to select it and press F9.

If you move or rename the Excel workbook that contains the source data for linked Excel data in Word, you have to tell Word where to find the file. To do so, follow these steps:

1. Select the linked object in Word.

2. Choose **Edit**, **Links** to display the Links dialog box.

3. Click the **Change Source** button, navigate to and select the workbook in the Change Source dialog box, click the **Open** button, and then click **OK**.

The Change Source dialog box also contains a Break Link button. Use it if you want to disconnect the data in your Word document from the original Excel data so that it no longer updates when you revise the data in Excel.

Embedding Data from an Excel Worksheet

Another option is to *embed* the Excel data in your Word document. When you use this technique, double-clicking the embedded object displays the Excel interface—menus, toolbars, and so on—within the Word window, so you can use Excel controls to revise the data without ever leaving Word. When you embed data, the Excel data "lives" in the Word document and is not linked to original data in Excel. When you edit the data in the Word document, it does not get updated in the original Excel worksheet, and vice versa.

To embed Excel data in a Word document, follow these steps:

1. In Excel, select the cells that you want to copy to Word and issue the **Copy** command.

2. Switch to the Word document, move the insertion point to the desired location, and choose **Edit**, **Paste Special** to display the Paste Special dialog box.

3. Mark the **Paste** option button, choose **Microsoft Excel Worksheet Object** in the list in the middle of the dialog box (see Figure 20.5), and click **OK**.

FIGURE 20.5

Choose Paste in the Paste Special dialog box to embed the pasted data in the Word document.

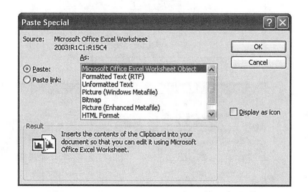

4. Switch back to Excel and press the **Esc** key to turn off the marquee around the copied data, and then close the workbook.

Just as when you link the data, embedded data is pasted into Word as an object. However, Word responds differently when you double-click an embedded object. Instead of displaying the source data in Excel, it displays the Excel interface in the Word window, as shown in Figure 20.6.

You can also start an embedded Excel worksheet from scratch in your Word document instead of beginning with data that you pasted from an existing Excel worksheet. To do so, click the Insert Microsoft Excel Worksheet toolbar button in the Standard toolbar, drag across the number of cells that you want to start out with in the drop-down grid (see Figure 20.7), and release the mouse button. You can now use your Excel skills to create a worksheet within the Word document.

20

Excel controls

FIGURE 20.6

You can use Excel controls to edit the embedded data in your Word document.

FIGURE 20.7

To start an empty embedded Excel worksheet, use the Insert Microsoft Excel Worksheet button in the Standard toolbar.

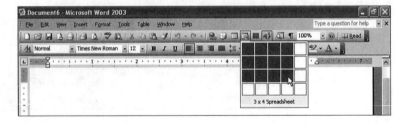

Inserting PowerPoint Presentations and Slides

You can, of course, use a no-frills approach to getting text and slides from a PowerPoint presentation into your Word documents. Simply use the standard Copy and Paste commands. If you go this route, your pasted data maintains no link to the source data in the PowerPoint presentation. If you want to get a little fancier, try one of the other options described here.

If you want to export a PowerPoint presentation to a Word document, you can paste your slides and notes into the Word document as embedded or linked objects. If you embed the slides, they are not linked with the original presentation. When you double-click one of the slides, the PowerPoint interface appears in the Word window. In contrast, if you link the slides, double-clicking one of them in the Word document opens the source slide in PowerPoint. If you edit the slide in PowerPoint, you can tell Word to update it.

Follow these steps to send your PowerPoint presentation to a Word document:

1. Start PowerPoint and open the presentation (see Figure 20.8).

FIGURE 20.8

Open the presentation that you want to export to a Word document.

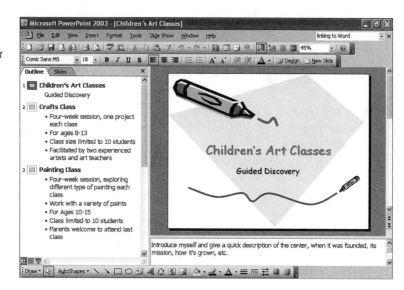

2. Choose **File**, **Send To**, **Microsoft Word** to display the Send to Microsoft Word dialog box (see Figure 20.9).

FIGURE 20.9

The Send to Microsoft Word dialog box lets you choose how you want the presentation to look in Word.

20

3. Mark the option button under **Page Layout in Microsoft Word** that most closely matches the layout you want to use.

4. Mark the **Paste** option button to embed the slides in the Word document, or mark the **Paste Link** option button to link them to the original slides in PowerPoint.

5. Click **OK**.

In a moment, the presentation appears in a Word document (see Figure 20.10). Note that Word has placed it in a table, so you can modify its appearance with all the techniques you learned in Hour 15. The Paste Link option was chosen in step 4 to create the document shown in Figure 20.10.

FIGURE 20.10

The PowerPoint presentation appears in a Word table.

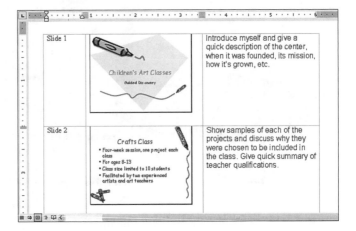

If you chose Paste in step 4, each slide in the Word document is an embedded object. When you double-click a slide, the PowerPoint controls appear in the Word window, as shown in Figure 20.11.

If you chose Paste Link in step 4, each slide in the Word document is an object that's linked to the original slide in PowerPoint. To edit the slide in PowerPoint, double-click it in the Word document. Unlike linked Excel data, linked PowerPoint slides don't update instantly when you modify them in PowerPoint. To update the slide object in Word, select it and press F9.

To ensure that the most current version of the slides always prints, follow these steps:

1. Choose **File**, **Print** in Word.

2. Click the **Options** button in the lower-left corner of the Print dialog box.

3. Mark the **Update Links** check box, and click **OK**.

4. Back in the Print dialog box, click **OK** to print or **Close** to close the dialog box without printing.

PowerPoint controls

FIGURE 20.11
*You can use
PowerPoint controls to
edit the embedded
slides in your Word
document.*

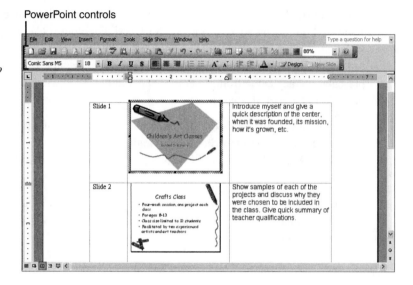

In addition to exporting an entire PowerPoint presentation to a Word document, you can also insert individual slides, either as linked or embedded objects.

Follow these steps to insert an individual slide in your Word document:

1. In PowerPoint, choose **View**, **Slide Sorter** to switch to Slide Sorter view.

2. Right-click the slide that you want to copy to Word, and choose **Copy**.

3. Switch to the Word document, move the insertion point to the desired location, and choose **Edit**, **Paste Special** to display the Paste Special dialog box.

4. Mark the **Paste** or **Paste Link** option button, and choose **Microsoft PowerPoint Slide Object** in the list in the middle of the dialog box (see Figure 20.12), and click **OK**.

FIGURE 20.12
*Choose Paste or Paste
Link in the Paste
Special dialog box to
embed or link the
pasted slide in the
Word document.*

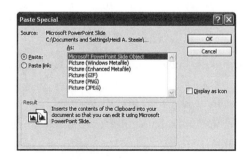

20

The Paste and Paste Link option buttons in the Paste Special dialog box function the same for PowerPoint slides as they do for Excel workbooks. Choosing Paste embeds the slide in the Word document, so you can double-click it to bring up the PowerPoint controls in the Word window and edit it there. The slides are not linked to the PowerPoint presentation they came from, so editing them in the Word window does not update them in PowerPoint, and vice versa.

Choosing Paste Link pastes the slide into the Word document while maintaining a link to the source slide in the PowerPoint presentation, so if you modify it there, it will be updated in Word when you select it and press F9. (You can't edit the linked slide in Word.)

Figure 20.13 shows a slide that was pasted from PowerPoint with the Paste Link option. Notice that it has selection handles around it, just as Excel data does when you use Paste Link (refer to Figure 20.3).

FIGURE 20.13

Choose Paste Link in the Paste Special dialog box to link the pasted slide with the original slide in PowerPoint.

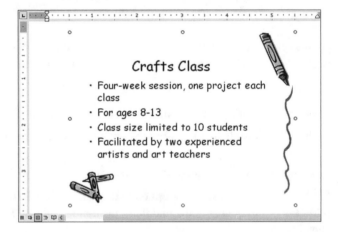

If you move or rename the source presentation for a linked Word document or for individual slides that you pasted with the Paste Link option, you need to tell Word what the new location and/or filename is. To do this, follow these steps:

1. Select all the slide objects in the Word document (see "Selecting Multiple Images" in Hour 17).

2. Choose **Edit, Links** to display the Links dialog box.

3. Select the objects in the Links dialog box (drag to select more than one).

4. Click the **Change Source** button, select the source presentation in the Change Source dialog box, click **Open**, and then click **OK**.

Inserting Data from Outlook

The most common reason to use Outlook data in a Word document is to insert an address from your Outlook address book into a document such as an envelope or label. Word displays the Insert Address button wherever it allows you to insert an address from Outlook. The Envelopes and Labels dialog box, shown in Figure 20.14, contains an Insert Address button.

Insert Address

FIGURE 20.14

Wherever you see an Insert Address button, you can click it to insert an address from Outlook.

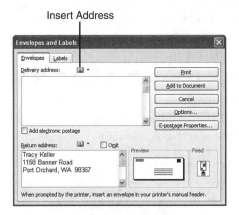

Clicking the Insert Address button displays the Select Name dialog box (see Figure 20.15) with the list of names from Outlook. (The first time you click this button, you may first see the Choose Profile dialog box, which asks which Outlook profile you'd like to use.) Select the name you want, and click OK.

FIGURE 20.15

Select the name of the person whose address you want to insert in the Select Name dialog box.

20

Word inserts the name in the Word dialog box (in this case, the Envelopes and Labels dialog box).

You can also click the down arrow to the right of the Insert Address button to display a list of names you have recently selected. If you see the one you want, you can click it and save yourself a trip to the Select Name dialog box.

Inserting Data from Access

In Hour 14, "Generating a Mail Merge," you learned that you can use an Access database as the data source in a mail merge. There might also be times when you'd just like to dump the contents of an Access table or query into a Word table. You might do this to include data from Access in a report you're preparing in Word, for example. To retrieve data from Access, follow these steps:

1. Move the insertion point to the location in which you want to insert the data from your Access table or query.

2. Choose **View**, **Toolbars**, **Database** to display the Database toolbar, and click the **Insert Database** button (see Figure 20.16).

FIGURE 20.16

Click the Insert Database button on the Database toolbar.

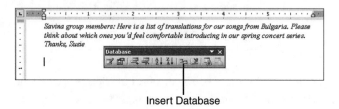

Insert Database

3. In the Database dialog box that appears, click the **Get Data** button (see Figure 20.17).

FIGURE 20.17

Click the Get Data button to select your Access database.

4. Word displays the Select Data Source dialog box. Navigate to and select your Access database, and click **Open**.

5. The Select Table dialog box appears (see Figure 20.18). Tables and queries use different icons to allow you to differentiate between them. Select the table or query whose data you want to insert, and click **OK** to return to the Database dialog box.

This is a query.

FIGURE 20.18

The Select Table dialog box lets you select the table or query that contains your data.

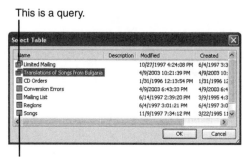

This is a table.

6. The remaining options in the Database dialog box have now become active (see Figure 20.19). Click the **Query Options** button if you want to further filter or sort your data before inserting it, or if you don't want to include some of the fields in the Access table or query. The Query Options dialog box that appears is almost exactly like the Filter and Sort dialog box you used in Hour 14 to filter or sort the records in your data source. The one difference is that the Query Options dialog box also contains a Select Fields tab (see Figure 20.20), which you can use to remove fields that you don't want to include in your Word document. (This does not remove the fields from the Access database; it just doesn't include those fields in the data that is inserted into your Word document.) To remove a field, simply click it in the Selected Fields list on the right, and click the **Remove** button. When you're done, click **OK**.

FIGURE 20.19

All of the options in the Database dialog box are now active.

20

FIGURE 20.20

The Select Fields tab in the Query Options dialog box lets you remove fields that you don't want included in the Word table.

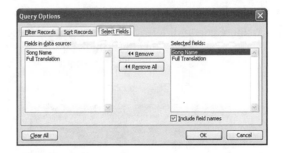

If you don't remove a field now, you can always delete it from the Word table later by deleting the column in which it is displayed.

7. Click the **Table AutoFormat** button if you want to apply a table style to your table. For more information on this, refer to the section titled "Using the Table AutoFormat Feature" in Hour 15.

8. Click the **Insert Data** button to display the Insert Data dialog box (see Figure 20.21). Mark the **From** button to specify a range of records if you don't want to include all of the records in the Access table or query. Mark the **Insert Data As Field** check box if you want the data to be inserted as a field that you can update to reflect changes in the Access database.

9. Click **OK**.

FIGURE 20.21

Use the Insert Data dialog box to specify a range of records if you don't want to include all of them, and optionally insert the data as a field.

Your data is inserted into a Word table (see Figure 20.22). If you inserted the data as a field, you can update it to reflect the current data in the source Access database at any time by pressing F9, or by right-clicking anywhere in it and choosing Update Field in the context menu.

If you insert Access data in a Word document as a field and then move or rename the Access database, or change its structure, it will break the field. (You will see an error saying that Word was unable to open the data source.) To fix the problem, you'll need to delete the current table in your Word document, and run through the preceding steps again.

FIGURE 20.22

This table contains data from an Access query. It was formatted using a table style.

Savina group members: Here is a list of translations for our songs from Bulgaria. Please think about which ones you'd feel comfortable introducing in our spring concert series. Thanks, Susie

Song Name	Full Translation
Dafino	This song is diaphonic, and has an improvised descant. Dafino, come out onto your balcony. Jano is planting his seeds in a big garden. He is growing white wheat.
Dimjaninka	This is a village song that's been taken and arranged for six parts, while still keeping the village harmonies. Dimjaninka is leading a horse to the well for a cold drink. She sees herself in the water and says, "How beautiful and fair I am. How ruddy and healthy-looking I am. If only I were taller and dark-eyed, then I could attract everyone."
Dumaj Zlato	A young man says, "Speak to your mother Zlata. Tell her I want your hand in marriage." She replies, "I have spoken to my mother, and she says that I cannot

Summary

In this hour, you learned how to enhance your Word documents with material that you created in other Office applications. The general principles of linking and embedding are not limited to Office 2003—they apply to all Windows applications. Feel free to take ideas from this hour and experiment with bringing data from other applications into your Word documents, or bringing Word text into documents in other applications. In the next hour, you learn how to work with documents that contain text in foreign languages.

Q&A

Q I have a lot of linked objects in my Word document, including PowerPoint slides, Excel data, and so on. Can I update them all at once?

A Yes. If you want to make sure that all linked objects in your document are current, select any one of them and choose Edit, Links. In the Links dialog box, drag over all of them to select them, click the Update Now button, and click OK. (You can also select all the objects and press F9.)

20

HOUR 21

Working with Foreign Languages in Your Word Documents

If you work with English-language documents exclusively, you can skip this hour altogether and go on to the next. The focus of this session is on working with non-English text in your documents. Whether you speak more than one language at home, are studying a foreign language, or work in an international office setting, you will find that Word provides a sophisticated environment for reading, editing, and formatting text in a huge number of languages. The information in this hour assumes that you are using an English version of Windows XP with an English version of Office 2003. If you are using different software, many of the concepts described here will be useful, but the step-by-step instructions may not apply to you.

The highlights of this hour include

- Understanding your options for configuring multilingual support
- Configuring multilingual support on your computer
- Reading and editing foreign-language text
- Using proofing tools for foreign-language text
- Using the multilingual services available in the Research task pane

Choosing Your Method of Providing Multilingual Support

Before you plow into the details of configuring multilingual support on an English-based system, it's useful to get an overview of the three main approaches for supporting multiple languages:

- Use the English versions of Windows XP and Office 2003 and configure them to support multiple languages. This setup works well for native English speakers because the user interface is in English. On the downside, the English version of Office only includes proofing tools for English, Spanish, and French (you have to buy proofing tools for additional languages, as described later in this hour). This is the approach covered in this hour.

- Use the *localized* (non-English) language versions of Office 2003 and Windows XP. The user interfaces of the localized versions are in the local languages, and they are designed from scratch to support the local language. They include proofing tools for the local language plus a few other appropriate languages. (For example, the localized Norwegian version of Office 2003 contains proofing tools for Norwegian, English, and German.)

- Use English versions of Windows XP and Office 2003 with the MUI (Multilingual User Interface) Pack. Microsoft developed the MUI Pack to provide user interfaces, help systems, and templates in more than 40 languages. The MUI Pack also includes the Microsoft Office Proofing Tools (described later in this hour). With this approach, a company could use the same installation in offices around the world. Each user then configures the MUI to use his or her language of choice.

Configuring Multilingual Support on Your Computer

In the context of configuring multilingual support on your computer, you can divide languages into three groups (keep in mind that these groups do not reflect similarities based on linguistic features; the languages in each group just have similar configuration requirements):

- Built-in languages—This group includes all languages other than those in the remaining two groups. You can read text written in these languages without making any changes to your Windows XP or Office 2003 installation. To input and edit text in these languages, you don't need to install any additional files, but you do need to make some configuration changes, as described in the next three sections. Figure 21.1 shows a portion of a folk tale written in Turkish, one of the built-in languages.

FIGURE 21.1

Turkish is an example of one of the built-in languages.

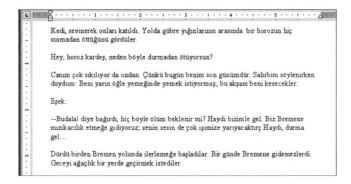

• Complex script and right-to-left languages—This group includes Arabic and Hebrew (right-to-left languages), as well as Armenian, Georgian, Thai, Vietnamese, and all of the Indic languages (complex script languages). You have to install additional support before you can read or edit documents in these languages. Figure 21.2 shows a note in Hebrew describing a company's mortgage services.

FIGURE 21.2

Hebrew is an example of a right-to-left language.

• East Asian languages—This group includes Chinese (both traditional and simplified), Japanese, and Korean. These languages can't be typed on a standard keyboard without using a special input system that converts keystrokes into phonetic and ideographic characters. You have to install these input systems, called *IMEs (Input Method Editors)*, before you can read or edit documents in these languages. Figure 21.3 shows the lyrics to a folk song in simplified Chinese characters.

21

FIGURE 21.3

Simplified Chinese is an example of an East Asian language.

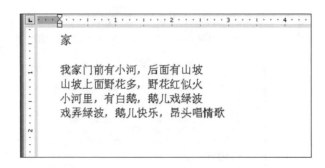

To prepare Word for typing, editing, and formatting text in one or more non-English languages, you need to configure support at three levels: Windows XP, Office 2003, and Word. The specific steps are described in the next three sections.

Windows XP Configuration

You must be logged on to your computer as a user with administrator rights to configure multilingual support for Windows XP. The support will be added for all users.

If you want to configure your computer to support a complex script or right-to-left language, or an East Asian language, follow this set of steps and the next. Otherwise, skip to the next set of steps:

1. Choose **Start**, **Control Panel**. If you're using Category view, click the Switch to Classic View link in the upper-left corner of the Control Panel to switch to Classic view.

2. Double-click the **Regional and Language Options** icon.

3. Click the **Languages** tab (see Figure 21.4).

4. Only if you are configuring your computer to support a complex script or right-to-left language, mark the **Install Files for Complex Script and Right-to-left Languages (Including Thai)** check box.

    Only if you're configuring support for an East Asian language, mark the **Install Files for East Asian Languages** check box.

5. When you mark either of these options, the Install Supplemental Language Support message box appears to tell you how much disk space the files will require and to inform you that the files will be installed when you click OK or Apply in the Regional and Language Options dialog box. Click **OK** to close the message box. Locate your Windows XP CD and insert it when prompted.

6. When you're asked to restart your computer, click **Yes**.

FIGURE 21.4

Use the Languages tab of the Regional and Language Options dialog box to add support for one or more languages.

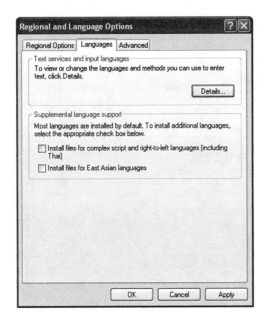

If you want to remove support for complex script and right-to-left languages, or for East Asian languages, simply clear the associated check box.

To install operating system services for your language, follow these steps:

1. Choose **Start**, **Control Panel**. If you're using Category view, click the Switch to Classic View link in the upper-left corner of the Control Panel to switch to Classic view.

2. Double-click the **Regional and Language Options** icon.

3. Click the **Languages** tab (see Figure 21.4).

4. Click the **Details** button to display the Text Services and Input Languages dialog box.

5. Click the **Settings** tab. This tab lists the services that are installed for each input language (see Figure 21.5). In Figure 21.5, Simplified Chinese has already been added.

6. To add an input language, along with its keyboard layout or IME, click the **Add** button.

7. In the **Add Input Language** dialog box that appears, select the input language that you want to add in the **Input Language** drop-down list, and then select a keyboard layout or IME in the **Keyboard Layout/IME** drop-down list**.** In Figure 21.6, Finnish will be added as an input language.

21

FIGURE **21.5**

FIGURE **21.5**

Use the Settings tab of the Text Services and Input Languages dialog box to manage your input languages and their keyboard layouts/IMEs.

FIGURE **21.6**

Use the Add Input Language dialog box to add the languages you want to be able to type and edit.

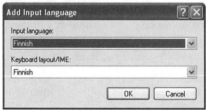

> If you or someone else has installed speech and handwriting support on your computer, you will see two additional drop-down lists in the Add Input Language dialog box.

8. Click **OK** twice to close the dialog box.

> If you are living or traveling in a region that uses a language other than U.S.-based English, or if you're just working with documents in the local language, you might want to switch the default formats that your programs (including Word) use for the dates, times, numbers, and currency to match local conventions. To do this, click the Regional Options tab of the Regional and Language Options dialog box and choose the desired language in the drop-down list.

Office 2003 Configuration

After you have added system support for your languages, as described in the preceding section, you need to tell Office about the languages as well. Taking the following steps will give your Office applications (including Word) the ability to detect when you're typing in a different language and to automatically use the appropriate proofing tools for that language. Various commands and options specific to your installed languages will also be added to the menu systems and dialog boxes of your Office applications.

To add Office 2003 support for your input language(s), follow these steps:

1. Click **Start**, **All Programs**, **Microsoft Office**, **Microsoft Office Tools**, **Microsoft Office 2003 Language Settings**. The first time you issue this command, you may be asked to insert your Office 2003 CD.

2. In the Microsoft Office 2003 Language Settings dialog box (see Figure 21.7), select the desired language or languages group in the **Available Languages** drop-down list, click the specific language in the list below, and click the **Add** button to add it to the Enabled Languages list.

FIGURE 21.7

Use the Microsoft Office 2003 Language Settings dialog box to add the languages that you want to be able to type and edit.

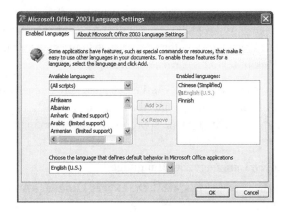

3. Repeat this step for other languages. Then click **OK**. A message box appears informing you that you need to quit and restart your open Office applications. Click **Yes**.

Now that you've completed the process of installing system support and Office support for your input language, you're ready to explore the details of working with your language in Word.

Word 2003 Configuration

After you've followed the steps in the preceding section, your Office applications will contain additional fonts, menu commands, dialog boxes, and so on. The specific changes

21

to your interface will vary tremendously depending on the language. For example, when Chinese support is installed, the Format menu contains an Asian Layout command, and the Options dialog box contains an Asian Typography tab. And if you install an Indic language, you will have additional Indic language formats for page numbers, numbered and bulleted lists, and so on.

There are a few options that you can change in order to make working with multiple languages easier and more efficient. This section explores the multilingual features that are available in Word.

If you want to automatically switch among keyboard layouts depending on where the insertion point is located, follow these steps:

1. Choose **Tools, Options**.
2. Click the **Edit** tab.
3. Mark the **Auto-Keyboard Switching** check box and click **OK**.

Now that you've completed these steps, when you click in text in a particular language in your Word document, the Keyboard Layout Indicator in the Language bar will automatically switch to that language (see "Using the Language Bar" later in this hour). (This assumes that you have followed the steps in the preceding two sections to install support for that language.) This saves you the step of switching languages manually when you want to edit a block of text in a particular language.

This next set of steps confirms that Word is set up to automatically detect the language of the text surrounding the insertion point (this is the default behavior). When this option is enabled, Word automatically uses the appropriate set of proofing tools for each language in your document.

1. Choose **Tools, Language, Set Language**.
2. In the Language dialog box, mark the **Detect Language Automatically** check box, and click **OK**.

When you click in text of a different language, the new language will automatically be listed in the Language field toward the right end of the status bar. In Figure 21.8, the insertion point is located in Spanish text, so the Language field indicates Spanish.

 Word can't automatically detect all languages. Here is the list of languages it can detect: Arabic, Chinese (simplified), Chinese (traditional), Danish, Dutch, English, Finnish, French, German, Greek, Hebrew, Italian, Japanese, Korean, Norwegian, Polish, Portuguese, Russian, Spanish, Swedish, and Thai.

FIGURE 21.8

Word's status bar lists the currently selected input language.

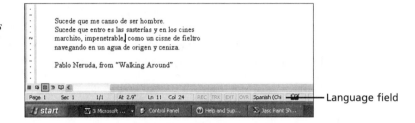

Language field

If you start a spelling or grammar check when a language other than English is listed in the status bar, Word will use that language's proofing tools, assuming they are installed.

Using the Language Bar

After you have configured support for at least one language other than English, the Language bar appears on your desktop. The Language bar is part of the operating system and is available to all programs, not just Microsoft Office. You use the Language bar to switch among the input languages that you have installed and, in the case of the East Asian languages, to adjust the way the IME behaves. The button at the left end of the Language bar, the Keyboard Layout Indicator, lists an abbreviation for the currently selected input language. (Depending on whether you have text labels showing, it may also list the full name of the language.) To switch to a different language, click the button and select the other language from the drop-down list (see Figure 21.9).

Keyboard Layout Indicator

Help

FIGURE 21.9

Click the Keyboard Layout Indicator button to select a different input language.

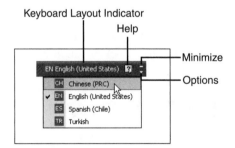

Minimize

Options

Figure 21.10 shows what the Language bar looks like when Chinese (PRC) is selected. Note the additional buttons used to configure the IME.

FIGURE 21.10

When Chinese (PRC) is selected as the input language, additional buttons appear on the Language bar.

21

To move the Language bar around the desktop, point to the vertical dotted line at the left edge of the Language bar and drag when you see the four-headed arrow mouse pointer. To dock the Language bar on the task bar, click the Minimize button in the upper-right corner of the bar. Figure 21.11 shows the Language bar after it's been docked.

FIGURE 21.11

Minimize the Language bar to dock it on the task bar.

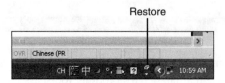

If you later want to restore it to the desktop, click the Restore button immediately above the Options button (or right-click the Language bar and click Restore the Language Bar).

To change the way the Language bar behaves, follow these steps:

1. Click the **Options** button on the Language bar, and click **Settings** in the menu that appears.

> If you don't see the Language bar, click Start, Control Panel. Double-click Regional and Language Options, click the Languages tab, click the Details button, and click the Language Bar button. Then go on to step 2.

2. Click the **Language Bar** button.

3. The Language Bar Settings dialog box appears (see Figure 21.12). Mark the **Show the Language Bar on the Desktop** check box to display the Language bar (this option is turned on by default).

FIGURE 21.12

Language Bar Settings dialog box.

3. Mark the **Show the Language Bar As Transparent When Inactive** check box if you want it to behave like a watermark when it's not active (when you aren't point-ing to it with the mouse). Figure 21.13 shows what the Language bar looks like

when this option is turned on. This option is only active when the Language bar is not docked.

FIGURE 21.13

Making the Language bar transparent keeps it from obscuring anything else on your desktop.

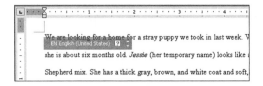

4. Clear the **Show Additional Language Bar Icons in the Taskbar** check box if you want to hide all the buttons on the Language bar except the Keyboard Language Indicator button.

5. Clear the **Show Text Labels on the Language Bar** check box if you want to see text labels on the Language bar buttons. This option is only active when the Language bar is not docked.

6. When you're finished making your selections, click **OK**, and then click **OK** again.

You can also access the same options as those shown in the Language Bar Settings dialog box by right-clicking the Language bar and clicking various commands in the context menu that appears. When the Language bar is not docked, the context menu also contains a Vertical command, which reorients the Language bar vertically on your screen.

The Key Settings button in the Text Services and Input Languages dialog box displays the Advanced Key Settings dialog box, which allows you to modify the keyboard shortcuts you can use to switch among your installed input languages.

To get more assistance with using the Language bar, click the Help button on the Language bar and then choose Language Bar Help. If you have installed an East Asian language and it's currently selected, the Help menu will also include a command to display the IME help. (The exact name of this command varies depending on the specific East Asian language that's currently selected.)

21

Typing Using Different Keyboard Layouts/IMEs

When you are using the keyboard layout for an input language other than English, the *keyboard mappings* for your keyboard will change to enable you to input all of the characters in that language. In other words, the character that appears onscreen when you press a particular key may not match the letter or symbol printed on the key cap. It can be difficult, especially at first, to remember which key inserts which character when you're using a keyboard layout for a language other than English. For example, when you use the Latin American keyboard layout, pressing the Shift key with the key to the left of the Backspace key inserts an inverted question mark (¿). Microsoft provides a free program called Visual Keyboard that displays a picture of a keyboard onscreen with the keyboard layout for the currently selected language (see Figure 21.14). In Figure 21.14, Spanish is currently selected in the Language bar, so the Latin American keyboard layout is displayed in Visual Keyboard. You can download Visual Keyboard from Microsoft's Web site. (To locate it, go to www.microsoft.com and search for *Microsoft Visual Keyboard*.)

FIGURE 21.14
The Visual Keyboard program gives you an onscreen guide to your keyboard layouts.

In many keyboard layouts, the *state* keys give you access to more characters. The most common state keys are the Caps Lock key, the Shift key, and the AltGr (Alt Graph) key, which is typically the Alt key to the right of the Spacebar. You press the state key while you press an additional key. To see what the state keys do, either click the keys in the Visual Keyboard itself, or press the keys on your keyboard while the Visual Keyboard is active. In Figure 21.15, the Shift key is pressed in the Visual Keyboard, so the keyboard shows you what other keys to press with the Shift key to display more characters.

Furthermore, some keyboard layouts contain *dead* keys. These keys are displayed in white in the Visual Keyboard (see Figure 21.15). They don't insert any character by themselves. Rather, pressing a dead key toggles you into a mode where you can access even more characters. In Figure 21.16, the dead key shown in Figure 21.15 was pressed and now a few new characters are available. When you're in the dead key mode, press the keys to insert the characters you want. To get out of dead key mode, press the dead key again. To see what a dead key does, click it in the Visual Keyboard or press it on your keyboard.

FIGURE 21.15

Use the state keys to produce additional characters.

Dead key

FIGURE 21.16

A dead key provides access to additional characters.

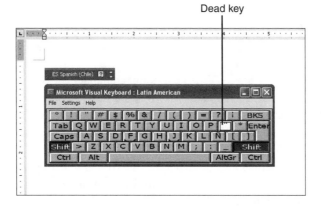

The Visual Keyboard program was written before Windows XP and Office 2003, so some of the instructions in its help system are not relevant to you. However, the keyboard layouts it can display have remained unchanged.

21

If you don't want to install the Visual Keyboard, you can also check out Microsoft's Windows Keyboard Layout page at www.microsoft.com/globaldev/reference/keyboards.aspx. This Web page contains a drop-down list from which you can select the keyboard layout that you want to view.

The available layouts include the new ones that were shipped with Windows XP. These are not available in the Visual Keyboard. Moving your mouse pointer over the state keys (Alt, AltGr, Shift, Caps, and so on) in the onscreen keyboard layout shows you what they do.

Editing Foreign Language Documents

When you have selected a language other than English in the Language bar, you can perform many of the usual tasks using that non-English language. You can save files using foreign-language names, create AutoText entries, check your word count, perform find-and-replace operations, and so on. Figure 21.17 shows the Find and Replace dialog box with Chinese text entered in the text boxes.

FIGURE 21.17

You can use any input language for tasks such as find and replace.

The proofing-related tasks—spell checking, grammar checking, and AutoCorrect—are one set of tasks that you cannot perform in non-English languages without buying additional software, unless you're using French or Spanish. The French and Spanish proofing tools are included with Office 2003. When you do a typical install, they are configured to be installed on first use. (If you start a spelling or grammar check on French or Spanish text using the Spelling and Grammar dialog box and select French or Spanish in the Dictionary Language drop-down list, Word will prompt you to install the necessary French or Spanish proofing files.)

If you know you want to use the French or Spanish proofing tools, you can install them on your computer now rather than waiting until you need them for the first time. To do this, follow these steps:

1. Place your Office 2003 CD in your CD-ROM drive, and double-click the **Add or Remove Programs** icon in the Control Panel.

2. Select Office 2003, and click the **Change** button.

3. Choose **Add or Remove Features**, click **Next**, mark the **Choose Advanced Customization of Applications** check box, and click **Next** again.

4. Click the plus signs next to **Office Shared Features**, **Proofing Tools**, and **French** or **Spanish**. Then click the desired proofing tools and choose **Run from My Computer** in the drop-down menu that appears.

5. Click the **Update** button.

If you want to use proofing tools for languages other than French and Spanish, you can buy the Microsoft Office Proofing Tools software package. This package, which includes proofing tools for 48 languages, is available at shop.microsoft.com (search for *proofing tools*). At the time of this writing, it cost approximately $80.

Multilingual Resources Available in the Research Task Pane

In Hour 11, you learned how to use the thesaurus in the Research task pane. In addition to this tool, the Research task pane also provides access to dictionaries and translation services. To check out what tools are available, display the drop-down list under the Search For text box. If you use the translation services, you'll have to bear with ads from WorldLingo, the company who provides the services in partnership with Microsoft.

> At the risk of stating the obvious, it's not a wise idea to rely on translations into a language that you don't understand. It's always best to find someone who reads that language to proofread the text for you before you actually use it in a document.

Summary

Although this hour is by no means an exhaustive discussion of multilingual issues in a Word environment, it should have given you a start exploring some new terrain. Have fun and be prepared to share your knowledge with friends and coworkers. This is an aspect of Word that some people find intimidating. It need not be if you approach it systematically and with a sense of adventure.

Q&A

21

Q Is there a default keyboard shortcut to switch among installed input languages in the Language bar?

A Yes. The default shortcut is Left Alt+Shift. This shortcut toggles you through the input languages in the order in which they appear in the Keyboard Layout Indicator menu. In addition, you can define keyboard shortcuts to switch into specific languages. To find out more, see the tip at the end of "Using the Language Bar" in this hour.

Q I write documents for readers in other English-speaking countries such as the United Kingdom and Australia. Do I need to install language support for them?

A Yes, if you want all of the language support that Windows XP has to offer. Windows XP supports 13 different "flavors" of English, all of which you install by following the steps in the "Windows XP Configuration" section earlier in this hour. If you want to work with documents written in Australia, Canada, or U.K.-based English, you will also want to install Microsoft Office support for the desired language option using the steps in the "Office 2003 Configuration" section.

Q I've installed Office support for U.K. English and turned on the Detect Language Automatically option for proofing, but Word doesn't seem to detect when I'm typing using U.K English versus U.S. English. What should I do to get Word to use the correct proofing tools?

A You can "manually" set the correct language. To do so, select the text and then choose Tools, Language, Set Language. In the Language dialog box, select English (U.K.), and then click OK.

Q Up until now my company has been using Word and TwinBridge for our East Asian language (Chinese, Japanese, and Korean) word processing. Can we continue to use it with Word 2003?

A Yes. TwinBridge works with Word 2003 and provides excellent East Asian font support. If you're already comfortable working with TwinBridge there is no reason to switch input methods. Check their Web site (www.twinbridge.com) for any updates.

Hour **22**

Using Word for E-mail

Word has powerful e-mail capabilities that make it a snap to compose and send e-mail from the Word window. One advantage of using Word for e-mail is that you don't have to leave the Word window to tell your e-mail program to send a message. Another advantage is that if you create e-mail messages in Word, you can make full use of Word features such as automatic spell and grammar checking, AutoCorrect, tables, and bulleted and numbered lists. In this hour, you learn three ways to use Word for e-mail.

The highlights of this hour include

- Understanding the system requirements for sending e-mail from Word
- Sending an e-mail message from Word
- Sending a Word document as an e-mail message
- Sending a Word document as an attachment to an e-mail message
- Sending any document as an e-mail attachment

What Programs Do You Need to Create E-mail in Word?

To create and send e-mail messages from Word, you have to have Outlook, which comes with Office; Outlook Express, which comes with Internet

Explorer; or a Microsoft Exchange Client. And one of these programs must be set as your default e-mail program. Outlook 2003 was used for the examples in this hour.

To send Word documents as attachments to e-mail messages, you aren't limited to Outlook and Outlook Express for e-mail. Most e-mail programs work just fine.

Composing and Sending an E-mail Message from Word

It's just as easy to send an e-mail message from Word as it is from an e-mail program.

To create and send an e-mail message from Word, follow these steps:

1. Choose **File, New** to display the New Document task pane, and click the **E-mail Message** link (see Figure 22.1).

FIGURE 22.1

Click the E-mail Message link in the New Document task pane to start an e-mail message in Word.

2. The new message opens in the Word window. You use the e-mail header to address the message. Type the recipient's e-mail address in the **To** text box, and optionally enter the e-mail address of a person to whom you want to copy the message in the **Cc** text box. Then type a subject in the **Subject** text box. (If the recipient is in your e-mail program's address book, you can just type his or her name in the To text box instead of the e-mail address.)

3. E-mail messages that you create in Word are sent in HTML format by default. (HTML is the format used to display Web pages, and it permits you to add text

formatting to your messages.) Most e-mail programs can read HTML-formatted messages. However, if you know your recipient's e-mail program can't handle HTML messages, or if you don't feel a need to beautify your text, you can display the Message Format drop-down list and choose Plain Text instead. Plain text messages cannot include any text formatting.

22

> If you're using Outlook, you'll also see an option for Rich Text in the Message Format drop-down list. This format also enables you to apply formatting to your messages, but it can only be read by recipients who use the Microsoft Exchange Client or Outlook. If you send a Rich Text message to someone across the Internet (as opposed to across a company intranet), Outlook automatically converts it to HTML format.

4. Type the e-mail message itself in the blank area below the Subject line (see Figure 22.2). When you're finished, click the Send button to send the message. (If you don't see a Send button, you have probably not yet set up an e-mail account in your e-mail program. When you have an account, the Send button will appear.)

Click to send the message.   Message format

FIGURE 22.2

Fill in the e-mail header information, choose your message format, and type your message.

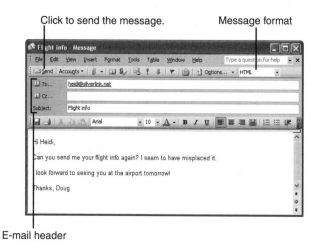

E-mail header

If you're not currently online, you may see a message prompting you to go online or informing you that your computer is connecting. After you're online, the message is sent out. The Word window remains open so you can continue using it.

When your recipient receives the message, it will look something like the one shown in Figure 22.3.

FIGURE 22.3

This message was composed and sent from Word.

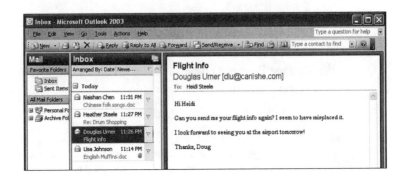

Adding a Signature

An e-mail signature is a block of text that is automatically appended to all of your outgoing messages. Typically, people include their names and contact information in their signature—the content is up to you.

If you want to create a signature that Word (and your e-mail program) will add to all of the e-mail messages that you send from Word, follow these steps:

1. Choose **Tools**, **Options**, and click the **General** tab.
2. Click the **E-mail Options** button.
3. In the E-mail Signature tab of the E-mail Options dialog box, type a title for the signature at the top of the dialog box, and then type and format the signature itself in the bottom half of the dialog box.
4. Click the **Add** button (see Figure 22.4). And then click **OK**.

Sending a Word Document in the Body of Your E-mail Message

In "Composing and Sending an E-mail Message from Word" earlier in this hour, you learned how to compose a new e-mail message from within Word. You can also send an existing Word document as the body of an e-mail message. When you use this method, Word converts the document to HTML format before sending it out. Unlike the traditional plain-text e-mail messages, HTML messages can contain graphics and other types of formatting, so your Word document retains much of its formatting when it is sent. The recipient does not have to have Word to read the message, but he or she must have an e-mail program that can handle HTML messages.

FIGURE 22.4

You can create a signature that Word adds to all your e-mail messages.

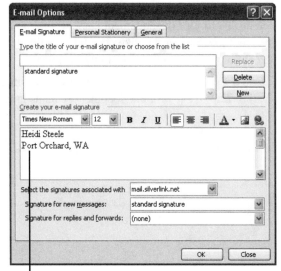

└─This signature will be appended to all of your messages.

22

Follow these steps to send a Word document as an e-mail message:

1. Create a new Word document or open an existing one, and then click the **E-mail** button in the Standard toolbar (see Figure 22.5).

E-mail

FIGURE 22.5

Click the E-mail button to send the active document as an e-mail message.

2. An e-mail header appears at the top of the document. Fill in the header information. By default, Word uses the document name as the subject of the message, but you can change it to whatever you like. The Introduction text box (available in Outlook) gives you a spot to add a note to the recipient.

3. Click the **Send a Copy** button to send a copy of the document as an e-mail message (see Figure 22.6). (The original document remains in its current location on your computer system.)

Click to send the Word document as an e-mail message.

FIGURE 22.6

Fill in the e-mail header and send the message.

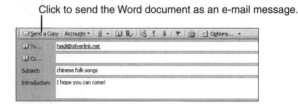

Your computer connects to the Internet, if you aren't already online, and then Word sends the message. When the recipient receives it, it looks something like the message shown in Figure 22.7. HTML can't duplicate Word formatting exactly, so you can expect the HTML-formatted message to differ somewhat from the original Word document. In Figure 22.7, you can see that the page border was removed from the document when it was converted to HTML.

FIGURE 22.7

This message is a Word document, now formatted in HTML.

If you want to see what your document will look like on the receiving end, follow these steps, but send a test copy of the message to yourself by putting your own e-mail address in the To text box before clicking the Send a Copy button.

After you've sent a Word document once as an e-mail message, when you open it in the future and click the E-mail toolbar button, all the e-mail header information that you filled in the last time you sent the document is already inserted for you. This makes it easy to send regular updates of a document to the same recipient. (You can, of course, change the e-mail header information to send the document to someone else if you need to.)

Sending a Word Document As an E-mail Attachment

Another option is to send a Word document as an attachment to an e-mail message. The advantage of doing this is that the formatting of your Word document remains intact. However, the recipient must have Word to open the document.

Follow these steps to attach a Word document to an e-mail message and send it:

1. Create or open the document that you want to send as an e-mail attachment.

2. Choose **File**, **Send To**, **Mail Recipient (As Attachment)**.

The File, Send To command also includes a Send to Mail Recipient (For Review) command. This command sends the document as an attachment, automatically creates the subject line *Please review 'document name,'* and inserts the text *Please review the attached document* in the body of the message. It also attaches a high-priority indicator to the message (a red flag) that will appear next to the subject line in the recipient's e-mail program.

3. A message window in your default e-mail program opens. Note that the attachment is listed in the Attach line in the Outlook message shown in Figure 22.8 (your e-mail program may use a slightly different label). Fill in the rest of the e-mail header information, and type the e-mail message. If your e-mail program lets you send HTML messages, you can choose to modify the message formatting.

Attached Word document

FIGURE 22.8

The Word document is attached to the e-mail message.

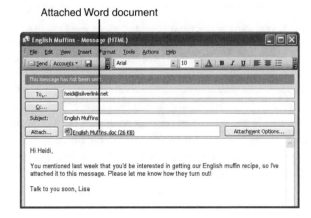

4. Click the **Send** button (or whatever button your e-mail program provides for sending messages).

Your computer connects to the Internet, if you aren't already online, and then it sends the message and its attachment. Figure 22.9 shows a message with an attachment as it will appear on the receiving end. Most e-mail programs use a paper clip icon to indicate that a message has an attachment. Use the command for saving an attachment in your e-mail program (usually something like File, Save Attachments) to copy the attached Word document to a folder of your choosing on your computer or network. You can then open it in Word in the usual manner.

The message lists the name of the attachment.

FIGURE 22.9

Most e-mail programs use a paper clip icon to indicate that a message has an attachment.

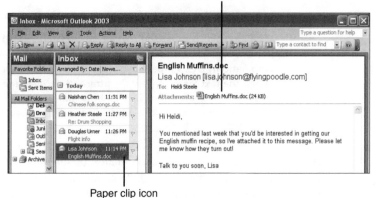

Paper clip icon

Sending Any Document As an Attachment to an E-mail Message

22

You aren't limited to attaching Word documents to e-mail messages. If you create a message in Word, you can attach any document to the message, including Excel workbooks, PowerPoint presentations, or files created in other programs.

Follow the steps in "Composing and Sending an E-mail Message from Word" or "Sending a Word Document in the Body of an E-mail Message" earlier in this hour, but in step 2, add this procedure:

1. Click the **Insert File** button in the e-mail header (see Figure 22.10).

Insert File

FIGURE 22.10

Click the Insert File button to attach any document to your e-mail message.

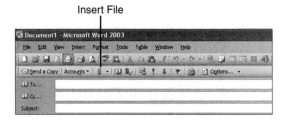

2. In the Insert File dialog box, navigate to and select the document that you want to attach. In Figure 22.11, the file is a PowerPoint presentation. Click the **Insert** button.

FIGURE 22.11

Select the file to attach in the Insert File dialog box.

3. An Attach line now appears beneath the Subject line in the e-mail header (see Figure 22.12). Attach any additional documents to the message if you like, and then finish the remaining steps in "Composing and Sending an E-mail Message from Word" or "Sending a Word Document in the Body of an E-mail Message" to complete and send the message.

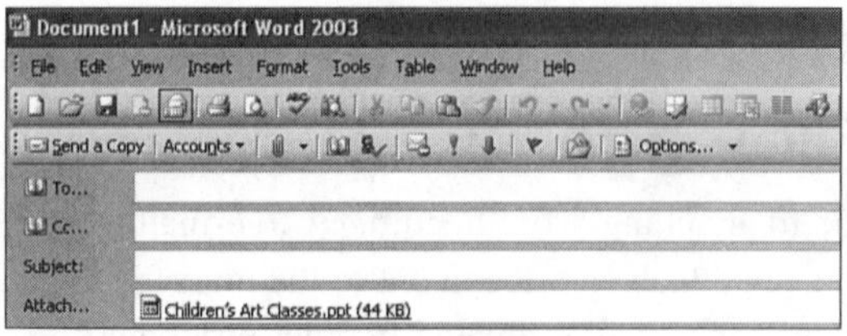

FIGURE 22.12

The files you've attached to the message are listed in the Attach line.

Summary

Word offers several convenient ways to create and send e-mail without leaving the Word window. If you do a lot of e-mail, at least one of the approaches explained in this hour will probably become an indispensable part of your repertoire. In the next hour of this book, you explore Word's Web page features.

Q&A

Q I want to send my message to more than one person. How do I do that?

A In the To box, type each person's e-mail address, separated by semicolons or commas in the To or Cc boxes.

Q I created a beautiful e-mail message with fancy formatting, but when my friend received it, it looked horrible. What went wrong?

A If the formatting disappeared, the most likely problem is that your friend's computer doesn't have the same fonts that you used to compose the message. If the message was filled with cryptic codes, it's likely that your friend's e-mail program can't handle HTML-formatted messages.

Q I added two signatures in the E-mail Options dialog box, one for business use and one for personal use. How can I switch between them?

A When you compose a new e-mail message in Word (by clicking the E-mail Message link in the New Document task pane), Word automatically inserts the signature that is selected in the Signature for New Messages list at the bottom of the E-mail Options dialog box. To change the signature in a particular message you're composing, right-click the signature in the body of the message and choose the one you want from the context menu that appears. (If you have Outlook configured to use Word to edit e-mail messages—via Outlook's Tools, Options dialog box, Mail Format tab—and you use Outlook to reply to or forward a message, the signature selected in the Signature for Replies and Forwards list at the bottom of Word's E-mail Options dialog box will be used.)

Hour 23

Word and the Web

Word gives you a host of options for integrating Word and the Web. You can turn Word documents into Web pages, turn Web pages into Word documents, and create Web pages from scratch in Word. And if you are responsible for making Web pages accessible to other people on an intranet or Internet site, you can even handle this task from the Word window. In this hour of the book, you get a sense of what you can accomplish when Word and the Web work as a team.

The highlights of this hour include

- Converting Word documents to Web pages
- Converting Web pages to Word documents
- Making your Web pages available to others

Converting Word Documents to Web Pages

If you have information in a Word document that you want to let a large number of people read, you can convert the document to a Web page and then post the page on a Web site, either on the Internet or on your company intranet. Before you convert your document, however, check with your network administrator to see whether it's necessary. In some cases—depending on the browser your company uses and the software used to run the Web server—you can put Word documents on company intranets without changing the document format at all.

Follow these steps to save a Word document as a Web page:

1. Open the Word document that you want to convert or create a new document now (see Figure 23.1).

FIGURE 23.1

Open the document that you want to convert to a Web page.

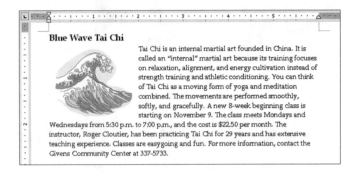

2. Choose **File**, **Save As Web Page** to display the Save As dialog box.

3. If you like, you can click the **Change Title** button to revise the title that will appear in the title bar for the page. A descriptive title will help search engines to catalog your page and help readers get a sense of what the page contains. Then specify a name and location for the page (see Figure 23.2), and click the **Save** button.

FIGURE 23.2

Choose a name and location for your Web page.

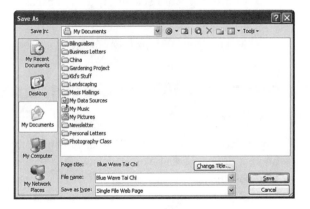

4. You may see a message such as the one shown in Figure 23.3 stating how Word will modify formatting that can't be rendered in a Web page. If you do, click the **Continue** button.

Figure 23.3

Word tells you if it can't convert all the formatting in the Word document.

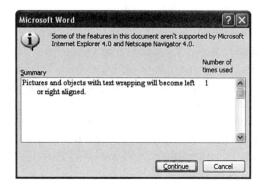

5. The newly converted Web page appears in the Word window (see Figure 23.4). Word automatically switches to Web Layout view (View, Web Layout) whenever it displays a Web page. If you want to see what the page will look like when viewed in a browser, choose **File**, **Web Page Preview**.

Figure 23.4

Word displays your Web page in Web Layout view.

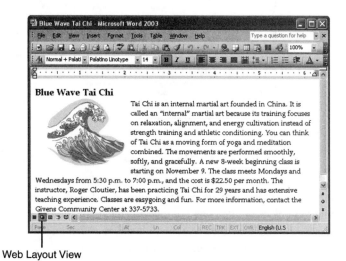

Web Layout View

6. Your browser opens and displays the Web page. In Figure 23.5, the Web page is displayed in Internet Explorer. Close your browser when you're finished viewing the page.

By default, Word saves Web pages in a format it calls *Single File Web Page* (see the Save As Type drop-down list in the Save As dialog box shown in Figure 23.2). These files have an extension of .mht (for MHTML). The MHTML format is convenient because it saves all of the components of a Web page—text, images, other graphical elements, and so on—in one file. However, it is not supported by all browsers. For this reason, it is only a good choice if you're planning on posting your page on a company intranet where everyone uses the same browser. If you are going to post your page on the Internet, you should choose Web Page in the Save As Type list instead. This option saves the files in the standard HTML format, which can be read by all browsers. Keep in mind, however, that if you save the file in HTML, you will need to upload any images or other components of your Web page to your server separately, and these components will need to be stored in the locations referenced in your Web page. If this raises more questions than it answers, ask your system administrator or a Web-savvy friend for help.

FIGURE 23.5

You can view your Web page in your browser to see how it will look to others.

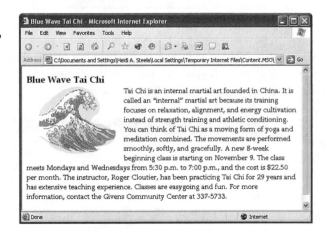

Converting Web Pages to Word Documents

Once in a while, you may want to save a Web page as a Word document. Perhaps you found a recipe on a Web site and want to edit the text in Word, or you discovered a Web page about woodworking and want to take advantage of Word's formatting and printing capabilities to spruce it up a bit. When you convert a Web page to a Word document, Word does its best to preserve the formatting in the page.

If you want to use content you found on the Web for other than your own personal use, it's a good idea to contact the author for permission because the usual copyright rules apply.

Follow these steps to save a Web page as a Word document:

1. Display the Open dialog box, type the address for the Web page in the File Name text box, making sure to type the complete address for the page you want to open (although you don't have to type the http://), and click the **Open** button (see Figure 23.6).

FIGURE 23.6

Type the complete address for the Web page in the File Name text box.

2. Word prompts you to connect to the Internet if necessary, and then opens the Web page in the Word window (see Figure 23.7). Choose **File**, **Save As** to display the Save As dialog box.

> If Word displays a message box asking if you want to make Word your default Web page editor, you can answer either no or yes and still have the page open in Word. However, if you're planning on creating more than a very occasional Web page, you probably want to answer no and use a full-fledged Web page editing program to create your pages.

3. Choose a location for the document, and type a name in the File Name text box.
4. Display the Save As Type list and select **Word Document** (see Figure 23.8).
5. Click the **Save** button.

The Web page is saved as a Word document, and all the graphics are included in the document itself (see Hour 16, "Inserting Images, Drawing Shapes, and Creating Text Effects with WordArt," and Hour 17, "Manipulating Images," if you need help working with them).

FIGURE 23.7

Word can display Web pages as well as Word documents.

FIGURE 23.8

Choose Word Document in the Save As Type list to save the Web page as a Word document.

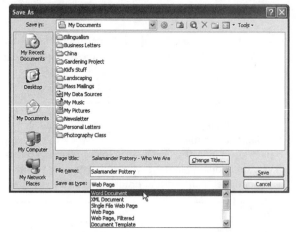

Step 1 in the preceding steps describes how to open a Web page directly from the Internet. You could also use your browser to save the page to your hard disk, and then open it from your hard disk. If you use this latter method, make sure to select All Files in the Files of Type list in the Open dialog box so that the Web page will be visible. (By default, Word shows only Word documents in the Open dialog box.)

Making Your Web Pages Available to Others

To make your Web pages visible to others, you have to copy (*upload*) them to the Internet Web site or intranet site where they will "live." If you aren't sure where they should go, ask your system administrator.

You typically upload pages to a Web or intranet site by using a *protocol* called FTP (File Transfer Protocol). So telling Word where you want to upload your Web pages involves defining an FTP location. You have to do this only once. From then on, you will be able to choose the FTP site in the Save As dialog box.

23

Follow these steps to set up an FTP location for uploading your Web pages to a Web site on an intranet or the Internet:

1. Choose **File**, **Save As**, and then select **Add/Modify FTP Locations** in the Save In list (see Figure 23.9).

FIGURE 23.9

Choose Add/Modify FTP Locations in the Save In list.

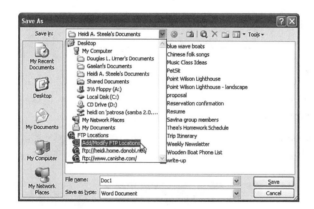

2. Word displays the Add/Modify FTP Locations dialog box. Type the name of the site in the **Name of FTP Site** text box. Although FTP addresses begin with ftp://, you don't need to type this at the beginning of the name. So, for example, you can just enter ftp.twoducks.com, not ftp://ftp.twoducks.com. (If you aren't sure of the name, ask the system administrator at the site.)

3. If you don't have a personal account at the site, mark the **Anonymous** option button. If you do have an account, mark the **User** option button, and enter your username and password. Then click the **Add** button to add the site to the list of FTP sites at the bottom of the dialog box (see Figure 23.10) and click **OK**.

Many companies let people who don't have personal accounts log in to their FTP site as anonymous users. Anonymous users have access to only certain public areas of a site, generally for download purposes only, and they may not be permitted to upload files at all.

FIGURE 23.10

Use the Add/Modify FTP Locations dialog box to tell Word about your FTP site.

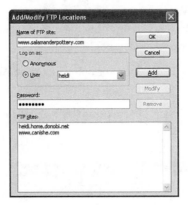

4. The new FTP location now appears under FTP Locations in the Save In list (and in the Look In list in the Open dialog box). Select it if necessary, and then click the **Open** button.

5. Word connects to the Internet (or your intranet) if you aren't already online, and displays the contents of the folders at the FTP site (see Figure 23.11).

FIGURE 23.11

The contents of the FTP site appear in the Save As dialog box.

6. Navigate to the folder in which you want to save the Web page, type a name for it in the **File Name** text box (use all lowercase), and click the **Save** button.

Word saves your Web page at the FTP site. It is now in a location where other people can access it with their browsers. (Note that in Figure 23.11, the option in the Save As Type drop-down list was changed from Single File Web Page to Web Page so that the Web page will be stored on the Web server as a standard HTML file.) If you need help with this process, ask your network or system administrator.

Summary

23

In this hour, you took a tour of Word's Web-related features. You now have the skills to create simple Web pages and make them available to your friends and coworkers. In the next hour, you'll learn about two new features in Word: XML and Smart Documents. These features can expand Word's usefulness in many ways.

Q&A

Q I created a Web page in Word and put it on my Web site, and it looks really different in my friend's browser. What is going on?

A Unfortunately, not all browsers interpret the underlying HTML (or MHTML) code in Web pages the same way. You can expect some differences in how Web pages look in different browsers. Ideally, you should open your Web pages in several browsers to see how they look and only upload them to a Web site when you are satisfied.

Q I'm creating my Web page in Word and I want to add a background color to the page. What command do I use?

A Choose Format, Background, and click the desired color in the submenu that appears.

HOUR **24**

Smart Documents and XML

With Word 2003, Microsoft extended Word's capabilities in two major areas. First, Word is now *XML-enabled*, meaning that you can use it to read, create, and save documents in XML (Extensible Markup Language). Second, software developers can create *Smart Documents*—highly interactive XML-based documents that are tightly integrated into a company's business processes. If you work with highly structured documents that are an essential part of your organization's products or services, if you frequently need to present the same document in multiple formats—perhaps as a Word document, a Web page, a PDF file, and online help—or if your company has informed you that it is converting to XML, you will probably find the information presented in this hour useful. If you don't work with Word in these ways, you might still want to skim this hour for general edification, but don't get hung up on the details.

The highlights of this hour include

- Knowing how much you need to know
- What is XML?
- What are Smart Documents?
- What is WordML?
- How can Smart Documents and XML help me do my work?

- Walking through an application of XML in the workplace
- Where to go for further information

How Much Do I Need to Understand?

The amount of detail you need to understand when working with Smart Documents and XML depends on whether you are a developer or an end user. If you are a developer, you will need to understand all of the content in this hour, and then you will need to build on that foundation with further study.

If you're an end user, you can ignore quite a number of the details. For example, you don't need to remember all of the files associated with an XML document, nor do you need to be familiar with all of the XML-related options—menu commands, dialog boxes, and so on—in Word's user interface. (Some of these will be touched on in this hour, but you will not learn about all of them.) What matters to you are the overall concepts. If they make sense to you, when your company asks you to start using a Smart Document instead of your familiar old .dot template, you'll have some idea of what to expect. Keep in mind that Microsoft designed these features to enable developers to hide XML from end users almost entirely. It's quite possible to use XML documents or Smart Documents without even knowing it.

What Is XML?

XML (and its parent SGML) is an open, international standard that has been under development for a number of years. Originally envisioned as a language for describing traditional documents and facilitating their conversion between different media (for example, a printed manual and an online help system), XML has proved to be invaluable for a huge variety of tasks where information must be described and shared between different applications. Today XML is being used in applications that vary from bank and stock transaction processing, to Web pages, and of course to document processing. XML has reached a level of maturity that enables its use in "mainstream" businesses, and it is starting to assume a prominent role in the processing of business documents.

What distinguishes XML documents from other types of documents is that the document is marked up to reflect the structure and semantics of the content. The way the document is presented to the user is handled separately through the Extensible Stylesheet Language (XSL). (XSL Transformations, which are also called *style sheets* or *transforms*, are discussed more later in this hour.)

To apply the XML structuring to a document, the author encloses discrete pieces of content—address, phone number, author, filename, part number, you name it—within *tags* that indicate what type of data each piece of content (or *element*) represents. (The tags and other XML-related information in an XML document are known collectively as *XML markup*. If you're familiar with HTML, you will note the similarity between XML tags and HTML tags.)

The structure of an XML document and the elements it may contain are defined in an associated file called a *schema*. The schema enables Word and other programs to *parse* the document—validate its structure and identify its components. Programs can then take actions based on the content (elements) defined in the schema and tagged in the XML document (for instance, text in the document tagged as a part number could be automatically checked to ensure that the part number was valid). You can associate multiple schemas with an XML document, each of which defines different aspects in the XML document. For example, a typical XML document in Word will have the document's own schema, which describes the content (or data) of the document, plus Word's internal schema (called WordML), which describes the formatting applied to the document, document properties such as the author's name and protected regions, plus tracked changes.

24

In the world of XML, people often talk about a document's *presentation* rather than its *formatting* because in some applications the document may not be "formatted." For example, a document that is used to drive a text-to-speech application would not contain formatting in the usual sense.

The presentation of XML documents is defined by XSLT style sheets (transformations), which are essentially lists of instructions telling Word and other programs that process the XML documents how the various elements should look and what should be done with them. If a developer wants to output an XML document to multiple media, such as a Web page, online help, and a PDF file, he or she creates a separate style sheet for each type of output. For example, a style sheet that is used to transform an XML document into a Web page might include instructions that convert the e-mail address elements in the document into HTML mailto links, and the style sheet that you use to output the same document to a PDF file might contain instructions for formatting the email address element in boldface.

XSL Transformations convert the source XML document into a customized XML version of that document that is geared toward a particular output (or other use of the information in the document). In many cases the actual conversion of the document to its final output media, say a PDF or an online help file, is handled by an application that reads the transformed XML file and generates the final output.

The complex range of possible transformations of a document can be quite overwhelming. In Word, Microsoft uses the concept of a *solution* to package the components involved in a transformation. Word solutions can also incorporate Smart Documents (described in the next section) to further simplify the process.

Standard Word formatting can, optionally, be saved saved in an XML document. Word uses XML elements defined in the WordML schema to store formatting information. In addition to formatting, WordML provides a way to store document metadata, such as tracked changes, protected regions, and document properties while maintaining XML compatibility. The WordML schema definition is not stored in the Schema Library with your XML schemas, so you won't see it when browsing schemas. As you'll see later in this hour, when you save an XML document you can specify whether to include the WordML information in it. If you save an XML file without applying your own schema to it, Word saves the document in WordML (in other words, it applies the WordML schema to it). When you save an XML file as XML (by choosing XML Document in the Save As Type list in the Save As dialog box), the file is stored on the disk in plain text. You can also save an XML file as a Word document or Word template. If you save the file in either of these formats, the file is stored on disk in Word's binary format and, although the XML markup in the file is preserved, the file will not be accessible to other applications that process XML files.

What Are Smart Documents?

Smart Documents are documents that use behind-the-scenes programming to assist the user during each step of working with the document. Performance reviews, proposals, and other frequently used structured documents are candidates for conversion to Smart Documents. Smart Documents typically sport a Document Actions task pane that includes information, guidance, and options for such tasks as completing, editing, and routing the document.

Smart Documents are made possible by XML, which enables them to parse the contents of the document and take actions based on the content. Smart Documents are always based on XML, but XML documents do not necessarily have to be Smart Documents.

Another valuable feature of Smart Documents is that they are able to keep themselves up-to-date with the latest versions of their components. This greatly simplifies the task of managing the documents that support a business.

Because Smart Documents can do significant amounts of processing "behind the user's back," Microsoft has taken great pains to make Smart Documents secure. Smart Documents are cryptographically signed to ensure that you always know the source of the document and that you're assured of its integrity.

Advantages of Smart Documents and XML

XML helps businesses to solve many of the thorny problems of creating, validating, managing, and exchanging data between applications and between businesses. Smart Documents go a step further by enabling developers to create documents that "understand" how they fit into a business process. The XML in Smart Documents enables the workers to interact with their users to streamline the business process and enhance the efficiency of "information workers," while at the same time insulating the workers from the complexities of XML. Here is a list of the key advantages of using Smart Documents and XML:

- You can take a single source document and transform it for many different media types, such as print, Web, text-to-speech, Braille, and online help. This helps to solve the problem of trying to maintain similar content in different documents, reducing both errors and duplicated effort.

- With the content in a document tagged, you can both pull data into the document from external data sources and export data from the document into external data sources. This makes it possible to do things like fill in elements based on tags in the document—for example, entering a customer number into an XML form could pull up the customer's shipping information or order history.

- Because XML documents are highly structured, they can be integrated efficiently into a company's business processes, and users can handle them with greater accuracy. Word and other XML-aware applications can validate the structure and contents of a document, so documents are more likely to be complete and correctly structured. In turn, other applications can access information that was previously trapped in Word documents. For example, a product specification in a Word XML document could be parsed by an external application to generate a list of components.

- Other programs can create Word documents. This enables applications to generate Word documents automatically, greatly eliminating the drudge work of some tasks. For example, a software company may use structured comments in its source code as the basis for technical documentation of its products. Now an application can extract this information from the source files and create an initial Word document that is the start of a manual. This enables a much higher level of automation of this process.

- Document management can now be automated more efficiently. When Word loads a Smart Document, the Smart Document will check to ensure that it is the latest version, greatly reducing the overhead of managing business documents. XML tagging also makes it possible to do things like automatically generating (and updating) a list of document authors and then push it into Smart Documents as needed.

24

This means you can keep customers supplied with up-to-date and consistent information.

What Files Are Associated with an XML Document?

As you have probably gathered from the preceding sections, an XML document (`*.xml`) depends on a number of files that collectively define the document and the operations that can be performed on it. If you work directly with XML documents, you will need to know what these files are. If you don't, you may still want to skim this section simply because you may run into references to these files in the Word interface. Here are the key files you'll encounter:

- Word templates (*.dot)—An XML document is often based on a Word template that contains all the XML markup, or at least the initial markup. As with standard Word documents, basing an XML document on a template keeps users from accidentally overwriting the boilerplate document and keeps all of the documents based on that template consistent. Smart Documents are also capable of checking to ensure that you are using the latest versions of the document template (and the other files that make up the document).

- Schemas (*.xsd)—The schema defines the structure of the XML document and the elements contained in it. Word and other applications that process the XML document also use the schema to *validate* the document, that is, to check that the document is correctly composed. You can have multiple schemas associated with a document.

- Style sheets (*.xsl or *.xslt)—The style sheet (transformation) defines the way in which the document elements will be formatted for presentation. A document that will be presented in different media (in print, in Braille, as a PowerPoint presentation, as a Web page, in an online help system, via a text-to-speech system) would have multiple style sheets. In XML parlance, applying a particular style sheet to an XML document when you save it to generate a particular type of output is called *applying a transform*. A document may also have additional style sheets to define alternative views of the document. For example, an assembly manual may have a view that presents the list of parts referenced in the manual as part of a quality control procedure.

- Manifest files (*.xml)—These files are XML-structured files that define the components of a Smart Document solution. And yes, it's confusing that manifests also use the .xml extension.

What Are Some Applications for XML and Smart Documents?

To get you thinking about ways in which you or your company might use XML and Smart Documents, here are three examples of documents that could benefit greatly from conversion to one of these solutions:

- Catalogs—Using XML for a catalog would enforce design rules and ensure that all of the information has been entered correctly. An XML-based catalog could be interfaced with databases, typesetting software, and Web design systems. It would streamline the process of outputting the catalog both in print form on the company's Web site. Word would provide a familiar and convenient interface for writing the copy in the catalog.

- Performance Reviews—A performance review that was built as a Smart Document could provide employees with guidance when they are filling it out. It would be able to automatically fill in some information by pulling it from the employee database (for example, if the employee entered his or her employee ID number, the Smart Document could then fill in the employee's name, address, department, years of employment, and so on). The document could route itself to the next person in the review process. It could provide a high level of security for confidential sections of the review, and it could automatically enter information from the completed review into the employee database.

- Books—Using XML for a book would enable more effective indexing and cross-referencing. Furthermore, the XML markup would make it possible for applications to extract the structure of the book for use in PowerPoint. You could use different transforms for hard copy books and e-books.

24

An XML Walkthrough

There are a myriad of ways in which you might encounter XML files and Smart Documents, and it would be impossible to cover all of them. One likely possibility, however, is that your company will make the decision to start using XML and you will be asked to help with this process. This section uses this scenario to walk you through using Word 2003 to perform some common XML-related tasks. If you are not facing the prospect of converting documents to XML yourself and don't feel a need to investigate the XML-related nooks and crannies of the Word interface, you can skip to the "Where to Go Next" section at the end of this hour. If, however, you have been, or think you might be, asked to do some of this work, you will probably want to read this section and poke around the Word interface as you go.

To set the scene for this section, let's say you are a tech writer at a software company, and one of your tasks is to prepare technical notes for your field engineers and customers. The technical notes are usually distributed via your Web site and on paper at trade shows. Until now, you have used a Word template for these documents and have managed them by hand, tracking when the software they describe changes, tracking new releases of the software, getting approval for drafts, determining whether a technical note is ready to be publicly released, and so on.

Your company has now decided to start basing your technical notes on XML. A consultant or someone from your documentation support group has already created the schemas and style sheets you will need. Your job is to convert your template to XML, associate the appropriate files with it, protect the regions of the template that you do not want to be modified, and so on.

After you have converted your template to XML, you will use it to create a technical note. As a part of this process, you will learn how to work with an XML-structured document, fixing validation errors you encounter, editing the document with track changes, and saving the document with and without a transform.

Converting a Standard Word Template to an XML Template

The general steps for converting a standard Word template to an XML template are as follows:

1. Open the Word template and attach the XML schema you want to associate with the new XML template.
2. Insert XML tags in the template to label each element of the document. This enables Word to check that documents based on the template are properly structured and to perform some validation on the element contents.
3. Protect the XML tags so that they cannot be revised or deleted.
4. Optionally, replace the default placeholder text for each element with text that will provide element-specific guidance when using the template.
5. Save the template.

Depending on the length of your template, this process can be pretty laborious. Luckily you only have to do it once.

In this section and the three that follow, you'll notice that the Word interface (and hence the text in this book) uses the term *document* in a general sense to refer to XML documents and templates.

These steps walk you through this process in more detail:

1. After opening the template you're converting to XML, choose **Tools, Templates and Add-Ins**. In the Templates and Add-Ins dialog box, click the **XML Schema** tab. Mark the check box for the schema that you want to attach to your template, in this case Technical Notes (see Figure 24.1). (These steps assume that one or more schemas have already been created for you and stored in your schema library, so they appear in this list; this would typically be part of the work done by the folks managing the migration to XML.) Under Schema Validation Options, mark the **Validate Document Against Attached Schemas** check box.

FIGURE **24.1**

Select the schema that you want to attach to your template.

24

2. Click **OK**. The selected schema is now attached to the template and the XML Structure task pane appears (see Figure 24.2). This task pane is organized in two sections. The top section, Elements in the Document, displays a map of the structure of the document. Initially there are no elements in the document, so the message "No XML elements have been applied to this document" appears.

3. If necessary, mark the **Show XML Tags in the Document** check box so that the XML tags you add to the template will be visible.

4. The bottom section of the task pane contains a list box from which you select an XML element to apply to a selected region of the document. Initially, this box lists only the top-level element (also known as the *root element*) defined in the attached schema. If it does not, mark the **List Only Child Elements of Current Element** check box under the list box. When this check box is marked, the list of elements that appears in the list box is narrowed to those that could be used to tag the

current selection. In this view, the elements are presented in the order in which they are declared in the schema. When the check box is cleared, all of the elements defined in the schema(s) are listed in alphabetical order, with a red slashed circle icon next to those elements that are not children of the element in which the current selection is located, and thus cannot be used in the current context. For complex schemas, this list can be very large.

FIGURE 24.2

When the XML Structure task pane first appears, the Elements in the Document list is empty.

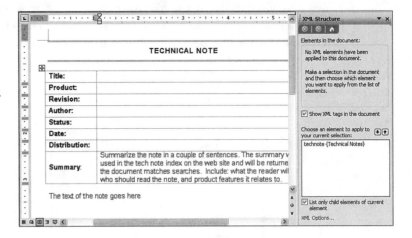

 Although Word does full validation of the XML elements applied to a document, in this release of Office 2003 it does not do the analysis necessary to show you only the elements that would be correct to add to the document at the insertion point, even when you have marked the List Only Child Elements of Current Element check box. This means that when this check box is marked, you may still see elements in the element selection list that will cause validation errors when you apply them to your document. For example, in the schema used in this section, the *author* element includes the child elements *name*, *title*, and *email*. Each of these elements can appear only once in the author element. When the insertion point is within the author element, Word will include all of the child elements even if one or more has already been applied, and it would be an error to include it again.

5. Select the whole document (**Edit, Select All**), and then click the top-level (root) element displayed in the element selection list. The Apply to Entire Document dialog box appears because this is the first element to be applied to the document (see Figure 24.3). The top-level element is the "container" for the entire document, so click the **Apply to Entire Document** button.

FIGURE 24.3

FIGURE 24.3

Click the Apply to Entire Document button to enclose the entire document in the root element tag.

If you have made a selection smaller than the whole document (perhaps because some of the text in the old template will not be included in the new one), be sure to click the Apply Only to Selection button instead—and remember that the root element must enclose the whole document by the time you are done.

24

6. Click anywhere to deselect the document. A pair of purple XML tags representing the root element of the schema now bracket the document, and the name of the root element appears in the Elements in the Document list. The element solution list changes to display the children of the root element. Because all but the simplest of documents will be incomplete, and thus violate their schema, a schema violation marker (a purple wavy line) will appear in the document window, and a yellow schema violation icon will appear next to the root element's name in the task pane (see Figure 24.4). If you find the schema violation markers distracting, you can turn them off by marking the **Hide Schema Violations in This Document** check box in the XML Options dialog (accessible from the bottom of the XML Structure task pane).

7. To investigate the schema violation, right-click the purple line. A message box appears describing the violation and offering some possible actions (see Figure 24.5). When the schema violation is within an individual element, Word may display the marker under the element (though if the element is in a table, the marker remains in the margin). In the task pane, you can hover the mouse pointer over the schema violation icon to display a brief description of the error.

As you work through the document tagging individual elements, the purple line will eventually disappear—the way in which the schema was written determines the exact manner in which the marker behaves. If the schema specifies constraints on the contents of individual elements, those elements will continue to be marked as violations until their contents are acceptable. You can either choose to fill in the elements with an acceptable default or leave the element empty so that Word will flag the omission.

This icon indicates
a schema violation.

Opening XML tag

FIGURE 24.4

*XML tags now bracket
the top-level element of
your document.*

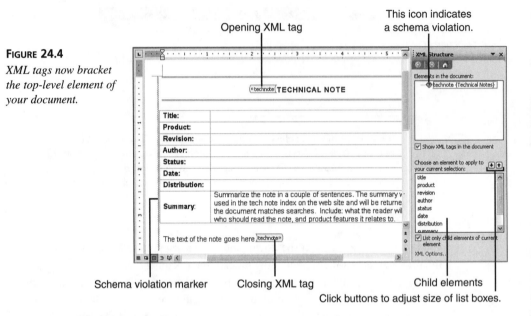

Schema violation marker   Closing XML tag   Child elements

Click buttons to adjust size of list boxes.

FIGURE 24.5

*A message box gives
you information and
suggestions about the
schema violation.*

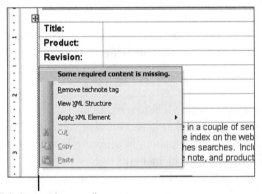

Right-click the purple wavy line.

It can be difficult to position the insertion point between the tags for two
adjacent elements by clicking the mouse. Word seems to prefer to place the
insertion point within one of the elements. However, you can easily move
the insertion point in between two tags using the arrow keys.

8. Continue marking up the document by selecting elements in the document window and then clicking the element names in the element selection list. Each time you do this, the element selection list changes to reflect the list of element tags that can be added to the document in the context of the current element. In some cases, the element selection list will be empty. As you add tags, the element names will appear in the Elements in the Document list (see Figure 24.6), showing the structure of the document. When you are finished, continue with the next set of steps to protect the tags you've added.

FIGURE 24.6

This document has been marked up.

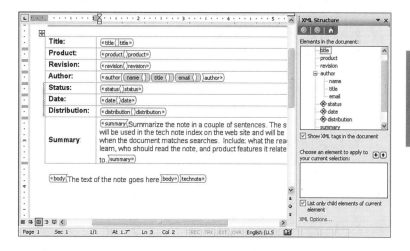

Word uses a variety of icons to indicate errors in the structure of an XML document. If one or more errors are present in your document, you can't save the document as an XML document unless you mark the Allow Saving as XML Even If Not Valid check box in the XML Options dialog (accessible from the bottom of the XML Structure task pane). You can still save the file as a Document Template (*.dot) or as a Word Document (*.doc) when there are validation errors. Until a document validates, it cannot be processed by other XML-aware applications.

Protecting the XML Template

After you have tagged all of the XML elements in the template and decided how you want to resolve any schema violations (by supplying acceptable defaults, or by leaving them to ensure that someone creating a document based on the template will have to supply valid contents for the elements), you could save your work, but because you are creating a document template, it makes sense to protect the XML tags first. By doing this you ensure that the tags will not be accidentally deleted when they are hidden from view. (For most users, you will want to hide the tags from view to make the document "friendlier.") To protect the template, follow these steps:

1. Choose **Tools, Protect Document** to display the Protect Document task pane.

2. Under Editing Restrictions, mark the **Allow Only This Type of Editing in the Document** check box, and leave the default option selected in the drop-down list below the check box (No Changes [Read Only]).

3. Create exceptions where you want the user to be able to enter text. One by one, click a tag for each element in the document where text must be entered. This will select the area between the element's tags. Then, in the Protect Document task pane, mark the Everyone check box in the Groups list under Exceptions. In the case of nested elements, in most cases you will want to only create exceptions for the innermost elements (for example the name element within the author element). This ensures that text can be entered between the tags, while protecting the tags themselves.

4. After you have marked all of the exceptions, scroll down to the Start Enforcement section, and click the **Yes, Start Enforcing Protection** button.

5. In the resulting Start Enforcing Protection dialog box (see Figure 24.7), select the desired protection method. **Password** requires you to enter a password (twice) to restrict the users that are allowed to remove document protection. For many purposes this will be adequate. If your site is using Microsoft Information Rights Management technology, you can also choose the **User Authentication** option. This provides significantly stronger protection for your document. When you are finished, click **OK**.

FIGURE 24.7

Specify the type of protection you want to use and enter a password.

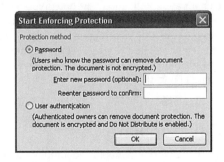

6. The Protect Document task pane now displays information about what regions the user can edit (see Figure 24.8). When you click in different areas of the document,

the text at the top of the task pane updates to inform the user whether the area is
editable.

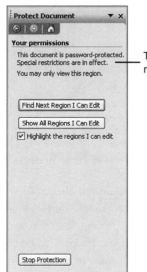

FIGURE 24.8

*The Protect Document
task pane tells the user
whether he or she can
edit at the location of
the insertion point.*

This text changes to
reflect your permissions.

To preserve protection, you must save the document as an XML document
(`*.xml`) with WordML included (the Save Data Only check box must be
cleared in the Save As dialog box), as a Word document (`*.doc`), or as a document template (`*.dot`). If you save the document as an XML document
with the Save Data Only check box marked, the protection information will
be lost.

Displaying and Customizing Placeholder Text

By default, when you hide the XML tags in your document, placeholder text appears to
help the user edit the document. Follow these steps to display the placeholder text.

1. Display the XML Structure task pane. (If the Protect Document task pane is still
   displayed, click the Back button at the top of the task pane. Otherwise, choose
   View, Task Pane and if necessary, click the down arrow in the upper-right corner of
   the task pane and choose XML Structure from the Other Task Panes list that
   appears.)

2. Click the **XML Options** link at the bottom of the task pane. In the resulting XML
   Options dialog box (see Figure 24.9), mark the **Show Placeholder Text for All
   Empty Elements** check box and click **OK**.

FIGURE 24.9

*The XML Options dia-
log box gives you
options for customizing
the behavior of your
XML document.*

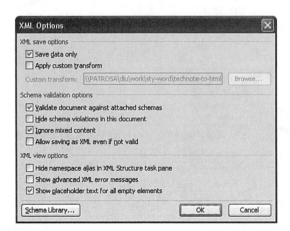

3. Clear the **Show XML Tags in the Document** check box in the XML Structure
   task pane (or press Ctrl+Shift+X). For many users this view may be easier to work
   with. By default, the empty XML tag pairs contain placeholder text (highlighted in
   purple) that lists the name of the element. If you marked the Highlight the Regions
   I Can Edit check box in the Protect Document task pane (refer back to Figure
   24.8), the regions of the document that can be edited will be enclosed in beige
   square brackets, as shown in Figure 24.10. If an element is empty and placeholder
   text is not displayed, the square brackets will overlap, forming an I-beam shape.

FIGURE 24.10

*The XML tags are hid-
den and the default
placeholder text
appears instead.*

Default placeholder text ——

These brackets indicate you can type here.

4. Click the **Forward** button to return to the Protect Document task pane.

> If you clear the Show XML Tags in the Document check box without marking the Show Placeholder Text for All Empty Elements and Highlight the Regions I Can Edit check boxes, you will be unable to tell where to enter text in the document.

In some cases you might want to use more informative placeholder text. For example, the XML date format would display the date October 30, 2003 like this: 2003-10-30. You might want to provide placeholder text that reminds users of the form of the format, or provide any other information that would help them in working with the template. To create custom placeholder text, follow these steps:

1. Choose **Tools**, **Unprotect Document** (or click the Stop Protection button at the bottom of the Protect Document task pane) to temporarily remove protection from the document. Enter the document password if you are using password protection.

2. Press **Ctrl+Shift+X** to display the XML tags if they are not already showing.

3. Right-click the tag to which you want to add custom placeholder text, and choose **Attributes** in the context menu (you can also right-click on the element in the Elements in the Document list of the XML Structure task pane).

4. In the **Attributes for [element name]** dialog box (see Figure 24.11), type the text you want to appear as a prompt for the element in the **Placeholder Text** text box. You can enter up to 253 characters. When you are finished, click **OK**. The text you entered is now displayed as a placeholder when the element is empty and XML tags are not displayed.

FIGURE 24.11

Use the Attributes for [element name] dialog box to specify custom placeholder text.

24

To preserve custom placeholders, you must save the document as an XML document (*.xml) with WordML included (the Save Data Only check box must be cleared in the Save As dialog box), as a Word document (*.doc), or as a document template (*.dot). If you save the document as an XML document with the Save Data Only check box marked, the custom place-holders will be lost.

At this point you have added the XML structure to your template, protected the template, hidden the XML tags, and added custom placeholders. Now all that's left to do is save the template in the usual way (the template will remain a *.dot file). After you've saved the template, you can put it into production, as described in the next section.

Creating a Source Document Based on the XML Template

When you work with an XML template, you'll typically want to use it to create one document that you'll fill in, save, and then use as both your print output and as the basis for other documents that you'll create using File, Save As with various transforms to create different types of output.

To create this source document, start a new document based on your XML template (choose File, New, click On My Computer in the New Document task pane, select the template in the Templates dialog box, and click OK). You'll see a document that looks much like a normal Word document, with the editable regions highlighted and/or enclosed in brackets (depending on whether the Highlight the Regions I Can Edit check box is marked in the Protect Document task pane, and on whether the document is displaying placeholder text). Each of the regions that you can edit is between a pair of hidden XML tags. The tags themselves are protected, so you don't need to worry about accidentally deleting a tag.

Start filling in the editable regions. Because the XML schema of the document may specify constraints on the content of the tags, you might see schema violations (purple wavy lines) as you fill in the various elements. To investigate a violation, follow these steps:

1. Display the XML Structure task pane.

2. In the Elements in the Document list, point to the yellow schema violation icon. A ScreenTip appears with a description of the problem (see Figure 24.12).

FIGURE 24.12

A ScreenTip gives you information about the nature of the violation. This tip shows the effect of marking Show Advanced XML Error Messages in the XML Options dialog (compare to Figure 24.5).

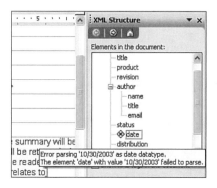

24

You can also investigate a schema violation by right-clicking the purple wavy line in the document instead of using the XML Structure task pane.

The amount and type of detail about the violation that Word provides is controlled by the Show Advanced XML Error Messages check box in the XML Options dialog.

If your document contains regions of "free" text—for example in an annual report, or a technical manual, or even in the descriptive text of a catalog—you will want to tag any elements that you add to this section. To do this, follow these steps:

1. Select the text that you want to tag.

2. Either display XML tags (Ctrl+Shift+X) or display the XML Structure task pane.

3. If XML tags are displayed, you can right-click the selection. If the attached schema contains elements that can be applied to the selection, the Apply XML Element command will appear in the context menu. Point to this command to display the submenu of available elements, and then click the one you want to tag (see Figure 24.13). If you're using the XML Structure task pane, select the item from the Choose An Element To Apply To Your Current Selection box in the XML Structure task pane.

Saving Your Source Document

When you have finished editing your source document, follow these steps to save it:

1. Choose **File**, **Save As**.

2. In the Save As dialog box, select either **Word Document (*.doc)** or **XML Document (*.xml)** in the Save As Type drop-down list. This choice depends on two factors:

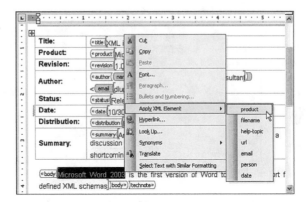

FIGURE 24.13

Select the element you want to tag in the Apply XML Element submenu.

- If the document will be processed by other XML-aware applications, you must save it as an XML document.
- If the document is partially edited and contains schema violations, you must save it as a Word document (unless you have allowed the option of saving documents that contain schema violations as XML documents).

3. Navigate to the folder in which you want to save the file, and type the filename in the File Name text box.

4. If you have chosen XML Document (*.xml) in the Save As Type drop-down list, the Apply Transform and Save Data Only check boxes will appear in the Save As dialog box (see Figure 24.14). Mark the **Save Data Only** check box if you want Word to discard all of the information contained in WordML. Because this includes document metadata such as tracked changes, XML placeholder text, document properties, and document protection information (in addition to Word's formatting), you will rarely want to do this when saving your source document. Marking the **Apply Transform** check box activates the default transform and also allows you to select an alternate transform using the Transform button (which displays the Choose an XML Transform dialog box). In most cases you will want to save the source document "as is" to preserve all of its content and then apply any necessary transforms later.

> If the Save Data Only check box is marked by default in the Save As dialog, you can change this by going to the XML Options dialog and clearing the Save Data Only check box.

5. When you've made your selections, click the **Save** button.

FIGURE 24.14

You can select options for saving an XML document in the Save As dialog box.

Using Transforms to Output Your Source Document in Different Ways

24

After you have created a source document, you can use transforms (also referred to as XSLTs, Extensible Stylesheet Language Transforms) to create additional views of your document. This process enables you to use one document for many purposes. For example, you could use the same source document to create a printed catalog, populate a database for an online catalog, and load short product descriptions into your company's order processing system. The process for doing this is simple (when the style sheets that define the transforms are created and installed on your computer).

When you apply a transform to an XML document, any content not used by the transform is omitted in the resulting document. Thus you always want to take care when applying a transform to a document so that you don't unintentionally overwrite your source document with the transformed one.

To create an output document, follow these steps:

1. Open the source document in Word and (if you want) edit it.

2. Choose **File**, **Save As**.

3. Type a new name for the file so that you don't overwrite your source document.

4. Choose **XML Document (*.xml)** in the Save As Type drop-down list.

5. Mark the **Apply Transform** check box.

6. If you only use one transform, a default transform may be available. If a default transform is not available or it is not the one you want to use, click the **Transform**

button. In the Choose an XML Transform dialog box, navigate to and select the transform file that you want to use, and click **Open**.

7 Click the **Save** button. If you have marked Save Data Only or Apply Transform in the Save As dialog box, you will be prompted to confirm that you want to do this (see Figure 24.15). Click **Continue** to confirm your choice.

FIGURE 24.15

*Click Continue to pro-
ceed with your save.*

Where to Go Next

Although XML is just now becoming a "mainstream" technology, it has been in use in a wide variety of applications for some time. If you're yearning to know more about XML, a great place to start is on the Web—just open up your browser and fire off a query to your favorite search engine. The result is likely to be overwhelming. For Word-specific questions, try the Word online help system. For many topics, Microsoft has also developed training materials that are available via the help system (though at the time of this writing there are none for XML). Browsing the technical section of a good bookstore or your library is also a good way to find up-to-date XML resources. You might want to check out *Sams Teach Yourself XML in 24 Hours*.

Summary

XML solves many problems of managing documents and information for organizations of any size. In the past, the use of XML and its predecessor SGML was often limited to large enterprises that could afford the resources to implement an overall document strategy. But the benefits of XML are just as relevant to small businesses, and as XML becomes more widespread, you can expect to find more and more "canned" XML packages. The support of XML in this release of Word is bound to accelerate this development.

Q&A

Q When should I use XML, and when should I use forms?

A For simple applications such as mail merge, forms are probably easier. For complex applications where you're integrating with other applications, XML—particularly in conjunction with Smart Documents—is probably the way to go.

For form-based enterprise applications, Microsoft InfoPath is an XML-based tool specifically designed for collecting information with forms.

Q   What about ActiveX controls? How do they fit in?

A   They can be used in conjunction with XML and Smart Documents, just like in standard Word documents.

Q   What is the difference between XML and WordML?

A   XML is a generalized language for describing the markup of data (also known as documents). It is the language in which a document-specific schema is defined, and it is also the language in which WordML is defined. WordML enables Word to describe both a document's metadata and the formatting applied to it in a way that is compatible with other XML applications, and which allows Word documents to be generated by applications other than Word.

24

APPENDIX A

Modifying and Repairing Your Word Installation

Please see the book's Web site at www.samspublishing.com. Type the ISBN (excluding hyphens) in the Search field and follow the links to the book page.

INDEX

Symbols

Change Case command (Format menu), 146
Change Case dialog box, 146
Change Source dialog box, disconnecting data source files, 442
Change Text Direction button, 355, 395
changes, undoing, 256
changing. *See also* editing
  fonts, 136
    color, 142
    defaults, 146-147
    Font dialog box, 138-139
    Font list, 137-138
    size, 139-140
  letters, case, 146
  margins, 184-186
  orientation (paper), 187-188
  paper size, 188
character styles, 206
characters
  formatting, 206
  hidden, paragraph marks, 39
  spacing, 143-145
  special characters
    ^ (caret symbol), 264
    finding/replacing, 264-265
    inserting, 270-272
check box form fields, 429
check box list form fields, 426
Check Grammar As You Type check box, 247
Check Spelling As You Type check box, 244
checkers
  grammar checker, 246-249
  spell checking, disabling, 244
  spelling, 247-249
checking
  grammar, 247-249
  paragraph formatting, 178-180
  spelling, 247-249
choosing
  folders (default), 85
  printer paper trays, 199-200
  views, 81-82
Clear Formatting command, 207
click-and-type features, 50

Clip Art images, inserting, 367-370
Clip Art task pane, 367-369
Clip Organizer, 370-371
Clip Organizer Help command (Help menu), 371
Clipboard icons, 40
Close command (File menu), 34
Close Side by Side button, 106
closing documents, 33-34
codes (field codes), viewing, 268
collapsing outlines, 284, 287
colon (:), 293
colors
  fill color, images, 389
  fonts, 142
  text colors used in tracking revisions, 414-415
Colors dialog box, 142
columns, 337-341
  adding/deleting, 350
  balancing, 341
  breaks, 340
  resizing, 352-355
  section breaks, 338
  vertical lines, 340
  width, adjusting, 340
Columns button, 339
Columns command (Format menu), 339
Columns dialog box, 339
combining, 104
commands. *See individual command names*
comment feature, 409
comments
  adding, 409
  balloons, 411
  deleting, 410
  editing, 410
  inserting, 409-410
  Reviewing pane versus balloons, 411
  Reviewing toolbar, 409
Compare Side by Side dialog box, 106
Compare Side by Side with command (Window menu), 105
comparisons (filters), 330

composing e-mail messages, 472-473
concordance files, 292
condensing text, 143
configuring
  multilingual support, 456
    built-in languages, 456
    complex script languages, 457
    East Asian languages, 457
    Office 2003, 461
    right-to-left languages, 457
    Windows XP, 458
    Word 2003, 461-462
consistent formatting, 206
Contemporary Fax template, 124-126
context menus, showing, 17
Continuous section break, 202
contrast (images), 390
control buttons, 12, 28
conventions
  filenames, 72
  naming conventions, macros, 280
converting
  documents to Web pages, 481-484
  documents to XML, 497-507
  endnotes to footnotes, 275
  fields to regular text, 268
  footnotes to endnotes, 275
  templates, 498
  Web pages to documents, 484-486
copying
  documents, 90
  files, 76
  formatting
    fonts, 147-148
    paragraphs, 177-178
  items between templates, 234-235
  text, 58-60
    drag-and-drop, 60-61
    multiple items, 61-64
  Web pages to the Internet, 487-488
copyright, images, 362

disabling
  grammar checker, 247
  spell checking, 244
disk drives, 72
**Display for Review drop-down
  list, tracking revisions, 412**
displaying. *See also* **showing**
  placeholder text in XML doc-
    uments, 505
distributing images, 401-402
Do Not Show Styles, 211
docking
  Language bar, 464
  toolbars, 22
Document Map
  documents, navigating,
    283-286
  formatting, 286
  troubleshooting, 215, 284
Document Map button, 284
**Document Map command
  (View menu), 284**
**Document Recovery task pane,
  78**
documents
  closing, 33-34
  converting to Web pages,
    481-484
  converting to XML, 497-507
  converting Web pages to,
    484-486
  copying, 90
  creating with a template,
    124-127
  creating with wizards,
    128-130
  default settings, 38
  deleting, 89-90
  editing, Print Preview view,
    108
  e-mail attachments, 477-478
  embedding Excel data,
    442-443
  foreign language documents,
    editing, 468
  inserting Excel worksheets,
    440
  inserting slides, 447-448
  large, managing, 97

linking, 300-302
long documents, managing,
  202
main, mail merges, 306-307,
  314-316, 331
margins, 185
moving, 76, 90
navigating, 283-286
opening, 79-81
outlines, viewing, 283-286
parsing, 493
planning, 288-289
previewing, 107-108
printing, 107-110
protecting from modifica-
  tions, 417-419
recently used, 81
recovering, 77-79
renaming, 76, 88-89
saving, 71-75
  periodically, 75
  as templates, 231
scrolling by page, 97, 107
sending in body of e-mail,
  474-477
sending PowerPoint presentations to, 445-446
splitting, 102-104
starting, 88
  based on existing docu-
    ment, 118-119
tiling, 104
toggling, 85-87
unsplitting, 103
viewing
  multiple, 104-107
  splitting, 102-104
views, 50, 94
watermarks, 392-395
zooming, 101-102
dot leaders, tabs, adding, 161
dotted lines, 40
**dotted underline (hidden text),
  292**
double-headed arrows, 352
drag-and-drop, 53
  text, 60-61
dragging scrollboxes, 44
Draw Table button, 344-345

drawing
  shapes, 371-375
  tables, 344-346
  text boxes, 374
Drawing button, 372
drawing canvas, 397-399
  deleting, 398
  resizing, 398
drawing canvas tools, 399
Drawing toolbar, 371
drop-down list form fields, 426
  adding, 429-430
drop-down lists, 24

E

Edit menu commands
  Find, 260
  Go To, 48
  Replace, 262
Edit Wrap Points button, 385
editing. *See also* **changing**
  comments, 410
  data source (mail merge),
    313-314
  Dictionary, 249-250
  documents
    accepting/rejecting revi-
      sions, 416
    finalizing changes,
      416-417
    Print Preview view, 108
    restrictions to, 417-419
    tracking changes, 411,
      415-416
  entries, AutoText, 259-260
  foreign language documents,
    468
  headers/footers, 193
  headings, Outline view,
    286-287
  linked data, 441-442
  macros, 279
  merge fields (mail merges),
    316
  PowerPoint presentations in
    Word, 446